WORLDS OF WOMEN

P9-CKR-470

WORLDS OF WOMEN

THE MAKING OF AN INTERNATIONAL WOMEN'S MOVEMENT

Leila J. Rupp

PRINCETON UNIVERSITY PRESS　PRINCETON, NEW JERSEY

Copyright © 1997 by Princeton University Press
Published by Princeton University Press, 41 William Street,
Princeton, New Jersey 08540
In the United Kingdom: Princeton University Press,
Chichester, West Sussex
All Rights Reserved

Library of Congress Cataloging-in-Publication Data
Rupp, Leila J., 1950–
Worlds of women : the making of an international
women's movement / Leila J. Rupp.
p.   cm.
Includes bibliographical references and index.
ISBN 0-691-01676-3 (cloth : alk. paper). —ISBN 0-691-01675-5
(pbk. : alk. paper)
1. Feminism—International cooperation—History.   2. Women's rights—
International cooperation—History.   3. Women in politics—History.
4. Women—Societies and clubs—History.   I. Title.
HQ1154.R86   1998
305.42'09—dc21   97-14449   CIP

This book has been composed in Sabon

Princeton University Press books are printed
on acid-free paper, and meet the guidelines
for permanence and durability of the Committee
on Production Guidelines for Book Longevity
of the Council on Library Resources

http://pup.princeton.edu

Printed in the United States of America

10 9 8 7 6 5 4 3 2 1

(Pbk.)

10 9 8 7 6 5 4 3 2 1

IN LOVING MEMORY OF

Sidney Stanton Rupp
(1912–1995)

AND

Walter Howard Rupp
(1909–1997)

WITHDRAWN

SEP -- 1999

WITHDRAWN

Contents

Illustrations

Preface

THERE'S something about finishing a book and sitting down to write the preface that makes one think about how much has changed since the beginning of the project. I don't mean just how vastly different the end result can be from what one envisaged at the beginning, but how much one's life can have changed as well. In the course of my research, I spent a lot of time at the New York Public Library, and I stayed with my parents in New Jersey. One evening at dinner, as I chattered on about some exciting find in the papers of Rosika Schwimmer, my mother remembered that she and her sister, as young members of the Westtown Friends Meeting, had stuffed envelopes for the American Friends Service Committee on behalf of Schwimmer's citizenship case. And now my mother is dead. I miss her sorely, cherish this small connection between her and the past I have studied, and dedicate this book to the memory of her boundless love, beauty, and gentleness.

Researching and writing this book has been an adventure in so many ways, and I am more grateful than I can really put into words to the many people and institutions that have made it possible. A yearlong fellowship from the American Council of Learned Societies in 1993, a sabbatical, and two quarters of release time from teaching, as well as grants from the Lilly Foundation Teaching Fellowship program, the Ohio State University Office of Research and Graduate Studies, the College of Humanities, the Department of History, the Center for Women's Studies, and the Mershon Center, facilitated my research in archives in the United States, England, the Netherlands, France, and Germany. In London, I reconnected with my old friend Chris Dymkowski and got to know Pauline Gooderson, and my trips there wouldn't have been nearly so enjoyable without our excursion to the country, good meals, and late-night conversation. Mineke Bosch in Amsterdam became a sort of *zielsvriendin*, and she and Jo Radersma made both Amsterdam and Paris even more magical places than I could have imagined. I will never forget our late-night bicycle ride home from Saarein, a weekend with the cows in Benschop, lingering over coffee and cognac, giggling over the various translations on a sightseeing boat on the Seine, eating songbird bodies by mistake at Le Télégraphe, and so much more. Claude and Hudson, from the Hôtel Louxor in Paris, practically saved my life when I was robbed, and they didn't even know me.

Archivists Eva Mosely, Anne Engelhart, and Susan Von Salis at the Schlesinger Library smoothed the way when the library was in the process of moving. Edith Wynner and Melanie Yolles always made sure that the boxes I needed were waiting for me at the New York Public Library, and Edith Wynner graciously invited me to dinner and shared her priceless knowledge of Rosika Schwimmer. Susan L. Boone at the Sophia Smith Collection made working there a special pleasure and even allowed me to stay a bit after hours. David Doughan and Anna Greening likewise made the Fawcett Library in London a kind of home away from home. Harold Sander at the Indianapolis Marion County Public Library kindly xeroxed a number of letters in the amazingly thoroughly indexed May Wright Sewall papers. At the International Archives of the Women's Movement in Amsterdam, Annette Mevis, Annemarie Kloosterman, and Yolande Heutenaar brought me tea and made me want never to leave. Sheila Green, general secretary of the National Council of Women of Great Britain, and Jacqueline Barbet-Massin, general secretary of the International Council of Women in Paris, made priceless letters and minutes available to me, and Mrs. E. E. Monro, ICW archivist, Gesa Heinrich of the Landesarchiv Berlin, Irène Paillard of the Bibliothèque de Documentation Internationale Contemporaine, and Annie Dizier of the Bibliothèque Marguerite Durand kindly provided helpful information that eased my research.

A number of colleagues around the country and beyond generously shared their work with me, sent me references, wrote countless letters of recommendation for grants and fellowships, and read and provided perceptive comments on articles and chapters. They include, some in more than one capacity, Bonnie Anderson, Emary Aronson, Margot Badran, Mineke Bosch, Victoria Brown, Antoinette Burton, Catherine Candy, Nupur Chaudhuri, Blanche Wiesen Cook, Nancy Cott, Drude Dahlerup, Jennifer Davy, Myra Marx Ferree, Estelle Freedman, Ute Gerhard, John Hoberman, Takeko Iinuma, Karin Lützen, Maggie McFadden, Karen Offen, K. Lynn Stoner, Carl Strikwerda, Margaret Strobel, Verta Taylor, Ian Tyrrell, and Ulla Wikander. Mineke Bosch and Ellen DuBois read and commented on the entire manuscript, helping to improve it (I hope) immeasurably. I am grateful also for the support and sage advice of Brigitta van Rheinberg and for the meticulous and inspired copyediting of Alice Falk. Closer to home, I have benefited from the advice of my Department of History colleagues Kenneth Andrien, Michael Les Benedict, Michael Berkowitz, John Burnham, Carter Findley, Carole Fink (who also generously allowed me to read microfilm on her reader without interruption), Susan Hartmann, Irina Livezeanu, Carla Pestana, Claire Robertson, Stephanie Shaw, and Birgitte Søland. I have learned so much from students who have worked on various aspects of the international women's movement—Sheila Darrow, Anene Ejikeme, Mala Mathrani, Michelle Mohr, Ayfer Karakaya Stump, Sue Wamsley, and Charlotte Weber—all of whom have opened my eyes to fresh angles. As research assistants, Irene Ledesma, who translated Spanish sources; Jutta Liessen, who transcribed difficult-to-decipher German and French letters; and Ayfer Karakaya Stump, who proved a marvel of persistence and ingenuity in a wide range of tasks, all lightened my load. My colleague in the Department of German, Helen Fehervary, advised me on some difficult translations. Long lunches at Flying Pizza, complete with discussions of feminism and history with, respectively, Mary Margaret Fonow and Carla Pestana, cheered me on. It would be hard to say enough to thank my friends and colleagues Susan Hartmann and Birgitte Søland, who have read every word I have written on this project (and more than once!), who have listened and advised over numerous trips for cappuccino and tea, and who, along with Claire Robertson and Stephanie Shaw, have made being a women's historian at Ohio State the joy that it is.

Even closer to home, I want to acknowledge two of the dogs in my life who helped me through this project. Jessie, who came to me while I was still in graduate school, saw me through great changes, including my move to Ohio, and spent many hours in my office when she was too old to stay home. She died in 1989 and kindly bequeathed me to Emma Lou, who has taken over the job of grudgingly letting me leave on research trips, welcoming me home, and reminding me how important it is to be silly.

I can never truly acknowledge the debt I owe to my father, Walter H. Rupp, who has always treasured the past and valued writing. He and my late aunt, Leila H. Rupp, who taught history in the Pittsburgh public schools, both instilled in me a love of history and of writing. My father and my mother were always interested in what I was doing, and I cherish memories of countless long conversations around the table in Stone Harbor, Mountainside, and Vero Beach. My father has continued to be a constant source of support, even when I know that he sometimes wonders why I didn't have enough sense to become a chemical engineer. Between copyediting and proofreading, my father was diagnosed with cancer and now he, too, is dead. I decided to leave the preface (which I had already shown him) largely as written, but I add his name to the dedication in gratitude for his powerful love, intellect, and passion for the past.

Finally, there is Verta Taylor. What can I say about the woman who shares my life, who has taught me everything I know about social movement theory and collective identity, who has sharpened my thinking in so many ways, whose endless and brilliant work on her own book on postpartum depression and women's self-help not only allowed me late hours at the computer while I waited for her to call it a day but revealed more connections than I ever could have imagined between two apparently disparate subjects, and who is, simply, the sunshine in my life?

INTRODUCTION

1

The International First Wave

> [W]omen have been protesting their exclusion
> from the elite task of "imagining the nation" and
> simultaneously demonstrating that historical acts
> of imagination, translated into oppressive and
> violent social systems, have material
> consequences which must be resisted and
> transformed through acts of political will into
> very different systems which may or may not
> need nations to support them.
>   *(Ailbhe Smyth, 1995)[1]*

IT IS HARD to imagine, in the last years of the twentieth century, the women of warring countries crossing enemy lines, gathering to try to end bloodshed and bring about peace. Yet this, in broad strokes, is what women from Europe and North America did in 1915. The Congress of Women, bravely convened in The Hague during the first year of the Great War, is probably the most celebrated (and was at the time also the most reviled) expression of women's internationalism, but it is neither the beginning nor the end of the story. *Worlds of Women* explores the complex process at work as women from far-flung countries came together in transnational women's organizations and constructed an international collective identity. Divided by nationality and often fiercely loyal to different organizations, women committed to internationalism forged bonds not only despite but in fact through conflict over nearly every aspect of organizing. By understanding how they did this and how the dynamics of mobilizing interacted with the economic, political, and social changes that swept across the twentieth-century world, we can contemplate the limitations and possibilities of internationalism.

I focus here on what I believe can be considered the first wave of an international women's movement because I believe that its history is instructive for understanding the very different—but connected—story of the second wave. The Second World War, which nearly severed international connections among women, marked the end of the first wave and the lull before the swell of the second. The emergence of a bipolar world out of the ashes of the war, the spread of national liberation movements throughout the formerly colonized countries, and the emergence and resurgence of national women's movements around the globe in the 1960s and 1970s profoundly transformed the context for an international women's movement. Transnational interaction jumped out of the well-worn transatlantic tracks. Adding to the gatherings of preexisting and emergent organizations, the United Nations–sponsored Decade for Women conferences and their accompanying nongovernmental gatherings met in Mexico City in 1975, Copenhagen in 1980, and Nairobi in 1985.[2] The latest chapter in this story unfolded at the Beijing conference in 1995.

But when I began the research for this book, I had no such grandiose scheme in my head. What originally piqued my imagination, in the course of my research first on the U.S. National Woman's Party in the 1950s and then on the life of Doris Stevens in the 1910s and 1920s, was the discovery of U.S. women's involvement in the transnational struggle for equal rights. In the wake of the United Nations–proclaimed International Decade for Women, I wondered why there was so little in print about the history of the international women's movement. Hungry for information, I learned for the first time of the International Council of Women and the International Alliance of Women from Edith Hurwitz's pioneering article in the first edition of *Becoming Visible*.[3] There was not much else to find and a great deal of what was available—with the exception of the in-house histories of major organizations—focused on national participation in international bodies.[4] This was more than the usual paucity of attention to women: historians in general seem to have clung so tenaciously to topics defined by the nation-state that international organizations of any kind have been left to the political scientists.[5]

I began my research knowing that I wanted to shift the focus to the international structures of the transnational organizations—not attempt a study of the extensive national sections—and that I did not want to write an organizational history. Although I started out interested in all international women's groups that I encountered, it quickly became clear to me that three major bodies, open (at least technically) to all constituencies of women from every corner of the globe, held center stage. These were the International Council of Women, the first surviving general group, founded in 1888; the International Alliance of Women, originally the International Woman Suffrage Alliance, an offshoot of the Council that was officially established in 1904; and the Women's International League for Peace and Freedom, which grew from the International Congress of Women at The Hague that met in the midst of the wrenching Great War in 1915. A multitude of regionally organized bodies, groups composed of particular constituencies of women, and single-issue organizations sprang up around these three, especially in the years between the wars, and the whole universe of transnational women's organizations interacted in a variety of ways, especially through coalitions comprising delegates from the different groups. Thus, by focusing on the three major organizations and their cooperation and competition with this vast array of bodies, including socialist women's groups, we are able to understand the workings of the international women's movement.

I considered qualifying my description of the international women's movement by adding such terms as "bourgeois" or "Euro-American." But, as I have argued elsewhere with regard to the U.S. women's movement, I see two viable strategies for responding to the critiques of the limitations and biases of women's movements raised originally by working-class women and women of color within the United States and by "Third World" women on the world scene.[6] One is to expand the definition of women's movements to encompass a range of activities by women who might not themselves have envisaged their commitments in that way. The other—the one I employ here—is to give precedence to women's own definitions of their interests and to lay bare the conditions that made women's movements exclusive rather than inclusive. As a result, I consider the most crucial characteristic of women's movement organizations the inclination to align with other women's groups. That was what distinguished such socialist groups, for example, as the International Cooperative Women's Guild, which functioned as part of the women's movement, from the Socialist Women's International, which did not. On the individual level, socialist women who belonged to the Women's International League for Peace and Freedom saw their interests very differently than those who refused to work with bourgeois women. Thus the international women's movement *was* bourgeois and dominated by women of European origin, and we must understand why this was so and what consequences flowed from the nature of the movement.[7]

I recognize that my focus on the international structures, which made the organizational records and the papers of the core participants my central sources, privileges those at the center—primarily, as we shall see, elite, Christian, older, European-origin women. I do not pretend to tell the stories of all of the national groups that participated in the international bodies, although I look forward to such work from other scholars, knowing how important it is to view international women's organizations from every angle. I have been struck, for example, with the picture Margot Badran has painted of the role of the International Alliance in the lives of Egyptian feminists Huda Sha'rawi and Saiza Nabarawi. They eagerly anticipated their travels to international congresses and remembered their connections with friends with great warmth. Yet the written record does not document any reciprocal pleasure in their company. This is an important reminder that no one angle of vision is complete.

I began this research with a framework firmly embedded in the historiography of U.S. women's history in the 1980s: the attempt to create "international sisterhood" out of the multitude of conflicting interests that women from different nations brought to the international arena. I at first envisaged this as the story of conflict and community juxtaposed. Over time—in part through my involvement in designing and teaching world history classes, in part through the development of women's history (including the impact of poststructuralism), and in part through continued exposure to social movement theory—I came to conceptualize my topic in a more complex way.

First of all, I see my work as part of a transnational history that we are only beginning to write in our increasingly interdependent world. The story of international organization—both through official bodies such as the League of Nations and United Nations and through structures created by a wide array of constituencies—is an important part of world history and needs to take its place alongside economic, military, and political interactions on the global level. The recent flowering of work on nationalism as an identity that is created rather than inherent in living in a certain place or speaking a particular language has been particularly inspiring. Benedict Anderson's concept of nations as "imagined communities" has caught the eye of the historical community, but a whole raft of literature on nationalism has made the same observation.[8] This work focused my attention on the process of constructing internationalism, an infinitely more difficult task in a world of nation-states. Audre Lorde's classic pronouncement that "the master's tools can never dismantle the master's house" raises provocative questions about the persistence of nationalism in liberation movements fighting against nationalist imperialism.[9] Thus, I see connections between the work on nationalism and such large historical questions as the viability of alternative methods of organizing peoples in the modern world.

Second, the notion of "sisterhood" versus conflict has come to seem far too simplistic in light of poststructuralist emphases on competing discourses, the dissolution of binary oppositions, and attention to the ways that meaning is constructed in specific historical contexts. I have come to view conflict and community within the international women's organizations not as opposites but as part of the same process by which women came together across national borders to create a sense of belonging and to work and sometimes live together. Just as the cohesiveness of the international women's movement flowed from its exclusiveness, so too did women's solidarity find expression in their struggles over the best means of achieving their broadly defined goals of equality and international understanding.

Finally, the concept of collective identity, developed by scholars of the "new social movements" of the 1960s and 1970s, helped make sense of this process. Understanding how groups define "who we are" provides the link necessary to explain how discontented constituencies mobilize for political action.[10] Collective identity is "the shared definition of a group that derives from members' common interests, experiences, and solidarity," and—perhaps most important—it is constructed and sustained within social movement communities. In analyzing collective identity within social movements, I make use here of the framework developed by Verta Taylor and Nancy Whittier.[11] In their scheme, collective identity consists of the boundaries that mark off a group; consciousness, or the ways of defining a group's common interests; and personalized politics, embodied in symbols and actions that challenge received wisdom about the way things are. Although my book is not heavily theoretical, I have used this model for analyzing collective identity to structure my analysis of the contentious process by which women from different nations came to define and work together for common goals.

In weaving the separate strands of the three organizations I explore here into the textured cloth that was the international women's movement, I found some threads far stronger and thicker than others. In some instances this reflects differences among the groups, but in others it is an accident of the sources. The organizational papers that have survived vary greatly in coverage for the different bodies. The headquarters of the International Council of Women, which followed the president from country to country, landed in Brussels in 1936, and when the Nazis invaded Belgium they sacked the office. In 1944, the Council got back its Belgian headquarters but found that all of the documents had been removed and, presumably, destroyed.[12] Likewise, in 1954 the president of the Alliance reported, "So much of our material was destroyed in London during the war," despite attempts to preserve the historical record.[13]

I knew that some of the papers of the International Council and the Alliance had been spirited away to safety in the United States, but I could not have written about the life of these organizations without some lucky finds. The official history of the International Council of Women mentions some letters of longtime President Lady Aberdeen held by the British National Council, and when I contacted that group while in London, I found that they possessed a substantial collection of International Council material, which they kindly let me use in their London office. The Helene-Lange-Archiv in Berlin also includes a large collection of International Council papers on microfiche. In addition, David Doughan of the Fawcett Library let me know that the International Alliance had donated many boxes of material, and he very generously agreed to let me see the collection before it had been catalogued. Most was from the post-1945 period, but I found detailed minutes of board meetings from the 1930s as well as other records that proved extremely enlightening. My most exciting discovery came at the headquarters of the International Council of Women in Paris. I went there to read the early rare issues of the Council *Bulletin*, not expecting to find any archival material at all. When the general secretary opened a large cabinet to get me the issues I had asked to see, I noticed several boxes of materials marked "Minutes" and found in them handwritten Executive Committee minutes from 1897 and 1898, as well as a great deal of other important material.

The Women's International League for Peace and Freedom is another story altogether. The Microfilming Corporation of America has made available the official records, moved from Geneva headquarters to the University of Colorado Library in the 1970s and 1980s. The microfilmed papers, well organized and indexed, are extremely rich. Such are the advantages of locating headquarters in a neutral country!

The papers of individual leaders—especially presidents and other key players—supplemented what could be found in the organizational collections. Rosika Schwimmer's papers at the New York Public Library are a veritable gold mine of information; invaluable, too, are the various collections of Carrie Chapman Catt's papers, Margery Corbett Ashby's material at the Fawcett Library in London, the papers of Jane Addams, available on microfilm, and the extensive collection of Gabrielle Duchêne at the Bibliothèque de Documentation Internationale Contemporaine at Nanterre. The collections at the Internationaal Archief voor de Vrouwenbeweging (International Archives of the Women's Movement) in Amsterdam, especially Aletta Jacobs's and Rosa Manus's, are a treasure. The archive, founded in 1935, like the International Council headquarters fell to the Germans, who reportedly burned its contents.[14] But recently a cache of Rosa Manus's papers has turned up in Moscow, giving rise to the possibility that more international women's movement material was taken by the Germans and captured by the Russians.[15]

It is important to point out that the women committed to the international women's movement understood the importance of the documentary record. The same impulse that led to the establishment of the International Archives of the Women's Movement in Amsterdam emerged in the United States in the form of the World Center for Women's Archives, which was launched by Rosika Schwimmer, taken over by Mary Beard, and eventually, in a transformed state, embodied in the Schlesinger Library at Radcliffe.[16] As Schwimmer put it in 1935, "Now that women start to slide down from the peak of achievement, it seems to me of historical importance to gather all documentary material connected with that marvelous epoch in which woman's struggle for their rights and for world peace reached an unprecendented height, in the last decades."[17] Without such historical consciousnesss, this research would have been impossible.

Although this is a history that ends with the Second World War, connections between past and present have been very real to me throughout the process of research and writing. I mean not to suggest a transhistorical sameness, but rather to evoke some personal connections to the political and historical. The dusty documents first came alive for me in 1990, at Sostrup Castle outside of Aarhus, Denmark, when my partner, Verta Taylor, and I spoke at a Nordic Women's Studies conference on "New Theoretical Perspectives on the Women's Movement." The problems of translation, even in our technological age, came home to us when, after a series of keynote addresses in English, the language for the proceedings shifted to the Scandinavian tongues. A small group of us—including some of the Finns and a Chinese woman studying in Denmark after the events of Tiananmen Square—were supposed to have simultaneous translation through headphones. But not only did the equipment fail: the conference organizers had been unable to find a feminist or even female translator, so we sat around the only male in the room, who whispered his translation as we strained to hear. Even when we could make out his words, we often could not understand. The Scandinavian audience would laugh and we would look at each other. Or we would laugh (at, for example, the translation of "feminist" as "women's lib") and they would turn around to wonder what was so funny. It was both an amusing and sobering experience that made me think of Lady Aberdeen and Jane Addams rebuking International Council of Women and Congress of Women participants for their unruly behavior during the translation process.

On Saturday night, we celebrated with a special dinner and impromptu entertainment. It began with offerings of characteristic songs from our cultures: not, I hasten to add, our national anthems, but folk songs in Icelandic, a chilling performance of Chinese opera, a rousing round of "We Shall Not Be Moved." I began to understand the phenomenon of creating an international bond through national rituals and symbols. I recalled that Rosa Manus performed a traditional dance in wooden shoes with a group of other young women at the Amsterdam conference of the International Woman Suffrage Alliance of 1908. As I danced a polka later that night with Ulla Wikander, whose research on international women's congresses had already inspired me, I thought of the stirring memories of conferences that women cherished for decades.

In the course of my research I forged other international ties that gave me glimpses of what the women I have studied, as different as we might be, might have experienced. At the 1987 Berkshire Conference, I went to hear a paper given by Mineke Bosch on women's friendships within the International Woman Suffrage Alliance. I marveled at the richness of her data and analysis and sought her out to learn more about her book,

Lieve Dr. Jacobs, published in Dutch to celebrate the fiftieth anniversary of the International Archives of the Women's Movement. As a result of that conversation, I worked to have the Ohio State University Press publish a revised English version of that stunning book and Mineke and I became friends. She put me up when I traveled to Amsterdam to do research at the International Archives in 1992 and, as a break from putting the final touches on her dissertation, came to Paris in 1993 when I went to do research there. I came to understand the depth of feeling that can grow from just a short time together engaged in mutual work. In Paris I found a letter from Lida Gustava Heymann to Gabrielle Duchêne, telling of her trip home to find Anita, her partner, and their dog in good health, and Mineke and I laughed about the inevitability of my repeating the phrase when I returned home to Verta and our dog Emma. When I send Mineke books or flower seeds for her and Jo's Benschop garden or reminisce about our bicycle ride through the cow pastures or the dinners we shared in Paris or place a picture of Mineke and Jo sitting by an abandoned windmill on my bookshelf, I think of the gifts and letters and pictures that flowed back and forth across the Atlantic earlier this century.

Worlds of Women addresses such dynamics within the international women's organizations in order to understand what it meant to be a woman committed to internationalism in a half century rent by two world wars and transformed by the Bolshevik Revolution, the decline of European dominance, the global depression of the 1930s, the rise of fascism, and the emergence of national liberation movements around the globe. Chapter 2, "Building an International Women's Movement," details the history of the three organizations and their patterns of interaction with other multinational groups, interweaving a sense of the ebb and flow of women's organizing through years of war, economic crisis, social transformation, and political revolution. This chapter points out that the trajectory of the international women's movement—emerging in the late nineteenth century and gaining in strength after the First World War, when national movements in the Euro-American arena stagnated and those in countries beginning to shake off European dominance picked up—forces us to rethink the history of the women's movement from a global perspective.

The remainder of the book, after this introductory chapter, is divided into three sections corresponding to the elements of collective identity. The first section, "Boundaries," focuses on the lines drawn between members and nonmembers. Chapter 3, "Who's In, Who's Out," explores the processes of inclusion and exclusion that shaped the membership of the international women's organizations as primarily elite, Christian, older, European-origin women. Detailing both the nature of participation and assumptions of Euro-American superiority that perpetuated the relative homogeneity of membership in the face of an ideal of universal inclusiveness, this chapter portrays these boundaries as both unintended and under attack, especially by women from colonized countries who challenged the "feminist orientalism" of internationally organized women. Chapter 4, "The International Bonds of Womanhood," explores the explicitly endorsed, if also occasionally disputed, notion of women's fundamental difference from men as the raison d'être of women's international organizing. Embodied both in ideological convictions and in the practice of separatist organizing, the line between women and men formed the keystone of women's international collective identity, even as barriers between the sexes began to break down in different parts of the world as the century wore on.

The next section, "Consciousness," analyzes the interests of internationally organized women. "Forging an International 'We,'" chapter 5, explores the concepts and symbolic expressions of internationalism, detailing conflicting positions on the relationship between nationalism and internationalism, a wrenching dispute over pacifism within the Women's International League, and ongoing struggles in all three groups over the nature of international representation. Chapter 6, "How Wide the Circle of the Feminist 'We,'" considers differing positions on the meaning of feminism, suffrage and the use of militance, special labor legislation for women, the nationality of married women, and the issue of moral standards as a way of understanding what women saw as their gendered interests. By focusing in this section on the conflicting positions taken by women who shared a basic consciousness as feminist internationalists, I emphasize the dynamic nature of women's international collective identity and the difficult process of defining goals and planning collective action as the organizations sought to expand their reach beyond the Euro-American world.

The final section, "Personalized Politics," begins with "International Ground," a chapter focusing on the international headquarters, committees, congresses, and publications that served to knit together the international community of women. Chapter 8, "Getting to Know You," explores the politics of personal interaction. Within the institutions detailed in chapter 7, women took their first tentative steps toward international participation, encouraged by friends and acquaintances; grew increasingly committed to organizational life; devoted themselves to international leaders; formed friendships across the borders of nationality; and even became part of international "families." This final section shows how the same forces that unified internationally organized women reinforced by their very nature the unintended boundaries surrounding the movement. Since attendance at congresses, participation on international committees, and travel to international headquarters or to visit the homes of other members played such a crucial role in the formation of a collective identity, those who lacked resources or skills, lived too far away, or felt excluded could not or chose not to participate. Yet for those who could and did, the experience could be intense and life-changing.

The conclusion steps back to ask: did it matter? In chapter 9, "International Matters," I discuss, first, the impact of the international women's movement through its work with the League of Nations and the newly formed United Nations, including the struggles to involve women in the making of international policy and to capture men's attention on such issues as disarmament, labor legislation, nationality, and the status of women. Neither the League of Nations nor the United Nations would have been quite the same without the efforts of internationally organized women. But even more important, I argue, are the successes and failures of the project of constructing a gendered internationalism. The first half of the twentieth century was a critical period for the question of what might unite women from around the globe, for as some women won access to the formal political process and increased entry into previously male worlds, the common bond of political powerlessness dissipated. Furthermore, women from countries struggling to free themselves from imperial subjugation embraced nationalism at the same time that women from the dominant powers reviled national rivalries as the motor force of war.

Yet women did reach out across the fortified borders of their countries to make common cause with other women. Although the international women's movement reproduced the dynamics of global power relations, and women's international collective identity incorporated limitations on its universality, the persistent challenges to the assumptions and structures of exclusion, from both within and from outside the movement, ensured the continuation of the process of defining what it meant to be a feminist internationalist. The members of these international organizations may not have changed the world, but their understanding of what women from different countries might have in common—an understanding made more complex as women outside the Euro-American cultural tradition came onto the international scene—holds out hope for the kind of alternative visions Ailbhe Smyth, as quoted in the epigraph, imagines. Internationalist moments, however fragmentary or flawed, are an important part of our global history.

2

Building an International Women's Movement

[F]ired by all this "getting-togetherness,"
Mary Dingman boldly conceived the idea of a
super "get-together" wherein all the "get-
togetherers" would "get-together" once again,
centrally and all-embracingly.
  (B.P., 1939)[1]

WITH THESE WORDS, an admirer credited Mary Dingman, chair of the
Peace and Disarmament Committee of the Women's International Organisations, with forging the interorganizational cooperation that served
as the heart of the first wave of an international women's movement.
Women began to organize across national borders in the late nineteenth
century, formed a variety of groups that cooperated and competed with
each other, and by the 1920s began to shape new structures designed to
facilitate interaction at the rarified heights of transnational organizing. In
the language of social movement theorists, individual groups came
together in a "social movement industry" that we call the international
women's movement.[2]

When Dutch Alliance activist Rosa Manus wrote to a German colleague of "die internationale Frauenbewegung" or when the Czech
Council and Alliance leader Františka Plamínková spoke of "the international women's movement," their colleagues knew what they meant.[3]
There were clearly recognizable insiders and outsiders, discernible in the
Alliance's objection to a French government appointee to a League of
Nations committee on the status of women in 1938. Alliance officers
protested—"not that we do not recognise that she is a distinguished
lawyer, but because she has not been so far closely identified with the
woman's movement."[4] More indirectly, organizations drew the movement's boundaries through patterns of interaction.

In order to understand the larger context in which the International
Council of Women, the International Alliance of Women, and the
Women's International League for Peace and Freedom operated, I
explore here the process of building an international women's movement.
As we shall see, these three groups might be seen as grandmother, mother,
and daughter, as one gave birth to another. Once grown, they took on

distinct personalities, yet their lives continued to intertwine. I consider each organization's origins and character separately, then focus on the "family history" resulting from their interaction. Women expressed intense loyalty to their groups and fought for turf, but even in their conflicts they recognized their connections to one another. I argue that both the cooperation and competition of organized women on the world stage, shaped by the economic, social, and political transformations of the twentieth-century world, staked out an international women's movement, albeit one that followed the patterns of global power.

Early International Connections

The roots of the international women's movement can be traced to a variety of connections forged across national borders, creating what social movement scholars call a "preexisting communications network" for the international women's movement.[5] Women travelers, migrants, missionaries, and writers—of books, newspaper articles, and letters sent off across the lines that divided nations—made contacts that prepared the way for more formalized interactions.[6] A variety of movements, including abolitionism, socialism, peace, temperance, and moral reform, called women's attention to the cross-national character of their causes and brought together women from different nations in mixed-gender meetings. The World Anti-Slavery Convention held in London in 1840, which refused to seat women delegates elected by their home societies, has gone down in history as the spark that ignited the U.S. women's rights movement. But it and similar meetings also set the precedent for the formation of the international women's organizations.

With the first stirrings of organized feminism in the United States and Europe, international connections among women solidified.[7] Works such as Mary Wollstonecraft's *Vindication of the Rights of Woman* (1792), translated into French and German, had already roused women on both sides of the Atlantic, suggesting that feminist analyses and demands might transcend national contexts. Radical women activists across Europe and in the United States stirred to each others' proclamations and translated each others' words. The transnational development of a feminist ideology led to formalized contacts among women—committed to women's rights rather than some other cause—at conferences unattached to any permanent body. The first international women's congress, the Congrès international de droit des femmes, convened in Paris in 1878 in connection with the World Exposition.[8] All of this activity laid the groundwork for the founding of international women's organizations, which institutionalized and perpetuated the impulse to work on behalf of women on the international stage.

The International Council of Women

As it turned out, the second international women's conference, called by the U.S. National Woman Suffrage Association in Washington, D.C., in 1888, gave birth to the first lasting multipurpose transnational women's organization, the International Council of Women.[9] The Council's origins reach back to 1882–83, when U.S. suffrage leaders Elizabeth Cady Stanton and Susan B. Anthony traveled to England and France, met with women reformers, and set up a committee of correspondence to form an international suffrage association.[10] Little came of the idea until the U.S. suffrage group, prompted by Anthony, invited international representatives to attend its 1888 meeting. Despite the suffrage connections, the call went out to "all women of light and learning, to all associations of women in trades, professions and reforms, as well as to those advocating political rights," reflecting an attempt to broaden the meeting's base of support to include literary clubs, temperance societies, labor groups, moral purity socities, peace organizations, and professional groups.[11]

The International Council, designed to bring together all existing women's groups in individual countries first organized into National Councils, was, as the German secretary Alice Salomon later described it, "built on air," for there were not yet any National Councils for women to join.[12] The 1888 meeting gave birth to the National Council of the United States, but council building elsewhere proceeded slowly. By the first quinquennial congress of the International Council in 1893, only Canada had formed a national body. Elections for a president—British suffrage leader Millicent Garrett Fawcett had been chosen in 1888 but refused to serve—produced the name of Lady Aberdeen, a Scottish aristocrat then living in Canada as the wife of the governor general. Aberdeen had never heard of the International Council when asked to lead it in 1893, but she took on the job and stuck to it with a vengeance, serving until 1936 with only a five-year break from 1899 to 1904 and another two-year gap from 1920 to 1922.[13] Shortly after taking office, she dispatched her French- and German-speaking private secretary, Teresa Wilson, to Europe to build councils. As a result of Wilson's efforts, Germany, Sweden, Great Britain, Denmark, and the Netherlands, as well as Australia, joined by the next quinquennial congress. By 1914, twenty-three councils had affiliated, by 1939 thirty-six (see table 1). In a pageant performed at the 1929 congress, a young child with a star of hope on her forehead represented the organization in 1888, while the "tall figure of a beautiful young woman" symbolized the full-grown Council.[14] Adding together all of the women who belonged to the local groups constituting the National Councils, the ICW claimed to represent four to five million women by 1907 and thirty-six million by 1925.[15]

TABLE 1
National Sections of the International Women's Organizations

International Council of Women		International Alliance of Women		Women's International League for Peace and Freedom
United States	1888			
Canada	1893			
Germany	1897			
Great Britain	1898			
Sweden	1898			
Australia	1899			
Denmark	1899			
Netherlands	1899			
Italy	1900			
New Zealand	1900			
Argentina	1901			
France	1901			
Austria	1903			
Switzerland	1903			
Hungary	1904	Australia	1904	
Norway	1904	Germany	1904	
		Netherlands	1904	
		Sweden	1904	
		United States	1904	
		Great Britain	1904	
Belgium	1906	Austria	1906	
		Canada	1906	
		Denmark	1906	
		Hungary	1906	
		Italy	1906	
		Norway	1906	
		Russia	1906	
Bulgaria	1908	Bulgaria	1908	
Greece	1908	Finland	1908	
		South Africa	1908	
		Switzerland	1908	
		Belgium	1909	
		Bohemia	1909	
		France	1909	
Finland	1911	Iceland	1911	
Serbia	1911	Serbia	1911	
South Africa	1913	China	1913	
		Galicia	1913	
		Portugal	1913	
		Romania	1913	
Portugal	1914			

TABLE 1 *(cont.)*
National Sections of the International Women's Organizations

International Council of Women		International Alliance of Women		Women's International League for Peace and Freedom	
				Austria	1915
				Belgium	1915
				Canada	1915
				Denmark	1915
				France	1915
				Germany	1915
				Great Britain	1915
				Hungary	1915
				Italy	1915
				Netherlands	1915
				Norway	1915
				Sweden	1915
				United States	1915
				Australia	1919
				Bulgaria	1919
				Finland	1919
				Ireland	1919
				Poland	1919
				Switzerland	1919
Iceland	1920	Argentina	1920		
		Greece	1920		
		Poland	1920		
		Spain	1920		
		Uruguay	1920		
Estonia	1921			Greece	1921
Romania	1921			New Zealand	1921
				Poland (readmitted)	1921
				Ukraine	1921
Latvia	1922				
Chile	1923	Brazil	1923		
		Egypt	1923		
		India	1923		
		Ireland	1923		
		Jamaica	1923		
		Japan	1923		
		New Zealand	1923		
		New Foundland	1923		
		Palestine	1923		
		Lithuania	1923		
		Ukraine	1923		

TABLE 1 *(cont.)*
National Sections of the International Women's Organizations

International Council of Women		International Alliance of Women		Women's International League for Peace and Freedom	
Czechoslovakia	1924			Belgium (readmitted)	1924
Ireland	1924			Czechoslovakia	1924
Poland	1924			Haiti	1924
				Japan	1924
India	1925				
Peru	1926	Bermuda	1926		
		Cuba	1926		
		Luxembourg	1926		
		Peru	1926		
		Puerto Rico	1926		
		Turkey	1926		
Brazil	1927			Finland (readmitted)	1927
		Ceylon	1929	Mexico	1929
		Dutch East Indies	1929		
		Syria	1929		
		Rhodesia	1929		
Lithuania	1930				
				Tunis	1932
				Yugoslavia	1934
				Egypt	1937
South West Africa	1938				

Source: The information on the ICW comes from *Women in a Changing World* 1966. I relied on the list compiled by Bosch 1990 for the IWSA; Bosch made use of the congress reports, and the information sometimes conflicts with that of Whittick 1979. For WILPF, I am grateful to my research assistant, Ayfer Stump, who plowed through congress reports, minutes of meetings, and official correspondence to come up with this list, which reflects some ambiguities about when sections actually joined.

Guidelines for organizing councils in new countries called for the circulation of ICW literature to prominent women workers in religion, philanthropy, social reform, art, music, literature, and education. The next step was to hold a meeting, which should include "representatives of all churches and all sections, races, and parties." A provisional committee would then organize an inaugural public meeting, at which leading men would indicate their support and approval. The meeting might end with the singing of the national anthem.[16] Such guidance reveals a cautious approach to organizing elite but not homebound women.

As National Councils formed and affiliated with the ICW, the international body itself remained shadowy, with little responsibility beyond planning the next congress five years down the road and, in a general sense, "stimulat[ing] the sentiment of Internationalism among women throughout the world."[17] The international structure began to solidify— and the ICW to take on substantive issues—only at the 1899 congress. Inspired by the first intergovernmental conference on peace and disarmament, called at The Hague for 1899, the ICW leadership formed an International Standing Committee on Peace and International Arbitration, a subject that became increasingly central to all of the international women's organizations. Although the presenter of a resolution on arbitration at the 1899 congress claimed universal support for such a goal, since "nothing touched a woman's heart so much as this," the Swedish delegates refused to vote on what they considered a "political" question.[18] According to Lady Aberdeen, reflecting back on the early commitment to peace from the vantage point of 1936, they had not "departed from the rule against attaching the I.C.W. to any one propaganda" but had merely observed the "Golden Rule," the group's guiding principle.[19] But not all members agreed. In 1925, the Washington congress blew up over the issue of pacifism, which, according to one observer, had positive connotations for Europeans but to Americans evoked disloyalty and defeatism.[20]

The other issue-oriented standing committee established in 1899, dealing with the legal position of married women, evoked far less feeling. Over the years, International Standing Committees—including "Suffrage," "Equal Moral Standard and Against Traffic in Women," "Trades and Professions," "Public Health and Child Welfare," and "Emigration and Immigration"—pursued the substantive work of the Council. The list of resolutions from the 1933 congress in Stockholm, which called for everything from an end to the narcotic drug traffic to control of water pollution endangering sea birds and sea bathing to disarmament, gives a sense of the breadth of the ICW's concerns.[21]

The Council's wide-ranging program, or what Corresponding Secretary Teresa Wilson referred to in 1899 as a "certain vagueness about both our methods and aims," served as "at once our stumbling-block and our pride—our stumbling-block because of the difficulty we experience in explaining precisely by rule and measure what we are and what we want, and our pride because this very vagueness enables us to be all-embracing."[22] The International Council's intention to remain a truly general women's organization echoes in its claim, after the First World War, to the title of "Women's League of Nations."[23] As other transnational women's groups emerged in the first decades of the twentieth century, the International Council conceptualized them as "new independent bodies which hived off to concentrate on a programme of their own."[24]

Aware of its reputation as "old-fashioned and out of date as compared with some of the younger international societies," the ICW prided itself on retaining its broad program in the face of increasing specialization.[25] The Council was, in fact, the most conservative of the major international bodies of women. Lady Aberdeen, as president, asserted in 1899 that "we hold fast to the belief that woman's first mission must be her home."[26] The ICW also had a reputation as an aristocratic body, in part because its longtime president Aberdeen was a marchioness (see figure 1) and her successor a Belgian baroness. In 1899, Lady Aberdeen even worked, unsuccessfully, to engineer the election of the German Empress Victoria as president of the Council. If it could not be the empress, Aberdeen's secretary Teresa Wilson in a letter marked "private" wrote to the president of the German body, "then can your Council not nominate some well known & outstanding German woman, of rank & social position," someone such as Austrian Baroness Bertha von Suttner or Finnish Baroness Alexandra Gripenberg?[27] Perpetuating the Council's association with the ruling classes, May Wright Sewall proposed an international campaign to express sympathy to Queen Margherita of Italy on the occasion of the assassination of King Umberto by an anarchist in 1900. Such an action, she argued, would show that "the women of advanced thought who are working for the promotion of human liberty and for the augmentation of women's influence are a *conservative* and not a *destructive* force."[28]

Members of other women's groups expressed virtually unanimous agreement throughout the years that the Council was conservative. The secretary of the Union Mondiale de la Femme pour la Concorde Internationale, founded by an American-born Swiss businesswoman, approvingly referred to the Council as "perhaps the oldest and most conservative" of all the women's groups.[29] Cor Ramondt-Hirschmann, a Dutch member of the Women's International League for Peace and Freedom, referred sarcastically to the "very advanced! point of view" to be put before the 1925 quinquennial meeting of the ICW.[30] According to Gertrud Baer, a left-leaning WILPF member, the Council "has always been so conservative, that we never could work with them in Germany."[31] As early as 1908, Dutch International Alliance activist Martina Kramers had complained to Hungarian pacifist and feminist Rosika Schwimmer that the Council was "a dumb thing and its meetings have not the least importance," while Austrian WILPF member Yella Hertzka in 1930 pronounced the ICW congress "the most boring in the world."[32]

The International Council of Women steadfastly maintained its self-image as the all-encompassing organization representing the diverse interests of women throughout the world. By trying to chart a course acceptable to all women, it failed to please many. Early on, the unwill-

Fig. 1. Portrait of Marchioness of Aberdeen and Temair, longtime president of the International Council of Women, in her regal garb. After a portrait by the Baroness Barnekow, 1930. Reproduced from the ICW *Bulletin*, January 1931.

ingness of its leadership to confront controversial issues led to the "hiving off" of the second major international women's organization, the International Woman Suffrage Alliance.

The International Alliance of Women

Ironically, the International Council of Women, which Elizabeth Cady Stanton and Susan B. Anthony had originally intended as a suffrage organization, assiduously avoided taking a position on contentious issues—including, in the early years, the vote. At the 1899 congress, the Council leadership insisted that antisuffragists deserved a hearing at a session on women's political rights, prompting German suffragists Lida

Gustava Heymann and Anita Augspurg to call an alternative meeting that advocated the founding of an international women's suffrage organization.[33] In 1901 Carrie Chapman Catt, then president of the U.S. National American Woman Suffrage Association, proposed to her board the calling of an international suffrage congress in conjunction with their annual meeting in Washington the next year. Invitations went out to existing suffrage organizations, National Councils of Women, missionaries, and U.S. ambassadors and consuls.[34] At this 1902 gathering, delegates from ten countries made plans to hold a meeting in Berlin during the next ICW congress and there form a permanent organization. As a result, the International Woman Suffrage Alliance, consisting of national women's suffrage auxiliaries pledged "to secure the enfranchisement of the women of all nations," came into being in Berlin in 1904.[35]

May Wright Sewall, herself a suffragist, tried to present the Alliance as the fruit of the ICW and worked to ensure that things would go smoothly in Berlin.[36] She wanted nothing to "give color to any charge that unworthy divisions exist among the women who are working for human progress."[37] But Margery Corbett Ashby, who would serve as president of the Alliance from 1923 to 1946, later insisted that the new organization had been "conceived of separately and only concluded in Berlin because so many people were gathered there."[38] Further distinguishing the two organizations, she called the Alliance the oldest *political* union of women organized on an international and nonparty basis.[39] But in fact the ICW not only gave birth to the Alliance but also responded to the separation. At the Berlin congress, the Council formed a Standing Committee on Suffrage, a highly controversial move that Alice Salomon called "revolutionary" in light of the fact that the organization was "bound to be cautious, as it included women from the most outlying villages as well as from those regions better prepared for an energetic policy in favor of the franchise."[40]

Unlike the International Council of Women, the Alliance defined a clear goal from the outset. In the early congresses, held every two years in different countries in order to stimulate national suffrage activity, the vote remained the sole concern. At the 1909 congress, delegates debated the question of whether or not national auxiliaries had to have suffrage as their sole object, ultimately deciding that they did.[41] The list of national auxiliaries grew from the six originals—four from Europe, the United States, and Australia—to twenty-six in 1913 to fifty-one in 1929, including South Africa, China, Argentina, Uruguay, Brazil, Egypt, India, Palestine, Jamaica, Bermuda, Cuba, Peru, Puerto Rico, Japan, Turkey, Ceylon, Dutch East Indies, Syria, and Rhodesia (see table 1).

But even before the First World War, as the first countries granted women the right to vote, the Alliance took up questions in addition to suffrage. Beginning in 1913, congress resolutions and international commissions addressed a wide range of issues, including prostitution, peace, equal pay and the right to employment, the nationality of married women, and slavery. By 1920, with a rash of postwar enfranchisements, enough women had the vote to create a division between "haves" and "have-nots." Although the 1911 congress in Stockholm had resolved that the nations with suffrage "feel their work is not done . . . as long as the women of any country remain disfranchised," women voters seemed increasingly eager to move on to other questions.[42] Carrie Chapman Catt, Alliance president from 1904 to 1923, assumed that the Alliance congress in the aftermath of the Great War would "probably be a meeting for the purpose of disbanding or forming some new organization" and confided in her Dutch friend Aletta Jacobs that she hoped for the establishment of an International League of Women Voters.[43] Public discussion of the future of the Alliance focused on the fact that many women—especially women of the "East," "probably needing our help more than any others"—remained voteless.[44]

Not surprisingly, given the tenacity to which people cling to established groups, the 1920 congress affirmed life for the Alliance. Divided into enfranchised and unenfranchised sections, the organization would continue to work to secure suffrage "and such other reforms as are necessary to establish a real equality of liberties, status, and opportunities between men and women."[45] The call to the 1926 congress, held not coincidentally in Paris, capital of the last major power where women remained voteless, emphasized enfranchisement.[46] Alliance leaders continued to present the organization as distinguished by its commitment to "the civil, moral, and economic enfranchisement of women."[47] But an organization of women working together for their rights is quite different than one in which some women are working for the rights of others. And the fact that, with some notable exceptions, the countries without suffrage tended to be those in Latin America, Asia, and Africa created further divisions within the Alliance. The Finnish feminist Annie Furuhjelm warned that "the Enfranchised Women must take up a line of their own in the Alliance or else drop out of it altogether."[48] As it turned out, that line would be peace.

For some Alliance members, the campaign for peace grew naturally out of suffrage: women had argued for the vote, after all, at least in part on the grounds that they would use it on behalf of such grand goals. As a reflection of the new direction, the group took on the name "International Alliance of Women for Suffrage and Equal Citizenship" (which involved just an addition, rather than a rearrangement, in the French and German versions of the earlier name). But, as in the International Council, the shift to peace did not go uncontested. One member insisted in 1928 that peace had to be "incidental to the Alliance's essential task of obtaining and safeguarding equality."[49] British member Nina Boyle angrily denounced the Alliance's embracing of "the two most dangerous rivals and foes of Feminism—Peace and the Social Reformers."[50] These views—expressed in letters to the editor of the Alliance journal, *Jus Suffragii*—set off a flurry of responses. German member Marie Stritt argued the inextricable link between feminism and pacifism: "We are Pacifists because we are feminists."[51] But Boyle insisted that "those of us who have honourably refrained from bringing our Imperialism into the movement, are deeply wronged by those who will not refrain from dragging in their pacifism."[52] As war clouds increasingly darkened the skies over Europe in the 1930s, the Alliance had to tread ever more lightly in its advocacy of peace. A conference planned for Poland in 1937 had to be put off. "They are terrified of a peace conference, the nation is in a panic of rearmament, the head of the society is a militarist (though a feminist)," Margery Corbett Ashby explained.[53]

Despite the insistence that peace work flowed naturally from the Alliance's central commitment to "suffrage and equal citizenship," the increasing concentration on peace threatened the group's distinctiveness. As early as 1918, Annie Furuhjelm had suggested that the Alliance could unite with the newly formed International Committee of Women for Permanent Peace (later the Women's International League for Peace and Freedom).[54] Carrie Chapman Catt thought that if there were a great international women's peace organization of young women (she dismissed WILPF as a candidate for the honor), it could replace both the Alliance and the Council.[55] The Alliance was, in fact, in trouble in the 1930s. The worldwide depression, of course, affected all organizations; both the Council and the Alliance had to cancel meetings because of lack of funds.[56] Carrie Catt declared herself ready to see the group "close its doors" if only France would give women the vote, and Rosa Manus found everything "so hopeless and difficult."[57] But despite her fears that the Alliance would indeed fold, Corbett Ashby publicly asserted the need to continue. "No other general feminist organisation exists to take our place, with a programme neither too wide on social or philanthropic lines, nor too specialised," she asserted, distinguishing the organization implicitly from the ICW and the host of groups focused on single issues or open to particular constituencies of women.[58] But its prospects looked increasingly dim. In the final meetings before the European war broke out, board members debated the possibilities for the Alliance in an environment in which feminism had come to seem anachronistic. Corbett Ashby insisted that the Alliance was a "specialised political body" that had "broeken [*sic*] away from the I.C.W. on this point," thus harking back to the organization's origins in her attempt to conceptualize its future.[59]

These crises within the Alliance help place it in relation to the other international women's organizations. Founded as a more political and more feminist group than the International Council, it took progressive and controversial positions on such issues as the rights of single mothers. Yet members of organizations such as Equal Rights International, which focused single-mindedly on legal equality, found the Alliance "old-fashioned and no more up-to-date," "a heavy and conservative body," "highly fossilized."[60] In fact, by the period between the wars there seemed little reason, except for history and the Alliance's explicit commitment to feminism, to maintain both the ICW and the International Alliance. Despite—or because of—their mother-daughter relationship, the two organizations had attempted from the very beginning to cooperate, especially to coordinate meetings in order to accomodate their extensive overlapping membership.[61] As early as 1920, Lady Aberdeen referred to her "dream that the day might come when a working union might be effected."[62] At several junctures in the interwar years, the organizations explored the possibility of a merger. Carrie Chapman Catt even longed to unite all the international women's organizations in one association that would hold a single congress at which individual groups could hold public meetings and also gather to discuss common work. "I have no doubt that such a union would engage in civil war before many years had rolled around," Catt wrote privately, "but to my mind it might cover a period of difficulty meanwhile, and if it did not lead to civil war it certainly would teach the world a big lesson in tolerance."[63]

But it was a pie-in-the-sky plan, for the Alliance itself wriggled out of every embrace initiated by the Council. The Council approved cross-representation, joint meetings, and a common publication, but the most the Alliance would agree to was the exchange of three voting members at congresses and council meetings. Some of the opposition came from national member societies, where organizational loyalty waxed strong. But the Alliance leadership also saw the Council as too conservative.[64] In 1925 Corbett Ashby expressed her hope that the groups would merge at some unspecified later date, although "at present the pace & temper of our two bodies is too different. . . . I am afraid by any amalgamation we should lose our feminist character & become the benevolent charitable debating society that the I.C.W. is apt to be."[65]

So the Alliance maintained its separate existence, even though its work increasingly overlapped with that of the Council. The international leadership's pride in the organization's history, and specifically its explictly feminist commitment, was too strong. Despite their common concerns, especially with the issue of peace, the two bodies saw themselves as having profoundly different characters. And in fact they did.

The Women's International League for Peace and Freedom

It is ironic that the International Alliance came to concentrate so fiercely on peace in the interwar years, for that was the very issue that did for the Alliance what the suffrage question had done for the Council: divided its members and led to the birth of a new organization, the Women's International League for Peace and Freedom.[66]

When the First World War broke out in Europe in 1914, most of the work of both the International Council and the International Alliance ground to a halt. Lady Aberdeen thought it best "if the women of every country do what appears to them to be their duty as citizens of their countries and that beyond that we hold ourselves in readiness" for the time when international work would again become possible.[67] In fact, all regular communication between the International Council and the National Councils stopped for six years, leading to a "loosening of the ties of common work within the international body."[68] Even after the fighting stopped, "objections which arose to every possible place of meeting from the point of view of one section or another" delayed a gathering of the Executive Committee.[69]

The Alliance did better than the Council in maintaining contact, in part because it had a journal and in part because its international structures had developed more fully. Women in neutral countries facilitated, as best they could, an exchange of information among those in belligerent lands.[70] Still, the Alliance dropped all international suffrage work, and the location of headquarters in a warring country proved problematic. Carrie Chapman Catt hoped that "whatever happens the hard years of work done for the Alliance will not be entirely lost, and that we shall be able to pull it together and go on from the point where it was dropped."[71]

The Alliance's congress, scheduled for Berlin in June 1915, had to be scuttled when war broke out in August 1914. But there were those unwilling to give up the idea of an international meeting. "Day and night I trouble my brains what we can do to stop this scandalous bloodshed," the Dutch suffrage leader Aletta Jacobs wrote to other Alliance members. "Ought not the women of the whole world send a strong and serious protest" to the men responsible?[72] Following up on this proposal, Jacobs issued an invitation welcoming the Alliance to her country. But opposition to meeting in wartime, especially from the British suffrage leader Millicent Garrett Fawcett, axed the idea of Alliance sponsorship.[73] As Carrie Chapman Catt pointed out from her American perspective, "No one enjoys travelling in mine-strewn seas and under the uncomfortable arrangements which now exist for ocean travelling."[74] And Anna Howard Shaw had "not the least hope that it would be possible to hold such a meeting even among the neutral nations, a spark would create a blaze in a moment that would make any future meeting of the Alliance impossible."[75]

At the same time that Jacobs made her proposal, both Hungarian pacifist Rosika Schwimmer and English suffragist Emmeline Pethick-Lawrence were working feverishly for peace in the United States, and German pacifists Lida Gustava Heymann and Anita Augspurg were appealing to Swiss colleagues to call a conference of women from the neutral countries as an expression of the solidarity of women.[76] Inherent in all of these initiatives was the burning desire to do something, which culminated in the decision to move ahead without Alliance support. In response to Jacobs's invitation, women from the Netherlands, Belgium, Britain, and Germany met in Amsterdam "in warm sympathy and the best harmony" in February 1915 and issued a call for an International Congress of Women to be held at the end of April in The Hague.[77]

The planning meeting addressed a "Call to the Women of all Nations" to women's organizations, mixed-gender groups, and individual women, soliciting participation from female delegates who agreed with two major resolutions: that international disputes should be settled by pacific means and that women should have the vote.[78] One big question was who would chair the congress. Women at the preliminary meeting wanted either Carrie Chapman Catt or Jane Addams. If Catt, as president of the Alliance, could not accept, then they would have to persuade Jane Addams, who had just become head of the new U.S. Woman's Peace Party. As Anita Augspurg saw it, "the selection of capable chairs from the neutral countries is so small, that the success of the entire congress may be linked to Mrs. [sic] Addams' coming or not coming."[79] Addams did, in fact, preside.

The Hague Congress, which met from April 28 to May 1, was a remarkable wartime gathering of women from the neutral and belligerent countries, including Austria, Belgium, Britain, Canada, Denmark, Germany, Hungary, Italy, the Netherlands, Norway, Sweden, and the United States. Although there were those who stayed away, hopes both for the congress's symbolic impact and for practical results ran high.[80] Annie Furuhjelm, unable to get out of Finland, thought that "the mere fact that women of belligerent countries want to meet as sisters seems to me like the dawn of a new time promising [sic] a better future for

humanity."[81] Those who could attend passed a series of resolutions calling for, among other things, continuous mediation, enfranchisement of
women, the establishment of an international society of nations, the convening of a congress of women at the same time and place as the peace
conference, and—Rosika Schwimmer's controversial contribution—the
sending of envoys from the Congress of Women to the belligerent and
neutral nations to try to end the war.[82]

In order to ensure the holding of a women's congress in conjunction
with the peace conference and to organize support for the other resolutions, the Hague Congress established an International Committee of
Women for Permanent Peace made up of five members from each represented country. Recognizing the need for work at the national level,
International Committee members planned for the growth of national
branches. Aletta Jacobs and Rosa Manus took responsibility for setting
up and running a central office in Amsterdam, which began in July 1915
to issue a *News-Sheet*. But wartime communication proved difficult and
relations at the Amsterdam office tempestuous.[83]

At the same time, the leading role played by Rosika Schwimmer in
both the International Committee of Women for Permanent Peace and
the controversial Ford Peace Ship project had ramifications for the bud-
ding organization.[84] Schwimmer, when the war broke out, found herself
an enemy alien at the London office of the Alliance. She scrounged
enough money for passage to the United States, where she labored to win
support for a plan of continuous mediation. A passionate advocate of
peace, Schwimmer seemed to get embroiled in one conflict after another.
She left her paid position at Alliance headquarters on bad terms with the
staff and resigned after a short stint as international secretary of the U.S.
Woman's Peace Party in response to "animosity to my personality."[85]
And things went no more smoothly in her dealings with the new International Committee of Women for Permanent Peace in the wake of the
Congress of Women. Criticism of her use of funds, her high-handed
ways, and her inability to get along with people wounded her deeply. To
her devoted friend Lola Maverick Lloyd, Schwimmer wrote en route
from Europe that "I am looked upon as a criminal. . . . [I]f our Boat
should be torpedoed you may be sure that I will not fight for the best
places in the rescuing boats."[86] Back in the United States, Schwimmer
had a complete and permanent falling-out with Aletta Jacobs, leading to
mutual charges of instability and insanity.[87]

It was in this context that Schwimmer announced in November of
1915 that Henry Ford had agreed to give $200,000 to the International
Committee of Women for Permanent Peace.[88] But European pacifist
women expressed unease about the connection with the ill-fated Peace
Ship, and Jane Addams recommended that the International Committee

keep itself separate from the Ford expedition.[89] When Schwimmer could not produce even the first installment of the Ford money—Ford apparently regularly reneged on such promises—Schwimmer resigned from the International Committee, blaming Jacobs for spreading stories about her misuse of the funds. "I just cannot wish anything but to be dead," Schwimmer confided to Lola Lloyd.[90] Although Schwimmer continued to devote her life to the cause of pacifism, she never again worked harmoniously with the international women's organizations.

Despite such controversy, the International Committee of Women for Permanent Peace survived and, at war's end, worked to make good on its resolution to meet in conjunction with the peace conference. When it became clear that the negotiations would take place in Paris, a location closed to the women of the defeated countries, the committee scrambled to find an alternate location, although a group of suffragists from the Allied nations did descend on Paris to try to influence the Versailles conference.[91] Vacillating between the Netherlands and Switzerland, the leadership finally settled on Zurich. At the Zurich congress, the organization rededicated itself to its twin goals of peace and the emancipation of women, decided to move headquarters to Geneva (home of the new League of Nations), and took on its lasting name of the Women's International League for Peace and Freedom. As Aletta Jacobs and Rosa Manus put it, "we trust that our League will prosper and develop very soon into a real WORLD'S WOMEN'S PEACE MOVEMENT."[92]

Emily Greene Balch, an American pacifist fired from her job at Wellesley College for her activism during the war, agreed to serve as the secretary of the new Women's League.[93] Dutch activist Cor Ramondt-Hirschmann packed the files in Amsterdam and transported them to Geneva, and Lida Gustava Heymann and her partner Anita Augspurg traveled to the new headquarters after attending a big socialist conference held in Lucerne. "Seldom have we taken part in a working community where so beautiful a spirit of mutual understanding reigns. . . . The office in Geneva has already become an international center," Heymann reported to Jane Addams.[94] Not all members expressed such contentment. Aletta Jacobs told Emily Balch that she was glad to have no more responsibility for the organization's work and asked why the Zurich congress had decided on the new title: "What an awful name!"[95]

Unlike the other two major international women's organizations, WILPF started with a functioning international structure and had to build national sections. Beginning with thirteen sections in 1915, it grew to twenty-two in 1921, mostly in Europe and North America. Like the other groups, it sought to expand its geographical reach in the 1920s and 1930s (see table 1). In contrast to the International Council, which hoped for wide membership and eagerly totaled up the numbers in its

National Councils to claim broad representation, the League lacked membership figures and even an accurate list of national sections, although *Pax* estimated a roster of fifty thousand members in 1926.[96] From the outset, the League asserted that the "importance of a movement like ours is measured, not by numbers but by moral power and the genuine devotion of each individual member," and leaders debated the desirability of increasing membership, given the danger of diluting basic principles.[97] Strong sentiment existed for remaining "*in the van*," "avant garde," not falling "back to the level" of other societies that did not dare to oppose the powers that be.[98] Given this prevailing attitude, leaders recognized the disadvantage of publishing membership figures that "would then be in danger of seeming very small indeed."[99]

A debate over absolute pacifism in the 1920s—whether or not the organization opposed all war, including "defensive war"—pitted proponents of vanguardism against those who wanted to recruit more broadly. The British section argued that an absolute pacifist position would make WILPF "a little band of those who are already extremists," further alienating women like those in the Turkish group, who chose to affiliate with the Alliance instead.[100] The French and German sections, in contrast, insisted that WILPF was for "pioneering in politics," not for "awakening and conducting women in distant countries, who only just begin to realize pacifism as quite a new and uncommon thought."[101]

True to its origins, the Women's International League maintained its vanguardist self-conception, radical if contested politics, and controversial reputation. The Zurich congress denounced the Versailles treaty and called for revision of the League of Nations. By the 1930s, the organization nearly split apart over the question of the necessity of revolutionary social transformation. WILPF consistently took more radical positions than the other organizations on issues including the "minority question" and imperialism. In contrast to the Council and the Alliance, both of which sought to protect the autonomy of their national constituent groups, the League prided itself on its willingness to meet during the First World War, to speak out against fascism in the 1930s, and to take strong positions on the eve of the Second World War. The ICW reported with regard to an interorganizational Conference on Prevention of the Causes of War held in 1924 that the Women's International League "did not feel able to actively co-operate whith [*sic*] us when our Board of Officers passed a resolution asking all speakers 'to refrain from mentioning incidents of the last War by way of illustration, or any of the political controversies arising therefrom.'"[102] This sort of difference caused Brazilian Alliance member Bertha Lutz to dismiss WILPF as "rather amateurish and very much divorced from reality."[103]

From the very beginning, the League steered a perilous course as a radical but nonsocialist group. A number of leading members of the League—including Emily Greene Balch, Lida Gustava Heymann, Anita Augspurg, Gertrud Baer, Gabriele Duchêne, and Camille Drevet—identified at some point as socialists. After the Zurich congress in 1919, Balch reported that Alice Salomon of the ICW had noted the "radical character" of the resolutions, which expressed sympathy for "the purpose of the workers who are rising up everywhere to make an end of exploitation." Balch added that "many people considered them to have a party character," by which they meant socialist.[104] Aletta Jacobs thought it "highly probable that a large part of the membership of this congress belong to the Social Democratic or Communist party."[105] In 1922, Balch commented on the difficulty of being "so bourgeois that we are not acceptable to the working people and so to the left that we are not acceptable to the bourgeois groups."[106] Australian member Vida Goldstein argued that they had to have the "moral courage to face the charge of 'Bolshevism' which is levelled against those who are opposed to the capitalistic system & in favour of the pure Communism of the Sermon on the Mount."[107]

Over time, the issue of communism became more troublesome within the League and threatened to prompt the withdrawal of the British section. British International Secretary Mary Sheepshanks worried because most speeches were "communistic" at a special WILPF conference held in Frankfurt in 1929 and expressed concern about League participation in congresses organized by communist groups.[108] Likewise British member Edith Pye opposed sending a delegate to an antiwar demonstration in 1932 because the organizers "are known to belong to a party *which considers class warfare admissable as a remedy* for many of the ills from which humanity is suffering."[109] Jane Addams believed that both communists and fascists could belong to the League, as long as they embraced pacifism, and even encouraged Bolshevik feminist Alexandra Kollontai to organize a Russian section, but she, too, expressed concern should "the Left . . . walk away with the international office."[110]

The crux of the issue in the 1930s was the rise of fascism and the appropriate pacifist response. The British section shied away from anything smacking of "class war" and objected to working against fascism when the League had never protested the evils of communism.[111] In contrast, the French section, supported by German members, increasingly emphasized the need to place the fight for social justice and against fascism above all else. The British section feared that "the collaboration of some Members and Sections with those who are working to bring about a social revolution by methods of violence" would lead people to believe that the League condoned the use of force.[112] The issue came to a head at the 1934 congress, which accepted a Franco-German formulation that because the goals of WILPF could not be attained "under the present system of exploitation, privilege and profits," their first duty should be to hasten the social transformation that would bring about "social, economic and political equality for all without distinction of sex, race or opinion."[113] According to Camille Drevet, "We do not want to help to spread slogans of violence, but we do want to march with the masses towards great world liberation."[114]

As a result of such pronouncements, as well as WILPF's progressive character, the organization suffered periodic attacks from right-wing groups and the media. In 1928, a Geneva-based group known as the "Entente Internationale contre la IIIe. Internationale" published a pamphlet listing the League under the "Agitation and Propaganda Section" of the Comintern.[115] The charge, traced to a Russian emigré lawyer who headed the Entente and carried in the conservative *Journal de Genève*, seemed to be based on Gabrielle Duchêne's having attended a meeting of the Anti-Imperialist League in Brussels and visited Russia and on the League's having soft-pedaled criticism of the Soviet Union.[116] WILPF hired a Geneva attorney and demanded a retraction, but the best they could get was a declaration that the offending pamphlet was not meant to suggest that the League was affiliated with the Comintern, only that there were members who spread Bolshevik propaganda. Adding insult to injury, the WILPF attorney, a personal friend of the Entente's head, demurred from taking any further legal action.[117]

That such accusations had consequences became clear when Pauline Chaponnière-Chaix, former president of the ICW, referred to the Entente charges in explaining why the other women's organizations ought not to have dealings with WILPF.[118] Furthermore, the allegations reached the Finnish section in 1931, making work almost impossible, for that country was struggling to maintain its independence from the Soviet Union. In 1936 the Finnish section was still begging the Geneva office for evidence of "our political independence, especially from Moscow."[119] Charges leveled in 1933 at French International Secretary Camille Drevet—described even within the League as having "very strong leaning to Russia and to the Soviet forms of Government"—resulted in the revocation by the Swiss authorities of her permit to reside in Geneva, a decision that WILPF successfully fought.[120] As the chairmen put it, "Although the refusal to renew the Permit was personal to Madame Drevet, . . . since her actions had been in conformity with the principles of the League, the League itself was involved."[121] Perhaps as a result of these associations, international cochairman Gertrud Baer responded defensively to a letter from the Bulgarian section: "The W.I.L.P.F. has nothing to do with political parties. It has as little in common with the Communist Party and its tactics as with any other party in any other country."[122]

The Women's International League survived such right-wing attacks, but the tension involved in supporting the twin goals of peace and freedom in the face of the rise of fascism in the 1930s proved almost too much. All three organizations confronted the fascist threat, condemning both Nazi repression of women and oppression of the Jews.[123] The German National Council of Women disbanded rather than accept Nazi principles, and the ICW refused to accept a new Nazi organization in its place.[124] The German branch of the Alliance also refused to submit to the Nazi Party or to adopt the required racial clause excluding Jewish women, leading to its dissolution as well.[125] Because of the pacifism and radicalism of the Women's International League, members faced real danger. Nazis raided the home of Lida Gustava Heymann and Anita Augspurg, prompting them, like many other members, to flee Germany.[126] Nazism threatened League members in Czechoslovakia and Austria as well.[127] Although WILPF organized to fight fascism, the Bulgarian section in 1937 defended Hitler as Europe's savior from communism, provoking Gertrud Baer, one of the joint chairmen, to proclaim in a draft of a response that the League "refuses fascism in whatever form it masquerades and in whatever country it may appear. . . . It refuses fascism, because fascism contradicts everything for which the League has stood since its origins and for which it fights today." Another of the chairmen, Dutchwoman Cor Ramondt-Hirschmann, apparently proposed adding a line indicating that members were free to hold their personal opinions, to which Baer responded incredulously: "Dear Frau Ramondt, I assume that this is a misunderstanding on my part or a slip of the pen on yours. Because it is surely not possible that you are of the opinion that a member or president of a section can have the opinion that fascism in certain countries is justified."[128] In fact, the League as an organization vigorously fought fascism wherever it reared its head, even joining communist-dominated coalitions and thus helping further to fuel charges of extremism.

The Women's International League, then, was the most radical of the three major organizations, remaining true to its wartime origins. Despite internal conflicts and the defection of those who abandoned pacifism as another war—and one more clearly connected to the defense of freedom—threatened, the League hewed to the course laid out in the 1915 Congress of Women, continuing to work toward the achievement of peace and the full emancipation of women.

Getting Together

These three major international women's groups—with related origins but different natures and trajectories—cooperated and competed with a host of other bodies. Reaching out across the borders of their nations, women came together as socialists; as advocates of single issues, such as equal rights; as members of occupational categories; as adherents of different religious traditions; and as inhabitants of different regions of the world.[129] Some of these multinational bodies interacted on a regular basis with the Council, Alliance, and League, while others kept their distance. In coming together internationally, women marched in step with a whole range of constituencies who founded transnational groups; the establishment of such groups began in the latter half of the nineteenth century and reached a crescendo between the wars.[130] Despite the crippling global depression, the intensification of nationalism embodied both in fascism and in the communist shift to "socialism in one country," and in what seems in retrospect the inexorable march toward war in the 1930s, the years between the world wars represented the high tide of internationalism.

The most troubling gap for those who longed for the unity of women was the chasm that yawned between the bourgeois and socialist women's movements. At an International Council of Women meeting in Berlin in 1896, socialist Lily Braun attacked "the bourgeois lack of understanding in allowing her only twenty minutes for a labor problem," and socialist women refused an invitation to participate at the 1904 International Council congress.[131] Not surprisingly, the Socialist Women's International, which was organized by Clara Zetkin in 1907, rejected any cooperation across political lines, making its position clear from the outset: "The socialist women's movement of all countries . . . pursues its struggle not in coalition with the bourgeois women's rights advocates, but in partnership with the socialist parties."[132]

Because there were women in the bourgeois organizations who identified with socialism and sought to win socialist support for their goals, the Socialist Women's International could not succeed in cutting off all contact. Dutch International Council and Alliance member Martina Kramers was especially active on this front in the years before the First World War. In 1901, she warned Council leader May Wright Sewall not to write the widow of assassinated U.S. president William McKinley on behalf of the Council, "for many of our thinking members are socialists."[133] Kramers, involved in a long-term relationship with a married male socialist, joined the socialist party and worked to defend her politics to the women's movement and to "make the Socialists realize that the women's movement is not hostile to theirs."[134] Despite her efforts, Kramers often despaired: "Here the SD [Social Democratic] women refuse to take a leaflet from the hands of a woman with the badge of the suffragists, although it is an appeal written by Bebel [author of *Women under Socialism*] himself," she wrote in 1911.[135] Nor did Clara Zetkin's implacable opposition endear her to the suffragists. Kramers referred to her "dictatorship," and one of Kramers's coworkers found Zetkin "a very peculiar woman" who "in true Jesuit spirit does 'everything for the greater glory of God.'"[136]

Opposition to war formed a fragile thread between socialist and nonsocialist women, and not surprisingly WILPF had the most success in making a connection. The International Conference of Socialist Women, held in Berne at the end of March 1915, sent greetings to the Hague Congress, an unusual expression of support across the lines of party politics.[137] In return, the new International Committee of Women for Permanent Peace greeted the Zimmerwald conference of antiwar socialists and printed its manifesto in its news sheet.[138] After the war, delegates from the newly formed Women's International League for Peace and Freedom took the resolutions of their 1919 Zurich congress to the International Socialist Conference.[139]

The success of the Bolshevik Revolution further divided bourgeois and communist women, although limited cooperation revived during the period of the Popular Front, as fascism forced reluctant liberals and communists into a strained embrace. One vehicle for this was the Comité Mondial des Femmes contre la Guerre et le Fascisme, formed at a Paris congress in August 1934. According to Dutch WILPF member Cor Ramondt-Hirschmann, the call to this gathering left "no doubt whatever" about the "absolutely communist character" of the plan.[140] Nevertheless, the organizing committee invited a range of individuals and groups. Gabrielle Duchêne, a moving force behind the congress, reported that an "indescribable enthusiasm" gripped the gathering, which brought together "the women that race, geographical situation, social milieu, intellectual formation, religion, philosophical conviction, individual or general interests, everything, finally, had separated until now."[141] A delegation from the Women's International League attended and called a special meeting of all pacifist representatives.[142] Although, according to one of the WILPF members, "undoubted efforts were made to prevent this meeting being a Communist Congress," the songs, cheers, slogans, and salutes to heroes all revealed "the powerful current of Communist sympathy."[143]

The other popular front organization that brought together bourgeois and communist women was the Women's Commission of the Rassemblement Universel pour la Paix, which was founded in 1936, in the wake of the Italian invasion of Ethiopia.[144] Organized women responded enthusiastically to the RUP, priding themselves on winning a guaranteed seat on the Executive Committee.[145] In an appeal signed by women leaders and organizations, the RUP called on "all women, manual workers and intellectuals, housewives, school teachers, mothers of families from towns and the countryside, of all countries, of all classes, of all political opinions," to support the campaign and attend a peace congress organized by Rosa Manus.[146] An emergent "Section Féminine" announced a women's gathering just prior to the opening of the congress and held a big women's demonstration in the congress's aftermath, giving rise to an ongoing "Commission Féminine."[147]

As with the Comité Mondial, the issue of communist involvement proved controversial. Mary Dingman, chairman of the Peace and Disarmament Committee, worried that "the left element is so strong that the Congress will take on that colour almost exclusively."[148] Rosa Manus argued that if "the people from the right and the organisations who have never worked with communists and socialists and who have tried to come into the Rassemblement, are now leaving all at once, we are giving the others all the opportunity but we may not blame them for taking everything in hand then," apparently winning Dingman over.[149]

Clearly, cooperation across the lines of politics was fraught with difficulty. Despite uneasy coalition work in the atmosphere of the Popular Front, socialist and nonsocialist women tended to eye each other with suspicion and to organize separately. As a result, socialist women's groups remained almost entirely outside the fold of the international women's movement.

Among the bourgeois groups, getting together took a number of forms. On the most basic level, groups regularly welcomed "fraternal" delegates from the other bodies to their congresses, although even such minimal interaction sometimes raised the fear that outsiders would infringe on organizational autonomy. The three major bodies tried to plan the timing and location of their meetings to facilitate attendance of women who belonged to more than one group and who had to travel from overseas. Groups sometimes shared office space: when Equal Rights International ran out of money, it used the Geneva office of the International Alliance; the Alliance itself later opened temporary Geneva headquarters in the office of the Disarmament Committee; and the Disarmament Committee, in turn, had initially met in the Geneva offices of the World Young Women's Christian Association and had also used the International Council's London office.[150] Organizations exchanged publications and reported each others' news, and the International Alliance, in 1920, offered other groups the possibility of printing a supplement to *Jus Suffragii*, though only the World Young Women's Christian Association worked out an arrangement to do so.[151]

One way that the groups tried to minimize potential conflict was by carving out special areas of expertise. While these might be clearly defined for the more specialized groups, as peace work took center stage in the period between the wars it became harder and harder to distinguish the spheres of activity of the big three. Leaders tried to do so. Emily Greene Balch proposed in 1921 that "the 3 middle class organisations of women" affiliate, "the Alliance taking suffrage and women's rights . . . , the Council taking social and moral reform, and we taking education & internationalism."[152] Others saw nothing wrong with all groups devoting themselves to peace. In fact, the most successful cooperative ventures focused on peace.

If the diverse bourgeois international women's groups sometimes jealously guarded their autonomy and sometimes competed with each other, they also managed, in the 1920s and 1930s, to forge an institutional form for cooperation. Formal coalitions represented the epitome of the process of "getting together."

The Superinternational Coalitions

As transnational women's organizations proliferated in the period between the wars, it made sense to create structures that would concentrate their efforts. Laying claim through their very titles to represent "the women's international organisations," four coalitions in the 1920s and 1930s added a new strata of superinternational organizing.

In 1925 the International Council of Women, exercising the privilege of inviting other groups "to unite and confer with us as to how best to mobilize the potential motherhood of the world," took steps to form what came to be known as the Joint Standing Committee of the Women's International Organisations to push for the appointment of women to the League of Nations.[153] Representatives from a number of groups attended the organizing meeting in London, where—an indication of the boundaries of the movement—"it was felt that only those should have been asked to join which were definitely feminist or concerned quite specially with women's interests" (see table 2).[154] The Secretariat of the League of Nations, according to a staff member, wanted the committee "to be truly representative of all women's organisations and thought that representatives of the Catholic women and Labour should be added," but the committee had no luck in widening its circle.[155] The International Union of Catholic Women's Leagues declined an invitation to an "undenominational international body" and demanded separate representation at the League of Nations, and neither the working-class International Co-operative Women's Guild nor the women's section of the

TABLE 2
Superinternational Coalitions and International Women's Organizations

Organization	Founded	Membership in Coalition:			
		JSC	WCCN	LC	PDC
International Association of Women	1868				
International Federation for the Abolition of the State Regulation of Vice	1875				
World Women's Christian Temperance Union	1883	X		X	X
Union Internationale des Amies de la Jeune Fille	1887				
International Council of Women	1888	X	X	X	X
World Young Women's Christian Association	1894	X		X	X
International Union of Women	1895				
International Bureau for the Suppression of Traffic in Women and Children	1899				
International Council of Nurses	1899	X			
International Woman Suffrage Alliance	1904	X	X	X	X
International Socialist Women's Committee	1907				
International Union of Catholic Women's Associations	1910				
International Council of Jewish Women	1912				
Women's International League for Peace and Freedom	1915	X	X	X	X
Union Mondiale de la Femme pour la Concorde Internationale	1915	X	X	X	X
International Association of Police Women	1915				
Pan American International Women's Committee	1916				
International Federation of University Women	1919	X	X	X	X

TABLE 2 (*Cont.*)
Superinternational Coalitions and International Women's Organizations

		Membership in Coalition:			
Organization	*Founded*	*JSC*	*WCCN*	*LC*	*PDC*
International Movement of Girl Scouts and Girl Guides	1919			X	
Medical Women's International Association	1919				
League of Jewish Women	1920				X
International Women's Secretariat (Comintern)	1920				
Women's International Zionist Organisation	1920				
International Federation of Working Women	1921				
International Co-operative Women's Guild	1921				X
Pan American Association for the Advancement of Women	1922				
World Council of Jewish Women	1923				
Inter-American Commission of Women	1928		X		
Pan Pacific Women's Association	1928				
Soroptimist International Association	1928				
International Federation of Women Magistrates, Barristers and Members of other Branches of the Legal Professions	1929			X	
Ligue Internationale des Méres et Educatrices pour la Paix	1929				X
Open Door International	1929				
Equal Rights International	1930	X	X	X	
International Federation of Business and Professional Women	1930			X	X
Associated Country Women of the World	1930				
Soroptimist International of Europe	1930				X

TABLE 2 (*Cont.*)
Superinternational Coalitions and International Women's Organizations

Organization	Founded	Membership in Coalition:			
		JSC	WCCN	LC	PDC
Union for Oriental Women's Congresses	1930				
Zonta International	1930				
All Asian Women's Conference	1931		X		
St. Joan's International Social and Political Alliance	1931			X	
Comité Mondial des Femmes contre la Guerre et le Fascisme	1934				
International Association of Altrusa Clubs	1935				
Commission Féminine de Rassemblement Universel pour la Paix	1936				
World Woman's Party	1938				
Women's International Democratic Federation	1945				

Source: Based, in part, on Reinalda and Verhaaren 1989.
Notes: JSC: Joint Standing Committee of the Women's International Organisations. WCCN: Women's Consultative Committee on Nationality. LC: Liason Committee of the Women's International Organisations. PDC: Peace and Disarmament Committee.

International Federation of Trade Unions could be coaxed to join.[156]

The Joint Standing Committee launched its work by soliciting names of women qualified to serve on committees of the League of Nations, honoring women active in the League, and working with these figures to lobby for the appointment of more women. Contacts within the League of Nations included Dame Rachel Crowdy, chief of the Social Section from 1919 to 1930 and the only woman to head a section; Princess Gabrielle Radziwill, member of the Secretariat in charge of relations with voluntary organizations; and Martha Mundt of the International Labor Organization.[157] The Joint Standing Committee claimed some success in winning appointments of women to various committees, generally those concerned with women and children, despite its objection to "the assumption that women were only interested in humanitarian subjects."[158]

Succumbing to pressure from organized women, the League of Nations in 1931 established the second coalition, the Women's Consultative Committee on Nationality (see table 2). How to handle the thorny problem of the nationality of women married to citizens of another country had become a contentious issue within the international women's movement in the 1920s and 1930s. Even before the initial meeting, the delegates quarreled over whether to wait to meet until a room came available at the Secretariat or to forgo such official sanction in order to begin work early enough to draft a comprehensive report.[159] It did not bode well for the group's future. And in fact the trouble escalated when U.S. National Woman's Party founder Alice Paul, who trailed conflict in her wake, schemed to expand the scope of the Consultative Committee and win it official League of Nations status.[160] For U.S. women, cut off from direct access to the League of Nations because of their country's refusal to join, such a body would serve an important purpose. But Paul's plan encountered serious opposition, in part because of her domineering ways and in part because a broadened committee stepped on the toes of existing organizations.

The Liaison Committee of the Women's International Organisations, the third coalition, took on the broad range of issues that Paul had in mind for the Consultative Committee. Why the organizations belonging to the Joint Standing Committee decided to form a new coalition rather than extend the focus of the old remains a mystery (see table 2).[161] Whatever the reason for its inception, the new group, established in 1931, quickly took on a life of its own and began to threaten the turf of other bodies. The disputed minutes of an early meeting reported Lady Aberdeen claiming that the Liaison Committee could be "considered as a Committee of the I.C.W.," although Aberdeen denied having said this.[162] In any case, she did think that "[o]ur job was filched away when the Liaison Committee was formed."[163]

One child of the Liaison Committee, the Disarmament (later Peace and Disarmament) Committee, rapidly declared its adulthood, serving as the fourth coalition. Although ICW member May Ogilvie Gordon envisaged the Liaison Committee functioning "like a parent body keeping control" of each temporary offshoot, other members approved of ad hoc committees attaining independence.[164] Organized in 1931 to promote the success of the League of Nations–sponsored Disarmament Conference, the new body encompassed more diverse groups than the other coalitions, including the League of Jewish Women and the International Co-operative Women's Guild (see table 2). According to a delegate from WILPF, "collaboration between these people, of sometimes very different opinions, is indeed marvelous and in the very best spirit owing greatly to

the tact of our chairman, Miss [Mary] Dingman, one of the well known
workers of the Y.W.C.A."[165] So closely associated did the chair become
with the work of this organization that many referred to it simply as "the
Dingman Committee."

As early as 1932, Mary Dingman was explaining to the ICW leadership that any member group that wanted to take some action with regard
to disarmament ought first to raise it with her committee.[166] In 1935, the
Peace and Disarmament Committee sent joint deputations with its supposed parent body to the president of the Assembly of the League of
Nations, an act that suggested a parallel rather than subordinate status.[167] And by 1938, according to one critic, "Miss Dingman's Committee behaves as though it were a member of the Liaison Committee."[168]
The major project of the new coalition when it formed was coordination
of a mammoth worldwide petition campaign. In February 1932, in a
carefully planned ceremony, women representing the Disarmament
Committee and its constituent international organizations carried to the
League of Nations petitions with eight million signatures collected in
fifty-six countries.[169] Originally intended to last for just one year, the
committee decided that it "could not give up its work."[170] In 1935 Mary
Dingman went to work on a full-time basis for the newly renamed Peace
and Disarmament Committee with the task of exchanging views and
information and coordinating actions among the transnational women's
organizations.[171]

In contrast to the Women's International League for Peace and Freedom, one of its often-impatient constituent members, the Peace and Disarmament Committee avoided radical stands and found friends in high
places. Powerful Genevan men not only wrote letters of appreciation but
also donated funds to rent and furnish the office.[172] Clara Guthrie d'Arcis, the businesswoman founder of the Union Mondiale, launched a plan
to win financial support from large corporations. As a first phase, the
Peace and Disarmament Committee published a "Peace-Roll of Industry" in which corporations such as General Motors (d'Arcis and her husband distributed GM cars in Switzerland), U.S. Steel, and Shell Union
Oil declared peace essential to prosperity. In contrast to the anticapital-
ist rhetoric of the Women's International League, the "Peace-Roll of
Industry" hoped to "refute the assumption now widely held that, if not
actually and secretly conniving for war, business is at least complacent
about war."[173] This dramatic difference in perspective, as well as the
Peace and Disarmament Committee's expansion of activities in conjunction with its name change, brought the coalition into direct conflict with
WILPF. As one of the cochairmen put it, "It is completely improper, how
the Dingman Committee now poses as an independent organization; it
was not founded as such, but as a clearinghouse of international organi-

zations."[174] But the Peace and Disarmament Committee hung on even as world events mocked attempts to move toward disarmament.

The formation of these four coalitions marks the high tide of the international women's movement before the Second World War. Like mixed-gender or male transnational organizations concerned with a vast array of questions, from agriculture to law, women's societies multiplied in the interwar years as the League of Nations opened up new opportunities for members to converge on Geneva and importune delegates. Although relations within and among coalitions proved stormy, with intense debates about degrees of constituent-group autonomy and battles over turf, the desire among women's groups in the interwar period to coordinate work is striking. Rather than being a sign of discord and decline, the proliferation of transnational organizations provided strength and stability to the international women's movement.

But women did not always see it that way, and the positive consequences of organizational reproduction did not lessen one whit the fervent loyalty that members lavished on their individual groups. Despite overlap and senescence, no body ever moved to disband. Margery Corbett Ashby thought the Alliance had "a terrible habit of continuing committees whether they are good or bad," while Carrie Chapman Catt complained in 1945 of the "good many organizations of women that are now quite old and, I believe, out of date."[175] Faced with the emergence of a new body or the extension of work into a new area—as we have seen in exploring the relations among the coalitions and their constituent groups—women proclaimed their allegiances. "For my part I feel convinced that Chinese walls will only give way before long-built-up organisations," wrote Martina Kramers in 1917.[176] According to Cor Ramondt-Hirschmann, "it can only harm the real work for peace to have new bodies springing up continually."[177] And when Carrie Chapman Catt, Rosa Manus, and Bertha Lutz heard a rumor that Alice Paul's World Woman's Party expected the Alliance to die and planned to take its place on the international stage, they resisted the very thought. "[T]he idea of the Alliance going out and Alice Paul picking up the members, makes my hair stand," wrote Manus. "THIS MAY NOT HAPPEN and I shall fight for it."[178]

Women's identification with a particular organization—even when they belonged to more than one—tended to be strong. When Alice Salomon came to visit the new Women's International League headquarters in Geneva in 1919, Emily Greene Balch reported that Salmon seemed impressed by their work and friendly, "though mainly loyal to the I Council of W."[179] Pauline Chaponnière-Chaix, president of the International Council from 1920 to 1922, regretfully declined an invitation to the Women's International League's 1921 congress because "I feel

I must, for this year at least, concentrate absolutely upon my work for the I.C.W."[180] Likewise, Renée Girod, who took the presidency of the ICW in 1940, declined to serve on the council of the World Woman's Party because "I do not feel that it is possible for me to work actively in another international organisation."[181] Differentiating the work of competing groups, Clara Ragaz commented about a colleague that "she does excellent work, to be sure, but not exactly in the style of the League."[182] Ramondt-Hirschmann reported to Jane Addams that she had gotten back in touch with the International Council and International Alliance "and there again it struck me how far more congenial I felt with regard to the W.I.L."[183]

Organizational loyalty played a powerful role in keeping groups alive. "People get so proud of and devoted to their own organizations," Margery Corbett Ashby told an interviewer in 1976.[184] Emily Greene Balch tried hard "not to be a chauvinist with regard to a given organisation with which I am associated any more than with regard to my country," but she could not hide her loyalty to the Women's International League.[185] Making the same comparison, Doris Stevens referred to falling into "the trap of patriotism, in this case toward the corporate bodies with whom one works and comes to love."[186]

Loving one's international organization contributed to a kind of organizational identity politics, but such loyalty also facilitated interaction among groups in the context of the international women's movement: even conflict meant that women were talking to each other across the lines of both organizations and country. And in fact the identity politics of such organizations sometimes served as an alternative—or at least a complement—to national identity, in that way contributing to the construction of internationalism.

The Second World War and Postwar Reconstruction

Contact among the international women's organizations had been broken during the First World War, but that conflict paradoxically energized the international women's movement. The bulk of the diverse bodies devoted to women's interests on the international scene came into being in the interwar period, as did the coalitions, the "get-togetherers" getting together once again. The Second World War was a different story. Already battered by the Depression, which had threatened their treasuries, the transnational organizations simply hung on as best they could. According to Alice Paul, in Geneva in October 1939, "Practically all activity on the part of women's organizations has ceased here—and throughout Europe."[187]

But that was not entirely true. Marthe Boël, the Belgian president of the International Council of Women, in October 1939 appealed to her Executive Committee "to see that the link which has united us for half a century, remains as strong and firm as it has been during the happy years when we worked side by side."[188] With the invasion of Belgium and the sacking of the office in Brussels, the ICW passed the presidency and headquarters to Renée Girod in Geneva in May 1940.[189] The *Bulletin*, moved to a temporary London office, continued to appear until 1944. Despite difficulty in getting Council funds out of the Netherlands and England, the reconstituted Geneva office worked to maintain "a delicate and fragile thread" uniting the National Councils.[190] In May 1945 Boël resumed the presidency and reopened the Brussels office, and in December she called on revived National Councils to serve once again as centers around which "women of all opinions and tendencies can rally."[191] The Council came together in a conference in Philadelphia in 1946, responding to the horrors of wartime and to the new world order by condemning war, aggression, and crimes against humanity and demanding a more active role for women in national governments and the United Nations.

The International Alliance, too, survived the war, but with difficulty. Perhaps as a result of the long anxiety about the impending conflict, Margery Corbett Ashby sensed that it would be even worse than the Great War, although she, like the Council president, reaffirmed bonds of friendship and prayed "that when the horror is over we shall find, as we found in 1918, that our ranks are not broken."[192] When the Germans turned to the West, the London office closed and the British secretary, Katherine Bompas, ran both the headquarters and journal out of her home. The leadership sent some documents to the United States, Switzerland, and Brazil for safekeeping and made plans to pass offices to women in those countries in case of a German invasion of Britain.[193] As a result of wartime restrictions, the Alliance handed over *Jus Suffragii* to a British group called the Women's Publicity Planning Association in October 1940, a move that kept the paper alive but severed its international and feminist roots. Margery Corbett Ashby urged members to "keep alive, in your heart and in the minds and hearts of your closest colleagues, the hope and determination that the seed of the woman's movement shall remain alive, ready to germinate when spring comes again."[194]

Throughout the war, the Alliance worked toward a postwar meeting. Carrie Chapman Catt, despite her long commitment to the Alliance, doubted that the existing organizations, led "by women who are old," would take the lead. Nevertheless, the Alliance tried as early as 1942 to interest other international women's organizations in a joint congress after the war.[195] When the fighting stopped, the Alliance slowly resumed its work while grieving the news of Rosa Manus's death in Ravensbrück and Františka Plamínková's execution by the Germans in 1943.[196] Meeting in Switzerland in 1946, the organization took on the new shortened name of "International Alliance of Women" and adopted a program of peace, democracy, women's rights, and support for the United Nations.[197]

As the most progressive of the three organizations, the Women's International League began dreading war from the time of Hitler's rise to power in Germany.[198] The Maison Internationale, the organizational headquarters in Geneva, opened to pacifist refugees in April 1933. Once war broke out, helping those fleeing Europe became a central priority of the League as well as of other women's groups.[199] As Emily Greene Balch put it, "Ringed around by a wall of violence, we draw closer together."[200] Located in a neutral country, unlike the Council and Alliance, the League headquarters could remain open and try to facilitate communication among members on opposite sides of the battle lines, but the work continued only with great difficulty. Ramondt-Hirschmann and Gertrud Baer fled Geneva, Ramondt-Hirschmann going home to the Netherlands and Baer, who was Jewish and thus in great danger, relocating to the United States.[201] A mimeographed circular letter, published in New York by Baer, replaced *Pax*. Although the U.S. section offered hospitality to the international headquarters, European leaders felt that it was important to stay put. As Swiss Alliance member Emilie Gourd put it, it was crucial that "international life continues in Geneva."[202] Like the other organizations, the Women's International League planned for the coming peace and pulled back together when the war ended, meeting in Luxembourg in 1946 and restarting *Pax* at the end of 1949.

The world of 1945 was a different place for the international women's movement. Not only did the organizations have to reestablish contacts and deal with the loss of members and national sections, but the escalating bipolar rivalry between the United States and the Soviet Union split the international scene into hostile camps. A group of U.S. women, described by Carrie Chapman Catt as having "engaged in so-called war work" and dressed in "very becoming costumes," convened an International Assembly of Women in South Kortright, New York, in October 1946.[203] Organizers, with no relationship to existing international women's groups, invited prominent women and leaders of transnational bodies "who will not proselyte [sic] for any specific ideology" from countries all over the world to pool their knowledge and learn about the United Nations.[204] Women experienced in international organizing, like Catt, viewed the enterprise with skepticism. Margery Corbett Ashby, who attended, at first thought the assembly had "the requisite for success," but three days later she reported that the U.S. organizers "are conservative and completely inexperienced & therefore terrified of any possible pronouncements which will of course be 'red!' "[205] To Rosika Schwimmer the women were "a crazy lot" and the meeting "a tragic farce," since discussion of the "great problems of our time" was not permitted.[206] The Assembly, with its "free world" emphasis, marked the drawing into camps that was already taking place.

Earlier, in November 1945, on the other side of both the Atlantic and the ideological divide, the communist-dominated Union des Femmes Françaises had called an international congress in Paris that gave birth to a new organization, the Women's International Democratic Federation. The preliminary program of the congress, from the International Alliance's perspective, showed "much feminist policy but also support for democracy and anti-fascism"—in this context, code words for communism.[207] Although the general secretary of the Alliance, echoing the lament of Carrie Chapman Catt about the International Assembly of Women, complained that members of the new group "feel they are the first women who have ever thought of having an international women's conference," she reported that Corbett Ashby thought that "this may be the new form of the women's movement, and that if it is not boycotted at the start by the older women's societies, some form of co-operation may be possible, or at least opposition avoided."[208] Corbett Ashby herself found the conference "intensely interesting," the program regarding equality as advanced "as the most old-fashioned feminist could require." But the keynote was fear of fascism. "We who have been free for a thousand years, how can we criticise their first steps!" she asked.[209]

As it turned out, the Women's International Democratic Federation continued the well-worn socialist tradition of hostility to the bourgeois women's movement. Well-funded and claiming to speak for eighty million women, the WIDF even challenged the right of the older organizations to represent women at the United Nations.[210] And so the cold war enveloped the world of international women's organizations, although rivalry between the two camps led to increased global organizing, especially as more and more countries fought for and won their independence from Western domination. The Second World War marked a turn, not an end or beginning, for international organizing among women.

The building of the international women's movement was, then, a process that lurched slowly into motion in the late nineteenth century, gathered steam at the end of the First World War, and nearly screeched to a halt in 1939, although the existing transnational groups reconstituted themselves in the late 1940s in a world transformed by bipolar rivalry and accelerated decolonization. In reflecting on the trajectory of the movement, one feels an insistent tugging at one's sleeve. "But the international women's movement seems to have flourished just when the

national movements of Europe and the United States slid into decline,"
a small voice whispers.

In fact, the pattern of growth of the international women's movement
challenges what has become a nearly hegemonic model of "first wave"
and "second wave," which is based on the rise of women's movements
in the Euro-American arena in the late nineteenth century, their ebbing
after the First World War, and their resurgence in the 1970s. For if we
pay attention to the world system beyond the industrialized core nations,
we see instead choppy seas, with women's movements emerging in countries newly free or struggling for political or economic independence in
the 1920s.[211] And we can witness the international women's movement
cresting in the interwar period, with new organizations springing up and
existing bodies adding sections in Asia, Latin America, and even Africa.

The three major groups, despite their differences, all began with
national sections in Europe or the "neo-Europes," areas of similar climate where European settler colonies succeeded.[212] The First World War
undermined European control of the world system and both stimulated
the growth of national women's movements in formerly dependent or
colonized countries and also encouraged attempts by international
women's organizations to expand their reach. Nevertheless, the patterns
of interaction among the whole range of transnational groups mirrored
the dominance of European or European-settled, Christian, capitalist
nations in the world system. It was within this context that members of
the international women's organizations came together across their
countries' borders and, through both conflict and cooperation, constructed a collective identity as feminist internationalists. We turn in the
next chapter to the boundaries, both implicit and explicit, that defined
who did and did not belong to the international women's movement.

Section I

BOUNDARIES

3

Who's In, Who's Out

[A]n international group is always very small
because we cannot bring you all from the
countries to sit there in Geneva.
(Mary Dingman, 1933)[1]

IN 1933, at the International Congress of Women in Chicago, Mary
Dingman addressed the paradoxical nature of international organizing,
distinguishing between the 45 million women who belonged to the Disarmament Committee through their national groups and the "faithful
group of women" who traveled to Geneva to do the work. In that way
she hinted at the often-unacknowledged boundaries that marked off the
circle of internationally active women.

In theory, of course, the three major transnational women's organizations welcomed women of all stations from every corner of the earth.
The constitution of the International Council of Women, drawn up in
1888 and revised in 1936, presented the organization as "a federation of
women of all races, nations, creeds and classes."[2] The International
Alliance issued a welcome in 1911 to women "of whatever race, nativity, or creed," and the 1915 Congress of Women at The Hague claimed
to speak for the "women of the world."[3] Ideally, no boundaries separated women from all continents of the earth.

But in fact, as we have seen, the major transnational women's organizations originated and grew primarily in Europe and the neo-Europes.
Despite grand pronouncements of universality, obstacles to the equal
participation of all groups of women belied the global ambitions of the
three organizations, creating a movement of predominantly elite, Christian, older women of European origin. In this chapter, we explore the
impact of class, religion, age, and ethnicity on the composition of the
movement. By examining the barriers that kept some women out, we can
see that the limitations on participation flowed from the nature of
transnational organizing and from unacknowledged assumptions about
the superiority and natural leadership of Euro-American societies. And
we can understand the complex consequences of the movement's boundaries. For the relative homogeneity of the international women's movement served as a source of solidarity for those within the walls. At the

same time, tension between the ideal of inclusiveness and the reality of exclusiveness, as well as increasing challenges to the unintended boundaries as European dominance of the world system declined, raised persistent questions about who was in and who was out.

A Gathering of the Elite

Although there were class differences among participants in the international organizations, elite status—through wealth or national prominence—served as one of the firmest lines dividing internationally active members from the masses of women around the globe. Participants' descriptions of gatherings make this clear. U.S. suffragist Matilda Gage depicted the audience at the founding meeting of the International Council, with its especially aristocratic reputation, as consisting of "the most eminent women."[4] The "leaders of the women's movement in their respective countries" attended the 1909 Toronto congress, according to Lady Aberdeen.[5] Even the Women's International League, with its radical reputation, seemed to a member of the League of Jewish Women an "important assembly of the feminine elite of the world."[6]

The women's organizations brought together a range of elite women, including aristocrats and solid members of the educated middle class. The ICW had the reputation for aristocratic pretensions, but the other organizations also attracted upper-class women, though perhaps to a lesser extent. Even if aristocrats did not dominate the leadership of the Alliance, the qualities of wealth and elegance did not hurt. Carrie Chapman Catt recommended an American coworker as an international officer because of her connections to rich women and her ability to raise money, and Bertha Lutz asked for "an elegant women [*sic*], with profound feminist convictions," to come to Buenos Aires.[7] The Women's International League, because of its radicalism, probably paid the least attention to the aristocracy, but it was still—as Gabrielle Duchêne, herself a wealthy woman and a socialist, put it—composed of "women of the privileged classes."[8]

The bulk of the membership of all of the groups probably came, as Gertrud Baer characterized WILPF members, "from the middle classes."[9] When Ghénia Avril de Sainte-Croix, a founder of the French National Council of Women, surveyed other countries in 1905 about their groups, she asked whether, like her own council, they were composed of "women belonging to the bourgeoisie."[10] Such women did not always have great wealth, but they did need sufficient income to travel. WILPF member Catherine Marshall, planning her trip to Paris for an Executive Committee meeting, wanted to stay in a small hotel another member had described "because I gathered that some of the poorer members of the Comm. could not afford the St. Pères & would be going to the other, & I do so *hate* the plan of dividing ourselves up according to what we can afford to pay for being comfortable!"[11]

Yet if members sometimes had limited resources, particularly in the economic hard times in the aftermath of the First World War and in the global depression of the 1930s, they were still unlikely to come from the working class. Margery Corbett Ashby explained in an interview that working-class women had their own international movement, meaning the International Co-operative Women's Guild.[12] That the three major organizations, and especially WILPF, sought to attract working-class women or to ally with groups that did indicates their awareness of their own class composition. In 1924, on board ship back to Europe from the WILPF congress in Washington, Lida Gustava Heymann insisted that third-class passengers be included in their peace meeting. According to a critic, "Frl. Heymann said that she was fearfully disappointed in our League only addressing bourgeois and jewelled people!"[13] Contemplating class differences in 1934, Emily Greene Balch recognized that her "academic manner" must seem as "alien and impossible" to a working-class group as the tone and manner of the congress of the Comité Mondial contre la Guerre et le Fascisme seemed to her. "I think it is such questions of taste and of way of doing things which (quite as much as questions of principle) make cooperation difficult between different social 'milieux.' "[14]

The class composition of the major international women's organizations resulted in large part from the demands of participation. Since members had to undertake lengthy and expensive travel to attend meetings, serve as officers, or participate in ongoing activities, only those with both the leisure and the independent means or with sufficient national or international stature to attract subsidies from organizations or individuals could take part. The top leadership roles required particularly extensive outlays of cash. During the early years of her presidency of the International Council, Scottish aristocrat Lady Aberdeen paid for all of the expenses of the organization, finally closing the purse strings out of fear of setting a precedent for future officers. No organization could be healthy, she argued, that relied so much on its president.[15] The American May Wright Sewall, pleading limited resources, refused to succeed Aberdeen until the Executive Committee agreed to pay her traveling expenses and explicitly accepted that she could not foot the organizational bills. In 1906 the ICW voted to provide travel grants to all of the leaders since "otherwise the choice of Officers would be limited to ladies of independent means."[16] But not until 1920 did the ICW adopt a plan providing for regular contributions from the National Councils "in order that the women most suited for the work of the council may be elected without consideration of their means."[17] To be elected, of course, required prior participation in the affairs of the organization, so the financial barriers to leadership remained.

Even simple attendance at congresses or meetings required access to financial resources. Delegates to the Hague Congress paid their own bills, although later the Women's International League subsidized travel expenses for "those in far-off countries who are not able to pay, if the money question alone would prevent them from attending an important meeting."[18] In discussing the cost of a hotel in Innsbruck booked for a WILPF Executive Committee meeting, Lida Gustava Heymann wrote Hungarian Vilma Glücklich, "Now I ask you, which of us can pay that? The English and Americans!"[19] Members of the Disarmament Committee paid not only for their own travel costs but even for the cups of tea they drank at meetings.[20]

Not all participants paid their own way. In some cases, friends, patrons, or national organizations came through with financial support for those deemed important enough to send to meetings. Rosika Schwimmer received funds from the Dutch feminist Mien Palthe and especially from her devoted American coworker Lola Maverick Lloyd.[21] Margery Corbett Ashby's father paid for part of Rosa Manus's trip to the Alliance's Istanbul congress in 1935 because he wanted her to travel with his daughter.[22] Often national sections, rather than individuals, picked up the costs for members they wanted to represent them.

The financial demands of participation ensured that international organizing remained an elite activity, even if some women lacked the personal wealth to support their travel. Although it is impossible to provide an accurate breakdown of the social characteristics of the most active members, the participation of educated, professional, and politically prominent women is striking. The organizations made much of their illustrious members, including Aletta Jacobs, the first woman doctor in the Netherlands; Germany's first woman judge, Anita Augspurg; Naima Sahlbom, a Swedish chemist; and Yella Hertzka, head of the first horticultural school for women in Austria. In addition, women writers, journalists, and activists in their national movements filled out the ranks of the leadership. Some of the first women to enter high-level government positions also graced these organizations with their presence, including Cécile Brunschvicg, the under secretary of state for education in France; Františka Plamínková, a Czech senator; and Rosika Schwimmer, the first woman appointed to the post of ambassador. Such achievements distinguished internationally active women even from the elite women most likely to be involved in national women's movements.

Elite status, then, bound together the women of the transnational women's groups even as it marked them off from nonelite women who lacked the access to resources necessary for participation. Yet the organizations early on recognized the need to overcome financial barriers to widespread attendance at international gatherings, even if they did little about it.

The Pervasive Christian Spirit

Although the Alliance journal *Jus Suffragii* proudly proclaimed in anticipation of the 1913 congress that "[f]or the first time in the woman movement, it is expected that Hindu, Buddhist, Confucian, Mohammedan, Jewish and Christian women will sit together[,] . . . uniting their voices in a common plea for the liberation of their sex from those artificial discriminations which every political and religious system has directed against them," this hardly described reality.[23] Religion—or perhaps "culture"—served as a second invisible boundary separating the overwhelmingly Christian women in the transnational bodies from those of other religious traditions.[24]

Christian assumptions so infused the organizations that the leaders often seemed not to perceive them. May Wright Sewall, in 1900, wrote to Marie Stritt of the German Council, expressing her hopes for world peace, since "any high state of civilization moulded upon the Christian ideal, or, indeed, approximating any lofty ethical ideal" would necessarily improve relations among the nations.[25] Yet she could also insist that the women's movement must "in a certain sense not [be] at all related to any . . . religious faith."[26] A fraternal delegate from the ICW addressed the congress of the International Federation of Working Women in 1921 and commented on the "Christian spirit which pervades the whole of the meetings," and Lady Aberdeen regularly described in biblical terms the spiritual nature of ICW meetings.[27]

A number of aspects of organizational culture reflected these deeply ingrained Christian assumptions, particularly in the case of the International Council. The ICW clung to the Golden Rule—"Do unto others as ye would that others should do unto you"—as its basis of action and motto (see figure 2). Although this ethical principle is common to most of the major religions of the world, the ICW expressed it in its New Testament form. Furthermore, members referred to the basic principles of the organization as the "I.C.W. 'Catechism.'"[28] The groups regularly celebrated Christmas but not other religious holidays. *Pax* described "Christmas at the Maison" in 1926, and Lady Aberdeen referred in 1931 to the

Fig. 2. "Souvenir of Allegorical Tableau arranged by Miss
Ruth Burchenal for the opening of the I.C.W. Meeting,
May 6, 1925," illustrating the centrality of the Golden
Rule in the ICW. Reproduced from the *Report on the
Quinquenniel Meeting. Washington, 1925.*

Christmas spirit affecting "us all."[29] Although the Toronto congress of the
International Council in 1909 arranged for special sermons at the local
synagogue on both Saturdays of the meetings, such awareness of religious
difference seems to have been more of the exception than the rule.[30]

The question of religious customs came to a head in the International
Council at the turn of the century. The early meetings opened with a public prayer, a practice objected to not by women from different religious
traditions but by European Christian women who found it an expression
of Anglo-American culture. The first compromise passed by the Executive Committee called for the substitution of silent for public prayer, but
this too, according to German women, smacked of Anglo-Saxon tradition. After extensive wrangling, the Executive Committee rescinded the
silent prayer provision and substituted opening remarks by the president.

But at the same time, the committee revealed its Christian bias by arranging for daily Church of England, Nonconformist, and Catholic services at nearby churches during the 1899 London congress.[31]

Jewish women encountered not only Christian assumptions and traditions but also anti-Semitism both within their organizations and from the outside. Yet, unlike other women outside the "Christian spirit," a number of Jewish women also held central leadership positions. As a result of this paradox, many soft-pedaled their Jewish identity, at least in interactions with non-Jewish women.[32] Martina Kramers matter-of-factly informed Jewish Alliance member Rosika Schwimmer in 1907 that the Czech feminist Františka Plamínková was anti-Semitic.[33] In 1921 Emily Greene Balch worried about sending Yella Hertzka to eastern Europe on an organizing trip because "the fact that she is Jewish would complicate things." "All that vague anti-Semitism renders our job much more difficult," she commented to Gabrielle Duchêne.[34] When Lady Aberdeen chose Alice Salomon, who had converted to Christianity, as her successor as president of the ICW in 1928, the leader of the German National Council told Aberdeen flatly that they could not support Salomon because of the spread of intolerance toward those of her "race."[35] And Rosa Manus, who worked tirelessly but often behind the scenes in the Alliance and other groups, almost always declined leadership positions because, as a friend put it after Manus's death in the Holocaust, "being a Jewess she did not want to come too much to the front. 'You have no idea how many people, even those of whom you would not expect it, are prejudiced against our race,' she would say."[36]

Even if Jewish women did not encounter direct anti-Semitism within their organizations, the larger societal context, especially with the rise of Nazism in the 1930s, placed demands on them that their Christian colleagues did not have to face and often did not understand. Lida Gustava Heymann worried about the health of Gertrud Baer, who was working too hard and confronting as well the increase in anti-Semitism. "G.B. takes very dark views and said she had to suffer a great deal from anti-Semitism and feels anxious going to Berlin," Heymann reported to Emily Greene Balch, who in turn passed the news on to Jane Addams.[37] In 1933, presumably in response to WILPF's activism against the rise of anti-Semitism, someone scrawled a swastika across the plaque at Geneva headquarters.[38] French Alliance member Cécile Brunschvicg, speaking at a WILPF study conference in Zurich, was pelted with an egg by a fascist man who called out, "We do not want Jews," prompting the Alliance to cancel a planned board meeting and study conference in Poland out of fear of similar attacks.[39] Even more ominous, the German secret police questioned Alice Salomon in May 1937 about her travel abroad, prompting her to flee Germany for the United States.[40] When Rosa

Manus devoted herself in the years before the outbreak of the war to helping Jewish refugees, and this work preempted her long-standing commitment to the Alliance, Carrie Chapman Catt tried to talk her out of resigning from the board: "I think, perhaps, you are feeling too sensitive about all the things that are happening to the Jews."[41] Once the war broke out, information about the concentration camps began to spread among organized women, increasing Manus's earlier fears that "'Not even in Holland and maybe not anywhere in the world we shall ever be safe.'"[42] Her words foreshadowed her fate.

If anti-Semitism forced Jewish women to tread carefully, their representation among the leadership is striking in comparison to Muslim women, the only other non-Christians explicitly acknowledged within the transnational organizations. The sole Muslim woman to play a prominent role was Huda Sha'rawi, a leading Egyptian feminist who served on the Alliance Board, although other Muslim women belonged to the bodies and participated in congresses.[43] Muslim women faced not only Christian assumptions but a pervasive characterization of Islamic societies as backward and particularly degrading to women. Deeply ingrained orientalism—the creation of a mysterious Eastern "other"—emerged especially clearly in the ongoing attempts within the international groups to organize women in Palestine.[44] Both the Alliance and WILPF sought to build branches in Palestine but came up against the division between Jews and Muslims. The leadership of the two organizations found the Jews, because of their primarily European origins, both more familiar and more interested in their endeavors. Muslim women, in contrast, seemed mysterious and oppressed. Carrie Chapman Catt and Aletta Jacobs, on their 1911–12 world tour, visited what Catt called in a report to *Jus Suffragii* the "fossilized humanity" of Palestine. "We wondered what the veiled women we met in the street were thinking," she noted, although after meeting in private with some Muslim women they decided that "the seeds of rebellion have already been planted in the hearts of those mysterious women behind the veil."[45] After the First World War, the Austrian-born physician Rosa Welt Straus worked to organize Jewish women in Palestine into the Alliance and reported in 1920 that the "Moslem and Christian Arab women are politically unborn, and are, especially among the Moslem population, treated as slaves and beasts of burden."[46] Millicent Garrett Fawcett visited Palestine for the Alliance in 1921 and contrasted the "progressive women" of the Jewish Women's Equal Rights Association to the "unorganised, inarticulate, little-educated Moslem women of Palestine."[47]

Both the Alliance and the Women's International League developed an analysis of the Palestine situation that emphasized economic over religious conflict and held Britain responsible for its contradictory promises to the Jews and Palestinians, as well as for its role in supervising Palestine under the mandate system of the League of Nations.[48] Despite the escalating violence in Palestine between the wars, internationally organized women held out hopes for peace and worked to bring Jewish and Muslim women together. After long discussion, WILPF sent Swedish member Elisabeth Waern-Bugge on a peace mission to Palestine in 1931. She found that even Arab women with European educations "have just begun to set their feet on the long path of experiences, on which the women of Western civilisation—and of course the European and American Jewesses of higher standing in Palestine—have been progressing for ages." Reaching only Christian Arab women, she found "the most obstinate chauvinism and the bitterest hatred against the Jews. It was obvious that they were only political tools of the men." She nevertheless held out hope that the small group of European Christian, Jewish, and Arab Christian women that she formed would eventually bring in Muslim women as well.[49]

In 1935 Margery Corbett Ashby, Rosa Manus, Germaine Malaterre-Sellier, and Christine Bakker van Bosse traveled to Palestine on behalf of the Alliance and reported the same difficulties. They had to meet separately with Jewish and Muslim women and found the Jewish Women's Union "small and intensely feminist" and the Arab Women's Union "nationalist to the exclusion of all other interests, violently anti-British and anti-Jewish." "We tried hard to persuade the Arab Women's Union to affiliate to the alliance," Corbett Ashby reported, "but difficulties are very great."[50]

That, of course, was an understatement, since the interests of Jewish and Muslim women, most immediately with regard to the level of Jewish immigration to Palestine, clashed directly. The Zionist perspective found expression in the international women's organizations, even though the Women's International League rejected an application from a Zionist group to form a Jewish national section in 1922 and the Liaison Committee in 1942 refused to admit the Women's International Zionist Organisation because "its scope was of a definitely national character in connection with Palestine."[51] Only Huda Sha'rawi, whom Margery Corbett Ashby described as "terrifically nationalist & tyrannical," voiced the concerns of the Muslim women of Palestine.[52] In 1933 she called on the Disarmament Committee to support the Arab demand for an end to Jewish immigration, and in 1938 she convened a Muslim women's congress on Palestine, prompting *Jus Suffragii* to editorialize that because of "our standing policy of neutrality on all national questions" and because there existed "a faithful feminist group among the

Jewish women of Palestine . . . , we could not express any opinion on the policy of the conference."[53]

The issue of Palestine exploded at the 1939 board meeting. In response to a call for a protest against anti-Semitism, Sha'rawi pointed out that the Muslims, too, suffered grave indignities, and "the Arab women sharply resent that the Alliance would not come to their aid in protesting the injustices and persecutions that they suffer in Palestine."[54] Sha'rawi, according to Rosa Manus, proposed a resolution against further Jewish immigration to Palestine and became furious when the board tried to rule it out of order as intervention in a national question. Manus reported that Corbett Ashby (herself in a difficult position as a British citizen) and Malaterre-Sellier worked hard to calm Sha'rawi down and persuade her not to resign from the board, while Manus stayed out "as I did not think it was wise for me as a Jewess to have mixed myself into it." But she finally asked Sha'rawi directly if she was "against me as a Jewess," to which Sha'rawi replied that "the Jewish question was not the matter but only the Palestine-Jewish question" and that the only board member she did not like was Emilie Gourd, who had said something fifteen years earlier that annoyed her. Manus concluded from this last that "the mentality of the Moslem woman is rather different to ours," suggesting the pervasiveness not only of conflict but also of cross-cultural misunderstanding.[55]

Although in the question of Palestine Jewish women fared better than did their Muslim counterparts, both Jewish and Muslim women—to say nothing of women of other religious traditions who may have taken part in these groups—were outsiders in primarily Christian organizations. Relative religious homogeneity served as a bond among the majority of internationally active women while it raised a barrier to truly global participation. Yet world events such as the rise of fascist anti-Semitism and conflict in Palestine brought to the fore challenges to the Christian assumptions and sentiments of the transnational groups.

Longing for Young Blood

Right from the beginning of international organizing, a generational boundary divided those who belonged and those who did not. Women of relatively advanced age predominated and had little success appealing to young women to join their ranks. In contrast to class, religious, and ethnic differences, the age gap had little to do with deliberate or structural exclusion. In fact, the older members often lamented the absence of young women and longed for fresh blood. But they never succeeded in attracting the younger generation; if anything, the chasm between old and young yawned increasingly wider over the years.

Young women who did participate attested to the prevailing pattern of participation. In 1900, at the age of twenty-six, Alice Salomon became the youngest-ever member on the Council board. The next youngest was already over sixty. "A novelist of the period had described the women at such meetings as 'black shadows,'" she wrote in her unpublished auto-biography, "and there I was—twenty-six years old, in a very short light dress, radiating eagerness and unbounded enthusiasm."[56] Similarly distinguishing herself, Rosika Schwimmer expressed pleasure at being called young in contrast to the usual accusations that feminists were "a lot of old sour spinsters."[57] And when Margery Corbett Ashby took over the presidency of the Alliance in 1923 at the age of forty-one, she felt "deplorably young to preside over a gathering of ancient suffragists." To her father she confided, "I wish my hair was white & my weight 12 stone instead of 8 1/2. I should then be perfect!"[58]

Rosika Schwimmer and Rosa Manus, both twenty-seven when they attended their first congresses in 1904 and 1908, respectively, shared the spotlight as the youngsters in the Alliance. Aletta Jacobs commented proudly that the good young women with courage and spirit were "always Jewish girls."[59] Older members regularly described both women as "my dear little friend," "young girls," "nice young people," and "the younger generation."[60] As they grew older—especially Manus, who remained an active participant in the Alliance—they continued to serve as symbols of youth. Carrie Chapman Catt wrote to Manus in 1931, remembering "the little Dutch girl who sat in the hall by the side of a blackboard in the beginning of this century and looked so cute as she took the names of the delegates who wanted to go on excursions."[61]

The longings—increasing as the years went by—for young blood attest to women's awareness of the dangers of an aging constituency. Madeleine Doty, an American "New Woman" and member of WILPF, called in 1926 for the recruitment and training of young women, "for we shall surely end in disaster if we depend only on those whom we have always had with us and who are now getting tired and a little worn out."[62] A young Jewish student from Palestine expressed shock that the Istanbul congress of the Alliance in 1935 provoked no discussion of the need to recruit young women. "It seems to me that every movement has to appeal to youth and educate it in its spirit; because having no young followers the movement has no future," she wrote in *Jus Suffragii*.[63] Despite her complaint, the groups did try to interest younger women throughout the years by forming special committees or planning events they thought would appeal to girls and young women. But such arrangements could be self-defeating, as they simply confirmed the assumption that the regular membership consisted of older women.

In addition to the prevailing conception of members as old, distrust of the younger generations no doubt contributed to difficulty with recruitment. U.S. suffragist Anna Howard Shaw, sixty-three in 1910, grumbled to Aletta Jacobs that "it is everywhere the same question—the young people come into the work with the greatest lack of respect for the older people; they think we have made great blunders all these years and have kept the work back; that now they are going ahead in their sweet and beautiful way."[64] Sometimes older women welcomed successors only if they took over the reins without changing the gait. Carrie Chapman Catt wanted carefully to choose and control those who would follow: "We must select them with a view to working harmoniously together."[65] The WILPF-sponsored summer schools, designed to appeal to young women, encountered the kind of generational conflict that would have to be negotiated for an age-differentiated movement to succeed. French member Andrée Jouve reported in 1923 that the young were happy with cheap, simple living accommodations but wanted more time for "excursions, sports and conversation," while the older League members who attended felt that they did not work enough but desired greater comfort because "one is not indifferent to agreeable living conditions when one is no longer twenty."[66]

The age composition of the international women's organizations can be linked to only one structural barrier, the financial demands of participation, for older established women were more likely to have the personal means or stature that would make travel possible. And once committed to international work, active members tended to stay, so even the women once joyously greeted as young grew gray in harness, reinforcing the image of internationally minded women as old. But other developments also played a part in lessening the appeal of membership to younger women: separatist organizing fell out of fashion in an increasingly heterosocial Euro-American world, and national interests unified women and men engaged in liberation struggles in other corners of the globe. Women's organizations had come to seem old-fashioned. By the 1920s and 1930s, with the proliferation of international organizations, young women surveyed a banquet of choices; and many who might have opted for, say, WILPF could be tempted by a mixed-gender socialist or peace group. The laments about the hopelessness of the younger generation hinted at a recognition that the world was changing and single-sex organizations and commitment to the cause of women might seem anachronistic. Patterns of organization and activity familiar to older women, including separatism, served as another boundary, then, that tightened already-existing ties but made recruitment of "new blood" more difficult.

TABLE 3

Nationality of the Officers of the International Women's Organizations

International Council of Women		International Alliance of Women		Women's International League for Peace and Freedom
Great Britain	1888			
United States–2				
Denmark				
France				
Great Britain	1893			
United States				
Finland				
Canada				
France				
United States	1899			
Great Britain				
Germany				
Canada				
Switzerland				
Great Britain–2	1904	United States–3	1904	1904
Germany		Germany–2		
Sweden		Great Britain–2		
France		Netherlands		
Netherlands				
Great Britain–2	1909	United States	1909	1909
Italy		Great Britain–2		
Austria		Finland		
Germany		Netherlands		
Sweden		Germany		
Canada		Sweden		
		United States	1911	
		Great Britain–2		
		Finland		
		Netherlands		
		Germany		
		Sweden		
		United States–2	1913	
		Great Britain–3		
		Finland		
		Germany–2		
		France		
		Sweden		
		Hungary		
		Belgium		

TABLE 3 (*Cont.*)
Nationality of the Officers of the International Women's Organizations

International Council of Women		International Alliance of Women		Women's International League for Peace and Freedom	
Great Britain	1914				
France–2					
Denmark					
Australia					
Germany					
Canada					
				United States–2	1915
				Netherlands–2	
				Great Britain	
				Denmark–2	
				Hungary	
				Sweden	
				Norway	
				United States–2	1919
				Germany	
				Great Britain	
				Netherlands	
				France	
				Switzerland	
				Austria	
				Norway	
Switzerland–2	1920	United States–2	1920		
Great Britain–3		France			
France		Great Britain–3			
Denmark		Germany–2			
Germany		Sweden			
Tasmania		Switzerland			
United States		Italy			
Norway					
Netherlands					
Canada					
Yugoslavia					
Belgium					
				United States–2	1921
				Germany–2	
				Great Britain	
				Netherlands	
				France	
				Austria	
				Denmark	
				Belgium	

TABLE 3 (*Cont.*)
Nationality of the Officers of the International Women's Organizations

International Council of Women	*International Alliance of Women*	*Women's International League for Peace and Freedom*
	United States–2 1923	
	Great Britian–2	
	France	
	Germany–2	
	Italy	
	Switzerland	
	Greece	
	Denmark	
	Uruguay	
		United States–3 1924
		Germany–2
		Great Britain
		France
		Netherlands
		Hungary
		Belgium
		Switzerland
		Austria
Great Britain–4 1925		
France		
United States		
Denmark		
Germany		
Czechoslovakia		
Romania		
Norway		
Netherlands		
Switzerland		
Canada		
	United States–2 1926	United States 1926
	Great Britain–2	France
	Germany–2	Great Britain–2
	Italy	Netherlands
	France–2	Germany–2
	Netherlands	Ireland
	Czechoslovakia	Hungary
	Switzerland	Norway
	Greece	Switzerland
	Denmark	
	Yugoslavia	
	Egypt	

TABLE 3 (*Cont.*)
Nationality of the Officers of the International Women's Organizations

International Council of Women		International Alliance of Women		Women's International League for Peace and Freedom	
		Uruguay	1926		
		Norway	(*cont.*)		
		Romania			
		Australia			
		Spain			
		Sweden			
		United States–3	1929	United States–2	1929
		Great Britain–3		Germany–2	
		Germany–2		Switzerland	
		Netherlands		Netherlands	
		France–2		Great Britain–3	
		Czechoslovakia		France–2	
		Switzerland		Austria	
		Yugoslavia		Canada	
		Egypt		Sweden	
		Denmark		Czechoslovakia	
		Uruguay			
		Romania			
		Australia			
		Spain			
		Greece			
		Sweden			
Great Britain–4	1930				
France					
Germany–2					
Norway					
Sweden					
United States					
Romania					
Czechoslovakia					
Netherlands					
Greece					
Yugoslavia					
Switzerland					
Canada					
				United States–3	1932
				Germany–3	
				Great Britain	
				France–2	
				Austria	
				Switzerland	

TABLE 3 (*Cont.*)
Nationality of the Officers of the International Women's Organizations

International Council of Women		International Alliance of Women		Women's International League for Peace and Freedom	
				Netherlands	1932
				Sweden	(*cont.*)
				Czechoslovakia	
Great Britain–3	1934				
France–2					
Germany					
Norway					
Sweden					
United States					
Romania					
Czechoslovakia					
Denmark					
Netherlands					
Switzerland					
		United States–2	1935		
		Great Britain–2			
		Germany–2			
		Netherlands			
		France			
		Czechoslovakia			
		Switzerland–2			
		Yugoslavia			
		Egypt			
		Denmark			
		Uruguay			
		India			
		Australia			
		Spain			
		Greece			
		Sweden			
Great Britain–3	1936				
Belgium					
Czechoslovakia					
Latvia					
Norway					
Switzerland					
Hungary					
Sweden					
United States					
India					
Australia					

TABLE 3 (*Cont.*)
Nationality of the Officers of the International Women's Organizations

International Council of Women		International Alliance of Women		Women's International League for Peace and Freedom	
South Africa	1936				
Netherlands	(*cont.*)				
Belgium					
Denmark					
				United States–2	1937
				Germany	
				Great Britain–2	
				Switzerland	
				Denmark	
				Sweden	
				Czechoslovakia	
				Austria	
				Norway	
				Netherlands	
				Sweden	
Great Britain–3	1938				
Belgium					
Switzerland					
Hungary					
Czechoslovakia					
France					
Sweden					
Netherlands					
Romania					
United States					
India					
Australia					
South Africa					
Belgium					
Denmark					
		United States	1939		
		Great Britain–3			
		Germany			
		France–3			
		Czechoslovakia			
		Netherlands			
		India			
		Sweden			
		Switzerland–2			
		Yugoslavia			
		Norway			

TABLE 3 (*Cont.*)
Nationality of the Officers of the International Women's Organizations

International Council of Women	International Alliance of Women	Women's International League for Peace and Freedom
	Egypt	1939
	Bulgaria	(*cont.*)
	Denmark	
	Australia	
	Brazil	
	Denmark	
	Poland–2	

Source: The information on the International Alliance comes from Bosch 1990 and is based on congress reports. I compiled the lists for the International Council and WILPF from congress reports, publications, and correspondence. Countries are listed in the order given in the officer lists.

We Women of Europe

The final—and perhaps most important—line between those who were inside and those who were outside the international circle was what, for lack of a more accurate term, we might call "ethnicity." By this I mean that the leading members of the Council, Alliance, and League almost exclusively claimed a European heritage, wherever they lived, although most in fact lived in Europe and the neo-Europes. As we have already seen, the three groups began in the United States or Europe, and until after the First World War they counted almost no sections in other parts of the world. And women from the United States, Great Britain, and western and northern Europe dominated the leadership. Although women from other continents got as far as the executive committees of the three organizations in the years after the First World War, the top positions remained in the hands of a small circle from a limited number of countries (see table 3). Ironically WILPF, the most radically internationalist of the groups, alone of the three never secured leaders from outside the Euro-American world, a result of its vanguardist self-conception and tightly knit leadership circle. The dominance of American and northern and western European leadership did not escape notice at the time. An Italian representative at the 1909 ICW congress described, from the perspective of the "Latin race," the event as uniting "the women of the Anglo-Saxon nation and race."[67] And as late as 1938, the Frenchwoman Germaine Malaterre-Sellier commented that "very often the Latin and

Oriental elements" felt isolated and estranged at the Alliance office, "where a spirit predominates that I will call Nordic, for lack of another name."[68]

The boundary of ethnicity, staked out by the origins and patterns of growth of the organizations in the context of a European-dominated world system, perpetuated itself through institutional arrangements. The physical devastation of Europe in the First World War and the emergence of the United States as the world's creditor meant that American money, in the form of both dues and donations, kept the international women's organizations afloat. Although individual financial support came from other sources as well—Huda Sha'rawi, for example, gave generously to the Alliance—reliance on the dollar gave U.S. women special leverage.[69] Not everyone was happy about that. Gertrud Baer "felt it contrary to her idea of international cooperation to be dependent on money from America only," and Cor Ramondt-Hirschmann agreed that true internationalism required broader financial support.[70] Alliance treasurer Frances Sterling's conviction that "rich Egyptians and Indians might be tapped but probably not without going to look for them" confirms that financial resources flowed most easily from the countries and individuals already centrally involved in the international organizations, thus prolonging Euro-American, and especially American, control.[71]

Language served as another reinforcement for the boundary of ethnicity. The international women's organizations conducted their business in English, French, and German, privileging native speakers of these European languages and making difficult the participation of women who knew none of these tongues. Members recognized the need to circumvent the barriers of language. Reporting in 1913 that Alliance members spoke twenty-two languages, *Jus Suffragii* envisaged what an "inconceivable impetus would be given the great international movements of the world, including our own, could all the languages of earth be suddenly melted into one, and the Babel which has kept races, tribes, and nations apart cease to be."[72]

Even though the publications of the major organizations attempted, to different degrees, to keep women abreast of developments in all three languages, English dominated. The Alliance's *Jus Suffragii*, launched in 1906, appeared mainly in English with, at various times, articles or columns or sections in French and occasionally in German; there was a French edition only from 1909 to 1920. The ICW *Bulletin*, first published in 1922, appeared regularly in English, French, and German editions, a format that the Council prized and insisted upon in unsuccessful negotiations with the Alliance over cooperating on a joint journal. *Pax*, WILPF's publication begun in 1925, also came in three editions until the

Depression made that financially impossible; only an English edition, with occasional articles in French and German, survived.

At congresses, too, the international groups had to balance the desire for inclusiveness against sheer logistics. When women met where languages other than English, French, and German were spoken, the organizations had to decide whether to add a fourth language for the daily proceedings. Could they reach local audiences if they did not? Katherine Karaveloff of Bulgaria welcomed the idea of a WILPF congress in the Balkans in 1927 but warned that "any successful work in Bulgaria requires a mastery of at least one Slav language."[73] Dealing in three languages caused trouble enough. Lady Aberdeen regularly urged International Council members to learn at least to understand all three official languages, but knowledge of a second, third, or fourth language, more common in some countries than others, generally assumed educational privilege accessible only to relatively elite women.[74] European imperialism and the historic shifts from one dominant Great Power to another ensured that large numbers of elite women from across the globe could indeed communicate in one or another of the official languages. But, as Alice Masaryk of Czechoslovakia pointed out in 1921, "sometimes a peasant has some idea that is well worth listening too [sic]"; or as Danish WILPF member Clara Tybjerg put it, "many working women would have liked to be here if it had not been for the difficulty of the different languages."[75] Thus the question of language reinforced the barrier of class as well.

Not surprisingly, given the composition and leadership of the organizations and the realities of global power, English often predominated in meetings as well as publications. May Wright Sewall apologized for the preponderance of English in the report of the 1904 Council congress, and Charlotte Despard "feared that the English language tended to swamp the other languages" at the 1913 Alliance congress.[76] Women in command of several languages sometimes noted the linguistic disabilities of their English-speaking colleagues. Giving voice to an all too common sentiment, Dutch activist Martina Kramers wrote Hungarian Rosika Schwimmer, in German, to tell her that she would translate Schwimmer's piece for publication "because the poor monolingual Americans must also know what is going on with you."[77]

Over the years, as Hitler's rise to power led to the dissolution of the German sections of the international organizations, German dropped more and more out of the congresses and journals. On the other hand, in response to interest in Latin America, Spanish became a "semi-official" language of the ICW in 1930. This meant that Spanish-speaking Council members could correspond in Spanish with the international office and that a Spanish version of the *Bulletin* was to appear when enough subscriptions had been gathered.[78] As a Latin American woman involved in one of the regional bodies pointed out, "it is a more sound policy to address the South American people in their mother tongue."[79]

Attempts to make meetings and publications linguistically accessible had their own costs. Congress participants often grew impatient waiting through two translations of speeches. Lady Aberdeen noted that the need for translations "induces whispering amongst the delegates," and Jane Addams had to remind delegates to the 1915 Hague Congress "to keep silent whilst the translation is given."[80] Congress organizers had to arrange for translators and multilingual or multiple stenographers, international offices required secretarial help able to cope with three languages, and organizations had to foot the bill to print minutes, congress proceedings, and publications in more than one version.

Use of an international language represented one potential solution, and the transnational organizations sporadically considered and then rejected this strategy. In 1909 the ICW debated a resolution calling for the National Councils to study the question in preparation for an interational discussion at the next congress. Proposed by a Danish woman speaking in Ido, or revised Esperanto, the resolution received support from an Australian delegate who pointed to the entrance into the group of women from China, Japan, Russia, and Hawaii. Alice Salomon opposed it, fearing that an artificial language "will never enable us to express our thoughts," although it might be useful for business and the tourist trade. May Wright Sewall responded that Dante, Goethe, and Shapespeare had all been translated into Esperanto, but despite her spirited defense of the literary qualities of the invented language, the resolution failed.[81] None of the organizations acted on recurring proposals to switch to Esperanto as linguistic diversity increased, and even well-meaning attempts to institute international languages overlooked their European basis.[82]

As the debate over Esperanto suggests, although members were not unaware of language barriers, they rarely thought beyond the European tongues. The staff of *Jus Suffragii* proudly announced in 1932 that language would be no obstacle to publication of news submitted from different countries, thus overlooking the significance of the fact, as the article stated flatly, that the publication could handle only roman alphabets.[83] That same year, the organizers of the WILPF congress in Grenoble invited a Chinese woman living in Berlin to come and speak briefly in Chinese, to which she responded, in German, that she could not undertake a lengthy interruption of her work "merely to speak for a few minutes in a language that probably all of the congress participants could not understand." She found this an "unreasonable demand that I cannot reconcile with my self-respect," and pointedly refused to be used in that way.[84] Her voice served as a reminder that language both unified and divided women on the international scene.

Further fortifying the boundary of ethnicity, international congresses and meetings of officers took place in Europe, primarily western and northern Europe, with occasional excursions to North America, discouraging those who hailed from other continents (see table 4). Suggestions or plans to hold meetings in other locations provoked shocked outcries that "such a far away place has been chosen."[85] Canadian women in 1909, and their U.S. colleagues in 1925, could coax European ICW members to cross the Atlantic only by raising money for expenses and guaranteeing hospitality for all delegates.[86] Even traveling to southern or eastern Europe seemed to many western or northern European women to be asking too much. Madrid, under consideration for the 1920 Alliance congress, seemed remote to a Finnish woman, and WILPF members complained about the expense of getting to Luhacovice, in Czechoslovakia, in 1937. To a Czech woman, Gertrud Baer explained that "we are all afraid that it is at the end of the world, where foxes and wolves say good night."[87] Traveling even farther afield provoked increased resistance. In response to a proposal to meet in Honolulu, Marguerite Gobat of WILPF exclaimed: "We have, we women of Europe, better things to do—alas, too much to do on our continent—to go so far, at enormous expense."[88] Although Gertrud Baer in 1940 noted on behalf of the League that "[w]e know only too well that Europe is not the world," only after the war did the international women's organizations begin to meet beyond the confines of Europe and North America.[89] Since, as an Australian woman wryly remarked in 1909, "the distance is exactly the same going out to Australia as it is coming," the location of conferences revealed assumptions about the global distribution of membership.[90]

But financial resources, language, and residence do not tell the whole story of ethnicity-based exclusion, for Euro-American cultural assumptions hindered the participation of women of color from both the neo-Europes and the rest of the world. Although a few elite African American women took part in international gatherings, Mary Church Terrell described herself at both the 1904 ICW meeting and the 1919 WILPF congress as the only delegate "who had a drop of African blood in her veins," prompting her to carry the burden of "representing the women of all the non-white countries in the world."[91]

For despite brave words condemning discrimination on the basis of race or color, dominant cultural assumptions made the international organizations no more hospitable than national groups for women of color living in predominantly white societies. After the First World War, when accusations of the rape of German women by African soldiers serving in the French army of occupation became an international cause

TABLE 4
Congresses of the International Women's Organizations

International Council of Women		International Alliance of Women		Women's International League for Peace and Freedom	
Washington	1888				
Chicago	1893				
London	1899				
		Washington	1902		
Berlin	1904	Berlin	1904		
		Copenhagen	1906		
		Amsterdam	1908		
Toronto	1909	London	1909		
		Stockholm	1911		
		Budapest	1913		
Rome	1914				
				The Hague	1915
				Zurich	1919
Oslo	1920	Geneva	1920		
				Vienna	1921
		Rome	1923		
				Washington	1924
Washington	1925				
		Paris	1926	Dublin	1926
		Berlin	1929	Prague	1929
Vienna	1930				
				Grenoble	1932
Paris	1934			Zurich	1934
		Istanbul	1935		
Dubrovnik	1936				
				Luhacovice	1937
Edinburgh	1938				
		Copenhagen	1939		
		Interlaken	1946	Luxembourg	1946
Philadelphia	1947				

célèbre, Mary Church Terrell explained why she could not sign a WILPF petition calling for the removal of African troops. As a member of "a race whose women have been the victims of assaults committed upon them by white men and men of all other races," she sympathized with any violated woman, but she did not believe that black men were any different than white men in propensity to rape and saw the petition as a direct appeal to racial prejudice.[92] The issue of race also came to the fore in 1921, when Mary Talbert, in Europe to represent the National Association of Colored Women at the ICW Kristiania congress, was barred from the dining room of the American Woman's Club in Paris.[93] African American singers scheduled to perform on a program of American music at the ICW congress in Washington in 1925 refused to go on, in protest against the segregation of black participants. Although the organization disclaimed responsibility, Hallie Q. Brown explained that "we could not be humiliated in the eyes of the foreign women who had come to believe that America was the land of the free and the home of the brave."[94] Such incidents, in addition to a sense of kinship and the articulation of a link between racism in the United States and South Africa, lay behind the formation of the International Council of Women of the Darker Races in 1920.[95]

But it was not just the question of color that privileged women of European origin. The discourse of what has been called "feminist orientalism," pervasive in the international women's movement, mobilized assumptions about backward, repressive, "Eastern ways" to threaten Western men with seeming "oriental" if they refused to accept the emancipation of women.[96] The image of the veiled, confined, and degraded woman of the "East" provided a startling contrast to the "Western" woman, also justifying her leadership in the international movement. The very constructs of "West" and "East," of course, polarized the world in a way that had little to do with geography and obscured the much more complex hierarchical rankings embodied in dominant assumptions about progress, civilization, and the emancipation of women. From the perspective of the women in charge, western and northern Europe and the United States represented the core, southern and eastern Europe a semiperiphery, and Latin America, the Middle East, Asia, and Africa the periphery of a feminist world system.[97] Such a vision placed women of European origin in the lead, offering a hand to their more oppressed sisters.

This was not an image designed to appeal to the women presumed to be so in need of help. A Dutch woman in 1920 referred to "even cannibals transformed into peace-loving people" in "our colonies," a report from Rhodesia noted "assaults on white women by natives," and a cartoon in *Jus Suffragii* depicted sexual slavery as a practice endemic to Asia and Africa (see figure 3).[98] The specters of cannibalism and unrestrained sexuality evoked a sense of peoples in need of civilizing external control. The "women of primitive race," African women "sold" to their husbands, veiled Muslim women, Asian women "more bound by tradition and faith than are we," and timid Latin American women controlled by their husbands and fathers all served to distinguish women of European origin as being well on their way to emancipation.[99]

Fig. 3. "Slavery in Asia to Slavery in Africa: They go on making speeches against us in Europe, but we still manage to find our prey!" Cartoon from *Jus Suffragii*, June 1931, illustrating a feminist orientalist view of sexual slavery.

When Carrie Chapman Catt and Aletta Jacobs traveled around the world in 1911–12, they reported on "women's awakening in the East," finding it "touching to think of these women, who lacked the simplest rights, seeking for help."[100] Although no "Asiatic" delegates came to the 1913 Budapest congress of the Alliance, *Jus Suffragii* expressed confidence that "these sisters of ours will come some day." In the meantime, "we must make them understand" that women's cause is the same throughout the world.[101] With such words, women of European origin shouldered the burden of protecting the women of the world, making it clear that they were in charge.

But at the same time, women in the international organizations sometimes recognized that the world was a more complex place than a feminist orientalist vision might suggest. Carrie Chapman Catt could write in 1912 of Burmese women's right to own property, engage in business, and vote in municipal elections as making them better off than women in the West in the same breath that she noted the languor of people in such sunshine.[102] "There are millions of women in the Orient who are held in the most pitiful tutelage, and denied every vestige of personal liberty, but we are finding that there are other millions who have always enjoyed more personal freedom than was accorded to most European women a century ago, and more than is now permitted to thousands of women under our boasted Western civilization," she concluded.[103] The organizations' journals reported that women on the Gold Coast of Africa were independent, engaged in trading, and sometimes very wealthy; that Islam was not oppressive to women; that "the projecting of the concepts and ideas of Western feminists upon the women whose lives we wish to study" had distorted research; and that African women were probably losing status under European influence as they were pushed out of agriculture and trade, kept out of local government, and "protected" morally.[104]

This counterdiscourse developed, as a participant described the 1924 WILPF congress in fine orientalist style, "when guests from [the] antipodes sidled in—as if direct from Gilbert & Sullivan & Mikado."[105] Recognizing their global limitations, the international women's organizations, particularly after the First World War, sought to recruit members and sections in parts of the world where they were not well represented. This process came to be called making the movement "truly international."[106] Using whatever contacts they had, leaders sought names of potential supporters in unaffiliated countries, sent members on organizing tours, made use of women from other continents (often students) visiting or living in Europe, and offered subsidies to help delegates come to congresses. Thus *Jus Suffragii* called on its readers in 1913 for the names of correspondents in South America "longing for the liberation of their sex from the thraldom of outgrown custom"; WILPF sent a mission to China and Indochina in 1927 and followed up with an interim congress in Honolulu; the Alliance board in 1933 co-opted Dhanvanthi Rama Rau, an Indian woman then living in England, to fill a vacancy; and the WILPF office in Geneva asked the Czech section to offer hospitality to the delegates of the Egyptian section during the 1937 congress in Luhacovice.[107]

In addition, the groups made some attempts to adjust their structures to suit conditions in other parts of the world. The Alliance changed its constitution in 1913 at the recommendation of Catt and Jacobs, following their world tour, to allow the formation of auxiliaries where there were no suffrage organizations because such agitation would be impractical.[108] Eager for broader representation at the 1921 Vienna congress, WILPF admitted delegates-at-large from Japan, China, and Mexico—all countries lacking sections—and in 1924 assured Japanese women that they had only to adopt the substance and spirit, not the letter, of the constitution in order to affiliate.[109] In the 1930s the ICW considered the possibility of admitting "countries not entirely self-supporting and in different stages of development" and amended the constitution to allow the Executive Committee to co-opt additional members "drawn from any Continent or geographical group of countries outside Europe."[110]

As a result of such efforts, the transnational bodies did expand their reach, creating challenges for women on both sides of the continental divides. Leaders had to recognize that they could not themselves organize outside the Euro-American arena. As an ICW member who visited Japan in 1907–08 put it, "as the movement must necessarily be conducted by Japanese, the ladies of other nationalities could only render passive assistance."[111] Likewise Catt, who came away from her world tour with such conflicting interpretations, argued that "Asia is not reaching out its weak hands to the West like a little child asking guidance of a strong man."[112] Yet the leaders sometimes doubted that women from other continents could handle the job themselves. When the Alliance held its 1935 congress in Istanbul, Margery Corbett Ashby and secretary Katherine Bompas worried about the ability of the local Turkish committee to organize properly but recognized that they might be "rather sensitive to any attempts to regard them as needing advice on matters affecting their local organisation."[113] Distrusting newly organized groups, the Euro-American leadership tried to pull unseen strings. Catt noted in 1925 that the "Latin Americans do not at all like to be told or shown how to do things, so I am planning to show them some things that I think will be useful without appearing to do so."[114]

From the other side, women confronted feminist orientalism and its manifold consequences within the international organizations. As national sections of the transnational bodies proliferated and as colonized and dominated countries began to shake loose from Europe's grip, diverse voices rose to challenge imperialism within the international women's groups. Not surprisingly, the Women's International League took the most radical position on imperialism, although conflict on the issue simmered within the organization. The French section, noted for its leftist tendencies, took a special interest in fighting imperialism, organizing a summer school in 1927 on the interracial problems of imperialism, contributing actively to the Colonial Commission established in 1931 "in view of the growing menace of imperialism and the sufferings and unrest among colonised peoples," and calling for independence and an end of military repression in the French colonies and mandates.[115] Similarly, the U.S. section took the lead in investigating and condemning the U.S. occupation of Haiti in 1926.[116] The British section, however, held more ambivalent views on the question of empire. In 1924 British leaders protested a telegram sent by International Secretary Vilma Glücklich denouncing the "merciless enforcement" of British reprisals in Egypt, newly independent and struggling to wrest control of its destiny from England.[117] Taking a similar line with regard to India, the British section in 1930 argued that British imperialism was wrong but not particularly cruel, an affront to those who could not forget the Amritsar incident of

1919, in which British troops fired on and killed nearly four hundred unarmed Indians celebrating a Hindu festival.[118]

But it was women from the colonized and dependent countries who raised the most insistent challenges to feminist orientalism.[119] To begin with, they insisted that they alone could represent themselves, explicitly rejecting the practice of European-origin women standing in for the women of countries in which they had settled. Taraknath Das warned Jane Addams that it would be "a great mistake" to allow British women to organize an Indian section of WILPF.[120] On behalf of Pandurgang Khanko, the secretary of the Indian News Service and Information Bureau, the American Agnes Smedley emphasized that "we do not wish British women to speak for the women of India. They are quite uncapable [sic] of it," adding a note at the bottom of the letter directing a reply to the bureau rather than Smedley.[121] That WILPF took such criticisms to heart is suggested by its dropping "India (British)" as a listed section after 1919, its hopes to add "a truly Indian Section" in 1921, and in 1936 its turning down the request to affiliate from a British-headed peace organization in Calcutta, as the League sought instead to see "whether an Indian Section of the League could be started by Indians themselves."[122] Margaret Cousins, an Irish woman known as the "mother" of Indian feminism, herself recognized in 1942 that "Indian national consciousness is much more touchy nowadays about non-Asians like myself taking any iniative or prominent part in Indian progressive movements."[123] Elsewhere, too, the WILPF leadership seemed finally to recognize the need for indigenous sections as well, working in 1929 "to get the Turkish women themselves," rather than European women living in Turkey.[124] The Tunis section of WILPF, founded that same year as a sort of subset of the French group, had as its original members almost all "Europeans or Jews," but a growing Muslim membership led to the formation of an independent section in 1932 "as a concession to the Arabs."[125]

Women from colonized countries also spoke out in forceful condemnation of imperialism, directly or indirectly tangling with European-origin women who defended their own countries' actions. At the 1933 International Congress of Women in Chicago, the Syrian Alice Kandaleft denounced imperialism in the form of the mandate system, provoking a French delegate to speak positively about her country's rule by pointing to Syria's history of external control and to the infrastructure the French had built. "The points that were taken by our friend, the French lady, that they have always been under some other authority is certainly no excuse, and you all know that. The second thing is the hospitals and schools and all that—again, you know that old story. We all know it," Kandaleft replied.[126] At the 1935 Alliance congress in Istanbul, Shareefeh

Hamid Ali of India, on behalf of "we of the East," warned "you of the west that any arrogant assumption of superiority or of patronage on the part of Europe or America, any undue pressure of enforcement of religion or government or of trade or economic 'spheres of influence' will alienate Asia and Africa and with it the womanhood of Asia and Africa."[127] Likewise, at the 1937 WILPF congress, the Egyptian Anna Tuby protested a Swedish proposal appealing to Great Britain to encourage and hasten development in the colonies, arguing that colonies could develop on their own and that "help" served only as a pretext for colonization. Even more forcefully, Shareefeh Hamid Ali denounced the assumption that imperial powers civilized backward peoples as "hypocritical and wrong." The "Ethiopians might as well some day pretend to go and civilize Italy, or China to civilize Japan. The civilization of peoples in Africa and Asia may be different from the European, but it has the same right of existence as that of Europe." Indians, she stated flatly, did not admire European civilization.[128] Hers was a particularly powerful voice questioning the very foundation of European imperialism.

Within the international groups, then, women of European origin, faced with the crumbling system of imperialism and their own contradictory evaluations of women in the rest of the world, struggled to come to grips with the consequences of organizational expansion. Although the structural barriers of finances and language and location, as well as the feminist orientalism so pervasive among Euro-American women, continued to block access for many women, the boundary of ethnicity came increasingly under siege, both from within and from outside the women's organizations. "International" took on new meaning as women gazed not just across the Atlantic, but in all directions.

The world of 1945 was a different place. No longer did Europe dominate the world system, no longer could colonies be kept in check. The global depression had proven a shocking illustration of just how interconnected national economies had become. In this context, the question of what the membership of an international women's movement might look like prompted very different answers.

The relative homogeneity of the international women's movement during the first wave served both as a source of solidarity for those within the fold and a barrier to the participation of others. The boundaries of class, religion, age, and ethnicity were never explicitly claimed by internationally organized women. On the contrary, members held dear the lofty ideal of universality. Nevertheless, the requirements of international travel necessitated access to financial resources, the ingrained assumptions about and ignorance of or hostility toward other religious traditions favored participation by Christian women, the preponderance of middle-aged or old women made membership of young women remarkable, and the dominance of European-origin women perpetuated itself throughout the years.

As we have seen, however, these unintended boundaries were far from impregnable. Although the transnational organizations could not pretend to represent the masses of peasant or urban working-class women from around the globe, voices did call out to challenge exclusion. Subsidies for members who lacked the means to pay for international travel, awareness of the rise of anti-Semitism and recognition of the interests of Muslim women (especially in Palestine), plans to recruit young women, discussion of the need for an international language, suggestions to hold conferences outside Europe, and strategies for making the organizations "truly international" all attested to the desire of some within the transnational groups to lower the barriers.

But the challenges of women outside the inner circle—and especially those from Asia, the Middle East, Latin America, and Africa—played the most important role in recognizing and breaching the exclusionary walls. The Chinese woman who refused to be put on display as an exotic at the Women's International League congress, the Tunisian and Indian women who insisted on representing themselves, the diverse voices of women like Alice Kandaleft and Shareefeh Hamid Ali raised in condemnation of Western imperialism and feminist orientalism—all called attention to the limitations on the universality of the women's international collective identity constructed within the transnational organizations. But by the very act of raising such challenges, women expressed confidence that the circle could be expanded.

If women in the international women's movement rejected, in theory, the notion of any limitation on the kinds of women who might participate, they enthusiastically embraced a different kind of boundary, that of gender. In the next chapter, we turn to a consideration of the ideological emphasis on women's difference from men that served as the explicitly heralded, if also occasionally disputed, basis for women's international organizing and to the separatist practices that continued throughout the first wave.

4

The International Bonds of Womanhood

Nos coeurs battent, à l'unisson des votres,
commes mères et comme femmes.
(Julie Siegfried, 1914)[1]

SHORTLY AFTER the outbreak of hostilities in 1914, Julie Siegfried, president of the French National Council of Women, wrote to Lady Aberdeen, "Our hearts beat, in unison with yours, as mothers and as women." It was as good an expression as any of women's sense of solidarity across the borders of different nations, even, though not in this case, nations at war with one another. Such professions of unity resounded throughout the international women's organizations. In 1899 a group of Dutch women addressed their "American Sisters," proclaiming it the moment "in which all Women ought to join hands and hearts and say of one accord: sense may separate us or mountains divide us, but our souls know no barriers."[2] As Dutch Alliance member Martina Kramers put it simply in 1917, "Long live the international solidarity of women!"[3]

Organized women around much of the globe, like the Dutch group quoted above, publicly and privately used the now-controversial language of "sisterhood" to forge such connections.[4] Hubertine Auclert, on behalf of all Frenchwomen, addressed the organizers of the 1888 founding meeting of the International Council of Women as her "sisters."[5] As the international women's movement mobilized before the First World War, women from the Netherlands, Russia, Canada, Italy, Germany, Scotland, Switzerland, Hungary, and the United States—in English, German, and French—used the terms "sisters" or "sisterhood."[6] This was not solely a usage by North American and European women: a Japanese student who attended WILPF's Vienna congress in 1921 dedicated herself to working for "universal sisterhood," a Chinese student at the 1929 congress addressed her "International Sisters," and an Indian woman reporting to the Peace and Disarmament Committee in 1938 wrote, in French, to "my sisters and collaborators."[7] Especially eager to claim such ties across the chasms of language and culture, members of the Women's International League greeted, expressed sympathy for, and congratulated their Japanese, Chinese, and Egyptian "sisters."[8]

As we have seen, not all women fit with equal ease into the family circle. But the self-professed bonds of sisterhood point to the one boundary—that of gender—which women not only acknowledged but embraced enthusiastically, with little difference among the three organizations. I explore here the line dividing women from men that members of the transnational groups drew both ideologically, by assuming fundamental gender differences, and practically, by organizing in single-sex groups and choosing, in some cases, to make their lives with other women. The international bonds of womanhood rested on the assumption that all women shared certain characteristics and thus naturally would flock together in women's organizations. And in fact women's potential for motherhood, women's systematic disadvantage compared to men of their group, and the seemingly universal threat of rape in wartime did forge bonds that transcended at least national differences.

Yet the boundaries we have just explored, if unacknowledged, still came into play, disrupting assumptions of commonalities. Particularly as changes in women's employment patterns, the granting of suffrage, and the breakdown of the social segregation of the sexes throughout the industrialized world took hold, women found themselves increasingly more divided than united on the questions of what they had in common and how best to organize and live their lives. Even so, the boundary of gender, shifting and contested as it might have been, formed the keystone of women's international collective identity.

The Ideology of Difference

Women's difference from men, long an ideological staple both in women's movements and in Western as well as other cultures around the world, dominated the discourse of the international women's organizations.[9] Even as the power of this idea began to wane in the outside world, with the increasing integration of women into previously male arenas, the aging women of the Council, Alliance, and League clung to what began to seem to young women an anachronistic vision. Turning upside down societal assumptions of women's inferiority, participants painted in broad strokes the superiority of female values. Anita Augspurg contrasted the "world of men," "built up on profit and power, on gaining material wealth and oppressing other people," to the "new world" women could build that would "produce enough for all and which would include the protection of children, youth and the weak." Augspurg's life partner, Lida Gustava Heymann, likewise condemned men's "lies and hatred and violence" and lauded the world women wanted to establish based on "love, right and mutual understanding."[10]

Although their British colleague Catherine Marshall did not fully embrace such ideas, she did agree that "women have a greater love for freedom for its own sake while men always tend to claim freedom for themselves but to oppress others."[11] *Pax* approvingly reported on a book that contrasted the masculine vices of lust, war, greed, drink, and slavery to the feminine virtues of patience, long suffering, purity, sacrifice, and love.[12]

Such contrasts between women and men came especially to the fore in discussions of what participants generally considered the male business of war and the female penchant for peace. Of the First World War, Mary Sheepshanks wrote: "Men have made this war; let women make peace— a real and lasting peace."[13] In the interval between the wars, Egyptian feminist Huda Sha'rawi proclaimed that "if men's ambition has created war, the sentiment of equity, innate in women, will further the construction of peace."[14] Putting it more bluntly, Carrie Chapman Catt insisted: "All wars are men's wars. Peace has been made by women but war never."[15]

Hatred of war unleashed a veritable barrage of antimale sentiment, already implicit in the hierarchy of female and male values. This, too, put a generational mark on internationally organized women and distanced them from younger women. The Hungarian Paula Pogány, during the First World War, had never in her life "felt more aversion against everything what [sic] carries the character of manhood."[16] U.S. suffragist Anna Howard Shaw, who already thought little enough of men, found their "war madness and barbarism" "unthinkable" and claimed that "I have not half the respect for man's judgment or common sense that I used to have, that they are such fools as to go out and kill and be killed without knowing why."[17] In the midst of the Second World War, Catt ventured that men had never wanted to end war: "They like to fight, they like the adventure, they like the prestige, and they certainly love conquest."[18]

Women's hatred of war, in contrast to men's desire for it, could, women in the international groups hoped, serve as the basis for common action. And it could make a difference in the world. In 1915 Rosika Schwimmer was "sure that millions of women in each country feel alike" and sought "to make a frame for this expression."[19] Czech WILPF member Lola Hanouskova believed that women could bridge national differences in southeastern Europe in the 1930s, and Gertrud Baer placed her hope in women's power to stop the violence between Ecuador and Peru in 1941.[20] Rosa Manus insisted in 1932, in the aftermath of the massive disarmament petition campaign, that "the women must stand strongly together and tell the statesmen that we do not care to which party and country they belong, but that no human lives may be offered again."[21] From this perspective, women's failure to save the world from a second great global conflagration dealt a grievous blow to women's confidence.

The conviction that women could make a difference serves as an international example of what we have come to call "maternalist politics": the construction of public positions on the foundation of women's biological and social roles as mothers.[22] In accordance with a long tradition, many internationally active women made the essentialist assumption that because of their biological capacity for reproduction, women were inherently pacifistic. As Germaine Malaterre-Sellier, a French suffrage leader, put it, "Women who have given life must always have a horror of war."[23] Milena Rudnycka, from Ukraine, asked the 1929 WILPF congress, "are we not as mothers of our children . . . steeped in the sacredness of each single human life through the mysteries of bringing forth life[?]"[24] Even more forcefully, a German-language appeal to women as mothers of sons demanded, "Have you forgotten the hour of his birth? No man can sympathize with that, for he has never with a hundred thousand pains borne a child."[25]

Maternalist pacifist politics might be rife with essentialist connections between the act of giving birth and horror of war, but women's roles as nurturers of children came into the picture as well. A "fraternal" delegate to the 1899 ICW congress assumed women's attraction to peace work because they "had committed to their care and charge the nurture of life."[26] Addressing the Pan-Pacific Women's conference, Jane Addams related women's proclivities for peace to their "nurture of living and growing things," both as the first food producers and as mothers.[27] Taking an unusual tack, a 1920 appeal "To Women of Palestine Who Love Peace" called on mothers as the socializers of children to use their power to help "their sons and daughters grow up free from religious and racial prejudice, free from all that is dwarfing in the wrong kind of patriotism."[28] In a startling action expressing the power of motherhood, the ICW wired Hitler four days after the German invasion of Poland, "evoking the cherished memory of Your Excellency's own Mother" to implore him to make peace.[29]

The emphasis on nurturing, not just bearing, children gave motherhood the potential to unite all women, even those who had never given birth. This move had great potential significance for organizations in which, as we shall see, many women had chosen not to marry and bear children. An Australian delegate to the 1924 WILPF congress emphasized "the pacifistic power of women as teachers, mothers, and journalists."[30] Marie Hoheisel insisted in the ICW *Bulletin* that the power to mother the world was inherent in all women, whether or not they had borne a child.[31] As Rosika Schwimmer put it, "Even women who are not physically mothers, feel all as the mothers of the human race."[32]

However they conceptualized motherhood, internationally organized women believed in its universal power. Referring to themselves as "mother-hearts," "guardians, nurses & preservers," "Mothers of the Human Race," "carriers of life," "MOTHERS OF THE NATIONS," "guardians of the new generations," women assumed that their gender united them behind the cause of peace.[33] Motherhood, biological or otherwise, was after all something that women all around the globe might share, making appeals to motherhood strategic as well as heartfelt. As Emily Greene Balch admitted in 1934, "I see value in sentimental appeals to 'the mother heart.'"[34] British suffragist Emmeline Pethick-Lawrence played on this theme during the First World War when she described women "who in every nation have shed their blood that men may be born" as "undivided by race or class."[35] Or as a participant in the 1913 Alliance congress had put it, "All this *concerns the mothers of the race, whether they be black or brown, white or yellow.*"[36]

Another powerful argument for gender difference targeted wartime sexual violence as a stark boundary separating women from men. The ICW Peace Committee protested in 1913 against "the horrible violation of womanhood that attends all war," and the quinquennial congress the following year appealed to the next international peace congress to take up the protection of women from rape in wartime.[37] During the First World War, such protests increased in intensity. In their petition to Woodrow Wilson, the women of twelve nations called on the U.S. president to mediate not only to save the lives of men but to prevent making of women "victims of the unspeakable horrors which inevitably accompany the bloody game of war!"[38] Picking up the theme of violence, the flyer announcing the upcoming Hague Congress of Women referred circumspectly to rape as one reason that women needed to come together internationally: "the moral and physical sufferings of many women are beyond description and are often of such a nature that by the tacit consent of men the least possible is reported. Women raise their voices in commiseration with those women wounded in their deepest sense of womanhood and powerless to defend themselves."[39] Quoting Lida Gustava Heymann, Jane Addams, presiding at the Hague Congress, proclaimed: "Worse than death, yes, worse than hellish, is the defenselessness of women in warfare and their violation by the invading soldier!"[40]

Violence against women, like motherhood, had the potential to unite women across cultures, since all women were fair game, especially in war. Carrie Chapman Catt pressured Mary Sheepshanks to collect evidence of "wrongs done to women" by any of the belligerents during the First World War.[41] But in fact the reports that surfaced followed predictable patterns, as we have seen in the furor over the African troops deployed in France. Catt mentioned rapes by Bulgarian and Greek soldiers in the Balkan war; Rosika Schwimmer learned of the rape of Hungarian women by Russian soldiers and the violation of French women by German troops; WILPF took up the issue of the rape and imprisonment of Armenian women by the Turks after the First World War; and a Western woman living in Japan told of the rape of women in China.[42] And Catt herself revealed her Euro-American vision of civilization when she deplored the fact that the "conditions of war subvert the natural instincts of many men of all races, who temporarily return to the brutal practices of the most savage primitive races."[43] The potential universality of wartime rape, as powerful a bond among women as it might be, could also be undercut by wartime animosities and assumptions about superior civilizations.

Other expressions of boundaries between women and men reflected the generational, class, and national composition of the membership and thus had less potentially universal appeal. One strand of discourse that developed in the years before the First World War called attention to women's domestic roles as shaped within Western bourgeois culture. Lady Aberdeen, assuming universality, argued in 1906 that devotion to the home brought women together across the chasms of class and race.[44] Finnish Alliance member Annie Furuhjelm saw the "motor force of the whole movement" in 1914 as the "intuitive comprehension of women that they have to go out of their own individual homes in order to make the big world more of a home."[45] But as women in industrialized societies moved into the labor force in larger numbers, and as women of European origin confronted divergent patterns of social organization in different parts of the world, this theme lost salience.

Likewise, the unifying potential of women's disfranchisement or lack of political power diminished over time, although a more generalized sense of oppression continued to serve as a basis of solidarity. At the founding congress of the ICW, U.S. suffragist Elizabeth Cady Stanton referred to the "universal sense of injustice, that forms a common bond of union" among "the women of all nationalities."[46] When U.S. women still lacked the vote, Carrie Chapman Catt saw Chinese suffragists beholding "the same vision which is arousing the women of all the Nations of the Earth" and, turning her gaze to the Balkans, asserted that there "are wrongs of countries and of classes to be righted, but the wrongs of women are common to all races and nations."[47] Sounding the theme of sexual slavery, Catt argued that the women of the East and the West had a "solidarity of interest" resulting from the traffic in women.[48] Mary Sheepshanks agreed in 1916 that oppression tied women together: "Unenfranchised, unequal before the law, suffering from innumerable disabilities and injustices, [women] will preserve the bond of their common sisterhood."[49] Siao-Mei Djang, a Chinese woman writing a pamphlet for WILPF, could still refer in 1929 to "the problems which are universal to womenhood."[50]

But oppression-based arguments that zeroed in on women's formal exclusion from the political system increasingly divided, rather than united, women. The granting of women's suffrage in the United States, Great Britain, Australia, and many of the European countries around the time of the First World War created new categories of enfranchised and still-voteless women. In 1915 Carrie Chapman Catt could express her doubts about the efficacy of the delegations sent out by the Hague Congress by pointing out to Aletta Jacobs that women "in no country have secured a position of political dignity."[51] But after the postwar wave of enfranchisement, the International Alliance, as we have seen, debated the best means of organizing when some auxiliaries had achieved suffrage and others had not, struggling to present a unified front.

Of course, women's continued exclusion from formal political power, even in countries where they could cast a ballot, blurred the lines between enfranchised and unenfranchised women. But women in the international organizations tended to view their outsider status in a positive light, focusing on independence from traditional political parties as a sign of superiority. "We have escaped party intrigues and precedents, and the awe for traditional conventions, which have tied men's hands," Mary Sheepshanks declared in typical fashion.[52] When Hitler came to power, WILPF issued a "Statement on Fascism": "We women, the greater part of whom are outside all political parties, and consequently not obliged to take the orders of any of them, can understand these events independently, with our simple common sense, and our sense of what is human."[53] Thus what might have been seen as a cause of women's continued inability to grasp the reins of power became a symbol of female values that could bind together those who had attained suffrage and those still far from reaching that goal.

There was great consensus, then, that women's difference from men—whether biologically or socially grounded—formed the basis for international organizing among women. The discourse of the movement settled variously on women's reproductive roles, the social roles of motherhood, violence against women, women's domestic roles, and women's relationship to the political process to explain the boundary that divided the genders. But isolated voices did sound a discordant note by questioning the assumption of women's difference. The world-famous peace activist Bertha von Suttner, who worked in mixed-gender rather than women's organizations, at the 1904 ICW congress argued against the notion that "because they are daughters, wives, and mothers . . . modern women want to undermine the institution of war"; she located their opposition instead in a rationality shared with men.[54] The crowd at the 1915 Hague Congress hissed down one woman for saying that "the average woman is no more for peace than men are," showing not only the existence of dissent but also the emotion invested in the dogma of difference.[55] The disillusionment of the First World War and the mounting threats to peace in the 1930s took their toll on some activists. A few articles in *Jus Suffragii* challenged the idea that women's nature is "differently organized" than men's and that biology accounted for a "differentiated sex psychology."[56] Although Bertha Lutz perceived "a very male-spirit rampant in the world" in 1933, she worried about women's ability to prevent a new war because "women are not really feminists and still less, pacifists."[57] And Rosika Schwimmer, in 1934, admitted that she, too, no longer believed in women's natural pacifism.[58]

But in general such unharmonious voices were drowned out in a chorus of acclamation for the idea that women had special qualities and with them important responsibilities for the future of the world. The ideology of difference, which formed the basis for the boundary between women and men, was the most fundamental underpinning of women's international collective identity.

Separatist Organizing

The ideology of difference found organizational expression in the woman-only membership of the three major international bodies and the coalitions they formed. But despite the nearly universal embracing of women's difference from men and the continuing practice of organizing apart from male colleagues, few women explicitly defended the practice. Perhaps, as the circle of membership expanded to take in women from societies less used to separatist organizing and as the exclusion of men came to seem anachronistic, even the older generation of women hesitated to publicize their old-fashioned preferences.

In the early years of the ICW, discussion of the role of men betrayed an unsure footing on the terrain of separatist organizing. In planning for the 1899 congress, the Committee of Arrangements agreed that men would be invited to speak and take part in discussions, but that some meetings would be open to women only.[59] Yet when the German National Council submitted a list of male speakers, the corresponding secretary told them plainly, "I do not think the Sub-Committee have selected men to speak, unless there is some very great reason why they should be chosen."[60] In her presidential address, Lady Aberdeen referred to separate women's organizations as a "temporary expedient to meet a temporary need" and hoped that they would not be allowed "to crystallise into a permanent element in social life."[61]

The Alliance, as the most explicitly feminist of the three organizations, seemed least troubled about separatist organizing, perhaps because of its origins as a group fighting for a right denied to women but enjoyed by men, at least in countries where men had some political rights. The IWSA encouraged the formation of a Men's International Alliance for Woman Suffrage and welcomed the male group to its Budapest congress in 1913, but the two organizations remained separate, with male delegates only at the men's meetings.[62] In a 1976 interview, Margery Corbett Ashby explained that the goal of women's organizations was to eliminate the need for women's organizations, although she admitted that it could be hard for some to accept this.[63]

The Women's International League, in contrast to the Alliance, grappled with the question of separatism from the beginning. At the Hague Congress, Dutch women called for the concentration of all forces, male and female, working for peace: "a special women's movement is not necessary and therefore undesired. The force of a movement where two sexes cooperate will come to better results than an organisation of one sex only," they insisted.[64] But not all agreed. Emily Greene Balch wrote to Aletta Jacobs in 1916 to report that the Neutral Conference for Continual Mediation, meeting in Stockholm, had decided to reorganize to exclude women on the basis that they mostly lacked the franchise. "I suppose I need not tell you that my interest and belief in our woman's organization is as strong as ever," she concluded.[65] Although WILPF constituted itself in 1919 as an all-female group, the question of separatism continued to provoke dissension. Reflecting the increasing integration of women into public life, the Executive Committee in 1920 considered "Reasons for a separate womens [sic] league—how long valid."[66] In answering the question, WILPF laid out publicly the whole range of ideas included in the ideology of difference, from biological motherhood to roles in education to lack of political experience. But there were several new twists. With regard to the possibility of making special appeals to women as "mothers and nurses of the race, as the natural guardians of life," a WILPF pamphlet weighed the "sentimentalism" of such an approach against the fact that it represented a "vein of feeling that quite spontaneously appears again and again among women from all quarters of the globe and of most various types." Furthermore, WILPF considered what would have been anathema to many—that women "may be even more chauvinist and belligerent than men"—but took this as "rather an argument for trying to organise them for peace than an argument the other way."[67] Finally, members pointed out that "in most joint meetings the men simply dominate the position, and the women sit silent, over-awed by the more aggressive personalities," considering this a good rationale for meeting without males.[68] For all these reasons, WILPF decided to remain a women-only organization.

Whether for ideological or practical reasons or out of unwillingness to break out of established patterns, neither WILPF nor the other two orga-nizations changed their policies on separatism, and the practice of gath-ering apart from men carried over into the coalitions. In 1938 the Liai-son Committee tabled the application of the Ligue Internationale Orient-Occident because it was a mixed-gender group.[69] But all of the international women's groups participated in mixed-gender congresses—such as international peace congresses—and coalitions—such as the Union of International Associations, the Central Organisation for a Durable Peace during the First World War, and the Liaison Committee of Major International Organisations. When the Disarmament Committee planned the presentation of petitions to the Disarmament Conference in 1932, the minutes record that only "reluctantly," because of material dif-ficulties, did the members agree to confine the procession to women.[70]

The question of separatism underlay a conflict within the international organizations about the appropriate relationship of women to the estab-lished political parties. As we have seen, independence from parties—that is, independence from male-dominated politics—signified female superiority to internationally organized women. As early as 1904, May Wright Sewall, invited to speak at the Berlin congress of the ICW on "the relationship of the women's movement to political and religious parties," explained that she interpreted the German word "relationship" (Ver-hältnis) in this case to refer to "independence" (Unabhängigkeit), which she strongly supported. The congress organizers took great delight in the fact that "you understand the topic exactly, to the dot of the i, as we say, as we do and will express our position on the question."[71] On the oppo-site side, at the 1925 congress an "animated discussion" on the best means of proceeding in the postwar world ended with the acceptance of a resolution presented by Betzy Kjelsberg of Norway recommending that women join political parties.[72]

The Alliance grappled with the same question. Debated at the 1911 Stockholm congress, the subject of a four-part article presenting both sides in *Jus Suffragii* in 1912, and brought to the floor again at the 1913 Budapest congress, the proper relationship between suffragists and men's political parties remained troublesome.[73] Some favored integration into politics, others separate women's lists and women's political groups. Although on Enfranchised Women's Day at the 1923 Rome congress,

"No woman could be found to advocate the establishment of a Woman's Party," members did not leap to substitute political participation in male-dominated parties for their own women's groups.[74]

Perhaps because it originated at the time of the first wave of enfranchisement and regularly took more progressive stances, WILPF's concerns focused on the danger of "not conserving its position of independence from all of the political parties," but especially from socialist and communist parties. A 1935 resolution proclaimed the nonparty character of the organization and its intention to work with the women of all parties or no party, as long as they agreed about WILPF's aims.[75]

Given the persistence of women-only organizations, the lack of vigorous defense of the principle of separatism is curious. Yet such silence speaks. It is possible that the need never occurred to those long committed to organizing in woman-only groups. But because the question of admitting men did arise, it is hard not to wonder if the silence was a sign of uneasiness over the old-fashioned associations of single-sex organizing in an increasingly heterosocial world. That separatist inclinations remained strong is clear from the apology of Eva Fichet, a member of the mixed-gender Tunis section of WILPF, who planned to bring her member husband to the 1934 congress. Noting that "his presence will offend some of our collaborators," she promised that "he will only make an appearance at public meetings, if there are any."[76] Still, the sentiments of British suffragist Catherine Marshall stand out in the records of the international women's movements: "It is always a pleasure to meet *Women fellow workers*. . . . I *do* like women best! Who was it said: The more I see of men the better I think of women!"[77] No other voice expressed such satisfaction with the practice of working with women, despite the widespread agreement about differences between women and men. In order to understand better the context for single-sex organizing and women's hesitance about defending it, we turn now to the different patterns of intimacy in the lives of women members.

Patterns of Intimacy

The discussion of separatism, I would argue, reflected patterns linking women's intimate lives with their political choices. Among the leaders of the international organizations, those married to supportive men stood as exemplars of cross-gender cooperation, those outside the boundaries of respectable heterosexuality served as warnings of the potential dangers of work with men, and those in couple relationships with women shone as beacons of the woman-committed life. An exploration of a number of

Fig. 4. Lord and Lady Aberdeen "at the door of the motor car that was given to them as a Golden Wedding present by many members of their large international family." Reproduced from the ICW *Bulletin*, November 1927.

women's relationships illustrates how connections between personal lives and attitudes about separatist organizing contributed to the drawing of the gender boundary in the international women's organizations.

For women who drew their husbands into their political work, separatist organizing seemed to be, as Lady Aberdeen put it, a "temporary expedient." Within the ICW, Lady and Lord Aberdeen served as a model of a couple committed to the same work, even though Lord Aberdeen in fact played no role in the organization. As they approached the fiftieth anniversary of their marriage in 1927, supporters within the ICW sent out appeals for contributions to purchase an automobile as a gift, and the *Bulletin* featured a front-page photograph of the happy couple with their shiny new possession (see figure 4).[78] Aberdeen's devoted friend Alice Salomon described their marriage as modern and ideal and insisted that the International Council was as much a matter of concern to Lord as to Lady Aberdeen.[79] The Council president herself described her husband's "never wavering support and . . . belief in the I.C.W." that had made possible everything she had accomplished.[80] Emma Ender, president of the German National Council, responded that she knew from her own experience "what it means, to live at the side of a man who totally understands and supports the life work that we have taken on."[81] Even after Lord Aberdeen's death, Lady Aberdeen referred to "the inestimable blessing of husbands who wish us to enter into all the fullness of life in service and responsibility."[82]

Like Lady Aberdeen, Aletta Jacobs brought her husband, Carel Victor Gerritsen, into her work with the ICW, Alliance, and WILPF. Despite her perception of marriage's injustice as an institution, Jacobs, the first woman doctor in the Netherlands, married Gerritsen in deference to his political career and their mutual desire to have a child. She described Gerritsen as "a feminist from the start," and when they married she kept her own name and they maintained separate quarters within the house they shared. Gerritsen actually took up Jacobs's cause not only by supporting her but by speaking himself in favor of women's suffrage.[83] Anna Howard Shaw, not known for her appreciation of men, added Gerritsen to her list of six men "of whom I say very often they have proved to me beyond a doubt, that it is possible to be as happy married as to be not married."[84] Rosika Schwimmer planned to write about Jacobs and Gerritsen in her book about marriage ideals and ideal marriages, although the final version, published in German, contained not a word about the couple, apparently because Jacobs did not approve of what Schwimmer planned to say.[85] When Gerritsen died in 1905, a friend wrote to Jacobs to express her understanding of how hard it was "to be deprived of the companionship of your dear husband, when you were so harmonious in all your tastes and thoughts," and Carrie Chapman Catt, who lost her own husband the same year, sent her sympathy for the loss of "so splendid and helpful a man."[86]

Aberdeen and Jacobs moved easily between their married lives and the female worlds of their organizations, but American WILPF leader Madeleine Doty, born over twenty years later, experienced more tension. A lawyer and emancipated woman who had lived in the bohemian community of Greenwich Village, Doty had an unconventional marriage to American Civil Liberties cofounder Roger Baldwin. Doty applied for the Geneva job of international secretary in the 1920s because Baldwin was taking a year off and planned to travel, leaving her "free to do."[87] When she left her work in Geneva to visit him in England in 1927, she reported that the staff at headquarters was "very severe," but Doty wondered "how good they'd be if they hadn't seen a husband in 15 months."[88] Baldwin's visits to WILPF headquarters prompted Doty to remark that "the Maison has much too feminine an atmosphere."[89] "He certainly made it lively here and we decided that one or two men are needed in this house of 'females,'" Doty wrote to Jane Addams.[90] Despite her commitment to an all-female organization, Doty seemed to prefer work in a mixed-gender environment. As a member of the younger generation (although in her forties in the 1920s), Doty seemed more ambivalent about the women's world in which she found herself in Geneva.

Tension also arose in the case of women perceived as too involved—or in improper relationships—with men, and criticism linked violations of sexual respectability to questionable political work with men. Martina Kramers, who maintained a long-term but unconventional liaison with a man, faced the censure of Carrie Chapman Catt in 1913. Bobbie, whom Kramers called her "left-hand husband," was a socialist and married man whose wife refused to divorce him. As president of the IWSA, Catt wrote to Kramers to recommend that she resign as editor of *Jus Suffragii* since her "moral transgressions" had provoked "horror and repugnance" among U.S. Alliance members.[91] Kramers reacted with incredulity and defiance, refusing to give up either her man or her work and insisting to Catt that she was not a "propagandist of free love."[92] But to no avail. Catt managed, as Kramers put it, "to throw me out of the whole movement" by moving the offices of *Jus* to London and appointing a new editor.[93] Kramers's improprieties extended to the political sphere, since she had joined the socialist party under Bobbie's influence and fought from within for her feminist principles. As early as 1908, she perceived that Aletta Jacobs suspected her of becoming more attached to socialism than feminism on account of Bobbie.[94]

Shortly before Kramers's tangle with propriety, a similar scandal broke out within the German women's movement and spilled over into international circles. Conflict within the German League for the Protection of Motherhood, the leading progressive sex reform association, led to revelations about the "free marriage" of Helene Stöcker and one of her major male allies, Bruno Springer, and Stöcker's countercharges that her opponent, Adele Schreiber-Krieger, was also sleeping with her male supporters.[95] In the aftermath of this affair, Aletta Jacobs reported, disgustedly, to Rosika Schwimmer that "Dr. Stöcker behaved in the Hague just as everywhere, always clinging on one of the men."[96] As with Martina Kramers, the Stöcker scandal involved the combination of sexual liaisons and political alliances.

Controversy also swirled around Doris Stevens, an American emancipated "New Woman" who lobbied vigorously on the international scene for equal rights for women. Stevens struck Bertha Lutz as a "sex-mad psychopath," a "nymphomaniac," and a "mentally deranged woman."[97] At the Montevideo conference of the Pan American Union in 1934, Lutz accused Stevens of "paying the mexican delegates in kisses . . . [and] luring the haitians with a french secretary she has." "She left many of the latin american men under the impression that feminists are like the greek women who shared the life and the loose living of the men of Athens," Lutz added. Two years later at a conference in Buenos Aires, Lutz thought Stevens put "all women to shame."[98] Once again, international colleagues associated Stevens's aberrant heterosexual relationships with political work with men. And in fact Stevens made her reputation—however one wants to interpret that term—in the international women's movement as a vocal advocate of both working with and playing with men.

In contrast to both conventionally married women and women in unorthodox relationships with men, some leaders of the international women's organizations made their personal and political lives with other women and found no need for a male presence in a "house of females." The ideology of difference and the creation of a women's world, at least upon occasion, made women's organizations welcoming to women who chose other women for their life partners or who did not form intimate relationships with either women or men.[99]

Members seemed to accept women's coupled relationships as romantic friendships or "Boston marriages" rather than lesbian love affairs, despite the fact that they had some familiarity with the discourse of "homosexuality" as it emerged in the late nineteenth century.[100] As early as 1904, in a speech to the Scientific Humanitarian Committee, the German homosexual rights group, Anna Rühling associated lesbians ("Uranian women," in the terminology of the time) with the international women's movement.[101] Although German feminists Klara Schleker and Käthe Schirmacher were the only couple to identify publicly as lesbians, Martina Kramers referred in 1913 to gossip about Anita Augspurg's as well as Schirmacher's homosexuality.[102] Aletta Jacobs wrote to Rosika Schwimmer in 1905 about Schwimmer's use of morphine in connection with her suppressed sexual desires and hoped that Schwimmer would one day tell her "that you had found a good friend, and then you can say whether you are sexually normal or abnormal."[103] Discussion within international women's movement circles of "fairies," use of the terms "queer" and "perverse from a sexual point of view," references to "MANLY-LOOKING" women and women who "went about together at the Hague, hair cropped short and rather mannish in dress," and a description of a schoolgirl crush as "hero-worship . . . but there was nothing sordid or exaggerated about it," suggest that at least the European women had taken in the work of the sexologists.[104]

Yet Anita Augspurg and Lida Gustava Heymann, one notable couple within the circle of internationally organized women, loved each other and made a personal and political life together without anyone batting an eye (see figure 5). Augspurg, a leading member of the radical wing of the German women's movement and the country's first woman lawyer, met Heymann, a social worker and trade union organizer, at an 1896 international women's conference in Berlin. Although early on they decided not to live together, they happily broke that promise. They moved to the country, where they launched a series of ambitious, and

Fig. 5. Lida Gustava Heymann, Charlotte Despard, and Anita Augspurg, Zurich, 1919. Courtesy of the International Information Centre and Archive for the Women's Movement, Amsterdam, the Netherlands.

successful, agricultural enterprises—a quite unusual undertaking for two women. One day a cattle dealer came to call with proposals of marriage for both women, explaining that the farm was splendid and lacked only a man. "It took all our effort to remain serious and make clear to the man the hopelessness of his desire. As he left, we shook with laughter," Heymann commented.[105]

As such an anecdote makes clear, Heymann and Augspurg presented themselves unself-consciously as a couple. Correspondents regularly sent messages to and received them from both women. Heymann sent "Heartfelt greetings from us both" to Rosika Schwimmer in 1919; "I hope you and Dr. Augspurg are not too tired after these strenuous days of Vienna," a friend wrote in 1921.[106] When leaders of the German section of WILPF put out a translation of the 1924 congress report, they replaced a photograph of Heymann with one of the two women together, since "our German members like that better."[107] Augspurg and Heymann stayed in double rooms when they attended congresses, entertained movement friends at their home in the country, and described a happy family life: "I had a very good journey home and found Anita and our dog in good health," Heymann wrote Gabrielle Duchêne on her return from a trip to Paris.[108] When Heymann planned to travel to Geneva for a meeting in 1930, a WILPF staff member reported that "she is coming without Dr. Augspurg which is scarcely believable!"[109] In 1933, the couple had to flee Germany and forfeit their property, prompting friends in WILPF to try to help them. Clara Ragaz, hoping to arrange hospitality at the Maison in Geneva, commented about Augspurg, who suffered from heart disease, that "it is a very hard time for her friend—and of course for herself."[110] When Heymann died in June of 1943, Emily Greene Balch worked to raise money to support "her life-long friend and co-worker . . . , for whom she had cared so devotedly."[111] But as it turned out, Augspurg did not survive long. "Did you notice that Lida Gustava Heymann and Dr. Anita Augspurg died within a few short weeks of each other?" Rosika Schwimmer asked a friend.[112]

Like Augspurg and Heymann, Jane Addams and Mary Rozet Smith lived together and worked together in the international women's movement, although Addams played a clearly leading role. The German women enjoyed the hospitality of Addams and Smith when they came to the United States for the WILPF congress in 1924, and in 1929 Heymann and Augspurg sent Addams "and Miss Smith many heartfelt greetings."[113] Addams and Smith sent and received messages for one another, made arrangements for rooms with double beds when they traveled, and took care of each other, although that responsibility fell more heavily on Smith. Addams would "suffer from your absence," Mary Sheepshanks wrote Smith when she was too ill to travel to Europe in 1929.[114] Smith, whom Addams described to Heymann as "[m]y most intimate friend," inspired a great deal of enthusiasm among Addams's colleagues.[115] "Will you kiss your dear friend, Miss Smith, for me and tell her that in sleepless nights and even in nice dreams I see her before me as a good angel," wrote Aletta Jacobs in 1915. "I have a remembrance of her as one of the sweetest women I ever met in the world," Jacobs added four years later. And, even more extravagently, Jacobs concluded in 1923 that "I always have admired her and if I would have been a man I should have fallen in love with her."[116] Despite its subjunctive and heterosexual form, Jacobs's enthusiasm suggests how easily women could make a life together in the international women's movement.

Not all relationships between women evoked such adulation. After her second husband died, Carrie Chapman Catt set up housekeeping with New York suffrage leader Mary Garrett Hay, who was not popular in international circles.[117] Martina Kramers referred to her cynically as "the eternal Hay," marveling that she was not accompanying Catt on a trip to Europe.[118] Anna Howard Shaw, herself known for her "strong and passionate attachments to other women," detested Hay and thought her "power over" Catt "tightened with passing days."[119] Shaw could not understand Catt "wanting to tie to herself as her most intimate friend a woman of such a common nature and such a trouble breader [sic]."[120] Kramers agreed with Shaw's description, referring to Hay as "a perpetual source of dissension." But Shaw did "not think there is any hope of breaking that affair off."[121] The American Rachel Foster Avery concluded in 1910 that Hay "really loves" Catt.[122] Despite their dislike of Hay, Catt's colleagues in the movement accepted the validity of the relationship. When Catt died in 1947, she was buried, at her request, not with either of her two husbands but next to her "unforgettable friend and comrade" Hay.[123]

In contrast to these pairs, Emily Greene Balch resisted becoming part of a female couple and identified as an unmarried woman. Balch's childhood friend Helen Cheever, a wealthy woman who provided financial support, wanted to live with her on a permanent basis. But Balch, who admitted that she both loved and was irritated by Cheever, balked. Perhaps, she wrote her sister, it was a result of Cheever's "giving me more love than I can quite digest."[124] Yet when Balch was in Geneva as international secretary of WILPF, her coworkers eagerly anticipated, on Balch's behalf, a visit from Cheever. "I think she is homesick and it would be very good if her friend from America came soon to keep her company and also attend a bit to her physical health," Lida Gustava Heymann confided to Jane Addams.[125] Suggesting how intermeshed personal and political life could be, three years later Cheever wanted to resign her offices in the U.S. section of WILPF in order to go to Geneva where "my usefulness to the W.I.L. will be confined to being with Miss Balch."[126]

Balch's recorded reflections on her unmarried state suggest the ambivalence she felt, especially as the work of the sexologists cast aspersions of sexual abnormality on women without men. "The intense love of children, the instinct for homemaking, the preference for the companionship of men over that of women—all these made themselves felt only when my path in life had irrevocably fixed itself," she wrote in a document she titled "Confessions of a Professional Woman."[127] In reply to an inquiry from Jane Addams about the new phenomenon of the unmarried career woman, Balch wrote that such women might have missed out on the most precious of women's experiences but that "there is no evidence that they themselves or those who know them best find in them the abnormality that the Freudian psychoanalysts of life would have one look for." Unmarried women thought strange, she said, the evaluation of "everything that is not concerned with the play of desire between men and women as without adventure."[128]

Balch was not alone in her public defensiveness about her singleness. In a 1931 German anthology on the modern single career woman, Elisabeth Busse explained that such women were not "amazonian," "inverts," or "homosexuals," although "they lived in women's unions," a term with the double connotation of partnerships and women's organizations.[129] So it is not surprising that ICW secretary Alice Salomon, a German Jewish pioneer in the world of social work who never married, apologized in her autobiography that "this book may sometimes seem as much a book about women as though I had lived in a harem." Actually, she assured her readers, "I always had men and women, old and young, rich and poor, and sometimes whole families as my friends." But in fact Salomon made her life in the female world of social reform and the women's movement. She apparently felt compelled to discuss why she never married, explaining that her work "estranged me from my background" and "made me reluctant to form a union which could not combine love with common interests and convictions."[130]

In the ICW *Bulletin* of 1932, Salomon published a defense of unmarried women, the first generation of independent women who pursued careers. She recognized that the discipline of psychology had changed attitudes toward single women—that they were reputed to be warped by celibacy—but quoted a woman of "international fame" to the effect that "they are alive, active, and they fully participate in present-day life by means of a thousand interests."[131] The U.S. founder of the International Federation of Business and Professional Women, Lena Madesin Phillips, likewise recognized that "[t]o live an old maid was . . . considered something to be greatly deplored," but insisted that she had "no complaints, no regrets, no fears" about her own unmarried but woman-coupled life.[132] Helen Archdale, a British equal rights advocate active in the international arena, reacted testily to a paean to marriage Doris Stevens apparently penned after her second wedding. "What you say about the beneficial effects of marriage on one's life rather puzzles me. Why should 'spinsterhood' be gray?"[133] Archdale shared a London flat and country home with Lady Margaret Rhondda, another international activist, in the 1920s.[134] Such defensiveness and defiance about living apart from men reflect the power of an intensified vision of married life as the only healthy choice for women. In this context, it was no wonder that separatist organizations offered an appealing haven for women who made their lives with other women, whatever the nature of their ties.

Despite the variety of intimate relationships that women formed, and the tensions that women not married to men expressed, women in the international organizations bridged more easily the difference of marital status or sexual identity than other characteristics that divided them. This was so despite national differences in attitudes toward sexual expressiveness. European women seemed more open to sexual expression than their Anglo-American colleagues. Alice Salomon suggested that Americans were affected by the "Puritan strain in their upbringing," but her American friends denied it, retorting that German women were oversexed.[135] Rosa Manus seemed to make the same assumption about "puritanical" American views when she and her parents took Carrie Chapman Catt to a show at the Casino de Paris in 1923, "a most shocking real Paris Veau de ville [sic, for vaudeville] with a quantity of naked women. She had never seen anything like that, and I think it was good for her education," Manus reported.[136] When Emily Greene Balch learned that gossip had begun to circulate about an innocent young American woman working in Geneva in the 1920s, she concluded that European women could not understand the peculiarly American combination of sexual restraint and an informal manner in relations with young men.[137] And Martina Kramers, facing condemnation for her relationship with Bobbie, noted that "nowhere in Europe, beginning with my own country, are people so convinced of my immorality as they seem to be in America."[138] Perhaps as a result, when Kramers wrote her Hungarian friend Rosika Schwimmer about this whole affair, she switched from their normal English to German. Such national differences may have dissipated among young women undergoing the transformations associated with the sexual revolution of the early twentieth century, but among the older women of the international women's movement they tended to linger.

The practice of separatist organizing did, as we have seen, elicit varying responses from women, some of whom believed in living and working with men and some of whom preferred all-female environments. But whatever their personal relationships and attitudes toward single-sex organizing, all remained committed to international organizations that admitted only women. In that sense, the boundary of gender held.

The embracing of women's difference from men and the practice of separatist organizing interacted with the boundaries of class, religion, age, and ethnicity to mark off those who belonged to the group of internationally organized women and those who did not. Although a specific history of sexual differentiation in industrialized societies underlay both the conceptualization of gender difference and the tradition of separatist organizing, some versions of the ideology of difference had far greater potential appeal. The Women's International League may have been right in arguing that appeals to women as mothers, as natural "guardians of life," struck a chord "among women from all quarters of the globe and of most various types."[139] Furthermore, the reality of worldwide violence against women, especially in wartime, might unite women across vastly different life experiences. And women's common experience of subordination, although it took many forms in many degrees, held the possibility of bringing them all together. On the whole, the strong consensus on women's difference from men in experience and values is striking. The "sisterhood" of which women spoke—however problematic in reality—rested on this belief in fundamental gender difference.

At the same time, although preexisting networks and patterns of interaction shaped the international women's organizations as separatist,
acceptance of single-sex organizing in principle came much harder for
some groups of women. National and generational differences are especially striking. European women tended to associate separatism, like sexual prudery, with the "New World." The president of the National
Council of Women of the Netherlands explicitly made this connection in
1909.[140] Danish women responded to the announcement of the Woman's
Peace Party in the United States and a call for the formation of similar
groups in other countries by asserting that "we preferred to work
together, men and women, in the same organisation."[141] German and
Austrian women trade unionists refused to send representatives to the
second congress of the International Federation of Working Women in
1921 because they were "opposed to taking part in a separate women's
trade union organisation" in the American fashion.[142] And an Austrian
woman noted with evident astonishment that the manless banquets of
the International Federation of Business and Professional Women
"would simply have been an unheard of thing with us."[143]

Likewise, women struggling side by side with men of their class or
national group for justice or independence looked critically at separatist
organizing. Women committed to the powerful socialist and social-
democratic parties of Europe had particular reasons for eschewing single-sex groups. Katherine Bompas, contrasting the "older" women's
movement to the Women's International Democratic Federation after the
Second World War, believed that the existing groups, by being nonparty,
had "in the eyes of working women seemed bourgeois and even perhaps
conservative."[144] Margery Corbett Ashby reported in 1935 that the enormous difficulties facing the nationalist struggle in Egypt "bring the men
and women nearer together" and found the nationalist Wafd movement
"quite progressive as regards women's position."[145] A Syrian woman,
speaking at the Istanbul congress of the Alliance, asserted her belief in
the necessity of working for prosperity and freedom in her country
shoulder to shoulder with men: "The economic and political situation of
my country is so desperate that it is extremely difficult for us women to
give our wholehearted energies to the cause of feminism alone."[146]

Generational differences on the question of separatism are also con-
spicuous. Young women experiencing firsthand the breakdown between
male and female social spheres in the twentieth-century world challenged
women-only groups more readily than did their older colleagues. Mary
Sheepshanks related in 1930 that young women at a Geneva meeting of
the International Federation of University Women announced that "we
are not going to join any more of these women's organizations."[147] The
Canadian Dorothy Heneker pointed out in 1931 that young European

women thought that women should work with men, and the Youth Committee of the Alliance reported in 1938 that the general feeling favored a mixed organization of young people.[148] Generational, like national, differences grew from distinctive patterns of homosocial versus heterosocial interaction.

The lines that divided women, and the gender barrier that unified them, defined a potential universe for the creation of a women's international collective identity. But even fervent apostles of "international sisterhood" always knew that women committed to transnational organizing were different from the bulk of women, that the boundary of gender did not place all women in their camp. How they defined their common interests—a process that reveals their internationalist and feminist consciousness—is the subject of the next chapters.

Section II

CONSCIOUSNESS

5

Forging an International "We"

[Sie ist] wirklich ein internationaler Mensch.
(Lida Gustava Heymann, 1925)[1]

RAISING INTERNATIONALIST consciousness in a nationalist age was no mean feat, even among those committed to the idea that their condition as women bound them together across the borders of their countries. So much could intervene. Just because women joined transnational organizations did not mean that they forsook loyalty to their countries. Nor did they leave behind the prejudices about and stereotypes of "foreigners" that flourish in every society. What is important is that they committed themselves to internationalism despite the pervasive imprint of nationalism. As the self-description of the World Young Women's Christian Association as "not only international but internationally minded" emphasized, there was a crucial distinction between a body merely composed of members from different countries and the quality of internationalism.[2] The ability to understand colleagues of different national traditions and work together toward international goals was what distinguished someone, in Lida Gustava Heymann's words quoted above, as "really an international person."

In order to understand all that an internationalist consciousness entailed, I first explore here the various attempts to define, in both words and symbols, the meaning of internationalism. I then consider the relationship between nationalism and internationalism, identifying three conceptualizations that coexisted within the international women's movement. Finally, we turn to the workings of the transnational bodies to see the impact of these different positions on the process of choosing representatives and acting collectively. The fact that women did not agree about the primacy of nationalist versus internationalist loyalties yet managed nevertheless to cooperate and to envisage themselves as part of a common endeavor reveals how difficult and contested the process of constructing an international collective identity could be. The scope of the obstacles they overcame makes internationalist women's accomplishments all the more impressive.

Defining Internationalism

Through words and symbols, women from the three international
women's organizations expressed a common understanding of what
internationalism signified. One way they did this was by directly deploy-
ing the language of "we" to refer to women similarly committed to an
internationalist ideal. Early in the history of the International Council of
Women, Corresponding Secretary Teresa Wilson defined "us" as "International workers."[3] With regard to a potential coworker, Emily Greene
Balch noted in 1921, "She appears to be of our way of thinking"; and in
reference to another recruit, a WILPF staff member inquired "if she is the
appropriate personality for us."[4] Austrian feminist Helene Granitsch
referred twice in one 1931 letter to "we international women."[5] What
they meant was that they shared the quality of being "internationally
minded."[6]

Internationalism, in the discourse of the organizations, emerges as
both a new—a twentieth-century—phenomenon and a spirit rather than
a formal ideology. Marjorie Pentland, Lady Aberdeen's daughter, pointed
out in a pamphlet which she compiled from her mother's papers that the
word "international," first associated with Karl Marx's working men's
association in the midcentury, had the lure of novelty in the 1890s. But
by 1920, when the League of Nations issued a handbook of international
organizations, five hundred groups, almost all new since 1900, claimed
the title.[7] Carrie Chapman Catt, at the IWSA congress in 1909, referred
to "that spirit of the 20th century which the world calls Internationalism," and other women in the 1930s referred to the "century of internationalism."[8] Institutions that transcended the borders of political entities—as the Catholic Church did—were nothing new, but emphasizing
internationalism as a twentieth-century force suggests that it represented
a response to the tension between the pervasiveness of nationalism and
the increasing integration of the world through trade, communication,
and other forms of interaction.

Yet internationalism remained a vaguely defined force. For Catt, it was
"a sentiment like love, or religion, or patriotism, which is to be experienced rather than defined in words."[9] As Annie Furuhjelm described the
Alliance, "The true spirit of internationalism . . . cannot be described; it
must be felt."[10] Words such as "spirit," "feeling," and "force" cropped
up again and again, suggesting the almost mystical quality of internationalism as an imagined community.

When women tried to describe internationalism, they conceptualized
it as a stitched-together quilt of existing differences rather than a wholly

new piece of cloth. Unity came out of the merging of diversity. "In spite of differences of tradition and climate, of race, religion, and language, we feel we have all something in common," as Furuhjelm put it.[11] The minutes of the Zurich congress that gave birth to WILPF noted "the differences of nationality and the divergence of political opinions (because among the delegates of the same countries are found conservatives and socialists)," the "class differences (in certain delegations, the great ladies visit with the workers)," yet the "perfect agreement" that "never ceased to prevail during all the discussions."[12] Likewise, Gabrielle Duchêne, in her contribution to a WILPF pamphlet titled "Messages of Europe, Christmas 1924," referred to "[t]he different languages, the varied accents, the arguments, presented calmly or with passion," merged into "a common thought, a collective spirit."[13]

Because the notion of differences fused into a common international-ism was so hard to define, it found its most vivid expression in symbols.[14] Only rarely did the organizations propose wholly new symbols, such as a purple, white, and yellow striped peace flag or an international song.[15] Far more pervasive was the juxtaposition of national symbols, especially flags and traditional costumes, in international ceremonies. The Stockholm hall that sheltered a 1911 ICW meeting was decked out with flags of the constituent countries in order of affiliation. In an added ritual, each National Council president stood up to speak, accompanied by a rendition of her country's anthem. Much to the horror of the German international secretary, Alice Salomon, who had taken great pains to get everything right, the orchestra struck up the German anthem when the French president arose, a mistake she feared would smack of German chauvinism.[16]

In addition to flags and anthems, international congresses featured performances, in national dress, of traditional songs and dances. Rosa Manus first came to the attention of the IWSA leadership when she participated in a dance in Dutch costume at the 1908 Amsterdam conference (see figure 6), and other congresses featured Irish, Austrian, Sinhalese and Indian, Czech, Danish, and Scottish singing and dancing.[17] Sometimes the committees organizing international congresses asked delegates to wear national costumes or colors. The Swedish auxiliary of the IWSA called on participants in the 1911 congress to dress in the colors of their country, and the Irish section of WILPF requested delegates to appear in national costume or a white dress with a ribbon in the national colors at the 1926 Dublin congress.[18] The Joint Standing Committee in 1928 proposed to ask representatives to wear national costumes at a future dinner and to stand up "so as to show the international character of the gathering."[19]

Fig. 6. Dutch dancers at the IWSA congress in Amsterdam, 1908. Rosa Manus is
on the left in the middle row. Courtesy of the International Information Centre
and Archive for the Women's Movement, Amsterdam, the Netherlands.

The irony of national symbols put to such use never seemed to occur
to participants. When things did not go awry, flag-bedecked halls and
national-costumed participants gave, according to WILPF secretary
Madeleine Doty, "a very international character" to the proceedings.[20]
As a description of the 1929 Alliance congress put it, "these symbols of
nationalism grouped under the banner of the Alliance became symbols of
world-wide cooperation."[21] Perhaps internationally minded women preferred to set national symbols side by side rather than create new ones
because such a procedure allowed them to harness the power of deeply
felt national loyalties.

These symbolic representations of internationalism made concrete the
spirit that drew together diverse women into an international "we." But
they also reveal conflicting conceptions of the relationship beween
nationalism and internationalism. Alice Salomon's fear of how listeners
might react to the playing of the German national anthem acknowledged
the powerful sway of national loyalties within international circles; the
search for new international symbols reflected a desire to transcend, even
eliminate nationalism; and the appropriation of national cultural expressions in international ceremonies conveyed the potential coexistence of

the two forces. We turn now to a consideration of these three different articulations in order to understand how contention over the proper expression of internationalism helped forge an international collective identity.

Nationalism on Top

Since all of the organizations professed a commitment to internationalism, the privileging of nationalism generally took subtle rather than forthright forms. Through setting out national goals, validating national autonomy, and defining what constituted a nation and a national section, the Alliance and ICW in particular gave expression to nationalist urges. But during the First World War and in its aftermath, every organization contained some women who gave vent to more bald nationalist sentiments.

International work could serve explicitly national purposes, as it did especially in the early years of the Alliance. Suffrage, after all, could only be attained on the national level, so the job of the Alliance was to use its international resources to bring pressure to bear on the governments of individual sovereign nations. Carrie Chapman Catt made this clear when she wrote in 1905 to urge the new Hungarian suffrage society to affiliate with the IWSA: "To show to Parliamentary Bodies that there is an International Alliance composed of the women of many countries, who are fighting for their political freedom, is one of the strongest arguments we can use," she insisted. "[W]e have found it of benefit even here, and I am perfectly positive you will find it of great benefit in Hungary."[22] The IWSA, while still devoted primarily to winning women the vote, sought to meet in places where the need for stimulation of the suffrage struggle was greatest.[23] Millicent Garrett Fawcett, in the aftermath of the London congress of 1909, thanked the Alliance, saying that the congress "had been the greatest help to Great Britain."[24] Every congress report emphasized the salutary outcome: the 1913 Budapest meeting "had had a very good effect upon Hungary," the "effect of the [1923] Congress on Rome and Italy was marked," and the 1926 Paris meeting, leaders hoped—in vain, as it turned out—"may have hastened . . . victory" in France.[25] The hope was that a victory in one nation would have international consequences, but the importance of winning suffrage in individual countries cannot be denied.

Even more important, because more pervasive, was the desire of the international groups, particularly the Council and Alliance, to avoid violating national autonomy. At the most basic level, all of the bodies were organized into national sections that, to different degrees, protected their independence of action. The constitution of the ICW stated from the outset that the central body had no power over its member groups, so that no National Council would "render itself liable to be interfered with in respect to its complete organic unity, independence or method of work."[26] Likewise the Alliance, in 1909, adopted a bylaw pledging "absolute neutrality on all questions that are strictly national" and promising to "respect the independence of each affiliated association, and to leave it entirely free to act on all matters within its own country."[27] In response to a conflict between the National Councils of Sweden and Norway in 1905, the ICW added a new article to the constitution specifically excluding all "political and religious questions of a controversial nature affecting the inter-relationship of two or more countries" from the jurisdiction of the international structure.[28] In accordance with these basic principles, the Alliance expressed its neutrality in 1914, since "any reference to political conditions may hurt national susceptibilities"; similarly, the Norwegian section objected to the ICW issuing pronouncements during the Munich conference of September 1938, which carved up Czechoslovakia in an attempt to appease Hitler.[29] Only during the Second World War did *Jus Suffragii* drop its pose of neutrality, editorializing about its "duty to express our horror of unprovoked attack" when Denmark and Norway fell.[30] And after the war, in response to the Holocaust, the ICW revised its constitution to exclude from the ban political and religious questions "affecting fundamental human rights and freedoms."[31] As the cases of the Council and Alliance show, respect for national autonomy could severely curtail international action. WILPF, as a body explicitly devoted to peace and justice, found itself less hampered in this way, but fear of infringement on national autonomy did occasionally arise.

Respect for national autonomy assumed agreement about what constituted a nation, but in a world of conquered, colonial, and dependent countries, the applicability of the label "nation" was not always obvious. Global politics intruded on the world of the women's organizations, shaping perspectives on the question of what entities were "nations" and could thus organize national sections. When formerly independent colonies with discrete national councils federated into the Commonwealth of Australia in 1901, the ICW rethought what it took to be a nation.[32] The majority of the Committee on Races and Nationalities agreed that possessing the "organs of national life"—defined, in a striking display of Eurocentrism, as a constitution and parliament—made a unit a nation "no matter whether this nation be enjoying a full autonomy or whether it have only a limited autonomy, being incorporated within a larger nation and not recognised as an independent diplomatic member."[33] According to Carrie Chapman Catt, the organizers of the IWSA solved the problem of defining "nation" at the outset by stipulating that a country possess the independent right to enfranchise women.[34] Nevertheless, the IWSA supported the right of Finnish women to affiliate when the ICW turned them down in 1904 because Finland was under Russian control.[35] Continuing its stricter application of the concept of nation, the ICW in 1925 concluded that the NCW-Ukraine could not continue affiliation because the rules made it "only possible to accept for affiliation National Councils in countries having a responsible Government."[36] Such regulations made the formation of national groups in colonized countries especially unlikely, thus contributing to the limited geographical reach of the transnational organizations. In response to an inquiry from a women's organization in East Africa in 1930, the ICW formed a committee to study how "organisations in non-autonomous countries" could get in touch with the international work.[37]

The question of what qualified as a national section of a transnational group took on special urgency in countries divided by ethnicity and religion. Marianne Hainisch raised the issue in the ICW in 1899, reporting that owing to the variety of "races" in Austria it would be impossible to have one National Council.[38] And, as we have seen, both the Alliance and WILPF tackled the hairy question of a united Palestine section with a notable lack of success. But it was WILPF in the interwar years that struggled most persistently with divisions within national sections. In connection with the Irish demand for representation independent of Britain, the Zurich congress resolved in 1919 that "[a]ny minority in a country which claims the status of a separate nationality may also form a National Section."[39] The Executive Committee agreed in 1920 that a minority nationality could form a section, "although the most desirable solution is for members of the different nationalities within a country to work together in the same organisation."[40] But by 1929, faced with the eruption of the "minority problem" in many of the countries carved out in the aftermath of the First World War, WILPF changed its tune. The amended constitution allowed for one national section in every "Nation, free or subject, every Colony and self-governing Dominion," with the proviso only that "[i]n countries where different languages are spoken the national union may take on a federal form if desired."[41] At the 1934 congress, Lida Gustava Heymann even opposed this exception because it might lead to "division into racial, confessional and other groups, which would split the unity of the League."[42]

What prompted this rethinking was the struggle to organize a national section in the Czechoslovak Republic. Early on, the question of whether more than one society could be admitted from the same country cropped up in Czechoslovakia because "women of German language thought it impossible to work together with those of Czech language."[43] Separate German and Czech groups—and by 1928 a Jewish group as well—emerged, prompting the international officers to work long and hard to bring them together. But according to Lida Gustava Heymann, both sides lacked the proper international spirit.[44] In 1928 Františka Plamínková of the Czech group demanded a public apology from the German society, which had sent a letter to China describing the German minority in Czechoslovakia as "oppressed."[45] Scheduling the 1929 congress in Prague, Cor Ramondt-Hirschmann hoped, might settle things down, but Mary Sheepshanks proclaimed cooperation between the two groups impossible. "I think that if we cannot have an absolutely harmonious and enthusiastic congress," Sheepshanks wrote, "that will be the signal of the end of the League."[46] The Czech body invited the German and Jewish groups to negotiate a union but insisted on Czech, French, and English as the official languages, much to the horror of the German women.[47] The International Executive Committee considered moving the 1929 congress away from Prague and continued its efforts to mediate, calling for recruitment in the Czech Republic of members "who do not care for their nation above other nations."[48] Although Lola Hanouskova wrote in 1929 that "we are no longer Czechs and Germans, we are all women of good will who are working for the same end," and the congress remained in Prague, divisions on the basis of nationality remained.[49] The Czech group, in effect, became the national section by opening itself up to all women regardless of nationality, religion, or politics, but the German and Jewish leagues remained even after this transformation.[50] A group of Sudetendeutsch women connected to Konrad Henlein even sought recognition as a section of WILPF in 1937.[51] Such difficulties within the Czech section revealed the persistence of nationalism.

In contrast to Hanouskova, who lamented her failure to achieve "the collaboration of women of different nationalities in one country," Milena Illová of the Czech society tried to explain to the leadership in Geneva why such collaboration was so difficult. "There is one feeling, that is so very difficult to understand by western nations—the feeling of to be less acknowledged and that plays its part and is the tone that makes the music all the time I try to bring our women nearer to the Geneva spirit. Don't you think, it wouldn't do better to let them feel, they are taken for full and the expression 'new nations' doesn't meant something humiliating in our sense?"[52] The problems of "new nations" indeed complicated the process of raising internationalist consciousness.

If all of these discussions represented somewhat subtle valorizing of nationalism, intemperate national loyalties surfaced and often swamped internationalism during the First World War, which, ironically, also stimulated the growth of transnational organizations. Some women seemed wholly to abandon internationalism. Marguerite de Witt Schlumberger wrote in an open letter to "Sisters of the Union" (Union Française pour le Suffrage des Femmes), published in *Jus Suffragii*, that this was no time for feminist demonstrations against the war, that Frenchwomen should show "that we are worthy to help to direct our country since we are capable of serving it."[53] The Central Committee of the Union Française pour le Suffrage des Femmes protested the inclusion of its name on a peace petition presented to U.S. president Woodrow Wilson, pointing out that "those who are fighting for our country and for our homes need all of our encouragement and all of our moral force."[54] And the French groups refused to send delegates to the Hague Congress. Eugenie Hamer of Belgium, who attended the Congress of Women but did not vote on the resolution calling for the end of the war, explained why: "In spite of the fact that my woman's heart knows that the war cannot continue, we cannot demand a peace at any price. First of all we must be given back our country, our prosperity, our well-being. That is all that I have thought of up to now. I cannot think as all of you do, I am Belgian above all."[55] On the other side of the battle lines, the Bund deutscher Frauen-vereine refused to participate at The Hague because, as Gertrud Baümer explained, "It is obvious to us that during a national struggle for exis-tence, we women belong to our people and *only* to them."[56] Even women of neutral nations looked out for their national interests. The Polish del-egation at The Hague presented an impassioned memorial reminding the gathering that peace for them did not mean a "blissful return to the safe tranquillity of home" but, rather, a return "to the daily grey, tragic bat-tle, waged without ceasing, for national existence."[57] Although women of the belligerent and neutral nations did sit down together at The Hague, their brave attempt to make peace gave rise to some vigorous expressions of nationalism that conflicted with, and superseded, interna-tionalism.

In the wake of the First World War, both the Council and Alliance encountered difficulty in coming back together. Although Lady Aberdeen proclaimed the ICW an "unbroken family" at its first postwar congress in 1920, the German National Council refused to send delegates unless the international body supported Germany's right to belong to the League of Nations, and the issue of German membership disrupted the 1925 Council meeting as well.[58] As early as 1915, Carrie Chapman Catt hoped "most of all that our women will not emerge from the war with such hate in their hearts that we cannot go on with our international movement," and she dreaded the first postwar congress.[59] The second postwar meeting had to be moved from Paris because public hatred of Germans was so strong.[60] During the 1922 Alliance board meeting, Catt complained of Italian member Margherita Ancona that "like everyone else in the world [she] is so nationalistic that every remark about Italy is regarded as an insult," concluding that "there was no longer any internationalism left in the Alliance."[61]

In contrast to both the ICW and Alliance, WILPF came together across the battle lines, but that brave beginning did not banish nationalism from the organization for ever after, despite its self-identification after the war as "the only genuine expression of world community among women."[62] When the Geneva office attempted to get a Belgian section up and running in 1919–20, a local consultant informed them that WILPF "will have no success in Belgium, because our people is not ready to come in close touch with germans or austrians."[63] Jane Addams felt compelled to apologize for the "currents of intolerance" delegates encountered at the 1924 congress in Washington, insisting that Americans are not "by nature and training less tolerant" but suspecting that it might have been too soon to hold an international gathering on U.S. soil.[64]

But the expressions of nationalism from the independent countries of Europe paled alongside those seeking the national self-determination promised by the wartime victors. Mary Sheepshanks, reporting on the Dublin congress of 1926, regretted "the use made of it as a platform for intense nationalist propaganda by representatives of one nation," meaning Ireland, and warned against "what is a misuse of what should be purely international and pacifist."[65] Even more troublesome was the situation in eastern and southern Europe where, according to WILPF member Mosa Anderson, the history of Ireland seemed to suggest that "you had to force your oppressor, if need be by violence, to recognise the rightness of your cause."[66] The problems, of course, were legion. It did not bode well that Emily Greene Balch felt compelled to remind a group of Ukrainian women hoping to organize a section in 1919 that WILPF supported "liberty for all the nationalities," or that a similar group of Polish women asserted as their first priority the defense of their country against enemy invasion.[67] Admitted in 1921, these two sections were soon at each other's throats.[68] By 1937 Clara Ragaz had concluded that the Ukrainian section was "no longer a Peace League, rather a progressively unveiled nationalistic movement."[69] Events seemed to confirm Kathleen Courtney's fears "that in Eastern Europe . . . [National Sections] are getting too national."[70]

But it was not just the Polish-Ukrainian dispute that provoked nationalist sentiments. The Poles and Germans wrangled about their newly drawn border, and Polish claims to what had been declared German territory provoked Lida Gustava Heymann to denounce the Polish women's "unfriendly spirit" as evidence that "[t]hese women do not belong to us."[71] WILPF regularly sent representatives to eastern and southeastern Europe to try to organize sections, often with little success. In 1925, Emily Greene Balch reported "great bitterness either against Turks or against Bulgarians or against both" among women in Greece, and from Constantinople lamented that "Turkey is now in the high tide of nationalist feeling."[72] Three years later, Mosa Anderson traveled to the Balkans in an attempt to meld together Croat, Slovene, and Serb women in a Yugoslav national section, but she found the women in Serbia "very much engrossed with national" activities and also hostile toward the Bulgarians.[73] Although a united society emerged from the National Council of Women in Yugoslavia, the International Executive Committee judged it "not far enough advanced" in 1930.[74] Camille Drevet reported after her 1929 journey on the hatred between Hungarians and Serbs, Serbs and Bulgarians, and Bulgarians and Greeks, concluding that there "is no international spirit."[75] As in the case of the WILPF section in Czechoslovakia, there were those who understood that conditions in a country such as Bulgaria could not be compared to those in, say, France. As Drevet put it, "The countries of Eastern Europe . . . , which have been recently created, can not have the same point of view on international questions as the people of the older nations."[76] A variety of women throughout southern and eastern Europe, like others engaged in a struggle for existence, saw international women's organizations as a means of asserting their national, rather than gender, identity.[77]

Nationalism tended to be particularly intense, then, where there was the least congruence between "nation" and state, although no group had a monopoly on nationalist sentiments. Milena Rudnycka, a Ukrainian member of WILPF, told her colleagues in 1929, "We must not forget that the fact that each one of us belongs to his or her nation, the kinship with one's people is not something synthetic, not the result of habit or education, nor of conventionality. On the contrary, it is something that touches our most intimate & secret self, it is something innate, it is undeniably a biological and psychological fact."[78] Such a proclamation, although perhaps unusually essentialist, was no different in kind from the principle behind the valorization of national work and national autonomy, or from the expressions of nationalism provoked by the First World War. In all of these cases, women committed to internationalism put a stronger and deeper loyalty to the land of their birth first. Yet they remained committed to the principle of internationalism, if not always as a first priority.

Transcending Nationalism

In contrast, other internationally minded women hoped to banish nationalism from the face of the earth. They expressed such a vision of triumphant internationalism in a number of ways: by explicitly claiming world citizenship, by forging solidarity with the women of "enemy" countries, by repudiating the policies of their own governments, by trying to replace nation-based organizing, and by participating in the international women's community in Geneva. Those who repudiated nationalism came from all of the organizations, although WILPF led the way in fostering a transcendant internationalism. In Madeleine Doty's vivid image, nations were like blocks of ice that would melt and mingle, then turn to internationalist steam.[79]

Not incidentally, many women who spoke out in rejection of nationalism did not fully identify with their countries of origin, often because they had had to flee persecution. Alice Salomon, who found that her conversion to Christianity did not distract the minds of the Nazis from her Jewish origins, proclaimed in her autobiography, "I wanted the whole world to be my country."[80] The WILPF member Helena Swanwick, "half Dane, quarter Irish and quarter only English," thought that people like her of mixed heritage claimed affiliations "according to our feelings and our beliefs and our work, rather than to the narrow boundaries where we happen to have been born."[81] In her failed bid to win U.S. citizenship, Rosika Schwimmer declared, "I have no sense of nationalism, only a cosmic consciousness of belonging to the human family."[82] And Lida Gustava Heymann and Anita Augspurg took comfort in their identification as "world citizens" when they lost their German citizenship at the advent of the Third Reich: "If we had lost our Fatherland, then the world had even more than before to become our Motherland."[83]

One way women acted on such an internationalist consciousness was to reach out to those supposed to be their enemies. In contrast to those French and German women who metaphorically wrapped themselves in their respective national flags during and immediately after the First World War, others engaged in repeated symbolic displays of bonds of what they called "sisterhood." The Alliance's *Jus Suffragii* published an open letter from German women in December 1914 calling on "our sister-women" to recognize that women in wartime share the same fate.[84] At the postwar Zurich congress of WILPF, French women unable to attend addressed their "German sisters," refusing to be enemies: "Because we are the same, because we are a single humanity, because our work, our sorrows and our joys are the same, because our children are the same children, we protest against the murderous invention of a 'hereditary enemy.'"[85] In what became a symbol of the possibilities of internationalism, Lida Gustava Heymann greeted newly arrived French delegate Jeanne Mélin with a bouquet of roses and a proffered hand, which Mélin clasped in friendship. "A German woman holds out a hand to a French woman," proclaimed Heymann, "and says in the name of the German delegation: We hope that we women will throw a bridge from France to Germany and from Germany to France." Mélin replied: "I take the hand of my German sisters; with them, we will work from now on, not against man, but for him."[86]

Similarly, when the Alliance reconvened after the war, the French-woman Marguerite de Witt Schlumberger and the German Marie Stritt sat side by side, embodying solidarity.[87] Recreating the scene between Heymann and Mélin, a French woman publicly embraced a German delegate who made a plea for peace at the 1926 Alliance congress in Paris.[88] That same year WILPF sponsored a solemn ceremony in which Camille Drevet, who had lost her husband during the war, and Frida Perlen, whose son had died fighting on the other side of the battle lines, together planted trees in the devastated region of France.[89] And in 1931 the French and German sections of WILPF issued a joint appeal to their governments and to the president of the Disarmament Conference convened by the League of Nations, stating their common desires: "Our peoples want *work* and *bread*. They want *peace* and *justice*."[90]

Internationally minded women also gave priority to internationalism over nationalism by self-consciously disclaiming actions by the governments of their own countries. Members of WILPF, in particular, took great pride in this kind of expression. Explaining the group's philosophy to an inquiring Cuban woman, International Secretary Mary Sheepshanks in 1930 recounted tales of the German section planting trees in devastated areas of France, the French section protesting its government's occupation of the Ruhr, and the British section objecting to the treatment of Ireland.[91] This was not just boasting: at the 1919 congress German women denounced the invasion of Belgium and Allied women spoke out against the blockade of Germany, and when Japan invaded Manchuria in 1931, the Japanese section apologized to their "Chinese sisters."[92] It became a "tradition in the Women's International League that, if a wrong has been done, it should be the Section belonging to the country which does the wrong that should appeal for right."[93] As the most radical organization, WILPF played a vanguardist role in lauding international loyalty above what traditional notions of citizenship might consider appropriate support for one's country.

WILPF also pioneered in considering proposals to do away with nation-based organizing, which fostered, some members recognized, continuing national identification. As early as 1915, a British woman wrote to Aletta Jacobs in Amsterdam to say that she and some of her friends wanted to belong to the organization without joining the British section, since there "is always a danger . . . of the national side being developed at the expense of the international."[94] Responding to developments within the Ukrainian section, the American Anna Graves proposed in 1923 moving away from the "undesirably national form" of organization.[95] In response to this kind of concern, the 1924 congress resolved to organize a World Section.[96] Such a section could have simply served the purpose of making room for women living in countries of which they were not citizens, individuals from countries with no national section, or women who did not get along with their own national groups. But some advocates saw the World Section as the first step to sweeping away national boundaries altogether. According to Madeleine Doty, who sought to get the World Section off the ground in 1930, the League ought "to have a group in its midst who belonged to no nation and called themselves world citizens." Realizing "that for the majority the way to internationalism or world unity is through nationalism, that there cannot be a League of People without first having a League of Nations," Doty nevertheless called on those who had "caught a vision of what a world section might be, . . . which sees the world as one," to serve as a "psychological laboratory" for world citizenship.[97] Thinking along the same lines, the author of an unsigned draft report on a "Suprainternational Republic" proposed what she called a "Mondial association" in WILPF, which might hold regional meetings to facilitate contact but whose sections would be named for geographical features that ignored national boundaries or, ironically, for "great men who were conspicuously non-nationalistic."[98] Congresses continued to discuss the formation of a "Mixed Section" or "Extra-territorial Section," but in 1935 Catherine Marshall referred to the World Section as "a still-born child."[99] Nevertheless, the concept of a World Section represented the organizational embodiment of a commitment to eliminating national thinking.

The gathering of an international women's community in Geneva both grew out of and contributed to an international consciousness that had the potential to transcend nationalism. Although WILPF was the only one of the three major groups to establish Geneva headquarters on a permanent basis, the Council and Alliance made an effort to open temporary offices there during sessions of the Assembly of the League of Nations. WILPF proudly proclaimed itself the first organization to follow the League of Nations to Geneva, "this little city, so full of traditions of a noble internationalism," and the headquarters staff claimed to have "struck root here and come to feel ourselves Genevese."[100] Geneva did indeed come to represent "the international centre of the world," as Cor Ramondt-Hirschmann put it in 1924.[101] In the 1920s, when the League of Nations Assembly was in session, the Alliance celebrated "our 'feminist international season,'" a time when international women's organizations gathered for meetings and social gatherings and, according to Emilie Gourd, one met more people on the streets from other countries than from Geneva.[102] Women did indeed come to Geneva from all over the world, sometimes remaining for years, and this "International Colony" seemed to develop its own international consciousness.[103]

Like all the other expressions of top-priority internationalism, the construction of Geneva as the world capital paid homage to the idea that nationalism had had its day. Not surprisingly, this position came more easily to women from countries where national identity could be taken for granted. This helps explain why WILPF was both the most Euro-American-dominated organization in its leadership and also the most radically antinationalist. Clamoring for an internationalist outlook that transcended nationalism was, to a large extent, a luxury reserved for the women whose countries' existence never came into question.

The Complementarity of Nationalism and Internationalism

Another line of thinking in the international movement juggled national and international identities with apparent ease, conceptualizing the two as complementary rather than contradictory. In her address to the 1899 ICW congress, Lady Aberdeen described the process of coming together "because whilst loving our own country we realise that a wider patriotism is needed, a patriotism which ignores all frontiers and raises us to a higher plane."[104] Emily Greene Balch described internationally minded women as "[l]overs of our own lands, . . . citizens of the world."[105] Addressing the Washington WILPF congress in 1924, Jane Addams welcomed the delegates as both an international officer and an American citizen, asserting, "To my mind these dual roles do not conflict."[106]

As is perhaps clear by now, the three articulations of the relationship between nationalism and internationalism that I have outlined here cannot be identified consistently with particular organizations or even individuals. These were not positions cast in stone but were tendencies that emerged in specific historical contexts. The kinds of crises that provoked some internationally minded women to put nationalism first prompted others to cling to their belief in the complementarity of the two forces. Minna Cauer, after the outbreak of the First World War, celebrated the loyalty of Alliance members to one another across national borders despite their "devotion to and love for their own fatherlands."[107] Making the same point, the German members of the preparatory committee for the Hague Congress claimed that by participating in the triumphal international gathering, they had "served their Fatherland well."[108] Balch, addressing the conflict between the Polish and Ukrainian sections, insisted that in every country "we are . . . a part of that *minority* who is alone persuaded that true patriotism and true international respect are the same."[109] The members of the Czech and Hungarian sections, which also had their differences, issued a memorandum in 1937 describing their conception of internationalism as a higher development, rather than a contradiction, of nationalism: "We can serve our own fatherlands and also the common fatherland of humanity."[110]

How this might work out in practice was not always clear. Kathleen Courtney criticized the false antithesis between nationalism and internationalism within WILPF at the 1929 congress, prompting Elisabeth Waern-Bugge to wonder if there might be some "divine inspiration which allowed people to know whether or not others were international," whether or not a person elected to the International Executive automatically became—that magic phrase—"internationally minded."[111] Mary Dingman of the Disarmament Committee pointed out in 1932 that they tried to "keep an international outlook on the whole problem and yet to take into consideration the various national points of view."[112]

The coexistence of national and international consciousness took on special significance for women from countries newly free from imperialist domination.[113] For them, national liberation was a prerequisite for internationalism, a view that women from long-established and often imperialist nations found hard to understand. Margery Corbett Ashby, for example, found the feminist movements in both India and Egypt "intensely nationalist."[114] But women involved both in a struggle for independence and in international women's organizations often saw no conflict. A woman from the Philippines wrote in 1920 that WILPF was "in keeping not only with the objects most dear to our women hearts but also to the aspirations of my people, to have freedom."[115] Edith Pye reported in 1928 that a group of women from the Guomindang or National People's Party in China wanted to start a branch of WILPF.[116] In India, Muthulakshmi Reddi explained to Helen Archdale, a national government—"a government representing the people's views and fully responsible to the people"—was a prerequisite for participation in the international struggle for equal rights for women. "I hope I have made our position very clear," she ended pointedly.[117] Women from the East, like women from the West, according to Alliance board member Huda Sha'rawi in 1935, ardently desired peace, "but they want it based on justice and respect for the rights of the people."[118] At the WILPF congress of 1937, greeted with warm applause, Shareefeh Hamid Ali of India called for support of "the just and legitimate aspiration of India and Indian women."[119]

Women accustomed to their own countries' national independence sometimes came to the defense of the aspirations of women from colonized countries, but dialogue across the chasm of sovereignty could also prove difficult. This was the case when the Egyptian section of WILPF organized in 1937. Provisionally accepted in April, the new section sent proposals for the upcoming conference in Czechoslovakia, making clear that it could not accept disarmament until Egypt had the capability to defend itself and that the issue of limiting and regulating state sovereignty had different ramifications for Egypt than for a nation such as Britain. "[T]he great imperialist powers . . . have often abused their state sovereignty to conduct an egoistic politics dangerous to peace," the proposals asserted.[120] This position provoked consternation in Geneva headquarters, since the joint chairmen, despite their understanding of the desire for self-determination and their eagerness to add an Egyptian section, could not accept support of the Egyptian army.[121] In response to a letter from Geneva explaining that if the section advocated armament it would not be in accord with the principles of WILPF, Egyptian spokeswoman Alice Jacot denied any conflict, insisting that universal disarmament did not mean unilateral disarmament without regard for whether a country were weak or strong, free or oppressed, aggressive or pacifist.[122] At the request of the Egyptian section, the Executive Committee took up the question. Anna Tuby explained for Egypt that the Anglo-Egyptian Treaty called, among other things, for occupation by the British until Egypt could itself defend the Suez Canal, leaving Egyptian women with the unpleasant choice of supporting either an Egyptian national army or the British occupation. They advocated the complete independence of Egypt, which alone would make possible peace and disarmament. Shareefeh Hamid Ali pleaded with the Executive Committee "not to lay too hard a responsibility on our young Egyptian friends," and in the end only one voice sought to keep them out.[123]

What is clear from this incident is that Egyptian women had a very different perspective on the meaning of disarmament, sovereignty, and internationalism than women from countries with secure national identities and independence. In union with women from around the world who claimed to be lovers of their own lands as well as citizens of the world, women from colonized countries such as India and dependent countries such as Egypt saw no conflict between patriotism or nationalism—both characterized by love of and loyalty to one's country—and internationalism, affirming both as positive forces that could coexist in a peaceful and just world.

Within the transnational bodies, a sometimes harmonious and sometimes cacophonous chorus of voices sang the praises of internationalism. None doubted the value of working together across national boundaries, if some, in some contexts, put national priorities first. Through the First World War, the emergence of new nations in Europe, the beginning of the process of decolonization, and the tensions that foreshadowed the outbreak of a new global war, women disputed the relationship of nationalism and internationalism. But, in doing so, they were talking to each other and affirming a common belief in the twentieth-century spirit of internationalism.

Struggling with Internationalism in Practice

Women's differing perspectives on the connection between nationalism and internationalism came into play as they wrestled with the troubling questions of representation within organizations and the initiation of international action. Did officers and members of the governing bodies of the transnational groups represent their national sections or did they take on a special international status? Could organizations act internationally over the objection of one or more national sections? There were no simple answers to such questions, but disputes over the choice of speakers and officers, over whom international officers represented, and over how much agreement was needed for international organizations to take action show how philosophical positions on internationalism worked out in practice.

One tricky issue of representation that cropped up was how much control national sections should have over the participation of their citizens in the international arena. When the Committee of Arrangements proposed a list of speakers for the 1899 London congress of the ICW, the leadership of the German National Council asserted their right to determine which German women might speak, rejecting Lily Braun (considered inappropriate for her attack on bourgeois women) as well as Minna Cauer and Anita Augspurg (public opponents of the council).[124] "It is scarcely to be believed, that the American or English Councils would not find it just as strange, if for the next Congress in Berlin any old American or English speakers were to be invited without first coming to an understanding with the countries in question," Anna Simson wrote pointedly.[125] In 1904 Alexandra Gripenberg of Finland conceded the congress committee's right to choose Finnish speakers whom she had not recommended, but she warned that she took no responsibility for them and pointed out that some people whose names were well known outside their country were not really qualified to take on such work.[126]

In the same vein, May Wright Sewall objected in 1899 to the practice of the president of the ICW appointing members of the Executive Committee without the prior endorsement of the National Council in question.[127] Heeding her own warning after her election as president, she cautiously requested that the German Council propose a name to replace the newly deceased German treasurer, assuring them that she had no intention of dictating what they should do.[128] Helena Swanwick of WILPF argued in 1916 that national organizations should approve citizens appointed to international committees since a person judged suitable by the international leadership might prove "extremely distasteful" to the national group, and Alliance officer Frances Sterling insisted in 1930 that "appointments are entirely a matter for the National Auxilary [*sic*] in each country."[129]

However appointed, international officers might speak as citizens of their country or as members of the international body. In 1899 May Wright Sewall argued for ICW officers being "international in spirit and in service."[130] That same year, leaders of the German section argued that the ICW should be based on the principle of the "alternation of control among the different nations," suggesting a concept of national representation.[131] A report on the 1925 ICW meetings assumed that members met "not . . . as individuals but as representatives of our National Councils to whom we must render account for all we have said and done," dubbing the work for country and ICW a "divided loyalty."[132]

Not surprisingly, WILPF struggled most intensely with the question of representation. A 1920 circular letter to the Executive Committee proclaimed that "we are each of us present as an international officer elected by the whole body and not as delegates of any national section."[133] Likewise one member in 1926 boasted that with their freedom from the responsibility of representing a government and their "international point of view," WILPF delegates could vote "individually across international lines," unlike representatives at the League of Nations.[134] But truly international representation was easier to announce than to implement. The comment of a French member who could not attend a meeting—that Gabrielle Duchêne "will accurately interpret the sentiments of French women, members of the League"—expressed the common assumption that women really represented their countries or at least countrywomen.[135] When Madeleine Doty, as international secretary, tried to sort out a conflict over the wording of the minutes between the English and French sections, she confided to Jane Addams that "I do not think most of our sections yet are *real internationalists.*"[136]

The question of representation came to a head in WILPF when the British section in 1926 proposed a constitutional change granting national sections voting membership on the International Executive Committee, the central administrative body. The French section strenuously opposed the plan, calling it "childish" and dangerous. Responding to the ongoing struggles in the new and newly independent nations, the French women feared that representatives from novice sections "in some cases would take their own national point of view and might submerge the other sections."[137] In response to Gabrielle Duchêne's arguments against the change, members of the British section accused her of setting up "an antithesis between 'national' and 'international' which does not and cannot exist in real life," argued that "we should each bring our national contribution of international spirit . . . rather than try to denationalise ourselves," and insisted that "our lives and experience in our

own countries are necessarily the basis from which we learn to understand the needs of other countries."[138] Clearly the differing perspectives
on internationalism that we have explored shaped this debate.

Although a committee set up in 1926 to consider the British proposal
recommended leaving the existing structure in place, British representatives continued to call for national representation. In the opinion of
Duchêne, "introducing national representation" would *destroy the
international spirit* that has always guarded our League until now."[139] At
an International Executive Committee meeting in 1928, Duchêne posed
the burning questions, which the committee decided to submit to the
national sections. Should WILPF, she asked, "regard the division of
humanity into nations as something that may be questioned and should
it hold that the division is *arbitrary* and *temporary*? Should it, on the
contrary, accept such divisions as incontestable?" Should the direction of
WILPF "be entrusted, as now, wholly to an *international body, internationally chosen*" or should it run the risk "by establishing the principle
of *national representation* of giving predominance in the direction of the
League to *national influences?*"[140] But no agreement could be reached on
these issues. Of the three organizations, WILPF grappled most agoniz-
ingly with the question of representation in large part because it was, in
its structure and history, the most international.

If the debate over the election of WILPF's International Executive
Council reveals competing perspectives on the nature of internationalism, it was only the tip of the iceberg of a larger divide that made visible
the problem of how groups could act internationally in the absence of
basic agreement. Within WILPF, a moderate Anglo-American-Scandina-
vian coalition and a more radical Franco-German bloc differed on substantive issues such as absolute pacifism, the necessity of revolutionary
social transformation, and the value of the League of Nations. The
polarization of German and French politics in the 1920s and 1930s,
together with the embracing of socialist views by German and French
WILPF leaders, helps explain this configuration. As the threat of fascism
loomed ever larger over the European landscape and war seemed increasingly imminent, the left wing of WILPF came more and more to wonder
if a pacifist position was viable, or if in fact revolution held out the only
hope for a future of peace and justice. Disagreement became so intense
that, as Emily Greene Balch put it as early as 1920, "in any such movement as ours, there is always the question of how wide to strain the
inclusiveness of a group and how to prevent the extreme right and left
from breaking apart."[141]

In such a political context, members had three choices: to compromise,
to act only with complete unanimity, or to impose majority rule. Well-
meaning members searched ceaselessly for compromises that could hold

the body together. When schism threatened over a "radical pacifist" reformulation of the object of WILPF in the mid-1920s, an agreement to use a short summary for purposes of publicity and to allow countries freely to choose whatever longer form they desired created an uneasy truce.[142] Another attempt to compromise focused on balancing the left and right wings in constituting the Executive Committee and electing the joint chairmen. In the process, it became clear that most members viewed individuals as representing at least a particular political tendency, if not a national position, rather than the international organization as a whole. Madeleine Doty complained that the Executive Committee in 1927 was weighted to the German-French side and admitted that "I do not believe that either the French or the German Sections can really act impartially and consider the British & U.S. point of view."[143] In 1933 Clara Ragaz of Switzerland, perceived as a centrist, became a third joint chairman because the two already elected represented the two wings of the organization, and from then on the Executive Committee sought to avoid choosing chairmen who reflected only one tendency.[144]

The most controversial proposal for reaching agreement on international action came from the British section, which called for unanimity on all policies. For the French and Germans, this violated the principle of majority rule and promised to paralyze the organization. Gabrielle Duchêne denounced a unanimity rule as undermining the very nature of WILPF and making the introduction of innovative ideas impossible. "We must choose," she insisted, "*action*, that is to say, struggle and decisions made *by the majority* or: unanimity on nothing."[145] Duchêne and her supporters insisted that a majority vote on any policy should bind all sections, regardless of their own preferences. Emily Greene Balch tried to downplay the division by suggesting that they already operated on the basis of a kind of a Quaker model of consensus: "We almost never 'majoritize' a decision against the real opposition of a member of the Board; we always *seek agreement* and generally substantially find it or yield."[146] WILPF devoted its 1934 congress, and innumerable Executive Committee meetings, to internal questions, hoping to find a way to act and to quash the possibility of either separation or demise. But the problem of international action remained unresolved. Even the question of whether they should discuss the constitution, or whether they should declare a truce in the face of the ever-worsening world situation, divided the 1937 congress.[147]

The call for unanimity, of course, came as a logical consequence of a belief in national autonomy. The British section sought to approve all literature before it could be sent out by international headquarters, a proposal that International Secretary Vilma Glücklich thought would threaten the "*international* character of our publications." "[I]f we only want to do what corresponds to our national habits and feelings," she asked, "what is the use of keeping up an international machinery at the cost of great sacrifice?"[148] In 1927 the British section again provoked outrage by interfering with a resolution approved by the International Executive Committee that called for the withdrawal of troops from China. Gabrielle Duchêne saw the British action as touching on "the fundamental question: our League has never been a federation of autonomous organizations, it will lose its character and, in my opinion, its principal *raison d'être*, if every possibility of international action is snatched away by the fact that the sections do not feel bound by the decisions of the congress and the Executive Committee and if those decisions can be defeated by the opposition of any one section."[149]

WILPF members, in what seems a blow to the spirit of internationalism, sometimes resorted to differences in "national temperament" to explain the schism. Madeleine Doty thought the "different National Sections have developed such forceful personalities that they find it more and more difficult to work together."[150] Arriving at the headquarters in Geneva in 1926, she reported that the "German Section felt the English Section was hopelessly reactionary and stodgy. The English Section felt the French and German Sections were wildly radical and quite impossible. The French Section seemed to be content with its own existence, and was paying no attention to anybody else."[151] Apologizing for the "vivacity" of a French delegate at the 1932 congress, Duchêne explained that "[i]f the French temperament shocked other delegates, their own impassivity, in some cases, made the French suffer."[152] Catherine Marshall considered British women absorbed with action, the French with "clear thinking," and the Germans with "right thinking." "I think we ought to recognize these different points of view & different natural aptitudes among our various national Sections & try to have an International programme that will give scope for them all," she concluded.[153] In the same hopeful vein, Doty thought that the "passion, . . . fire, . . . ability to stir the masses" of some members could combine positively with the "cold and intellectual type of mind" and "perfection in detail and statistics" of others.[154]

It was, of course, ironic, and perhaps the ultimate expression of internationalism, that French and German women joined together in opposition to the British section. Lillian Wald found it "somewhat humorous to have troubles come because the French-German alliance is so strongly knitted," but Emily Greene Balch was glad that the enmity did not lie between the women of the archenemies.[155] At least the divide did not follow the shape of mainstream European politics.

In the end, fraying at the seams, WILPF stayed in one piece despite polarized positions on substantive and procedural questions. What might have happened had the war not broken out is anybody's guess. The struggle over representation and national autonomy in all three groups, and especially the tangled dispute in WILPF over the policies for taking international action, shows how difficult it could be to translate internationalist consciousness into practice, even when only the English Channel and the Atlantic separated the disputing parties.

Internationalist consciousness—the forging of an international "we"— emerged out of never-resolved tensions over the relationship between nationalism and internationalism. Buoyed by the optimism engendered by the birth of a new century, women from the beginnings of international organization embraced what they perceived as the spirit of the twentieth century. They sought ways to express internationalism symbolically as the merging of the many into one. Yet they did not all agree about the significance of internationalism for the older ties of the nation, and with the rise of fascism disagreements grew more intense. Depending in part on individuals' attitudes toward the governments of their countries and those countries' places in the world system, internationalist women might view nationalism and internationalism as contradictory and pledge their first loyalty to one or the other, or they might see them as complementary. But the dispute was less over the salience of internationalism than it was over the value of nationalism. The wide variety of understandings of nationalism—from love of one's country to desire for sovereignty to the urge to dominate—reflected different historical traditions represented outside the international women's movement by leaders as diverse as Mazzini and Gandhi and Hitler. Internationally minded women could be nationalist or nonnationalist or antinationalist.[156] But all agreed that women could—and ought to—come together across national borders and work to make the world a better place, and that agreement is what bound them together.

The vision of multicolored flags and costumes juxtaposed to symbolize the spirit of internationalism was not, of course, unique to women. Beyond the tie of gender that brought them together, transnationally organized women shared a feminist, as well as internationalist, consciousness. We turn now to this second aspect of what defined these women as a group.

6

How Wide the Circle of the Feminist "We"

> "Feminism," as it is called, is a world-wide
> movement of the utmost significance.
> *(Jus Suffragii, August 1923)*[1]

THE WOMEN of the Council, Alliance, and League shared not only a desire to gather across national borders but also an interest in their status as women in both national and global arenas. As we have already seen, they perceived their femaleness as part of what defined the boundaries of their group. But their feminist consciousness went beyond any simple commonality of biology or socialization. Although they disagreed about precisely how to do so, women in the transnational organizations sought to improve their situation as women. Some proudly claimed the label "feminist," while others avoided it, in part because the meaning of "feminism" shifted in different contexts and over time. As we shall see, internationally organized women did not agree about any one aspect of the feminist program. They did, however, share a sense of themselves as a group with interests distinct from those of men; a perception that existing societal arrangements, differing as they did from country to country, disadvantaged women in relation to men; and a commitment to improving the situation of women. I call this "feminist" consciousness, despite women's struggle over the meaning of the word and over the best methods and proper goals for attaining equality, because none of the other possible terms—"gender consciousness" or "female consciousness"—really captures the critique of women's disadvantage and the intent to better women's situation that served as a unifying bond within the international women's movement.[2]

Just as conflict over the place of nationalism contributed to the process of constructing an internationalist consciousness, debates about the label "feminist" and disputes about what actions should follow the embrace of a feminist program on the international stage helped to define the feminist part of these women's collective identity. I explore here the evolution of the term "feminism" and the staking out of different positions on the issues of suffrage (including suffrage militance), sex-based labor legislation, married women's nationality, and the legislation of morality. In that process, through struggle over goals and means, women forged a set of common interests.

Grappling with "Feminism"

"Feminist," "*féministe*," "*feministisch*" took on a variety of meanings in international circles, differing among the discrete organizations and changing over time. As we shall see, groups especially founded to fight for equal rights legislation clung to the oldest sense of the word, evoking support for identical legislation for women and men. Among the three major groups, the Alliance claimed allegiance to feminism most publicly, although we can see a shift in meaning as the debate about labor legislation intensified and feminism came to seem anachronistic.

For some observers, feminism continued to connote, as it had in international circles before the First World War, the struggle for legal equality and equal opportunity in the labor market for women and men, particularly opposition to special—what was known as "protective"—labor legislation for women.[3] Cécile Brunschwicg, a founder of the Union Française pour le Suffrage des Femmes and officer of the Alliance, intended this meaning in 1912 when she recommended a French delegate for Correspondence Internationale, an anti–protective legislation coalition, as "une excellente feministe."[4] This connotation is especially strong in the claims by specialized international women's organizations devoted to winning equal rights for women. Such groups equated feminism with "equal rights" or an "equalitarian" position on legal rights. Equal Rights International, founded in 1930, distinguished itself as feminist compared to other members of the Liaison Committee and took pride in turning the discussions "into more feminist channels."[5] ERI welcomed the participation of the St. Joan's Social and Political Alliance, a "strongly equalitarian" international Catholic group, because members held "advanced feminist views."[6] In preparing a pamphlet, ERI looked to the definition of "feminism" in *Webster's International Dictionary*: "the theory, cult and practice of those who hold that present laws, conventions and conditions prevent the free and full development of women, and who advocate such changes as will do away with undue restrictions upon her political, social and economic conduct and relations."[7] Members of equal rights groups regularly described individual women they met as "a fine feminist," "conscious feminists," "a keen feminist," "an advanced feminist," or simply "ONE of us."[8]

At the same time, "equalitarian" organizations were not alone in seeing themselves as feminist, although those were most vociferous in claiming the appellation. Among the three major transnational groups, the International Alliance used the term most steadily, first in connection with the primary goal of suffrage and then after the First World War to refer to its broad "Programme of Woman's Rights," which included suffrage, abolition of slavery, married women's nationality rights, married women's property rights, rights of parenthood, widows' pensions, rights of illegitimate children, education, employment opportunity, equal pay, the right of married women to work, a single higher moral standard, and suppression of the traffic in women.[9] According to Chrystal Macmillan, the Alliance supported "Feminist policy on the civil, moral, and economic enfranchisement of women."[10] In 1916 *Jus Suffragii* embraced the role of "reflect[ing] faithfully the spirit of contemporary feminism throughout the world," and in 1920 the journal described a report of Corbett Ashby as "a kind of Feminist bible."[11] As suffrage receded in importance in the Alliance's program of the 1930s, the body claimed special status as a "general feminist organisation."[12]

The Women's International League did not use the term "feminist" to describe itself, but one of the conditions for participation in the original Congress of Women at The Hague was support for women's suffrage, and peace and equality for women remained twin goals. Rosika Schwimmer, who regularly identified herself as a feminist, insisted in 1915 that members of the International Committee of Women for Permanent Peace had to be "absolute pacifists and feminists."[13] At the 1919 Zurich congress, a Feminist Committee put together a "Feminist Programme" calling for equal rights in politics, nationality, marriage, and as parents; equal pay for equal work; equal moral standards; equal training and opportunity; and the endowment of maternity.[14]

The International Council, because of its desire for mass membership, was least likely to identify as feminist, although French member Avril de Sainte-Croix, reporting for the committee for an equal moral standard in 1908, referred to the point of view of the ICW as "feminist."[15] According to a colleague, president Lady Aberdeen "was not a feminist in the 'suffragette' sense" but early realized women's importance and believed that "only after having become citizens with equal rights would they be able fully to exercise their influence for the common good."[16] The ICW called together the first meeting of the Joint Standing Committee, conceptualized as a coalition for groups "which were definitely feminist or concerned quite specially with women's interests," and listed the meetings of the Liaison Committee and Peace and Disarmament Committee under the heading "Feminist Events" in its *Bulletin*.[17]

Obviously, a range of perspectives rated as "feminist" within the international women's movement, at least by the early twentieth century. The use of qualifying phrases, so pervasive among organized women, indicates that women understood the multiplicity of views. Rosika Schwimmer, in 1912, lauded an organization because it was "feminist in the highest sense."[18] Helen Archdale, a staunch British supporter of the equalitarian position, referred to herself and American equal rights advocate Alice Paul as "left wing feminists," clearly meaning that they were adamant about legal equality rather than that they were socialists.[19] Such usages referred to the insistence on identical rights for women and men. In contrast, Archdale, with some sarcasm, called the attention of Doris Stevens to a pamphlet published by the pro–special legislation U.S. League of Women Voters, written by a woman described by the Women Voters as "a feminist in the larger sense."[20] These two ends of the spectrum—feminism in the highest sense versus feminism in the larger sense—came to be called, by officials at the League of Nations revealing their strong preference, "extremist" versus "sensible" feminism.[21]

Partisans of these contrasting interpretations faced off directly in a debate published in *Jus Suffragii* in 1928. Here disagreement focused on the terms "feminist" and "humanist." One side argued for their compatibility, even envisaging humanism as a high evolutionary development of feminism, while the other brushed aside humanism as a diversion or betrayal. Thus in response to British member Nina Boyle's charge that the Alliance was moving away from its feminist commitment by working for peace, Carrie Chapman Catt identified as a "humanist" who had "not ceased to be a feminist."[22] As Margery Corbett Ashby put it, "we cannot, we dare not be only feminist, we must be humanists as well."[23] For Corbett Ashby, feminism was "much like love: a new love takes nothing from affection already given, it is an added enrichment of life. In the same way a feminist is no less a feminist because she has reached a point at which she dare develop every side of her human nature and natural interests."[24] Marie Stritt agreed, defining feminism as "the struggle against violence in every form."[25] Taking the opposing position, Helen Archdale objected to this usage, comparing "humanist" to the older term "social reformer." For her, a feminist "is one who works for the advancement of women's intellectual and social status," in contrast to a humanist, who "cares for the joys and sorrows of all humanity." Neither the ICW nor the Alliance were really feminist, in her opinion, although the retention of the name "International Alliance of Women for Suffrage and Equal Citizenship" gave Archdale hope that a "lingering gleam of feminism" remained.[26]

It was the broader view of feminism, however, that increasingly held sway in the Alliance, especially as the impending world crisis in the 1930s distracted many organized women from total concentration on issues of legal equality. Emilie Gourd defended participation in the Peace and Disarmament Committee against those who saw this as nonfeminist, and Germaine Malaterre Sellier insisted that feminists had to fight for liberty and respect for human dignity.[27] For the Alliance leadership, this did not mean *ignoring* women's rights. In 1936, in the face of mounting crises in Abyssinia, Palestine, and Spain, Corbett Ashby asked whether or not it was time to put aside feminism and answered with a resound-

ing "no," in the process incorporating women's issues into a larger political position: "Feminism is the faith of women who believe in individual
freedom and responsibility. It is but the women's side to the great doc-
trine of freedom of thought and speech, of ordered self-discipline, of self-
government, of free loyalty to the community, of equal opportunity and
mutual assistance."[28]

The redefinition of "feminism" as leading to humanism represented a
response not just to the world situation but also to the taint of antimale
sentiment that clung to feminism. In a world in which women seemed to
be moving into previously male domains—whether offices in the industrialized world or political movements in the formerly colonial countries—this made feminism seem old-fashioned, backward looking. In
1925 an editorial in *Jus Suffragii* on labor-saving devices in the home,
requested by Greek board member Avra Theodoropoulos, pointed out
that such matters interested feminists, "even . . . those rather mythical
ones who are still sometimes pictured in the general press as valkyries
with wild hair bent on riding down the whole of the male sex."[29] When
Martha Larsen Jahn, a Norwegian WILPF member, recommended a
countrywoman to the League of Nations, she identified her as a feminist,
but not an "obdurate" one—rather, "personally very agreeable, with
plenty of tact and amiability and I think that it will be easy for her to col-
laborate with the men."[30] During the Second World War, Alliance secretary Katherine Bompas suspected that feminism "sounded old fashioned,
anti-man or something odd."[31] And in fact Indian women involved in
international organizing, perhaps like women in other colonized countries, eschewed the term "feminism" because of what they perceived as
its antimale assumptions.[32]

In response to such associations, some women emphasized working
with men as part of humanism, or what was often called the "new" feminism. At the 1933 international congress in Chicago, the American
Emily Newell Blair identified two schools of feminism, both of which
saw women as the equals of men. To one, however, equality meant identity: "This brand of feminism would have women compete with men in
making their contribution to the social pattern." The other, to which she
subscribed, "holds that women may do different things from men in a
different way. . . . This brand of feminism would have women collabo-
rate with men in making the social pattern."[33] A report of the Liaison
Committee on the League of Nation's Committee of Experts on the Status of Women illustrates the importance of women's traditional roles to
the "new feminism." One of the women on the Committee, Mme. Paul
Bastid, "won the feminine hearts" of the members "by bringing with her
Mlle Bastid—aged three months! Such an example of the new feminism
could hardly be resisted."[34] Such stress on working with men rather than

fighting them continued in the postwar period. The American Margaret Hickey, at the first postwar international women's conference in Germany, talked up a "new feminism already at work in the world," not militant like the old but "far more concerned with establishing a partnership of obligation and responsibility on the part of men and women alike."[35]

Clearly, internationally minded women contested the legacy and use of the term "feminism." Yet however they defined the term in the changing political and social context, they by and large embraced it. As a result, we can cautiously describe their collective commitment to improving the status of women as feminist consciousness. But the struggle—not just over a label but over their central goals and methods—is as important as their agreement for the project of understanding the interests of women in the transnational organizations. For it was in the process of working out positions on the central women's issues of the period that differences and commonalities became clear.

Getting the Vote

The suffrage question, as we have already seen, was controversial enough in the early years of the International Council to result in the breakaway of the IWSA. But despite the inclusion of antisuffragists at the 1899 congress of the ICW, what really divided internationally organized women was not whether women deserved the vote but how they should get it. In exploring the history of conflict over suffrage questions in the international organizations, we can see that issues of national differences in methods of work, the form of suffrage laws, and, especially, militance took center stage.

The possibilities of demanding suffrage differed greatly from country to country, as the ICW Suffrage Committee recognized in a 1913 resolution that called for the right to vote "in all countries where representative governments exist."[36] Where men had no vote, a women's suffrage movement had no meaning. May Wright Sewall, as president of the International Council during the planning of the 1904 Berlin congress, kept in mind national differences as she tried to minimize any impression of conflict between the ICW congress and the founding of the Alliance. Herself a supporter of suffrage, she insisted that in "a Congress of International significance in which a score of different countries are to participate . . . it would seem unquestionably fair that nothing should be done to impair the effect of their united activity."[37] Anna Howard Shaw, who directed the ICW's suffrage work, emphasized the variety of positions on suffrage within the Council after the founding of the Alliance. In its bid to become an all-encompassing organization, the Council had to tread lightly. "The difficulty," according to Shaw, "is due largely to the fact that some organizations, who are members of the Council, are very progressive and others very conservative, and it will be impossible for us to push the work faster than the more backward members of the organization are willing to follow."[38] For Annie Furuhjelm, whose Finnish group joined the new Alliance after the ICW turned them down because Finland did not have an independent government, the Council's cautiousness hurt it. The 1904 Council congress was, she thought, "grand, brilliant, and full of interest, but there was something wanting in it to me—one big thing to bind the whole together, . . . and this big thing was Suffrage."[39]

In the wake of the founding of the IWSA, the suffrage issue continued to plague the ICW. At the 1909 ICW congress, held in Toronto, the host council proposed changing the name of the "Committee on Suffrage and the Rights of Citizenship" to "Committee on Citizenship" in order not to alienate women from conservative countries.[40] Anna Howard Shaw suspected a nefarious plot to suppress the suffrage question at the congress when Lady Aberdeen informed her that two foreign members would speak at the meeting devoted to suffrage. Shaw retorted that "if these foreigners whom she was to select delivered their addresses in a foreign language, that it would be a most uninteresting meeting to most of the people present," and she promised to violate her assigned role of chair by speaking herself.[41] At the Rome congress five years later, despite support from the Italian National Council, a resolution that would have given the host council veto power over the program went down to resounding defeat, and a suffrage resolution passed with enthusiasm. In Shaw's opinion, this "silenced any future attempt to eliminate suffrage from the program at any succeeding Quinquennial."[42] Employing a feminist orientalist image, Shaw called for the "progressive" nations to help raise "backward" ones to their level, invoking an image of "the beturbaned and befrocked men and the veiled women, the slavery and degradation of women" that she encountered during a visit to Algiers en route to the congress.[43]

If the 1914 resolution settled the question of whether or not suffrage advocacy had a place on ICW congress programs, it did not touch another controversial issue: the form of suffrage for which women would fight. This was a major bone of contention between the socialist and bourgeois women's movements. The Socialist Women's International came out firmly for women's suffrage only if it were universal, equal, and direct. In contrast, the Alliance waffled, in part because of a division of opinion in its ranks. At both the Amsterdam and London congresses, the organization passed resolutions intended to express its nonpartisan and nonsectarian character and to take *no* position on the form of suffrage that auxiliaries would pursue. But observers, socialists among them, interpreted—and attacked—these resolutions as calling for the extension of suffrage to women under the exact terms as granted to men, including in some countries "limited" or what the socialists called "lady suffrage."[44] An Executive Committee meeting encountered practical consequences of these measures prior to the 1911 Stockholm congress. A new suffrage group in Prussia, in favor of extending the limited suffrage in place for men to women, claimed that it, rather than the existing German suffrage organization which supported universal adult suffrage, followed Alliance policy.[45] In response, Catt reiterated the Alliance's position of national autonomy, which left "workers of each country entire liberty to determine" the form of suffrage most in harmony with national institutions.[46] As news of the first suffrage victories splashed across the pages of *Jus Suffragii*, struggles over the viability and most appropriate form of suffrage lessened (see figure 7).

At the same time, debate on the most controversial issue of all—the desirability of militant action—intensified as the Women's Social and Political Union's campaign in England heated up. The WSPU, symbolizing militance throughout the world, applied for membership in the Alliance in 1906, raising vigorous objections from Millicent Fawcett, then president of the mainstream National Union of Women's Suffrage Societies. Both sides of the militance issue in Britain sought the support of the international women's movement: the nonmilitant NUWSS hosted a demonstration in London before, and the WSPU one after, the Amsterdam congress in 1908, hoping to attract the participation of delegates from far-flung lands.

Just like British women, Alliance members divided on the appropriateness and wisdom of militant tactics. Anna Howard Shaw, according to her partner Lucy Anthony, "has so much sympathy with the Suffragettes," but Aletta Jacobs thought "[i]t would be a very bad act" to participate in a suffragette demonstration.[47] Carrie Chapman Catt professed it "a very fine thing" if the whole Alliance congress could go to London to see the suffragettes.[48] But by 1909, when the Alliance met in London itself, the tide seemed to be turning against the militants. Rosa Manus reported, "Everybody who at first thought they like the work of the suffragettes changed their opinion" when the militants disrupted a mass meeting held in conjunction with the congress.[49] Minna Cauer wrote later that year from Germany that people had grown indignant about the goings-on in England.[50] As attacks on property escalated in England, *Jus Suffragii* referred to "militant outrages."[51] Yet the ambivalence of individual women is suggested by the fact that Aletta Jacobs and Anna Howard Shaw both marched with the suffragettes in 1910.[52] Catt even reported that one group of suffragists in China "are inclined to the

Fig. 7. "Turkey and South Africa, as they enter the Universal Suffrage Coach: I say, boys, why don't *you* bring your girls with you?" Suffrage cartoon from *Jus Suffragii*, June 1930, celebrating the granting of suffrage to Turkish women and (white) South African women.

militant methods" employed by the English.[53] The Alliance tried to finesse the issue by insisting that it would be a violation of neutrality either to approve or condemn tactics about which British women differed.[54] As a result, the organization reaffirmed neutrality on the question of militance but went on to protest the argument put forth by opponents of suffrage that militance justified the withholding of the vote from the women of the world, since men's propensity to engage in riots, revolutions, and disorder had never led to their disfranchisement.[55]

Although Emmeline Pankhurst's obituary in *Jus Suffragii* in 1928 proclaimed that the "bitterness of the controversy over militant methods has long died down," a protest that same year rekindled the debate over militant tactics within the international women's movement.[56] An international collection of women—including French lawyer and prominent ICW member Maria Vérone, French Alliance leader Germaine Malaterre-Sellier, and British equalitarian Viscountess Margaret Rhondda and led by the controversial U.S. chair of the Inter-American Commission of Women, Doris Stevens—participated in what Stevens claimed was "the last militant act . . . to have been staged for women's rights."[57] Taking advantage of the gathering of plenipotentiaries from around the globe to sign the Kellogg-Briand Peace Pact at the French president's summer chauteau in Rambouillet, the women's delegation asked for a hearing on the Equal Rights Treaty, the brainchild of the Inter-American Commission of Women. When the dignitaries ignored their request, the women assembled at the gates of the chateau, unfurled a banner demanding equal rights, and asked to deliver their petition. The French police seized their banner, tore up the petition, and arrested the women, in the process winning the event international attention.[58]

Opinion within the women's movement on the success of this demonstration differed. Stevens reported herself "screamed at, yelled at, scolded, bullied somewhere along the line by practically every colleague with whom I was attempting to work," but insisted that the event was "brilliant" and "magnificent." In her opinion, "our methods [are] so far ahead of European methods."[59] Alva Belmont, Stevens's wealthy and autocratic American patron, proclaimed the scene at Rambouillet "foolish," while another American former suffragist thought it "lovely."[60] *Jus Suffragii* walked a careful line: "Whether one holds that the occasion was one where discussion of equal rights for women was relevant or not, one must regret that such discourtesy was shown," and one had to respect the commitment of "these feminists." In short, "Good judgment is a matter of opinion, but devotion to the woman's cause should not be called in question."[61]

The questions of suffrage and militance, then, divided internationally organized women who agreed in principle that women lacked political power. What kind of suffrage—restricted or universal—women should demand and how women should go about fighting for the vote and other basic rights were open to discussion. The transnational organizations attempted to accommodate as many women as possible: the Council both suffragists and antisuffragists, the Alliance advocates of all kinds of suffrage and both militants and antimilitants. But such a balancing act was extraordinarily difficult. Antisuffragists in fact had little place in the ICW, and the Alliance's hesitation irritated advocates of universal suffrage, especially socialists, and led both militants and moderates to accuse the organization of favoring their opponents. Nevertheless, the basic goal of empowering women in the political arena united women of disparate views. And by the period following the First World War, the question of suffrage was eclipsed by the most divisive issue in the movement.

Protecting or Discriminating against Women?

From the very beginnings of international organizing among women, the question of special labor legislation proved contentious. Did it protect or discriminate against women? Who should decide? In a 1976 interview, Margery Corbett Ashby insisted that this was the only real controversy she could remember on the international level.[62] Debate raged in the international congresses that surrounded the formation of the International Council of Women, spurred on after 1888 by the ICW's tactic, as in the case of suffrage, of seeking to avoid taking a position in the interests of attracting as broad a constituency as possible.[63] As we shall see, irreconcilable differences took an institutional form in the international women's movement and never were resolved.

Laws regulating women's labor became a truly international issue—not just a concern common among different countries—because of the international ties of the socialist and trade union movements and because governments, worried about unfair competition on the world market, increasingly came together to set uniform standards. In 1906, a conference in Berne sponsored by the International Association for Labor Legislation produced a multinational agreement to prohibit night work for women, and a later convention setting maximum hours laws for women failed to come into effect only because of the outbreak of war. The founding of the International Labor Organization at the 1919 Peace Conference testifies to the transnational character of labor issues in an increasingly interdependent world.[64]

The term "feminist" in international circles, as we have seen, originally conjured up opposition to special legislation for women. In 1911, at the International Alliance meeting in Stockholm, the Dutch feminist Maria Rutgers-Hoitsema recruited members for a group that took the name "Correspondance Internationale." Established to oppose "all legislation called protective of women's work" and to seek laws that would equally protect the work of men and women, Correspondance Internationale embraced what Rutgers-Hoitsema referred to as "feminist ideas concerning the industrial work of women."[65] Opponents of special labor legislation for women staked out an early claim to the label "feminist" and also to the goal of equality. But as the increasingly nuanced qualifiers attached to the word "feminism" suggest, supporters as well as opponents of such labor laws saw their work as feminist and leading to equality. The fight was, fundamentally, about means rather than ends, which is why I avoid what I see as a false dichotomy between "equality" and "difference."[66] Some women believed that only "equal rights" (meaning identical laws for women and men) would allow women to exercise their "special" influence on the world. And others saw "special" laws for women as leveling the playing field so that women could attain "equality."

We can see that women active in the international women's movement and supportive of special laws clung tenaciously to the goal of equality. At the first conference of the International Federation of Working Women in 1919, designed to prepare recommendations to present to the

ILO, participants heatedly discussed whether or not men should be included under the laws prohibiting night work. Cleaving to the idea that above all women had to be protected from the rigors of working at night, U.S. trade union delegate Rose Schneiderman insisted that "we cannot help thinking differently from some of our friends and some of our delegates here, that fierce equality that we talk about, equality of women to kill themselves by night work is no equality to us."[67] Even more directly, ICW member Louise C. A. van Eeghen claimed, in 1931, that she was an "ardent believer" in equal rights, even though "I am not against EVERY kind of protective laws for women in industry." For her, the fact that she was "certainly against MEN dictating laws to women" made the difference.[68] Taking an increasingly common position, Katherine Bompas, secretary of the Alliance, in 1947 labeled herself "distinctly 'equalitarian'" because she opposed special legislation for women except in the case of maternity.[69]

This kind of exception infuriated opponents of all special legislation. In 1928, equal rights advocate Helen Archdale insisted in *Jus Suffragii* that there could be "only one kind" of feminist and that the term "absolute equalitarians" was redundant because equality could only be absolute.[70] But the Alliance, with members on both sides of the question, referred to "the two groups of feminists," thus bestowing the label on opponents as well as supporters of special laws.[71] A 1930 article in *Jus Suffragii* labeled "protective" legislation the only question on which leaders of the "Feminist movement" differed in principle but then went on to identify the anti position as "the logical outcome of doctrinaire feminism."[72]

The volatile situation exploded at the 1926 Alliance congress, which rejected the application for affiliation of the U.S. National Woman's Party largely on the grounds of its opposition to special labor legislation. The U.S. League of Women Voters, the American affiliate of the IWSA, mobilized at once in opposition to the Woman's Party's application, even threatening to withdraw and cut off financial support.[73] Without a trace of irony and with more than a touch of orientalism, Catt assured Margery Corbett Ashby that she understood the need for the constitutional provision for more than one society per country "because personalities in all the Latin countries seem to enter so much more into their organizations than it does in the Northern countries."[74] Meanwhile, she worked behind the scenes to undercut her archenemies in the Woman's Party. Corbett Ashby tried, diplomatically, to prevent the Woman's Party from pushing the issue, but chairman Alice Paul refused to back down and insisted on a hearing at the Paris congress.[75] And so, as one newspaper headline put it, "Rival Suffragists Take Row to Paris. Feminism Is Real Issue."[76] The board, as expected, recommended against admission of the Woman's Party, prompting the British equalitarian Six Point Group to withdraw its application in protest. Debate on the floor turned to the question of special legislation. Rosa Welt Straus, a delegate from Palestine, pointed out that the IWSA Committee on Like Conditions of Work supported equal rights in industry; with regard to the Woman's Party, she argued, "We have accepted their spirit. If we reject their bodies, it is a great danger."[77] But reject their bodies they did. According to Lady Rhondda of the Six Point Group, the Alliance recognized the Woman's Party as "pure feminists and were afraid."[78]

In the wake of the contentious 1926 congress, the divide in the international women's movement took on an institutional shape as new groups formed, specifically devoted to fighting special labor laws for women. Hints of a possible new organization were realized in 1929 with the founding in Berlin of Open Door International, planned to coincide with the triennial congress of the Alliance.[79] Like Correspondance Internationale before it, Open Door International worked to see that "legislation and regulation dealing with conditions and hours, payment, entry and training shall be based upon the nature of the work and not upon the sex of the worker."[80] The group opened headquarters in London and an office in Geneva in order to concentrate on lobbying the International Labor Organization, perceived as the chief enemy in the fight for equal work for women, and regularly lobbied both the ICW and the Alliance.[81]

In 1930, yet another group emerged from the dissatisfaction of antiprotectionists with the Alliance. Founded in 1930, Equal Rights International took on the task of lobbying in Geneva for the Equal Rights Treaty, first proposed at the Havana Pan-American Congress of 1928 that gave birth to the Inter-American Commission of Women.[82] Doris Stevens, chairman of the IACW, described the formation of Equal Rights International as building "a new feminist front after the W.P. had been rejected at the Sorbonne."[83] ERI proudly claimed to be a vanguardist "feminist"—even "left wing" feminist—organization.[84] The original idea was to focus on one object only—the Equal Rights Treaty— to be "more energetic" than the larger organizations, "and to act quickly," "without red tape."[85] But Alice Paul sought to take control and broaden the focus of ERI, plunging the group into turmoil.[86] Resisting such a move, the leadership of ERI asked what would then differentiate them from the Alliance, "who claim loudly and often that they have as their chief objective 'equal rights.'"[87]

When ERI failed to meet the expectations of Alice Paul, she formed a third organization in 1938, the World Woman's Party, designed to "combine the various national efforts of feminists' movements in order to make a world movement to give women more power and to abolish all discrimination of rights on the ground of sex."[88] Like Equal Rights International, the World Woman's Party saw itself as a vanguardist, not a mass membership, organization. The World Woman's Party opened headquarters in Geneva and, despite enormous difficulties in such inauspicious times, claimed to have "on all occasions raised its voice when in the international field matters affecting women's rights were at stake and when it was necessary and useful to emphasize the equality demand."[89] In 1941, after the war put a halt to international activity on behalf of equal rights, the World Woman's Party merged with Equal Rights International, taking on the name "World Woman's Party for Equal Rights."

Although no new organizations emerged devoted to fighting *for* special legislation, in part because the ILO played that role, debate continued within the three major groups, especially WILPF and the Alliance. Even before the members of the National Woman's Party left Europe in 1926, they had lobbied the WILPF congress in Dublin and claimed credit, along with their Six Point Group allies, for passage of an equal rights or "industrial equality" resolution.[90] But WILPF continued to agonize. In 1930 ILO staff member Martha Mundt debated Open Door International representative Edith Rodgers at the Maison Internationale, where "feelings ran high" and the crowd expressed more support for pro-protectionist Mundt than for her opponent.[91] The 1937 congress vigorously debated a resolution on special legislation, pitting the protectionist British section against Dutch, Danish, and French representatives.[92] Despite a divided house on the issue, WILPF gained a reputation as an "equalitarian" organization, although chairman Gertrud Baer objected in 1938 that "my co-chairmen, not to speak of other members, would never allow" WILPF to be described as supporting "complete" equality between women and men, a reservation probably related to support for maternity legislation.[93]

The Alliance, too, continued to stamp out brushfires after the conflagration at the 1926 congress. At the 1929 congress, the Committee on Like Conditions of Work for Men and Women proposed for the next international gathering a special conference to "permit of different opinions being stated and discussed more thoroughly than is possible at a short committee meeting or at a Congress."[94] When the Depression postponed the holding of a congress in 1932, *Jus Suffragii* printed replies to a questionnaire on special legislation sent out in preparation for the planned debate.[95] Prior to the 1935 congress, special legislation advocate Josephine Schain worried about the "Women's [*sic*] Party point of view" coming to the fore and worked to get protectionist members on the Like Conditions of Work committee.[96] Jockeying for position, both sides sought a sympathetic chairman of this key committee. After sending out another questionnaire on the subject, the Alliance leadership determined in 1937 that a majority of auxiliaries favored identity of legislation for women and men and the protection of maternity through insurance.[97]

Both the Alliance and the ICW attempted to take a middle position by insisting that no laws different from those for men should be imposed contrary to the wishes of working women themselves.[98] Opponents of special legislation referred to this contemptuously as the "'Women Themselves' Fallacy," arguing that women workers who supported such legislation were too often controlled by male trade unions.[99] The problem was that this strategy just shifted the battle to the nature of working women's desires. What did working women want? Since, as we have seen, interaction across the lines of class was minimal within the international women's movement, most of the discussion took place on behalf of, rather than with, women employed in the industrial jobs subject to government regulation.

Who could speak for working women? The U.S. trade unionist Maud Swartz attacked an article in *Jus Suffragii* signed with a pseudonym spelled in Greek letters on the grounds that the writer ought to adopt a name readable by working women as long as she chose to speak for them.[100] Mary Sheepshanks wrote equally bluntly in 1929 that she supported the "self-determination of working women" and objected to the attempts of middle-class women living on their dividends to deprive working women of protection they desired.[101] At a debate on special laws at WILPF headquarters in Geneva that same year, Emilie Gourd noted that an IWSA resolution against legislation for women had aroused the ire of French working women who objected to "intellectual women involving themselves in something they knew nothing about."[102]

As a result of the tug-of-war over working women's interests, the participation of organized constituencies of working-class women came to play a key role. Members of the International Federation of Working Women lobbied hard at Alliance meetings, reporting in 1923 that they "succeeded in getting resolutions adopted which were not opposed to our aims."[103] The ICW in 1927, spurred on by British Labour Party member and cabinet minister Margaret Bondfield, resolved that no action should be taken without prior consultation with working women's groups.[104] As a correspondent reminded Helen Archdale of ERI, "workwomen pointed very severely out to Opendoor International, that they are disposing in public in the labour womens own affairs without asking their opinion before."[105]

The class issues involved in special legislation came clearly to the fore in the 1930s. The severity of the Depression led to attacks on women's right to employment, especially in the professions. Some parties came to accept the need for special legislation for women in blue-collar jobs but sought exemptions for women managers. Questioning whether the Berne Convention ever meant to prohibit night work for women other than manual workers, the International Council of Women sided with those who called for the exclusion of women in management positions. International organizations of business and professional women joined in the call for revision along these lines.[106] Open Door International and Equal Rights International, on the other hand, wanted the International Labor Organization to wipe out the entire Night Work for Women Convention.[107] At its 1934 conference, the ILO, in response to women's lobbying, did revise the convention on night work for women, allowing more flexibility on the hours of night work and excluding women in management.[108]

The fight over special legislation culminated in the stormy debate in the 1930s over the Equal Rights Treaty, known as the Montevideo Convention after Cuba, Ecuador, Paraguay, and Uruguay signed it at the Montevideo meeting of the Conference of American States in 1933.[109] Born in part out of the frustration of national activists with the struggle to win equal rights at home, the Equal Rights Treaty, if ratified, was to force governments to bring their laws into compliance with the principle of equal rights. Whether or not support of the treaty necessitated opposition to special legislation became a highly contentious issue within the international women's organizations. Emily Greene Balch supported the treaty but made clear that she did not "accept the interpretation which makes equal rights imply identity of laws as regards men and women."[110] Predictably, the Alliance congress of 1935 witnessed "acute differences of opinion" on the Montevideo Treaty "due to two conceptions of 'equality.'"[111] Although WILPF and the ICW both passed resolutions supporting the treaty, eight organizations from the Liaison Committee put together a Status of Women Group to pressure the League of Nations for an "International Convention on the Status of Women," intended as a gradualist alternative to the Equal Rights Treaty.[112]

At the outbreak of war, no consensus had been reached on the question of special labor legislation for women. Despite attempts to compromise—to "protect" manual workers but exclude managers or to eliminate special laws except those dealing with women's reproductive capabilities—the dispute raged on. The ratification of international legal agreements such as the Berne Convention, the establishment of the International Labor Organization, and the formation of specialized groups opposed to women's labor legislation institutionalized the conflict but did not much change the terms of debate. Though Margery Corbett Ashby exaggerated when she identified the issue of special legislation as the only controversy within the international women's movement, her comment probably reflected its capacity to arouse the most passion.

Nevertheless, the history of the struggle—especially the insistence that men should not make the laws for women—reveals the common ground (in this case, admittedly limited) that women in these organizations shared. This commitment to "equality," however defined, emerges even more clearly in the discord over another central issue, that of married women's nationality.

Losing Citizenship through Marriage

Traditionally, when a woman married a man of a different nationality, she lost her own citizenship and gained that of her husband. Although this was presumably not a dilemma that directly affected masses of women, the International Council of Women, spurred by its aristocratic and cosmopolitan leader Lady Aberdeen, took up the issue in 1905. The practice of depriving women of their nationality took on added significance after the outbreak of the First World War, when some women found themselves enemy nationals in the land of their birth while women born in enemy territory enjoyed full rights of citizenship. As a result, the International Alliance turned its attention in 1917 to what had become far more than a minor reminder of women's tenuous legal status. Alliance secretary Chrystal Macmillan, herself an attorney, took up the cause with gusto—consulting with the ICW, sending out a questionnaire to women lawyers in various countries, and publishing the results in *Jus Suffragii*.[113]

In the aftermath of the war, attempts by individual countries to remedy this inequity rendered some women, deprived by their own countries of their nationality but not granted that of their husbands, stateless. This intensified women's efforts to address the legal inequities that produced such an outrage but also set the scene for conflict about how exactly to fix the problem. Should both women's and men's citizenship remain in the country of their births? Should the couple jointly decide what citizenship to adopt, with laws allowing both women and men to choose? If a married woman and man held citizenship in different countries, how would their children's citizenship be determined? These were the questions that plagued those who sought to address the problem of nationality. All of the international organizations wanted women to have "equality" in this matter. But some placed highest priority on identical laws for women and men, advocating what came to be called "equal nationality" through an Equal Nationality Treaty, which like the Equal Rights Treaty was the brainchild of the Inter-American Commission of Women. Others feared that laws neutral on their face—for example, that couples could decide which nationality they would adopt—would in fact work to the disadvantage of women. These supporters of "independent nationality" called for each woman's right to choose which nationality she would adopt.[114]

The issue of nationality came into the international spotlight around the Conference on Codification of International Law held in The Hague in 1930. The Inter-American Commission of Women and the International Federation of University Women joined the ICW and Alliance in working for a change in the current nationality laws, although disagreement about how exactly a new law should be worded flared up.[115] Despite intense lobbying by women and a massive women's demonstration on behalf of independent nationality, complete with a procession of women in color-coded dresses and sashes indicating the state of their countries' laws on nationality, the Conference on Codification of International Law maintained the principle of a woman's nationality following that of her husband.[116] In retribution, organized women took up the fight against ratification of the entire convention.

Chrystal Macmillan convened an International Committee for Action on the Nationality of Married Women in early 1931. Comprising representatives of six international women's organizations, including the big three, the new committee sought the support of socialist and working-class women's groups as well. The object of the group, as formulated in its first meeting, was to urge delay of the ratification of the Nationality Convention and to work to ensure that any further convention would recognize equality of the sexes in matters of nationality: specifically, the nationality of a wife would not be affected by marriage or any change in her husband's nationality without her consent and the nationality of neither parent would carry any greater weight in determining the nationality of children.[117]

This new international committee, along with the Inter-American Commission of Women, successfully lobbied the League of Nations to place the subject of nationality on the agenda of the next assembly.[118] In this instance the League crumbled under women's pressure and invited nine international women's groups to constitute a Women's Consultative Committee on Nationality.[119] When, after a rocky start, the Consultative Committee finally settled on a first meeting date and a method of work, it produced a report that strongly opposed ratification of the Hague Convention and demanded an end to distinctions based on sex. But there agreement ended. Some of the delegates supported equal nationality while others insisted on independent nationality.[120] The lines were drawn a bit oddly because the equal nationality promoters included both the "identical laws" camp (ERI, the Inter-American Commission of Women, and WILPF, because it was represented by an Alice Paul supporter) and the ICW, which from a more conservative position opposed the possibility of individuals having different citizenship from their spouses. The Alliance strongly endorsed independent nationality. In a rather euphemistic vein, Margery Corbett Ashby described the meetings to the public as "very lively, since members differed greatly in their views."[121] In the end, the Alliance and International Federation of University Women, both under the sway of Macmillan, signed the report with the stipulation that they understood equal nationality to include the right of women to their own nationality, thus defining "equal" as identical to "independent" nationality.

This was the only common report that internationally organized women ever produced on the nationality question. When the League Assembly failed to make a decision in 1931, the Consultative Committee began to wrangle in earnest, and this time they assembled two separate and conflicting documents. The vehement disagreement over how best to solve the quandary of women's nationality greatly hampered the chances of success. "Our way is difficult enough just because we are women, so that we ought to at least be harmonious and firm in order to justify the confidence we desire," one woman wrote.[122] At the end of 1932 the League of Nations Assembly, disgusted with the inability of organized women to speak "with a united voice," recommended ratification of the hated Hague Convention.[123] Gabrielle Radziwill, the League of Nations liaison to voluntary organizations, set out to disband the Women's Consultative Committee, since, in her opinion, it was "doing the Women's Organisations a great deal of harm."[124] The Alliance and International Federation of University Women resigned in 1933 and called on the secretary-general of the League of Nations to deliver the committee's death blow.[125] In such an atmosphere, organized women could not prevent the ratification of the Hague Convention, complete with its shackles on women's nationality, in 1937. Only in 1957 did the United Nations establish independent nationality for women as the international norm.[126]

But the bitterness of the dispute about nationality—on which, after all, the sides differed far less than they did on special legislation—arose from more than a matter of principle. Alice Paul's attempts to control the Consultative Committee and to refocus the attention of Equal Rights International on the nationality question alienated women throughout the movement. Her actions confirmed what the Dutch activist Lily van der Schalk described as "the opinion that 99% of all the people whom I have met and who have had to deal with Miss Paul" held: that "A.P. can ONLY lead!"[127] Helen Archdale, the British chairman of ERI, labored to keep her organization working on equal rights and the Consultative Committee dedicated to nationality, but Paul fought her within both groups every inch of the way. Although Paul and Archdale had been friends, by

1933 the embattled ERI chairman concluded bitterly that many organizations, both national and international, "will never join or attempt to form any Committee of cooperation which it is possible for Miss Paul to enter."[128] From Geneva Archdale reported, in a somewhat more charitable moment, "It breaks my heart to see her here with a handful of stray followers; with all the womens [sic] organisations with their hackles and bristles out and up against her; with the delegates being horrid about her; with the Secretariat rigid to oppose her." However, she saw Paul as herself responsible for that opposition: "I wish I knew her reasons for believing in the value of antagonising people."[129] That Archdale was correct about hostility toward Paul from within the Secretariat of the League of Nations is suggested by the aversion of Hugh McKinnon Wood, senior member of the Legal Section, to those "very exasperating" feminists of "the Alice Paul group."[130]

On the other side, a devotee of Alice Paul traced the intensity of the conflict back to the Alliance's rejection of the National Woman's Party in 1926. Since Woman's Party leaders played a central role in the Inter-American Commission of Women, which in turn stood behind the Consultative Committee, the resignation of Alliance representatives from the Consultative Committee and the subsequent attempt to shut down the rump body could be viewed as a continuation of the earlier hostility. "I deplore to have to state it," Eugenie Miskoczy Meller wrote, but "personal antagonism has dimmed objective reasoning."[131]

Whatever the real cause, the hostility between Alice Paul and other internationally active women spilled over into the fracas over the Equal Rights Treaty, which had implications for the issue of nationality as well as for special labor legislation. Chrystal Macmillan, as the staunchest advocate of independent nationality, recognized the approval of the Equal Rights Treaty by four countries at the Montevideo conference as "a remarkable piece of work" but insisted that "I want a great deal more than that internationally."[132] A colleague from the Woman's Party responded with hopes that Macmillan would take up the cudgels for the Montevideo Convention, asserting that "Feminists could accomplish almost anything they want in the way of equality legislation if they unite."[133] But of course they could not unite. The Liaison Committee, unable to formulate a unified position, left the question to the Women's Consultative Committee; WILPF endorsed the treaty in 1934; the Alliance engaged in heated debate at its 1935 congress but continued to insist on independent nationality; and the ICW passed a meaningless compromise resolution in 1936 supporting "equal, including independent, nationality."[134]

Although internationally organized women could not agree on the appropriate solution to the problem of inequities in the citizenship of women who married across national border, they all agreed that something needed to be done. Ironically, in the debate about nationality male policymakers implicity endorsed the position that gender overrode national loyalties, leaving internationalist women to argue, contrary to their dominant line, that it did not. A "woman has the same feeling of love for and loyalty towards her country as a man and . . . this love and loyalty are not weakened by the fact that she has a husband," Chrystal Macmillan proclaimed.[135] The conflict between supporters of equal versus independent nationality was virulent, even though the differences in their positions do not appear profound. The argument that "equal" included "independent" cropped up often enough to suggest that a formulation could have been found to satisfy both sides. In this case, the animosity among individuals and organizations, with roots in the conflict over special labor legislation, raised seemingly insurmountable barriers to the creation of a united front on the question of nationality. But that women suffered from inequality was never in doubt.

Questions of Morality

The final issue—or set of issues—that both united and divided internationally organized women had to do with morality. Women had long mobilized across national borders in the interests of temperance and the abolition of prostitution. The World's Woman's Christian Temperance Union, founded in 1891, concentrated its efforts on global abstinence from alcoholic beverages but also embraced social purity, peace, suffrage, and socialism. Groups such as the International Federation for the Abolition of the State Regulation of Vice, which formed in 1875 in association with the famous British vice crusader Josephine Butler, the Union Internationale des Amies de la Jeune Fille (1887), and the International Bureau for the Suppression of Traffic in Women and Children (1899) focused on the evils of prostitution. The "traffic in women" took on an international dimension at the turn of the nineteenth century because of the practice of exporting prostitutes from imperialist countries to work in colonial brothels.[136]

The three major international women's organizations took up various questions of morality, generally agreeing that there was a double standard of morality and that women had a special responsibility to attend to moral reform. Few internationally minded women would have questioned the sentiments of a cartoon printed in *Jus Suffragii*—entitled, ironically, "Equal Moral Standard"—that showed a policeman arresting a prostitute as a gentleman in a top hat left the bedroom. As the policeman proclaimed to the prostitute in the caption, "The sin that ye do by two and two ye must pay for one by one—and you're the one."[137] And most would have shared the astonishment of Avril de Sainte-Croix, a future member of the League of Nations Committee Against the Traffic in Women, when an ICW member in 1907 objected that "women of self-respect and of good society in their countries would not listen to anything concerning" prostitution.[138] In fact an editorial in *Jus Suffragii* described the proposal for an investigation of the "white slave traffic" as the most important accomplishment at the 1913 Budapest congress.[139] "To whatever class women belong, it appears, they will be moved by the hope of moral reforms, or they will not be moved at all," according to Marie Vérone.[140]

As a sign of the presumed universality of the appeal of moral reform, both the ICW and the IWSA critiqued the use of the term "white slave traffic" as a misnomer that obscured the sexual abuse of women of color.[141] But in reality substituting the term "traffic in women" did not eliminate the racial and imperial overtones of the older phrasing. Whether focusing on men of color trading in women or women of color as helpless victims of sexual exploitation, portrayals of the sex trade often reflected and supported a feminist orientalist worldview. Reinforcing the message conveyed in the *Jus Suffragii* cartoon of the African and Chinese slavers (see figure 3 in chapter 3), WILPF focused attention in the post–First World War years on women captives in Turkish and Persian harems, and international organizations worked to persuade the League of Nations to include a (Western) woman on the Commission on Mandates because "[i]n all countries inhabited by races of different colours, the relations between the men of the governing race, and the women of the other are a source of difficulty and often an actual hindrance to good understanding."[142] Succumbing to pressure from WILPF and the Alliance, the Mandates Commission in 1921 appointed Anna Bugge-Wicksell, who asserted her ability to "feel as a woman for other women as well as for children" and who made it "her special business to care for and speak for that part of the native population."[143]

While such imperialist rhetoric assumed that Western women needed to take care of indigenous women in the colonized countries, it also asserted a bond of vulnerability among women that made morality their special province. But there agreement ended. On a number of questions—the urgency of moral reform, the line between protection of and discrimination against women, and the acceptability of birth control—organized women disagreed. Some saw moral reform as a secondary priority. Aletta Jacobs, herself a strong advocate of birth control, in 1906 hesitated to speak publicly about Malthusianism to a group of women doctors because "it would certainly hurt the cause of women's suffrage."[144] After the resolution on the "white slave traffic" at the 1913

Alliance congress, Jacobs wrote an open letter protesting this deviation from the central goal of suffrage. If women had such influence with governments that they could stop the traffic in women, she asked, why would they need the vote?[145]

On the other side of this debate, British moral reformer Nina Boyle lambasted the Alliance throughout the years for downplaying the traffic in women. In 1922 she portrayed herself as a gadfly and "a voice crying in the wilderness." As long as women concentrated on such issues as the League of Nations or labor legislation, she insisted, "we shall make very little headway in securing the real freedom of women."[146] Six years later she gave up in disgust, announcing her intention to turn to other organizations and publicly declaring, "It will be to the lasting discredit of the Alliance that I was forced to do so by the apathy of its members toward the cry of suffering womanhood."[147] In fact, the discourse of social purity did wane in the interwar period as the women's organizations shifted from insistence that men adopt women's traditionally higher moral standard to a demand that all laws "apply equally and legally to the male sex."[148] Increasingly the crusade for "the promotion of a high moral ideal in matters of sex" took on the flavor of a rearguard action in the more sexually permissive climate of the 1920s and 1930s.[149]

The international women's movement also divided over the protection of women and girls from sexual danger. As in the case of special labor legislation, some women advocated "protection" while others defined such policies as discrimination. Taking a conservative position in response to the changes in social and sexual behavior associated with the "sexual revolution" of the turn of the century, the ICW at its 1920 congress passed a resolution deprecating "the exaggeration in dress and dancing which has recently arisen in many countries" and also called for the segregation of "persons proved incapable of sex control."[150] Likewise, in 1922 the ICW Standing Committee for the Equal Moral Standard and for Public Health deplored the dangers "which lurk for young emigrants on board ocean steamers."[151] In contrast to such traditional fears of the sexual danger threatening unsuspecting women, other activists raised the specter of discriminatory control of women's sexuality. Paulina Luisi, a professor of medicine and founder of the National Council of Women of Uruguay, warned the Alliance in 1924 that legislation designed to protect young women traveling alone tended to limit the freedom of adult women.[152] Luisi continued to urge vigilance so that measures touted by the authorities as necessary for health did not become a means of regulating women's lives.[153] Similarly, the editor of *Jus Suffragii* pointed out in 1925 that the "ordinary decent woman" could suffer from police actions intended to curb prostitution and that internationally organized women should concern themselves not only with "a very helpless class of women" but also with "the liberty and security of all women."[154] As such warnings make clear, some women in the international organizations took what would now be called a "sex-positive" perspective, supporting birth control and sex reform.

Such differences emerge especially clearly in the debate over birth control in the International Alliance. Women such as Aletta Jacobs and Rosika Schwimmer who strongly supported birth control hesitated to publicize their convictions not only out of fear of attracting hostile outside attention but also because of opposition within the movement. Jacobs, in 1906, told Schwimmer that she did not know what her friend Carrie Chapman Catt thought about birth control, admitting, "it is strange, but I have never spoken of it with her."[155] But perhaps it was not so strange, considering the Alliance's reluctance to broach the question. Marguerite de Witt Schlumberger objected in 1917 to the recommendation of neo-Malthusian books in *Jus Suffragii*, provoking a flurry of responses.[156] English feminist Edith How Martyn insisted that any subject of interest to women should be fair game and accused de Witt Schlumberger of calling in the pages of *La Française* for French women to bear children for their country.[157] Invoking once again the national autonomy clause, Dutch Alliance member Maria Rutgers-Hoitsema reminded readers of the organization's commitment to leaving each auxiliary free to act on "difficult, complicated, and especially most delicate problems, partly national, partly international—such as patriotism, Chauvinism, internationalism, Neo-Malthusianism, depopulation, re-population, immigration, emigration, colonisation, imperialism, etc."[158]

In fact, after the 1917 discussion, the pages of *Jus Suffragii* bore no trace of the subject of birth control for eighteen years, until How Martyn put pen to paper in 1935 to argue that without the right to control motherhood and their own bodies, women could never hope for economic freedom.[159] In response, Vera Laughton Mathews of the St. Joan's Alliance, the Catholic feminist organization, ridiculed the notion that birth control and abortion would bring sexual equality when the physical side of parenthood differed so dramatically for women and men.[160] That the Alliance took seriously Catholic objections to birth control was confirmed by *Jus Suffragii* editor Karleen Baker, who revisited the 1917 debate in 1937 and stated flatly that the Alliance could not take a position because of the principles of its Catholic members.[161] But such caution was not enough to win over organized Catholic women. Throughout the years the International Union of the Catholic Women's Leagues, the international embodiment of the Catholic women's movement, attacked the Alliance for its positions on divorce, unmarried motherhood, sex education, and other issues contrary to the teachings of the Catholic Church.[162]

Neither the ICW nor WILPF devoted any significant attention to the question of birth control. Although some members of the ICW Committee on Equal Morals insisted in 1932 that the organization should not ignore "the most burning questions of sexual life," Lady Aberdeen ruled that birth control fell in the realm of religion and thus, according to the policy of the ICW, could not be considered.[163] Despite its progressive reputation, WILPF attempted to wriggle out of the situation using the strategy proposed in the conflict over labor legislation. Recommending that national sections take up the "problem of population," WILPF insisted "that above all in matters of birth control, full weight should be given to the judgment and opinion of women."[164]

In all of these ways, then, internationally organized women disagreed about the goal of moral reform, despite their common conviction that women had the right and responsibility to shape morality. For some, fighting the traffic in women seemed paramount; for others, this endeavor came in behind the winning of the vote and other basic political rights. Those who focused on the dangerous figures lurking in the shadows—threatening to seduce or enslave young women—saw little positive in the new social and sexual freedoms of the early twentieth century. But critics of restrictive laws and regulations and advocates of birth control emphasized the ability of women to control their own destinies. Equality of moral standards for men and women served as a rallying cry on the international scene, but whether that one standard should be closer to the traditional women's standard of "a high moral ideal in matters of sex" or the men's norm of greater permissiveness was up for grabs. Yet a general consensus that moral reform was women's work suggests the feminist consciousness that underlay the profoundly different interpretations of the appropriate moral climate for women in the tumultuous world of the early twentieth century.

Given the variety of positions that women in the international organizations took on the questions of suffrage, militance, special labor legislation, nationality, and moral reform, it comes as no surprise that the meaning of the term "feminism" ranged from a narrow description of a particular equalitarian position on political issues to a concern for women that broadened into humanitarianism. As women sparred over what divided them, matters of principle, strategy, and personality came into play, determining whether an individual or organization would support universal or restricted suffrage, militant protest or behind-the-scenes lobbying, identical labor laws for women and men or laws that took into account women's reproductive potential, independent or equal nationality, or laws to protect women from sexual danger or to provide women access to contraceptive information. In the earnest debates as well as in the hostile encounters, we can see a group of women working out their common interests, pointing to their collective disadvantaged status, and claiming their right as women to make decisions about how best to improve their conditions. In the process, they developed a collective, if far from monolithic, feminist consciousness.

This feminist consciousness not only developed in international interactions, of course, but mirrored developments within national borders as well. What was particular to the members of the international organizations was the combination of internationalist and feminist consciousness. Not only did women share a common belief in some sort of loyalty to an entity beyond their motherlands, but they believed that the international arena was the appropriate place to work to change the condition of women. While the original impetus for transnational organizing was fairly solidly based in national interests—help from abroad to achieve suffrage at home, for example—by the interwar period the growing interconnectedness of the modern world meant that questions of labor legislation, nationality, and the traffic in women could only be addressed on the international plane. Out of these realities, women's internationalist and feminist consciousness arose.

Women saw themselves as fundamentally different from men and came together on the basis of common class, ethnic, religious, and age interests; within those boundaries they developed their commitment to internationalism and feminism. But they expressed this identity as members of their particular groups. We turn now to the personalized politics of women's transnational organizing, looking first at the structural bases of their international communities and then at their personal interactions within those worlds.

Section III

PERSONALIZED POLITICS

7

International Ground

Almost 30 years have gone by since [the 1899
congress]; life with its passionate desires and
battles lies behind me—but the welcome memory
of those wonderful days and weeks in London is
as alive for me today as it was then.
    (Marie Stritt, 1927)¹

GREAT DISTANCES separated internationally organized women, so the
structures that brought them together on a periodic basis played a vital
role in making possible a politics of everyday life. Unlike members of
local or national groups, women in the Council, Alliance, and League
did not see each other on a daily, weekly, or even annual basis. Yet the
leaders and most active members did manage to find ways to make
what might be very intermittent contact into something quite pervasive
in their lives. Although women's commitment to internationalism
flowed across the perimeters of their organizations, most interactions
took place within discrete groups, to which members expressed intense
devotion.

Thus we begin our consideration of the structural bases of personalized politics by exploring symbolic expressions of organizational loyalty. I then turn to the "international ground" on which women gathered, sometimes face to face and sometimes metaphorically. Beginning
with the interactions involving the fewest women and moving to those
with the broadest reach, we consider international headquarters, committees, periodic congresses, and organizational publications. The most
intimate relationships flourished at WILPF's headquarters in Geneva,
where women lived as well as worked together. On the other end of the
spectrum, the Alliance's *Jus Suffragii*, the Council's *Bulletin*, and
WILPF's *Pax* knit together far-flung women through regular communication about what was going on in every corner of the international
community. Together, such structures facilitated the kind of everyday
actions that cemented women's international collective identity.

Membership Symbols

All three major international organizations created membership symbols that allowed women, in their everyday lives, to display their commitment to feminist internationalism. The International Council of Women set up a committee to develop a badge sometime after the 1899 congress and finally, in 1908, adopted a design with the intertwined letters "ICW" modeled on a brooch of Susan B. Anthony's, passed on at her death to Lady Aberdeen.[2] Throughout the long process of settling on a badge, various National Councils submitted and resubmitted designs, while committees evaluated the symbolic, artistic, and practical merits of each. Proposed symbols, all intended to convey a sense of harmony arising from diversity, ranged from a rainbow to a wheel "to whose balanced motion all the spokes equally contribute" to a chain "each link of which represents an organization."[3] President May Wright Sewall insisted that the time put into designing the perfect badge was worthwhile, for this was no trivial decision. "As compared with the actual work to be done by the International Council," she admitted, "it is true that the badge and insignia indicative of its intentions are trifling, but in themselves they are of vital importance. . . . It is my view that women like ourselves whose minds are occupied by great and serious subjects are too likely to underestimate the value of external signs and symbols." To her way of thinking, the badge had the potential to serve as an effective means of propaganda if worn by members scattered over the face of the earth. If even 10 percent of the seven million members wore the badge, the conversations it incited would publicize the ideas of the ICW in a way nothing else could.[4]

The International Council also created a banner in 1925 to replace one lost in 1914 with the outbreak of war in Europe (see figure 8). Made of silk in the organizational colors of white, gold, and purple, the new standard displayed the Golden Rule printed in Latin, with sunbeams streaming down from the motto onto a map of the world. According to Norwegian member Anna Backer, who conceptualized the banner, the design symbolized "the whole world benefitting of the sympathy, love and goodwill among women, . . . whose blessings like sunbeams overdazzle even the most outlying countries."[5]

The International Alliance similarly struggled to find an appropriate symbol. Neither the 1904 founding congress nor correspondence in its aftermath hit upon the perfect embodiment of internationalism, but the 1906 congress in Copenhagen adopted a badge portraying the figure of justice and the words "Jus Suffragii." "In order that this badge shall be truly international," according to the conference report, "suffragists

Fig. 8. The ICW banner, 1925. Reproduced from the
Report on the Quinquennial Meeting. Washington, 1925.

throughout the world should be encouraged to purchase and to wear it."
It would be cast in bronze rather than silver or gold so that "it might be
within the reach of every woman who believes in woman suffrage."[6]
That the Alliance leadership put less stock than the ICW in such membership symbols is suggested by President Carrie Chapman Catt's
description of a proposed flag and banner as a "purely sentimental fea-
ture of international work."[7] Nevertheless, in 1928 the Alliance
announced a competition for a new design to reflect the changed work
in the aftermath of the war and to allow "our younger women" to show
what they "can do with their modern training and opportunities."[8] Ten
years later, a member of the International Executive Committee argued

that "fashions have somewhat changed" and "people do not now buy or wear such things to the same extent as formerly," thus raising questions about the efficacy of badges as a fund-raising and consciousness-raising tool in the world of the mid-twentieth century.[9]

The Women's International League, too, despite initial refusal of a membership symbol, at its 1921 congress adopted a badge displaying the word "Pax." According to an English member, displaying the badge would give an opening to discuss peace, producing it would provide employment for women, and wearing it would allow members to "recognise each other in any country as sisters of the W.I.L."[10]

Displaying an organizational symbol at home, in everyday life, theoretically provided the opportunity for women anywhere in the world to identify with internationalism, both signaling organizational membership to other like-minded women and advertising the cause of international understanding. Although there is no indication in the sources that badges played the propaganda function their advocates attributed to them, such symbolic displays, at least in the early years, did serve as the quintessential expression of the personalized politics so critical to women's international collective identity.

Membership badges also symbolize the central role that organizations played in the building of an international community. Like the headquarters, committees, congresses, and publications of individual groups, badges served as expressions of both loyalty to a particular organization and a more diffuse commitment to internationalism.

International Headquarters

The Women's International League led the way in establishing truly international headquarters, located in Geneva, the historically international city and site of the League of Nations. Emily Greene Balch, involved in the creation of WILPF headquarters, wrote earnestly to an American coworker of her desire "to make this bureau a little centre of internationalism here as well as a radiating point for all our ideas all abroad."[11] In contrast, the ICW and Alliance were slow even to establish permanent central offices. The Council, with its original inchoate international structure, began with an office in the house of its president and a small appropriation for a secretary.[12] Only in 1925 did a real headquarters office open in London, designed to "lead to the Council more and more taking its rightful place as the big co-ordinating body internationally."[13] But because of financial constraints during the Depression, the office began once again to follow the president or move where rents were cheaper. Not until 1963 did the ICW again establish a permanent office, this time in Paris.[14] Likewise the Alliance opened an office in London only in 1913, just before the outbreak of war brought activity to a halt. Despite Secretary Katherine Bompas's assertion in 1935 that headquarters served as "the heart to which and from which the life-blood must run to the members," the central office never played such a critical function.[15]

The headquarters of all of the transnational organizations handled correspondence, sent out information and publications, received foreign visitors, and maintained communications with national sections, but WILPF headquarters did much more. According to Emily Greene Balch, reporting in 1920, "We make friends and receive and give ideas and information and sometimes are able also to do a good turn in some practical way."[16] At the same time she complained that volunteers tended to show up unannounced with the expectation that she would have suitable work for them to do. "It is like running a settlement," she confided to Jane Addams.[17] With a more jaundiced eye, Balch's successor Vilma Glücklich described headquarters as "a sort of refuge for people suffering from widely different misfortunes. . . . [M]any of the callers are in a most pathetic state of mind, so that one feels rather like a physician who has the duty of listening to a patient."[18]

But it was not just such services to needy people that set apart the WILPF's Maison Internationale (see figure 9) from the headquarters of the Council and Alliance. The fact that members and friends and family and women from other organizations came to stay or live at the Maison, a beautiful old house with rooms to let and space for receptions and meetings, made it, as the organization claimed in its publicity, "a little international centre where members and friends, passing through or staying in Geneva, can find a 'pied à terre' and strengthen the international ties that mean so much."[19] Members waxed positively lyrical about the Maison. One wrote a poem in 1922 describing the "green creepers" that invited one to climb the stairs, where "the house no more presents an austere front / but under graped-vined porch the wide-spread door / Welcomes all nationals of open heart."[20] According to Madeleine Doty, who arrived from her Greenwich Village studio to serve as international secretary in 1925, "It makes a fantastic little scene to turn in off the street where the automobiles are honking, climb the Roman wall, step into a dark little garden and see a bright light on the table and a group of people sitting around it under a tree."[21] "I love this old house and Geneva and already find myself very much at home," she wrote Jane Addams only a few days after her arrival.[22]

Such enthusiasm overlooked the fact that the house was, according to Mary Sheepshanks, "insanitary" and foul-smelling, with its one bathroom and lack of central heat.[23] Lida Gustava Heymann and Anita

Fig. 9. The Maison Internationale, headquarters of WILPF.
Courtesy of the Women's International League for Peace and
Freedom.

Augspurg, visiting in 1925, urged residents to care for their own bed-
rooms to spare "our one little maid" and in this way practice "community life" in a small way.[24] Not all felt welcomed with open arms.
Madeleine Doty experienced great disillusionment when she and her
father, recovering from surgery on his eyes, were turned away because
Doty's successor Sheepshanks was "fussy and ill and didn't want a man
in the house using the bath room." The incident, small as it was, convinced her that the Maison was not a refuge for all the women of the
world and left her wondering whether WILPF could really work for
understanding between nations.[25]

When the Depression and then the war struck, WILPF struggled with
the question of how to manage, mulling over the possibilities of renting
rooms to other international organizations, keeping only the office,

packing up and moving to another city, renting the house to American college girls on a junior year abroad program, or turning the Maison into a home for old women.[26] But they hung on, in part because the Maison was "so rich of memories," "the symbol of the W.I.L. and the last thing we have to cling to as it means very much to the people in Geneva."[27] Staff member Lotti Birch suspected in 1938 that "in America . . . the members have the impression that the 'Maison' is the most important part of the work in Geneva."[28] Despite all the worry, the League held on to its historic house until 1966.

As the emotions evoked by the Maison suggest, it functioned as more than a house for the members who lived and regularly visited there. The German feminist paper *Die Frau* reported in 1920 that the Maison Internationale was "no ordinary office, but rather a home for women."[29] At an Executive Committee meeting in Vienna in 1921, "The special importance of having a home like the Maison Internationale was pointed out."[30] And when Lida Gustava Heymann and Anita Augspurg fled Germany after the Nazi takeover, the Executive Committee offered them three rooms on the first floor, convinced that their presence would "make the Maison a real home for all."[31]

The "international family" that inhabited this home consisted of a number of different kinds of members. The headquarters housed the international secretary, a member paid to coordinate the work; member volunteers; a paid secretarial staff; and a paid housekeeping staff. But because members could not imagine viewing work for peace and justice as just a job, the lines between committed activists and paid employees were thin indeed. A young woman trained in shorthand and typing received a strong recommendation as a "keen Internationalist and Pacifist" for a staff position, and another assistant seemed to one observer useless because she was "not more than an intelligent clerk, without special interest for our cause."[32] Sophie Hattinga-Raven, the Dutch "directress" of the Maison for four years in the 1920s, worried before she arrived that it would be a "disadvantage that I am not so enthusiastic about the work of the League."[33] When Camille Drevet left as international secretary in 1934, her colleagues spoke appreciatively of "the way she had drawn the staff into close association with the W.I.L."[34] She, like some other WILPF officers with socialist leanings, worked to lessen status differentials at the Maison. Both Drevet and Vilma Glücklich called for more equal salaries and less job differentiation, goals their coworkers found very much "in the spirit of the W.I.L."[35] In reality, of course, although members thought that the work should be "done from idealism" and that "[i]t is all quite different from a commercial office where each is looking out for his own interest," the paycheck remained critical to the employees.[36]

That we now see the headquarters of WILPF, in contrast to those of the Council and the Alliance, as sheltering a vital women's community is in part an artifact of the far more detailed surviving organizational records of WILPF. But the existence of those documents is also, in turn, testimony to the more extensive role that headquarters played in the life of WILPF. The international offices of the ICW, Alliance, and WILPF served as their "hearts," pumping blood in the form of correspondence, reports, and publications to the national sections, but they also served as a location for the most active members to meet and interact face-to-face and, in the case of the Maison Internationale, to live and work together on an everyday basis. Although only a small group partook of such opportunities, more members met through their work on international committees.

International Executive Committees

All three organizations established an executive committee that met regularly to help govern the international body. The ICW Executive Committee, which first met in London in 1897, consisted of the officers, honorary vice presidents (as nonvoting members), and the presidents of affiliated National Councils. The constitution of the Alliance called for an Executive Board of Officers composed of the president, vice presidents, secretaries, and treasurer; the board was expanded in 1913 to include additional members, some of these from outside core countries, elected by the congress. The WILPF International Executive Committee consisted of the president and, originally, nine members elected at the congress from a pool of candidates nominated by national delegations. Thus these committees, reflecting basic differences in the three organizations' structures, ranged from a collection of national representatives to a body of internationally elected members.

Executive committees, in contrast to congresses, met "in the place most convenient for transacting business and not where it is convenient to do propaganda."[37] This meant that the committees met in major European cities with little attempt to move around to facilitate widespread participation. Geneva proved a particularly popular location, especially when the League of Nations was in session. From the perspective of WILPF in particular, "Members would have an opportunity to get a first hand acquaintance with the work of Headquarters, to see the *Maison Internationale* and to get a personal impression of the Assembly of the League of Nations."[38]

At executive committee meetings, members worked, debated, and socialized. Because the committees mediated between the national sections and the congresses, meetings could be contentious. German ICW member Marie Stritt hoped in 1903 that the "impending meeting of the Executive will put aside all existent differences, clear up all misunderstandings."[39] Margery Corbett Ashby claimed that "for years and years there were always cliques and jealousies on the ICW Executive whereas however much the members of the Alliance disagreed there was never anything but real friendship between members of the Board," an observation belied by the struggle over Palestine, to mention only one example.[40] In WILPF, the tensions and conflicts that built in the threatening atmosphere of the late 1920s and 1930s led to increased discussion of procedure, including clear rules, time limits for speakers and subjects, and opportunity for everyone to speak once before anyone took the floor for a second time.[41] When the British section objected to speeches given at the 1927 executive meeting, the Austrian section responded that a member of the Executive Committee "has the right to choose a subject and treat it according to her own conception so long as this conception is in harmony with the general principles" of WILPF.[42] Gabrielle Duchêne, in turn, called the British section to task, and the French section denounced the "irregular procedure" that "created a veritable state of anarchy in the League."[43]

As a result of such differences, meetings could turn into ordeals. When Yella Hertzka proposed inviting a Spanish woman interested in organizing a section in her country to a WILPF executive meeting, opposition came from those who feared that she would not come away with a good impression.[44] Edith Pye opened what she considered the "rudest letter I have ever received in my life" from Lida Gustava Heymann and retorted that the "apparent want of faith in the good intentions of comrades, expressed in the tone as well as in the matter of your letter (which perhaps reads more harshly in English than you intended)" was typical of what "makes the spirit of our meetings so unfriendly sometimes."[45] Emily Greene Balch blamed their hard work, without sufficient rest, for the "bad ways" and "rudeness" of committee meetings: "[W]e push ourselves unmercifully getting more and more unreasonable and *difficile*."[46] Yet at times WILPF members took heart. In 1929 Balch "felt renewed confidence in the friendliness felt by everyone," and a newcomer described a 1936 meeting in very positive terms: "No one seemed to question silently or aloud the right of each individual member of the Committee to have and to express an opinion. . . . Whether it was the quiet brave atmosphere of the Maison, the character and nobility of the women in the Committee or the singleness of purpose which had united us that was responsible for this tolerance, I cannot say, but I like to think that it was a combination of the three."[47] This description, printed in *Pax*, was, of course, for public consumption, but the surprise at the lack of hostility along with the insistence on the principle of free expression perfectly reflected the atmosphere within WILPF in the interwar years.

Despite the tensions, executive committee meetings were not all work. Regular social events provided an opportunity for members to see the sights in the city and relax over meals. May Wright Sewall organized a breakfast in Berlin in 1904 for the Executive Committee of the ICW, hoping to bring "Council workers together socially."[48] On the other hand, Lady Aberdeen discouraged entertainment during the 1905 meeting, reporting to Marie Stritt that she told "our English Council ladies" that "we wanted to have a really quiet time to talk over things and not to have to break up our meetings in order to have to go to parties."[49] The Alliance regularly reported lunches, dinner parties, receptions, and excursions. In 1924 the board met at the Normandy home of Marguerite de Witt Schlumberger, and the report in *Jus Suffragii* rhapsodized about the beauty of the old abbey and the countryside, as well as the opportunity to see French social life up close.[50] In Brussels in 1936, the Belgian auxiliary entertained the board at the Cercle de l'Avenue, a club "where the grey panelled walls, recalling Balzac's typical 'boiserie grise,' were in piquant contrast to a modern 'bar.' Not, let me hasten to add," as *Jus* put it, "that the Board, enjoying lively conversation after an excellent dinner, felt any need for additional stimulant!"[51] The WILPF Executive Committee, too, socialized together. In Dresden in 1923 for a meeting, they planned meals, including vegetarian options, and in Amsterdam in 1930 they traveled in a large motor bus to the fifty-two-room country estate of the Broese van Groenaus.[52] In the mid-1930s, when things had become especially tense, the minutes record an occasional "interval of 10 minutes for Tea."[53]

The minutes of executive committee meetings record the work, the debate, and the socializing, but they also reflect the conviction that what these bodies did was important. The Women's International League in particular took great pains with the minutes. Madeleine Doty complained in 1926 about having to send out the "volume" of minutes from the Paris Executive Committee meeting to the eighteen members present, incorporate all of their corrections, and then have forty-nine copies in three languages made and sent out to national sections.[54] Furthermore, the WILPF publicly offered copies of Executive Committee meeting minutes and, like other groups, circulated and published excerpts from them.[55] In 1928 the Executive Committee got in an uproar over a rebuke in the minutes by Lida Gustava Heymann to Helena Swanwick; the members finally agreed not to confirm the document and in future to confine the minutes to "recording decisions taken, except when by special request a note is made of statements."[56] In 1925 one Executive Committee member had already worried that the minutes were "rather too confidential to be printed," so the decision not to broadcast internal squabbles is understandable.[57]

Out of that same concern, the International Council of Women defined its Executive Committee meetings as private, thinking that the committee's business could best be discussed "under circumstances which allow . . . [the officers] to speak freely without any publicity."[58] The ICW considered Executive Committee members the "inner circle" and insisted that the *Bulletin* should only print what would be "palatable to the rank and file reader."[59] In contrast, the Disarmament Committee in 1934 considered shortening the minutes of meetings but reached unanimous agreement that this should not be done, for "those who are kept informed of our work through the Minutes are several times the number of those who are able to attend the meetings of the Committee."[60]

The meetings of committees, then, had the potential to affect more than the small number of women who attended them. But the major role of executive committees, like other international committees convened to deal with specific issues, was to provide a place where an increasingly diverse group of women came face to face in the cause of internationalism. May Wright Sewall referred to the Executive Committee members of the ICW as "the working force of the International Council" and sought to bring more women to the meetings, despite her fear that the "increased number of those present at the Executive will multiply the chances for dissention."[61] The Alliance journal described a meeting as bringing together "the leaders of the international Suffrage movement in the quiet, friendly atmosphere of a family party."[62] Emphasizing the importance of personal interaction in the process of running an international organization, Emily Greene Balch wrote in 1920: "it is hard, isn't it to get a real meeting of minds by correspondence?"[63] Vilma Glücklich insisted in 1923 that the Executive Committee meeting "has always been the most important event in the regular life of our League, even in less critical times than the present."[64]

International executive committees not only made important decisions for the organizations—how important, as we have seen, remained a matter of dispute—but they also created a space, if only once a year, in which women came together across national borders to argue, work, and socialize together. In their conflict as much as their agreement, in their partying as much as their painstaking work, women made internationalism part of their daily life. Expanding the circle beyond headquarters, executive committees gave women—after the First World War, even women from outside the Euro-American arena—a chance to enter the "inner circle" or "working force" of the transnational organizations.

International Congresses

Even larger numbers of women, including those from host countries with no previous experience on the international stage, had the opportunity to meet and work with like-minded colleagues at the periodic congresses sponsored by all three groups. Congresses, like committee meetings, were international affairs, although, as we have seen, they retained a national flavor as well. In 1899 Lady Aberdeen insisted that the ICW divest itself of responsibility for arranging the quinquennial congresses, handing over the charge to the National Council of the country in which the congress would be held.[65] But both the Alliance and WILPF kept their hands on the reins of the congresses, which under normal circumstances were held every two or three years.

Organizing an international congress could be a mammoth undertaking. First a location had to be found. As Europe teetered on the brink of the abyss in 1937, the WILPF leadership agonized about where they could meet. Bratislava was hosting a League of Nations Federation congress, the Scandinavian countries were preparing a conference for the Peace and Disarmament Committee, Finland, Austria, and the countries of southeastern Europe lacked free speech, England was too expensive, France was impossible on political grounds, Alsace was too near the German border, Switzerland had hosted the previous congress, the Belgian section was too unreliable, the members of the Luxembourg section had left for other countries, and the Netherlands was not keen to have it.[66] After settling on a place (in this case, Luhacovice in the Czech Republic), a local committee had to be gathered and trusted with taking charge. But international officers often worried about the competence of local organizing committees. ICW Secretary Alice Salomon scornfully described the efforts of Italian women, only a handful of whom had "kept pace with the women of other countries," to put together the 1914 congress.[67] Sometimes leaders took on the arduous preparations themselves. May Wright Sewall, in charge of the ICW quinquennial and "World's Congress of Representative Women" held in Chicago in 1893, reported that she and two others devoted nine months to the preparations, sending out over 7,000 letters and 55,000 printed documents in a number of languages.[68] Arrangements included not only locating appropriate rooms, hiring translators, contacting the press, and finding hospitality for delegates whose journeys would be especially costly but also such details as employing pages to see that the rooms were tidied and the waste baskets emptied, arranging flowers, and making signs for the doors and placards printed with "Silence" to be held up on the platform.[69] Describing her labors on the Budapest congress of the Alliance in 1913, Rosika Schwimmer, mixing her imagery, thought "a multimillionaire could more easily pass through the eye of a needle into heaven."[70]

The congresses themselves, bringing together a more diverse crowd of women than either headquarters or committees, could be by turns ponderous, conflict ridden, and celebratory. Relying on parliamentary procedure and rules of order when customs differed from country to country, and negotiating the use of three official languages—and the language of the host country as well, in many cases—bogged down proceedings. The Alliance urged members in 1913 to study the rules of order as a means of saving time and avoiding confusion at the next congress.[71] *Jus Suffragii* printed a critique of the Budapest congress as leaving "no time for the many little courtesies and attentions which would have added greatly to the enjoyment of the occasion."[72] As the organizations grew in size, problems multiplied. "We are too big now to do any business in a full session," Margery Corbett Ashby ruefully concluded in 1929.[73] As a result, women attending the congresses reported great fatigue. At the WILPF congress in Luhacovice, a spa in Czechoslovakia, Lida Gustava Heymann moved to close a session shortly before eight o'clock in the evening "as the delegates are too tired to go on with the work."[74] Perhaps the congress planners had taken seriously Cor Ramondt-Hirschmann's earlier caution: "We should watch out and not give our congress members the chance to go to the baths or they will fall asleep in the congress!"[75]

But congresses were by no means all tedium and sleepiness, for conflict increasingly threatened to erupt even at orchestrated displays of international harmony. In anticipation of a difficult, even "dangerous," discussion of absolute pacifism at the 1926 WILPF congress, Emily Greene Balch noted, "Overstrained nerves betray. Feelings may get hurt. Certain personalities irritate. People grow heated. They misunderstand one another especially if what has been said has been filtered through a translation. Then they say more than they feel or at any rate more than it is either kind or wise to express."[76] Attempting to put a positive spin on conflict, *Jus Suffragii* printed a gushing piece about the 1923 congress, insisting that "[t]here was argument enough to satisfy the most ardent fighter, but in essentials there was an amazing unanimity."[77] In the same vein, Lady Aberdeen asserted that ICW discussions were "lively" but "there was never any bitterness, but just the assertion of the right to all to hold their own opinions and to express their reasons."[78] But, especially as time went on, the tension in the expanding organizations could not be denied. In 1932 Jane Addams admitted that it might have been a mistake for WILPF to try to avoid misunderstandings by increasing the time between congresses. "We may thus have grown further apart and forgotten how difficult we are so that we have a fresh shock every time we meet."[79]

Congress sessions devoted to constitutional revision and other internal workings of the organizations were often both boring and contentious. Lady Aberdeen expressed surprise at the attention paid to organizational questions not usually considered "excessively interesting or attractive."[80] May Wright Sewall reminded ICW members that the organization had grown to encompass women of different "races" and different languages, who were accustomed to different constitutional usages.[81] As we have seen in the disputes about the nature of representation, technical questions often had substantive impact. Yet the feeling persisted that it was a "waste [of] the precious time available at our International meetings" to discuss "constitutional points of little importance."[82] Particularly as the world situation grew more ominous in the 1930s, leaders tried to keep constitutional questions from public discussion. When WILPF leaders devoted the 1934 congress to "the question in what form and how our work shall be continued" in view of the Depression and the threatening political situation in Europe, the Swedish WILPF section lodged a protest, finding it a "deplorable mistake" to enter into fruitless debate on constitutional details when the world situation was so serious.[83]

But congresses also had important positive consequences, propagandizing the cause of suffrage, peace, and internationalism and serving, as Anna Howard Shaw pointed out, as "inspiration for workers."[84] Lavish social events, the specialty of the International Council, entertained and rewarded attendees for their hard work. At the congresses, as at executive meetings, excursions, receptions, teas, pageants, dinners, and eventually even films filled the hours (or minutes!) not spent on business. Sometimes the organizations sponsored tours following the congress.[85] Carrie Chapman Catt urged national auxiliaries of the IWSA to send full delegations to Stockholm in 1911, promising "a refreshing and instructive vacation" to those who attended.[86] At the ICW congress in Kristiania in 1920, "the ladies had to change garments with marvellous rapidity if they aspired to wearing the exact right dress on each occasion."[87] Reinforcing the notion that international feminist activists were still, after all, women, *Jus Suffragii* attempted to lure delegates to the Paris congress of 1926 by offering time for sightseeing and—"dare we mention it?—to do a little of that necessary shopping which, even to ardent feminists, seems an almost necessary corollary."[88] Taking photographs of each congress gathering, which Jane Addams dubbed "the first ceremony in these modern times," marked such important occasions for posterity.[89]

But social events did not lack critics. Minna Cauer, describing the 1904 Berlin congress of the ICW for the German feminist periodical *Die Frauenbewegung*, questioned the "high society, salon, even courtly flavor" of such events, wondering why no one seemed to question the danger of a social movement giving this impression.[90] Crystal Eastman expressed a sense of wonder when the Hungarian guards banned women's hats from the 1913 Alliance congress. Marveling at the "hatless convention," which allowed speakers to address "a great company of intelligent faces, not . . . a stuffy thicket of hats, a bobbing, many-coloured wilderness of fruits, flowers, feathers, grasses, and plumes," Eastman approved the disappearance of "the last traces of the 'afternoon tea and culture club' atmosphere . . . from the serious councils of women."[91] Margery Corbett Ashby described the 1925 ICW congress in Washington even more bluntly in her diary. Dinner at the College Woman's Club was "the worst nightmare I could have had." As a guest of honor, she "shook hands until I had to change to my left. . . . It would be hard to find any occupation more calculated to dull one's senses. . . . We had songs, amusing parodies, we all sang. . . . More music . . . I had endured so much! I hoped I should creep on to the sleeper but no such luck."[92] At the same time, when the Czech section of WILPF, the organization least devoted to extravagant entertainment, planned "a serious business Congress and did not want the work hurt by social events," Mary Sheepshanks found the schedule "a little severe and lacking in the attractions which certainly help to make a Congress a pleasure."[93]

But even in WILPF, and even under the darkened skies of the 1930s, social events remained integral because they brought large numbers of women together for memorable moments in the cause of women's internationalism. For Marie Stritt, writing to Lady Aberdeen on the occasion of her fiftieth wedding anniversary, attendance at the 1899 International Council congress would always linger in her memory as her introduction to "a blessed new world."[94] At the outbreak of war in 1914, the Frenchwoman Julie Siegfried's thoughts turned to the ICW Rome congress, "where we sang all together the hymn of peace."[95] The Irishwoman Louie Bennett looked back, from the vantage point of 1934, to the first WILPF congress in Zurich "as an event—an inspiration—a source of refreshment."[96] Even those who experienced the ugly side of congresses tended to hold on to the uplifting moments. May Wright Sewall hoped that after her German colleague Anna Simson had time for reflection after the 1899 ICW congress, "the mistakes and the unpleasantness . . . will seem small as compared with the really fine work that was ultimately done."[97] Echoing her wish, Carrie Chapman Catt wrote Rosa Manus in the wake of the 1929 Alliance congress that "by and by you will forget the disagreeable moments and only remember what a fine Congress it has been."[98] Indeed, Františka Plamíková insisted in 1937 that only congresses "keep the current of the international women's movement flowing."[99]

The innumerable travel diaries—complete with membership ribbons, credentials, postcards, invitations, and souvenirs—preserved in archive

Fig. 10. Farewell Banquet, ICW Quinquennial Congress, Mayflower Hotel, Washington, D.C., May 13, 1925. Reproduced from the *Report on the Quinquennial Meeting. Washington, 1925.*

boxes throughout Europe and the United States give mute testimony to how important congress attendance could be to the women involved in the international movement. Lady Aberdeen proclaimed in 1920 that only attending an ICW meeting "really convinces people of the unique character and influence of this organisation," and Rosa Manus expressed no surprise when the U.S. auxiliary talked of pulling out of the Alliance, since its president "has never been at one of the congresses and therefore has never got the international thrill about it."[100] Almost all agreed that personal connections outshone all other beneficial aspects of congresses (see figure 10). Lady Aberdeen lamented her own inability to engage in "personal intercourse" during the ICW congress in Washington in 1925, but she rejoiced in "the personal understanding and friendship" fostered among those who had traveled or lodged together.[101] For Estonian Aino Kallas, "The world's map is, so to speak, now peopled for me."[102] The board of the Alliance considered time for informal talk "a very important aspect of international meetings," and Madeleine Doty thought the chief value of the WILPF Dublin congress "the way it got folks together."[103] In this way, then, congresses provided a setting in which dedicated workers and new recruits could meet face to face and establish the kind of bonds that held the movement together. The critical role that congresses played in solidifying commitment to internationalism underscores the significance of location in shaping the composition of the international women's movement.

Organizational Publications

For women who lived in countries that never hosted a congress and who could not travel far from home, reading paved the way to participation in the personalized politics of the international women's organizations. Organizational publications, accessible at least to those who knew the official languages, opened a window on the world of international activism to the widest circle of all.

The International Woman Suffrage Alliance was the first to start a paper, *Jus Suffragii*, launched in 1906 and known from 1930 as *International Women's News*, at least in part because, according to Anna Howard Shaw, the Latin name hurt sales in the United States.[104] After the war, the Alliance raised the possibility of publishing supplements for other international organizations, including WILPF, but given WILPF's political positions on "national" questions the Alliance withdrew the offer and, as we have already noted, only the World Young Women's Christian Association ever worked out an arrangement for a supplement.[105] The International Council of Women began publishing its *Bul-*

letin only in 1922 after an earlier attempt had ended in failure.[106] WILPF began by publishing a simple newsheet, *Internationaal*, the Dutch name chosen for its similarity to the English, French, and German versions of the word.[107] In 1919 WILPF changed the name to *Pax et Libertas* because the old name "suffered from being Dutch" and "might in some countries under not too improbable circumstances hinder our circulation."[108] After a brief interlude, WILPF launched a new *Pax* in 1925. Struggling to keep the journal afloat, Madeleine Doty raised funds in the United States in 1928, but when the Depression struck WILPF decided with reluctance to publish only the most-read English edition, with articles periodically printed in French and German.[109] Although Gabrielle Duchêne and Lida Gustava Heymann supported the decision, Gertrud Baer argued that "it is not really in our interest simply to exclude the non-English-speaking elements of our Women's League."[110] With the outbreak of war in 1939, *Pax* gave way to a mimeographed newsletter, coming back full circle to its origins.

All three publications combined reports from member countries with information deemed truly international, seeking a balance not easy to maintain. Emily Greene Balch described *Pax* as both "a pleasure and a care," admitting that "at best it is a very puzzling problem how to make an international organ LEAST UNSATISFACTORY."[111] At a 1936 board meeting, Polish Alliance member Anna Szelagowska expressed the view that *Jus* was not so much international as a collection of national news, an opinion with which a French and a Czech member agreed.[112] And WILPF debated the virtues of *Pax* serving as propaganda versus a record of "very private Meetings . . . , a report about our private discussions which take place in our own little circles."[113]

Thus the journals attempted to meet multiple needs. They carried reports on international conferences, information about other transnational organizations, articles about the birthdays or deaths of prominent women in the membership ranks, reports on substantive issues, and news of the activities of the League of Nations, as well as the ubiquitous reports from national groups. The papers reprinted articles from national publications and encouraged the reprinting of their own stories with proper permission. Regular columns ranged from *Jus*'s "The Bookshelf," which reviewed books on women and feminism, to the *Bulletin*'s "Parliamentary Column," to *Pax*'s "The National World" and "The International World." Regularly appealing for contributions and information, the journals featured articles on a wide range of topics, including "The Prevention of Venereal Disease," "Simplification de la Toilette Feminine," and the golden wedding anniversary of the Aberdeens, alongside more regular features on suffrage victories, the status of women, peace and disarmament, and international affairs.[114] *Jus*, the *Bulletin*, and *Pax* all accepted advertisements to help pay for the soaring costs of publication.

Like the periodic congresses, organizational publications served both to publicize women's international activities and to knit members more closely together, but they could have impact only if women read them. In the early years, the Alliance printed 700 English and 200 French copies of *Jus*, and by 1921 *Jus* reported 455 "honorary associate" members, 751 subscribers, and 192 issues exhanged or sent out without charge.[115] Even before the Depression worsened the situation, the Alliance worried about the circulation figures and costs of publishing. Editor Elizabeth Abbott begged members in 1925 to talk friends into subscribing, explaining that *Jus* was "dependent on the interest taken in it by feminists all over the world."[116] The ICW *Bulletin* in its first years stated bluntly that the cost of subscriptions was high because the paper was a "nursling" and could not be run as a commercial paper.[117] After three years, 2,000 copies circulated, although, like the Alliance, the ICW issued regular pleas for more subscribers.[118] According to the *Bulletin* in 1927, "our paper is arousing a good deal of interest and . . . our members find it useful and are anxious for its continuance."[119] And in fact subscriptions hovered around 1,500 in the mid-1930s, despite the Depression and worsening European situation; over half were sent out in English and the rest divided between the French and German editions.[120] Ironically *Pax*, in many ways the most in-house publication, and one sponsored by a self-proclaimed vanguardist organization, claimed the largest circulation. Perhaps this reflects the tighter bonds of a more radical group. The official history of WILPF credits Madeleine Doty with raising circulation to 12,000 in the three language editions of 1926, although organizational records for the 1930s place the figure closer to 3,000.[121]

For all who subscribed to or borrowed these papers, the experience of reading brought them into contact with the international women's movement. As a testimonial to *Jus Suffragii* put it in 1932, "International meetings must always be few and far between, the cost of travelling must always be prohibitive to many," but sixpence a month made participation possible for all.[122] And it was not necessarily a passive form of involvement, for the journals created a forum for an international exchange of opinion through letters to the editor and debates on controversial issues. Members contributed ideas on how to improve meetings and congresses and responded to surveys included in the papers' pages. *Jus* invited readers in 1930 to write in on some "vexed question" or to disagree with editorial opinions, in this way stimulating a "frank interchange of views which will be of great value to us all."[123] The Alliance journal in particular printed questionnaires on topics of international interest, inviting responses on such subjects as suffrage, women's employment, women in dentistry, and women typesetters. As ICW President Marthe Boël described the *Bulletin* in 1938, these journals could (or had) "become by degrees a platform where the different feminine tendancies [*sic*] and all those problems which apply to women could be ventilated and discussed, where the experiences of some, with their successes or failures loyally recognised, could become examples or lessons for others, where divergent opinions could confront each other for the wider development of ideas which we cherish."[124]

Publications also served as a strong but invisible cord tying women together across national borders, even—perhaps especially—during wartime. Jane Addams thought *Pax*'s predecessor, *Internationaal*, "has done so much to hold us together" during the First World War, and at war's end a contributor to *Jus Suffragii* insisted that "the thin gold link of our International suffrage Press has held us all together in one high sisterhood."[125] When the armies marched across Europe again, ICW members dubbed the *Bulletin* "the most dependable visible link which we now have."[126] But even in peacetime the journals seemed indispensable. According to Elizabeth Abbott, the editor of *Jus* in 1923, "without a regular propaganda paper it is more than conceivable that the blood pressure of such an International body as the Alliance would not merely fall below normal but tend to cease."[127] Likewise, *Pax* called for subscriptions and contributions in 1931, imploring its readers, "Please, do not feel you can do without *Pax*."[128] As the ICW put it, "as members read quietly in their homes the record of work of their colleagues in other lands, new ideas, new energies, new hopes and longings may spring within them and help them to go forward and have no fear of the future."[129] The WILPF member Annie Sterritt, in a 1927 poem titled "Unmet Friends," asserted that through reading *Pax* she "has come to feel in close touch with other members throughout the world," thus undermining the difference between face-to-face and text-mediated interactions.[130] Expressing the significance of shared bonds through organizational publications, Mary Sheepshanks hoped to make *Jus Suffragii* "a perfect expression of the International Women's Movement."[131]

As we have moved through a consideration of the different structures that facilitated contact among members, we have seen that as the women increase in numbers at each level, they interact less and less intimately. International headquarters, especially the Maison Internationale in Geneva, brought together women who devoted their lives, at least for a period of time, to the international women's movement; in some cases they built families and homes with their coworkers. Executive committees gathered in a slightly larger group of intensely committed members to struggle over the meaning of international representation and to work and play together. Congresses periodically mobilized large numbers of members, including those who played leading roles in the organizations, those who attended only sporadically, and at least some women from the host country who participated because the events unfolded on their doorsteps. The journals cast the widest net of all, making contact with the occasional reader and provoking responses from more involved members. Because of the transnational character of feminist internationalism, the movement relied more heavily than would have been true of national organizations on substitutes for face-to-face encounters. Without such means of communication, no international movement could have survived.

Despite the differences between the austere vegetarian meals of WILPF Executive Committee meetings and the high-society atmosphere of the International Council of Women, all of the organizations relied in a similar way on these various means of interacting. Although each organization designed its own membership symbols and fostered intense loyalty, by creating comparable structures they also helped create a sense of an international women's movement community. As we have already seen, that community had its limits, which were reinforced by the location and functioning of headquarters, executive committees, and congresses, as well as the language priorities of the publications.

The structures considered here were important in their own right, for it was, after all, at headquarters, in meetings and congresses, and through the monthly papers that members worked to make feminist internationalism a reality. But the central significance of the "international ground" created by the transnational organizations can be found in the personal interactions—ranging from intimate friendship to the "Unmet Friends" encountered on the written page—through which internationally minded women expressed their collective identity.

8

Getting to Know You

My own life has been marvellously enriched by
such friendships full of sacred associations. . . . It
is in the deep meaning of these bonds, and the
high purpose which unites us, that lies the secret
of our strength.
  (Ishbel Aberdeen, 1936)[1]

WHEN WOMEN traveled far from their homes to work with colleagues
from other nations, the bonds they formed not only cemented their sense
of "we-ness" but also represented a small step in the direction of internationalism. While a common language, shared culture and history, and
devotion to a particular landscape served as the basis for national loyalties, internationalism rested on a more abstract, though not more artificial, foundation. Only by creating ties that stretched across national borders could feminist internationalists enact their deep convictions.

We step here within the different worlds of women gathered at organizational headquarters, at international executive committee meetings,
at congresses, and—less tangibly—in front of open copies of *Jus Suffragii*, the *Bulletin*, and *Pax*. I consider the significance of women's interactions, the meaning of participation in women's lives, and the ways that
relationships ordinarily formed within one country but forged across
borders in the transnational organizations contributed to the internationalist project. Thus we look first at recruitment through friendship
networks; then at commitment and the costs and rewards of participation; and finally at devotion to international leaders, the cementing of
transnational friendships, and the formation of international "families."
In all of these ways leaders and even rank-and-file members engaged in
personalized politics, at least on an occasional basis, by making internationalism a part of their lives and identities.

Recruitment

The politics of personal interaction began with recruitment to the cause
of feminist internationalism. As in other social movements, friendship
networks and personal connections served as the most effective means of

bringing new members into transnational women's organizations. Yet most women's circle of friends did not extend far across the globe, making mobilization especially difficult. The written word certainly played its part in catching the eye of potential new members. Madeleine Doty, in a plan to win new converts to WILPF, sent international members two copies of *Pax* each month, requesting that they pass one along so that they could "make our band twice as big as it has ever been before, so that the sound of our voices in united chorus will become like some great rushing torrent, which cannot be resisted."[2] But as Czech member Lola Hanouskova put it, WILPF needed "not only . . . the written word but . . . the living word as well."[3]

As a result, tours by organization leaders gained great favor as a way of making contact with and recruiting members in parts of the world not yet well represented. Early in the history of the International Council, May Wright Sewall crossed the Atlantic to arouse interest in France, Belgium, and Germany.[4] When Carrie Chapman Catt traveled to the Balkans in 1908 to try to stimulate interest in the Alliance, Rosika Schwimmer offered her connections with the best families in Turkey and used national rivalries in writing to a friend in Serbia to suggest that her countrywomen would not want to fall behind Bulgarian, Romanian, Greek, and Turkish women in jumping on the women's movement bandwagon.[5] In the period between the wars all three organizations lavished attention on southern and eastern Europe. Recruitment travel both depended on and revitalized personal contacts. When Gabrielle Duchêne contemplated a trip to Sweden, where members felt "rather on the outskirts of our movement," Naima Sahlbom assured her that "your personal presence will stimulate and encourage at least our own members. Most of them cannot go to a congress, you know, and they need some new impulses and direct contact with the friends abroad."[6]

But while communication with a traveling member was desirable, attendance at a congress was best, for there a potential recruit could be immersed in a world of internationalism. Anita Augspurg read an article in a Vienna paper authored by Rosika Schwimmer and wrote to invite the young Hungarian woman to the 1904 Berlin congress. Schwimmer arrived a journalist and left a devotee of the Alliance.[7] Although by no means typical, Schwimmer's story illustrates the ideal outcome and the significance of personal interaction. A connection might be tentatively established when a woman read something that caught her eye or wrote a piece that attracted the attention of another like-minded woman, but unless that led to attendance at a congress or introductions to other members, it would likely come to naught. Once in the international women's movement network, one might be called on to serve as a hostess for visiting dignitaries, to come to a congress, or to compile lists of countrywomen who might be approachable. Like a snowball rolling down hill, the international women's organizations hoped to grow snowflake by snowflake.

Commitment and the Costs and Rewards of Participation

Once recruited, members settled in to different levels of commitment to the cause of internationalism. Without such devotion, no social movement can survive. Commitment comes easily when immediate and dramatic successes follow, but if results seem distant and meager, as they increasingly must have in the international women's movement by the 1920s, members' energies can flag without some other stimulation. What made the difference was a sense of benefiting from the very process of belonging and contributing. In order to understand the relationship between commitment and the costs and rewards of participation, I explore here the dynamics of personalized politics. As we shall see, members worked hard, sacrificed their health, and overcome obstacles that stood in the way of full-time commitment. In pledging themselves to internationalism, they found joy in their work. They also learned new skills, gained external recognition and confidence, and found fun, solace, and support in the process. The most committed individuals shaped their entire lives, if they could, around their organizational participation, merging work and personal life as part of their political project.

At bottom, commitment to an international women's organization entailed hard work that often took its toll on activists. After the Alliance congress in Geneva in 1920, Margery Corbett Ashby reported that she was "so exhausted that I slept soundly all the way home sitting up in a second class carriage." When her companions complained of a bad night's sleep, she "retorted that they had not worked hard enough."[8] Clara Ragaz described sitting at a typewriter at WILPF headquarters on a beautiful Whitsunday as "practically a 'sin against the Holy Spirit,'" and a year later wished for two lives in order to accomplish everything that needed to be done.[9]

Far too often women collapsed from overwork. Carrie Chapman Catt suffered from excessive menstrual bleeding as she went through menopause and came home from the 1909 London congress of the Alliance so drained that she could not even get out to the country where she had planned to rest.[10] At the same time that she confided her troubles to Aletta Jacobs, Catt tried to reassure Jacobs about the Dutch doctor's own heart trouble. Catt mistrusted doctors who called for total rest, she told Jacobs, since that was the surest way to kill someone. "I do not know but heart trouble may kill just ordinary people, but I am sure suffragists are too tough to be so afflicted; and with rest and not too hard work when you are at home I feel sure your heart will right itself." But she also admitted that "if you were an American your malady would be called nervous prostration. You have overworked, I am sure."[11] Secretaries of WILPF seemed especially susceptible to breakdowns blamed on overwork, perhaps because of the hothouse atmosphere at the Maison. Madeleine Doty, who herself headed to a sanatorium for a nature cure at the end of her term, commented sardonically that "you know you always do kill your Secretaries."[12] The litany of woes that plagued international leaders is testimony to their hard work and committed perseverence.

Women triumphed over a variety of barriers that stood in the way of full-time commitment. Physical inability to take up or continue with the work regularly merited apologies. When Gabrielle Duchêne came down with influenza, Vilma Glücklich sent her regrets and reminded Duchêne wryly that "that is against the constitution of our League!"[13] Family responsibilities, especially in the early days of the movement when women far less commonly traveled away from home, could also stand in the way of more extensive participation. A woman from Nuremberg explained that she could not attend the 1899 ICW congress because "the duties of an extensive household do not permit me to leave," from Geneva a woman apologized that "I have had a little son today 4 weeks ago and I nourish it myself," and a Canadian member wrote that to "cross the ocean without [her husband] would be such a departure from all that is expected of me that I must not even consider it."[14] Perhaps reflecting defensiveness about such literal and metaphorical departures, when the recording secretary of the ICW stayed home because of the marriage of two of her daughters, Lady Aberdeen proudly announced that this demonstrated that "Council women put home duties first."[15] Though leaving home to attend faraway congresses became less shocking as the years rolled on, married and single women alike continued to wrestle with conflicts between family responsibilities and their organizational work. Proving the truth of Carrie Chapman Catt's comment that "[i]t is always the unmarried one that the mother wants," ICW General Secretary Elsie Zimmern resigned when headquarters moved from London because she could not leave her ill mother, and Rosa Manus found that the death of her father added to the burdens of her work.[16]

As more women throughout the industrialized world moved into paid positions in the labor force, the demands of employment served as yet another barrier to women's participation. As early as 1904, Aletta Jacobs assured Rosika Schwimmer that she would be "a second [Charlotte] Perkins Gilman if you only had time to work. I mean, work for the cause, not work for your bread, that you do enough—too much."[17] So too Carrie Chapman Catt regretted "more than anyone else possibly can that you must turn aside from the work for which nature so admirably adapted you to look after the necessities of bread-earning," and she wished fervently that "God . . . would have filled the pockets well of all workers for women's emancipation."[18] That the conflicts Schwimmer experienced so painfully throughout her career erupted for many other women as well is suggested by the Alliance board's comment in 1926 that "professional and other circumstances make attendance difficult for many."[19]

In the face of these obstacles—illness, family responsibilities, and the demands of employment—some women did simply wear out, especially if they remained in harness in the increasingly difficult years of the 1930s. In 1934 Josephine Schain of the Alliance confessed that "I feel like throwing up everything and retiring to the country for the rest of my life!"; and after the outbreak of war in Europe in 1939 she told Rosa Manus, "I would kind of like to go off and vacate permanently."[20] Margery Corbett Ashby, whose passion in life was gardening, conceded in *Jus Suffragii* in 1938 that "I long to give up feminism and peace to grow roses and cabbages."[21] But that neither she nor the vast majority of women did in fact give up the cause testifies to their boundless commitment.

The very conceptualization of internationalism as "the cause"—a term borrowed from suffrage movements and thus especially common in the Alliance—suggests the passionate commitment that motivated women. When Carrie Chapman Catt's husband died, she told Anna Howard Shaw that "all there is in life for her now is our cause."[22] Shaw herself referred to "the cause which we both love" in thanking a Dutch friend for putting her up in 1913 and to "our cause" in expressing her regret at missing a visit from Aletta Jacobs.[23] And the Countess van Heerdt-Quarles thrilled to Catt's portrayal of the 1920 congress, which "filled us with a holy enthusiasm for the cause of woman."[24]

Even without claiming the "cause," women using other words expressed the same kind of single-minded devotion. Margery Corbett Ashby described her trip with her mother to the 1904 ICW congress in Berlin as setting "the direction of my life's interest."[25] The Austrian suffragist Marianne Hainisch longed for coworkers for whom the women's movement was a "purpose in life."[26] The Swedish delegation to the 1909 ICW congress in Toronto carried away "the ardent desire . . . to throw one's whole soul in the work."[27] Meeting that high ideal, in 1923 Rosa Manus declared, "*My soul is in* the Alliance."[28]

As a badge of commitment, women displayed their sacrifices. British peace activist Emily Hobhouse longed "to possess *nothing* & so to be set free for the service of humanity."[29] Rosika Schwimmer urged Emily

Greene Balch to give up her professorship, if necessary, at Wellesley College to come to Stockholm and join the Ford Expedition in 1916. "What is it to interrupt any important college work you may have on hand, compared to the work to which you are called? For humanity's sake I hope that you will give up everything, if necessary," a challenge that Balch in fact met, losing her position as a result of her peace work.[30] Reporting a painful sacrifice, Camille Drevet told of her father's refusal to see her before she left on a WILPF-sponsored trip to China in 1928 and her subsequent receipt of a telegram informing her of his death.[31] Bertha Lutz, torn between her desire to take care of her father and her commitment to the Alliance, hoped to "dedicate the remaining years to cooperation in a new burst of life and activity of the cause."[32] So engrained was the notion of sacrifice for the cause that Cor Ramondt-Hirschmann in 1937 assumed that a translator for the WILPF congress would be happy to serve without payment, a suggestion that made Gertrud Baer "deeply ashamed."[33]

Translating from dawn to dusk was not Baer's idea of a vacation for a nonmember, but activists in fact often described their work as joyful. Stepping down from the chairmanship of the Swiss National Council in 1911, Pauline Chaponniére-Chaix noted "what a joy & what a strength the I.C.W. has been to me during all those years & how happy I have been."[34] Marie Stritt, who rejoiced over an Alliance meeting "like a child over Christmas," extolled what the Alliance had given to its members, including "the joy of work, the faith 'that removes mountains' in the glory of our cause, and, above all, the joy of knowing that we are united in solidarity with all the women of the world who are striving and fighting in this strenuous battle for the greatest ideal of our time."[35] At the 1919 WILPF congress in Zurich, Aletta Jacobs reminded her colleagues that "the work was not just a burden, but also a joy."[36] Rosa Manus wrote Laura Dreyfus-Barney of the Peace and Disarmament Committee in 1932 that "I would simply love to start working with you all again, but I must keep this pleasure until a later moment."[37] In a tactic that suggests they took the "joys of participation" seriously, WILPF went about raising funds by emphasizing the pleasure of giving. Catherine Marshall insisted that members not go begging to potential donors, "asking them to give as a duty, but rather to make them so enthusiastic for our ideals that they *want* to give, as a joy and a privilege."[38] Likewise treasurer Cor Ramondt-Hirschmann called for increased international giving, reminding Executive Committee members that "you all know that it is a joy to give."[39]

The joy of giving was quite intangible, but some women reaped more concrete rewards from their commitment to internationalism. Inquiries about jobs or opportunities to lecture or write articles reveal the hopes of some women that international connections might boost their careers. A WILPF member living in Greece whose husband sought a job in Switzerland asked if she might find work with WILPF or another international organization in Geneva, and another member hoped she could work for WILPF in the United States in order to afford a trip there.[40] Having arranged lectures in Austria for Adele Schreiber, Rosika Schwimmer asked a German friend, in turn, to set up speaking engagements for her in 1912.[41] Alice Salomon called on Jane Addams for help in getting assignments to write for American magazines, and a German Alliance member hoped for the same kind of assistance with British periodicals from Margery Corbett Ashby.[42]

Members also learned how to lecture, write, organize, and speak foreign languages through participation in international organizations. Rosika Schwimmer, encouraged to develop her oratorical skills by Aletta Jacobs, inspired "amazement, gratitude and pride" in Carrie Chapman Catt, who remembered in the aftermath of the Budapest congress "the young girl who could understand no English and who knew little about the movement for the enfranchisement of women only nine years ago."[43] As bitter as she remained after her break with Aletta Jacobs, Schwimmer remembered with gratitude Jacobs's insistence that she could become a good public speaker.[44] Rosa Manus, too, declared herself "not a speaker" but learned to give speeches as well as organize conferences.[45] That international involvement might have provided recognition sometimes lacking at home is suggested by Aletta Jacobs's comment that Charlotte Perkins Gilman, a heroine in the Alliance, "is not honored in her own country. It is the same everywhere."[46]

For women unused to public roles, especially in the early years of the movement, such participation boosted their self-confidence. A participant in the 1909 ICW Toronto congress thought every woman "must have returned home feeling a better and stronger woman for having had this experience, and with her respect for her sex immensely increased."[47] From the 1911 Alliance congress, Anna Lindemann carried away courage from the "smart and nice women" she met.[48] A woman who attended a WILPF Executive Committee meeting in 1920 found it "tremendously heartening to go to such a meeting & one does come away better informed & full of energy."[49]

Commitment to an international organization also provided the pleasure of travel for those who could afford it. Lida Gustava Heymann and Anita Augspurg planned a journey to Dalmatia, Greece, and Palestine, indicating that they would try to recruit members for WILPF but making clear that this was primarily a vacation: "We are so happy in the sunny South!"[50] When Rosa Manus reported on her travels in Egypt, Syria, and Palestine in preparation for the Istanbul congress of the

Alliance, a coworker admitted, "I envy you your work."[51] In fact, members even touted international work and the travel connected with it as a healthful cure. Anna Howard Shaw headed for the Alliance meeting in Amsterdam when a doctor told her to take a vacation.[52] Carrie Chapman Catt talked up a trip to Stockholm traveling west from the United States through Russia, saying that she "wished to accomplish certain international things and . . . I believed I should recover my strength faster in that case."[53] And in fact Catt undertook her world tour with Aletta Jacobs when her physician suggested that she travel.[54]

As we have already seen, attendance at meetings and congresses involved both hard work and pleasure, and the fun of social events and sightseeing also counted as a reward of participation. Rachel Foster Avery anticipated the "nice times" Alliance members would have at the Copenhagen congress.[55] According to Margery Corbett Ashby's thank-you letter to her Dutch hostess in 1909, "My visit to Holland was full of pleasures but really my stay at the Hague was the most delightful climax to a long crescendo."[56] Fannie Fern Andrews's diary of her 1915 trip to Europe records visits, sight-seeing, shopping, and theater performances, and Alice Park's diary of the 1926 Alliance congress in Paris details a luncheon, shopping in the afternoon, and dinner with friends on a free day.[57] And Lida Gustava Heymann reminisced with Gabrielle Duchêne about a WILPF Executive Committee meeting in Paris: "I liked our open meeting, the evening in the Foyer des Etudiantes, our going to Arras, I enjoy everything in Paris—also Folies Bergère," which was not, she hastened to add, "in connexion with the business meetings of our ligue——"[58]

Work could also provide solace and support for members in need. When Carrie Chapman Catt and Aletta Jacobs lost their husbands, Catt advised her friend that work "will help you to bear the grief which has come to you," that "work must be our comfort and our duty."[59] Charlotte Perkins Gilman said the same thing, that "your work will hold you up."[60] Catt herself intended to "find my chief solace in my work."[61] Members suffering in other ways could also look to coworkers. WILPF members collected money to help secure Gertrud Baer's safety in the face of the rise of Nazism, and Vilma Glücklich tried "to overcome a stupid depression" by writing to Jane Addams.[62]

Women worked hard for the cause of internationalism, despite the varied barriers and costs, and received some minimal material rewards; but primarily they labored because they enjoyed intangible benefits from giving wholeheartedly to their organizations. Rosa Manus admitted that "I would myself die" if she took two weeks off, and Rosika Schwimmer, announcing her retirement from work for world peace in 1939, labeled it a "partial suicide."[63] Commitment entailed a very personal exchange of effort for the reward of satisfaction. By working themselves to exhaustion or going on work-related journeys as a way to recuperate from illness, by finding solace and support in work, by emphasizing the joy of giving, women shaped their lives to one degree or another around internationalism. Through their commitment, sometimes against all the odds, they engaged in a personalized politics that sealed their collective identity.

Leadership

In the everyday life of international organizations, the fact that members followed and revered, and sometimes criticized, leaders across the lines of nationality constituted an implicit affirmation of internationalism. In the normal course of events, leader-follower relationships existed within the boundaries of one country, so transnational leadership reconfigured the patterns of loyalty and challenge. As we have seen, leaders played an especially critical role in transnational organizing because there was really no way for most members to participate in between the periodic congresses, and many never could attend a distant event. I consider here three individual women who reigned as virtual queens of their groups in the period before the Second World War: Lady Aberdeen of the ICW, Carrie Chapman Catt of the Alliance, and Jane Addams of WILPF. For these leaders, as for the pantheon of lesser powers, the forging of ties of affection and reverence—as well as the occasional attacks—across national borders affirmed the significance of an international collective identity.

Ishbel Aberdeen, the grande dame of the ICW, took her post as a figurehead but became, in the words of her daughter, a "captain."[64] Her devoted secretary Alice Salomon described her as the central figure of the 1899 London congress, "more royal than anyone I had ever seen—like a queen out of a fairy tale."[65] The image of royalty cropped up often. Anna Howard Shaw, rather more cynically than Salomon, described Aberdeen at the ICW congress in Toronto as "in regal raiment," escorted by "the two aides who follow her about everywhere."[66] At the 1938 congress in Edinburgh, a participant described the eighty-five-year-old Aberdeen as "looking like Queen Victoria. All the countries paid her homage in French, German and English."[67] And a tribute on Aberdeen's death pegged her as "queenly and motherly."[68] She seemed like a queen because, as Salomon put it, "she belonged to a social circle that was remote for all of us," and also because she was "very tall with beautiful carriage" and "wore wonderful constantly varied clothes and jewels, tiaras, necklaces, brooches and bracelets." Although Aberdeen was an aristocrat, Salomon insisted that "she worked with the lowliest of us on equal terms."[69]

Aberdeen did, of course, have her critics. The best that a German member could say in 1929 was that Aberdeen would win reelection despite her "unsatisfactory performance" because "really no one more serviceable is running."[70] From outside the ICW, Lady Aberdeen could even strike observers as a bit of a ridiculous figure. Rosa Manus described her on the platform of the Alliance congress in 1926: she was "wrigged [sic] out in one of her beautiful get-ups, a dress with chiffon, silver and lace, long white gloves and on the top of her lightcoloured wig was seated a tremendous black chiffon hat, the form of a pan-cake and in three corners a big plum sticking out." Manus also confirmed Alice Salomon's pronouncement that despite Aberdeen's boast of her ability to go on very little sleep, she nodded off regularly during the day: "Unluckily after 10 minutes she dozed away and the plumes said 'yes' to one side and 'no' at the other side and almost wig and hat dropped off."[71]

But whatever criticism might be raised, the fact remains that the papers of the International Council are full of letters from women, written in English, French, and German, congratulating Aberdeen for successful congresses or expressing general appreciation. A woman from New South Wales, Australia, marveled that "you can make time for all you must have to do & yet keep a corner in your heart & thoughts for us so far away."[72] In Stockholm, a member suspected that it was "your personal influence[,] your own kind smile, and soothing, calming presence that is calling forth the amiable sides of all those very different women!"[73] And Countess Apponyi from Hungary admired Aberdeen's patience and endurance, finding her "a shining example of devotion to duty."[74] She struck one member as "the very picture of the mother and queen we love and never shall forget."[75] When Lady Aberdeen finally stepped down from the presidency in 1936, the "acclamations . . . almost brought the house down."[76] Her successor, Marthe Boël, penned a paean to "Grannie" on her eightieth birthday, and when Aberdeen died in 1939 the tributes knew no bounds.[77]

Carrie Chapman Catt held the same exalted place in the International Woman Suffrage Alliance, also earning the title "queen," although without all the trappings. According to an ICW member, Catt was "the uncrowned Queen of the American women."[78] The Swiss auxiliary, too, dubbed her "our uncrowned queen," and Mary Dingman of the Peace and Disarmament Committee called her the "queen of the occasion" at the Woman's Centennial Congress in 1940.[79] That she enjoyed playing with this role is suggested by her humorous responses to her devoted followers. On the eve of a trip to Hungary, she issued Rosika Schwimmer a "command from a superior officer" that "must be obeyed on penalty of loss of life," insisting that Schwimmer spend no time, energy, or money entertaining her.[80] In the same vein, Catt sent a thank-you letter for a badge she received at the Budapest congress noting that she was not, as described, the "uncrowned queen" but rather a "CZAR," and that she was very angry at her extravagent subjects and would boil them in oil after the congress and attend the mass funeral as the most sorrowful mourner.[81]

In the words of Annie Furuhjelm, Catt was a "born leader" with a "statesmanlike way" and "inner vision."[82] When she began to talk of resigning in 1913, Catt created an uproar. "What shall we do now?" Martina Kramers asked Schwimmer.[83] "We have many women who could give us some of what she gives, but none who could give it all," proclaimed Anna Lindemann. "Above all I know no one who could bestow on our congresses this inner light that emanates from her."[84] Chrystal Macmillan wanted Catt to call the 1915 Hague conference, insisting that "without a first class chairman whose qualifications should include international impartiality and international knowledge" it would fail and that "No one has these qualifications in so high a degree as MRS. CATT."[85]

Like Aberdeen, Catt also aroused some hostility. Belying her concern for how the Alliance would survive without Catt, Martina Kramers reported in 1907 that, in her opinion, for a long time Catt had left the Alliance in the lurch.[86] Anna Howard Shaw, in competition with Catt both at home and abroad, noted in 1913 that Catt had "never presided so poorly" as at the 1913 congress.[87] Catt's support of the U.S. war effort during the First World War changed the attitudes of many European women towards her. A Dutch woman described it as "indecent" and indelicate to have maintained her presidency of the IWSA, and after the war Catt seemed no longer in control of the organization.[88] She sought to move the 1923 congress away from Rome and lost that battle, reporting that Alliance headquarters in London "do not seem to find suggestions of mine agreeable as a rule."[89] It grieved Rosa Manus to see "the way they treated our beloved chief."[90]

Although Catt stepped down as president on this sour note, letters expressing love and reverence continued to pour in. Manus had adored her right from the beginning: "I suppose you will think me silly to talk in that way but really I am in one mass of admiration for such a great and noble woman," she wrote in 1909.[91] On the eve of their joint tour of Latin America in 1922, Manus received advice from Catt's secretary, Clara Hyde, who realized midstream that "I don't think I can tell you anything which your own love and affection plus much common sense will not dictate."[92] Manus took charge of organizing a celebration for Catt's seventieth birthday in 1929. She gathered recipes for national dishes, seeds for an "International Garden," and tributes for a birthday

Fig. 11. The Brazilian page of Carrie Chapman Catt's 70th-Birthday Book, 1928. Courtesy of the International Information Centre and Archive for the Women's Movement, Amsterdam, the Netherlands.

album (see figure 11).[93] The pages of the birthday book, carrying photographs and greetings from around the world, and the ceremony in which it was presented lauded Catt as "the greatest chief we have ever known," "A Beacon in the Storm," and, once again, "the Queen."[94] On Catt's seventy-fifth birthday Manus made a gramophone recording of messages of love, and for Catt's eightieth she threaded calling cards with greetings from different countries on a ribbon.[95] Catt's leadership had great personal meaning for many Alliance members. Annie Furujhelm wrote in 1930 to say, "I owe you very much. . . . [A]ll you gave me of friendship, advice and encouragement meant very much to me."[96] For Bertha Lutz, staying with Catt on visits to the United States made her feel "as if I had been privileged to live with the gods—or rather the goddess."[97] And Else Lüders wrote even more unrestrainedly that "you were my 'great love,' and you never can be forgotten by me, even if I am not to see you again."[98]

Jane Addams played the role of leading lady in the Women's International League. Rosika Schwimmer once wrote wistfully that she wished she could be such a respected power as Catt was among the women of Europe and Jane Addams was in the United States, but in fact she was understating the influence of Addams, who was also revered in Europe and beyond.[99] In 1916 a woman who had read about Addams wrote from Berlin, in 1921 a Croatian woman sent a missive expressing her disappointment that Addams had not visited Zagreb, and appreciative letters flowed in from all across the globe after the publication of *Bread and Peace* in 1922.[100] Following the Congress of Women in 1915, over which Addams presided, European women begged her to come to a variety of meetings. Chrystal Macmillan wrote in desperation to say *"how badly we want you in Europe as soon as possible."*[101] Aletta Jacobs insisted that Addams come preside over a special peace conference planned for The Hague in 1922, saying that they could not wait or Europe would be ruined.[102] Six years later, Lida Gustava Heymann worried that Addams's failure to sign her name to the Frankfurt Conference against chemical warfare would harm the cause.[103] When Addams brought up the subject of her stepping down as president of WILPF, Heymann pointed out that the organization "is so deeply connected with your personality that it is quite impossible that the League keep on without your name."[104] And when Addams refused to waiver, WILPF simply changed its constitution, substituting presiding officers for the president and making Addams "Honorary President."[105]

One of Addams's great contributions was as a peacemaker within WILPF. Aletta Jacobs and Rosa Manus urged her to come preside over the postwar meeting of the International Committee of Women for Permanent Peace because such a difficult task could only be fulfilled by a "clever and calm woman," and observers regularly noted her genius for presiding at turbulent meetings.[106] Jacobs described her at the 1924 Washington congress as "masterly" and "a wonder," and an Irish member had never "seen a woman preside over an assembly of women with so much patience, understanding, dignity or dexterity."[107] According to Madeleine Doty, Addams's "fine, tolerant spirit . . . brought out the best in us" at the 1926 Dublin congress.[108] Regretting Addams's absence at the Grenoble congress in 1932, Andrée Jouve noted that "[h]er great serenity enables her to keep the discussions at a level where all personal questions and conflicts of temperment disappear."[109]

But even saintly Jane Addams had her critics. Her illness during the First World War annoyed the staff at the Amsterdam office because her refusal to set a date for a meeting in Europe made their work difficult.[110] In Anna Howard Shaw's eyes, her penchant for compromise made her undependable: "You can never be quite sure what she is. . . . [Y]ou could not depend upon her taking a stand and keeping it."[111] And Rosika Schwimmer noted bitterly that "Jane Addams and her bunch want only people who will adore the leader and who will not have an opinion or criticism of their own."[112]

But such voices were the exception, and Addams's receipt of the Nobel Peace Prize in 1931 cemented her reputation. Although as early as 1920 Addams modestly demurred that "[o]n an individual basis I have no claim whatever beyond that of thousands of people who refused to bow the knee to Mars," her colleagues did not agree.[113] In contrast to Addams's insistence that the prize recognized women's collective work, Clara Ragaz praised "Miss Addams' personality, . . . the influence of her whole life work."[114] *Pax* devoted an issue to testimonials, and letters of congratulation filled Addams's mailbox.[115]

And Jane Addams did, indeed, inspire love among her followers. Olga Misar found her "spirit and way of looking at things was like a piece of a better world and I am sure it is not possible to work with you for a short time without feeling a little better for it."[116] Genevieve Tapping, working in Japan, found Addams's life an "inspiration."[117] The WILPF Executive Committee, meeting in Paris in 1926, sent their love, and later that year Madeleine Doty wrote to say, "Everyone is quoting you and loving you."[118] Addams gave inspiration and strength to Irma Tischer and helped Andrée Jouve "not to despair of women."[119] Eleanor Moore of Australia "felt drawn to you by something more even than our common interest in the great cause—a touch of that feeling of personal kinship."[120] And on Addams's birthday in 1930, Emily Greene Balch wrote "Dearest Jane" to tell her, "I hate to take your time to tell you what you know so well—that I love you very much and owe you more than tongue can tell. I do not believe you have any idea *how* much of the sunshine of my life comes through the fact of you being you."[121] When Addams died in 1935, the Executive Committee took time to mourn and *Pax* devoted an issue to her.[122] At the 1937 congress, Clara Ragaz honored Addams, who "through the greatness of her personality, her moral quality, her unfailing kindness and the clarity of her thought, . . . was the centre of the light of our movement, the impersonation of the primal spirit of the League."[123]

The aura that surrounded these three leaders—the "queens" of the movement—testifies to the strength of the cross-national ties between leaders and followers. But even criticism represented an acknowledgment of leadership that crossed national boundaries. Perceptions of—and complaints about—national styles of leadership make successful international leadership appear even more striking. In 1923 Margery Corbett Ashby garnered the presidency of the Alliance largely because the leading contender, Marguerite de Witt Schlumberger, was deemed "impossible, TOO OLD, TOO SLOW, TOO FRENCH."[124] WILPF's Maison seemed especially wracked by conflict over national differences in approaches to leadership. Cor Ramondt-Hirschmann, who criticized Vilma Glücklich's handling of WILPF's finances, seemed to Jane Addams to possess "Dutch thrift."[125] As Glücklich began to lose the confidence of the Executive Committee, she admitted that her twenty years of close work with the Hungarian section might have made her "too informal," and she attributed her struggle with Addams over the appointment of a house matron to "the difference of presidential functions between our two continents!"[126] She hoped that her successor, the American Madeleine Doty, would freshen up the atmosphere "with some American 'pep.'"[127] At the same time, Gabrielle Duchêne, as the vice president, worried a bit about Doty's lack of experience in Europe and urged her to maintain close contact with the Executive Committee in order to understand, among other things, "the psychological differences between the United States and the European countries."[128] Doty in fact took on the job of international secretary with gusto, longing for a "young and vigorous assistant . . . whom I could drive in true American fashion."[129] Sophie Hattinga-Raven, the "directress" of the Maison, told a countrywoman that "Miss Doty at first wanted to change everything and did make some changes in the house, but gradually she has found out that it is very difficult to Americanize a thoroughly European place."[130] Marguerite Gobat complained about the cold shoulder she received from Doty, blaming it on her nationality. "Madeleine always presents one with a 'fait accompli' and never listens to my advice and my experience, just as all other American women. . . . [A]s an American, she has the confidence of those who pay."[131]

Despite such differences in national styles, international leadership worked. The love, devotion, and reverence—as well as the criticism—directed at Lady Aberdeen, Carrie Chapman Catt, and Jane Addams, as well as at other lesser lights within the transnational women's organizations, embodied a commitment to internationalism that placed organizational loyalty above national ties, at least temporarily. Each time a member pledged her love for her leader, she forged a personal bond across the borders of nationality, and in that way enacted her commitment to an international collective identity.

Friendship

Love between leader and follower could be a rather distant form of heroine worship, but it could nevertheless be intense and even blossom into real friendship. Bonds of love and affection between members from different countries, like the personal relations of leadership, substituted international common ground for the tie of national identity. In making international friends, as in following international leaders, women expressed their identity as internationalists. To understand this dynamic, I consider here some of the loving friendships that developed within the international organizations (with particular attention to the case of the Alliance), the use of endearments to express such love, and the depths of despair when relationships broke apart.

Intense friendships sometimes developed out of the devotion directed at beloved leaders. Alice Salomon stated plainly that Lady Aberdeen "was to become my dearest and most intimate friend for life."[132] Cora di Brazza of the National Council of Women of Italy addressed ICW president May Wright Sewall as "Sister soul" and lamented, "I miss you daily. . . . You know how I love you do I need add anything more."[133] Sewall also received an extravagant letter of love and appreciation from a Syrian woman after the 1893 World Congress of Representative Women: "To say that I feel keenly your departure, to say that I miss so much the light of your eyes, the sweetness of your voice, the wisdom of your conversation, would be but a useless repetition. . . . I wish you could understand the Arabic languages[,] the language of romance, poetry, expression for then I would write you an Arabic letter where my love to you, my regard to your noble self, my appreciation of all your great glorious efforts and deeds, would find expression in words."[134] Catharine van Rennes, a Dutch composer who wrote the opening song for the Amsterdam Alliance congress, also "not . . . at ease IN ENGLISH," addressed Anna Howard Shaw in 1913 to say, "Be sure, dear heart, that I often, often thought and think of you, since I looked in your wonderful eyes, and you kissed me for my work."[135] On hearing that Rosika Schwimmer was sailing for The Hague in 1915, an American woman confided in her, "Strangely, you have entered into my life as no other woman has perhaps because I have been able to see the true nobility of your soul. . . . You may think anything you want to about this letter, that it is sentimental or anything else but only know that I am sincere in all I say and that I do care about you to a very high degree of love and admiration."[136] Appreciation for distant friends came from the German leader Minna Cauer, who, on the occasion of her eightieth birthday, thanked her "far-away foreign friends" who seemed "a glittery constellation sparkling through gloomy clouds."[137]

The intense and entangled friendships that blossomed within the International Woman Suffrage Alliance illustrate well the personalized politics of the international women's movement.[138] The complex threads running back and forth across the Atlantic secured Aletta Jacobs, Carrie Chapman Catt, and Rosika Schwimmer in a tightly woven web of friendship and competition.

Anna Howard Shaw competed vigorously with Carrie Catt for the friendship of Aletta Jacobs, and Shaw spoke quite plainly about the importance of her relationship with Jacobs. When Jacobs gave roses to Shaw and her partner Lucy Anthony in 1906, Shaw wrote that "never did I see roses last so long and keep so fresh I trust it is emblematic of our friendship."[139] Thanking Jacobs for putting them up during the 1908 Amsterdam congress, Shaw insisted that "I shall never be satisfied until I can 'cuddle' you up a bit in our own home."[140] Later that year she explained, "There are some friendships which demand that you shall be frequently told of their existence . . . [but] the friendship I have for you, and which I believe you have for me, is of a vastly different kind."[141] Shaw referred to a letter as a "little love note" and commented, "We are like lovers just as soon as a letter comes from you we want to answer it at once sending love and good wishes."[142] When the war stranded them on opposite shores of the Atlantic, Shaw longed to see Jacobs again, giving thanks for their bond since "there are so few real friendships in the world."[143] When Shaw died, a grief-stricken Jacobs wrote, "I do not know any person in the world I loved so much and I appreciated so much as our dearest friend."[144] She could scarcely believe that "I will never see her again, that I will never hear her sweet voice again and that I never will have another of her so highly valued letters."[145] And when, two years after Shaw's death, Jacobs received a photograph of her, "the tears came" when she realized that "we shall never have the happiness to see that nice dear face again, never see her laugh again, never kiss that happy looking mouth again."[146]

Carrie Chapman Catt also loved Aletta Jacobs, writing in 1906, "You are a blessed woman and I love you," although Catt elsewhere described herself as "a cold old icicle . . . [who does] not know how to gush."[147] Their trip around the world brought them even closer together, inspiring Catt to pen a poem, "To Aletta," in which Catt committed to "sail, till death shall part us two."[148] But in fact they seemed to grow apart after their journey, although Catt could still write, almost ten years later, "we shall meet again and I shall love you till we do—and after."[149]

Catt developed other transnational friendships, two of them with younger women, Rosa Manus and Bertha Lutz. Manus considered Catt "the greatest, loveliest and dearest woman in the world" and swore to "give her all the love that is in me."[150] After a tour of Latin America together, Manus longed to "cuddle her up for a week at our lovely country home in Holland," and she eagerly offered to take off with Catt again to Australia or Egypt, Greece or Hawaii.[151] In soliciting pages for Catt's seventieth birthday album, Manus described herself as "the special friend of Mrs. Chapman Catt," her "intimate friend."[152] Others described Catt to Manus as "your great friend."[153] As the years went by, Catt gently scolded Manus for showering her with presents, and Manus wished she could slip into Catt's bedroom to give her "a real birthday kiss with all my loving wishes."[154] "Thirty years of friendship with you how can I tell you again what your love has meant to me in my life," Manus wrote in 1938.[155]

Like Shaw and Catt for Jacobs, Manus and Bertha Lutz competed for the affection of Catt. Manus put it plainly when she noted, in the course of her Latin American journey, that Bertha Lutz was "green with jealousy that *I* am with Mrs. Catt."[156] After attending the Pan American Conference of Women in Baltimore in 1922, Lutz was transformed. "The days I spent with you were amongst the happiest not only of those spent in this country, but in my life," she wrote Catt.[157] In 1931 Lutz wrote that "I often think of you and all you have done for me" and sent Catt "very best wishes and love."[158] In 1938 Catt wrote that she was "glad if my love for you has any inspiration in it."[159]

Rosika Schwimmer also came into the movement as a young woman with great admiration and love for Catt. Catt first addressed Schwimmer in 1905 as "My dear little Hungarian friend" and then progressed to "Rosika," "My dear," or "My dear girl."[160] Unlike Manus, however, Schwimmer was not a one-leader woman, for she also had close ties to Aletta Jacobs, despite their later break, and she formed intimate friendships with a number of coworkers. Martina Kramers told Schwimmer in 1907 that she thought of her often, that "we understand each other without words."[161] Particularly intense was Schwimmer's relationship with the American Lola Maverick Lloyd, who addressed Schwimmer on "the happiest birthday of my life" in 1915 as "My Darling woman" and who longed to "give again to you all the immeasurable good gifts you have given to me."[162] Lloyd gave Schwimmer money and presents and begged her not "to waste one precious minute on me. You've done enough of that and I have a fund of memories to draw on, that will keep me going a long time."[163] Lloyd warned Schwimmer not to let a competitor, Rose Morgan French, who had also pledged her love for Schwimmer, be "a drag on you."[164] Others, too, worried about Schwimmer. Anna Wicksell reminded her, "If I have once given my heart to anybody I never take it back again," offering to serve as "a personal friend who loves you for your own sake" when Schwimmer looked tired and sad in 1916.[165] Schwimmer "thought with longing of the splendid bright winter in Sweden and the pair of magnificent bright women that I learned to value and love there" when she wrote to Naima Sahlbom in 1918.[166] And to her Dutch friend Mien Palthe, who put her up and missed her when she left, Schwimmer sent embraces, greetings to her husband and children, and signed off "with sisterly love."[167]

The kind of endearments so typical of women's friendships in the nineteenth century held a central place in international correspondence, at least in the early years of the twentieth century. Aletta Jacobs closed letters to Schwimmer by sending her a "sisterly kiss" or "love and kisses" or "many kisses," and Martina Kramers ended with "A kiss from your Martina."[168] Lola Lloyd signed a letter to Schwimmer "Madly yours" or "Yours for life."[169] To Jane Addams, Emily Greene Balch ended with "Always lovingly yours," and Aletta Jacobs with "Loving and adoring you."[170] After Katharina von Kardorff visited Rosa Manus in the Netherlands in 1930, they addressed each other, in German, with the intimate "Du," "Kathinka" writing to "Dear sweet Rosa" or "Dear best Rosa, the little rose of my heart," and closing with "loving and kissing you a thousand times."[171] Such endearments represent more than conventional usages: they express the depth of love and affection entwined with political work in the international women's movement.

Because the bonds of friendship grew so strong in the shared work for the cause, they had the potential to cause great misery when sundered. As we have seen, Jacobs and Catt broke with Martina Kramers over her extramarital relationship, and Schwimmer quarreled bitterly with Jane Addams and, especially, Aletta Jacobs. Carrie Chapman Catt believed that nothing could be done "to stop bitterness of feeling, nor to check gossip when it once gets started," and that it was difficult for women from other countries to understand quarrels that began on the national scene and spilled over into the international arena.[172] Such escalation could be very swift. Embroiled in a conflict at home in England and also shunned at the Amsterdam office of the International Committee of Women for Permanent Peace in 1915, Emily Hobhouse was shocked that "women *could* have behaved quite like it to one who like themselves was engaged in devoted work for a neutral & sacred cause."[173] Even Rosa Manus, with a reputation as an unruffled behind-the-scenes worker for the cause, would, according to her friend Mia Boissevain, occasionally cry out, "For Heavens sake what a 'stinker' that woman is!"[174] Aletta Jacobs minimized the seriousness of difficulties when she reminded Emily Greene Balch that "only dear friends are scolded. . . . [I]f you have not a wife or a husband you must use your dear friends for it."[175] But her formulation suggests how powerful both friendships and their rupture could be for women who built their lives around commitment to the movement.

In truth, whether women loved and admired each other or engaged in bitter quarrels, their relations expressed the merging of personal relations with political work. Like the ties between leaders and followers that in the normal course of events followed the lines of nationality, the international friendships that women forged grew out of and affirmed the significance of their international collective identity. To make a devoted friend from another nation represented one small victory for internationalism.

Families

Family ties, even more than leadership and friendship, ordinarily remained safely within national borders. Yet women in the international organizations regularly used family metaphors to express their connection, in this way proposing a conceptual reconfiguration of their worlds. By casting leaders in the role of mothers, by applying the language of family to various relations within the movement, and, most dramatically, by creating a family life within the WILPF's Maison, internationally organized women challenged the notion that the only families were national families.

The great leaders Aberdeen, Catt, and Addams all played the role of mother or, in the case of Aberdeen, grandmother. On the occasion of Lady and Lord Aberdeen's fiftieth wedding anniversary, the ICW took part since "their family has extended further than the usual ties" and "it is as members of this family that we may offer our congratulations."[176] When Lady Aberdeen stepped down from the presidency, her successor, Marthe Boël, sent "sisterly" greetings to "that large family" of the ICW and referred to Aberdeen as the "spiritual mother" who was becoming its "grandmother."[177] Aberdeen took on the new role right away, signing her Christmas and New Year's message "Your affectionate GRANNIE."[178] And when Aberdeen died in 1939, Boël, describing herself as one of "Aberdeen's daughters," thanked her on behalf of all of Aberdeen's children for her inspiration; Františka Plamínková praised her as "a mother, in bright days and in dark days," of the National Councils; and Karen Glaesel gushed over "My Grannie, our Grannie, . . . great enough to have a world of daughters."[179]

Catt, too, played the role of mother both to the Alliance and to individual women. *Jus Suffragii* referred to her as "the Head of a Great Family" on the occasion of her seventieth birthday.[180] Rosika Schwimmer wrote to Catt during her world tour with Aletta Jacobs to say, "We all are in unvaried love your obidient [sic] children and sometimes stepmothers."[181] Rosa Manus addressed her beloved Catt first as "my dearest stepmother" and later as "Mother Carrie." In 1909 Manus felt sad and sorry for Catt that she had had no children. "She always called me her little adopted daughter and she was really a perfect Mother to me," Manus wrote (see figure 12).[182] When Manus's mother died she wrote Catt, "I always thought of you both on the same level and now YOU ARE THE ONLY ONE."[183]

Manus had to contend with her rival, Bertha Lutz, who addressed Catt as "Dear (Step-) mother Mrs. Catt," "My dear (mother) Mrs. Catt," and "My dear mother (not step) Mrs. Catt," and signed herself as Catt's

Fig. 12. Carrie Chapman Catt and her "daughter"
Rosa Manus. Courtesy of the International Information
Centre and Archive for the Women's Movement, Am-
sterdam, the Netherlands.

"Brazilian daughter."[184] Lutz pulled no punches when she wrote to
Manus: "I am not goingt [sic] to put step-sister, because that either pre-
supposes that you are only a step-daughter, which you won't accept, or
that I am, and that I also can not brook. So be 'sister' straight away."[185]

Within WILPF, Jane Addams also served as a mother. Marguerite
Gobat called her "our beloved mother and the soul of our gatherings,"
and an Irish woman remembered her as the "dear lovable Mother whose
children were from every clime and every country."[186] Addams apologized for not writing more regularly to Emily Greene Balch, admitting

that "[n]eglecting you is a little like neglecting ones [*sic*] family."[187] Vilma Glücklich thanked Addams in 1924 for her letter, which "struck me like a motherly comfort to an orphan."[188]

The language of motherhood and familial relations reverberated throughout the movement. Schwimmer took the part of both daughter and mother, addressing one coworker as "My dear Motherly friend" and receiving letters to "My very dear 'Foster Mother,'" "My dearest Mütterchen," and "Dearest Big Sister."[189] Sometimes the relationships were more abstract. Aberdeen addressed the new ICW *Bulletin* as "but a baby" in need of nourishing food from "your many mothers," Madeleine Doty referred to *Pax* as "a little bit a child to me," and members called the Alliance Catt's child and WILPF Addams's.[190] In the same vein, the National Council of the United States promised a "mother's welcome to the far-travelled and long-separated daughter, who was now herself the proud mother of so many children," in inviting the ICW for its 1925 congress, and at the congress greeted the ICW "as a daughter, as an elder sister, and as a founder."[191] The ICW called "to its strong young daughters throughout the world" in 1924 and rejoiced in "seeing her children from all parts of the Globe" in 1930.[192] Marthe Boël called on "[e]ach member of our big international family" to "feel as free as in her family circle."[193]

The rhetoric and practice of family developed perhaps most fully at the WILPF's Maison, especially in the early years. The members who lived and worked in Geneva created a homelike atmosphere. The international staff of Emily Greene Balch, Marguerite Gobat, Anna Wössner, and Myrrha Tunas worried about each other's health and spirits and kept in contact when traveling on WILPF business, switching back and forth from English to French to German, sometimes in the same letter. Gobat, the daughter of a Swiss Nobel Peace Prize–winner, warned Balch of her replacement in Gobat's nephew Pierre's affections by a coworker to whom he gave a bouquet every day but assured Balch that when she returned Pierre would love her anew.[194] Wössner, in Vienna preparing for the upcoming congress, worried about Gobat back in Geneva, "all alone and abandoned, inundated with papers and letters, sitting hopelessly in the office!"[195] In Innsbruck before an Executive Committee meeting in 1925, Vilma Glücklich sent greetings back "to the whole house."[196] For these members, WILPF was their "happy family" or what they were wont to call "Famille Internationale."[197] And the metaphor could extend beyond the Maison to the entire organization, as when Jane Addams, in the midst of conflict in 1932, referred to their "family difficulties" or when Gertrud Baer, in 1940, expressed her "deep wish and hope that our family will stand unshaken by whatever may come."[198]

Whether leaders stood in as mothers (or stepmothers), daughters formed bonds among themselves, or organizations recreated a family atmosphere, the significance of the figuration is clear: international families ignored the biological and national bonds of traditional family life in favor of new transnational connections. Through such small steps was internationalism molded.

Is it possible to doubt the salience of personal interaction in the international women's organizations? Although the medium of the written word carried news, greetings, affection, and love from continent to continent, members prized face-to-face interaction above all. "How much better I should like [to] be sitting down to a good talk than to be writing," Emily Greene Balch wrote longingly to a friend.[199] Hoping that Madeleine Doty would come to England, Kathleen Courtney explained that "one gets so much more out of personal contact than by the exchange of letters."[200] And Rosika Schwimmer, longing for her friend Miel Coops, complained that "it is so hard to live thousands of miles from one's best friends. Writing is so cold in contrast to living direct conversation. But a substitute is better than nothing."[201]

Through such treasured personal contact, participants in the international women's movement enacted their politics by substituting international for national ties of love and friendship. May Wright Sewall claimed to "have seen prejudices fade and vanish under the influence of the Council, . . . a circle within which *those who are different are convened as peers*."[202] Likewise, a Japanese participant in a WILPF summer school emphasized the personal connections forged among different kinds of people: "We were all brothers and sisters utterly irrespective of race, colour, religion and manners."[203] German National Council president Emma Ender insisted that one could speak of the value of international women's work only if one had herself experienced an international congress, if one had seen "that the women of the whole world, with their social concerns, with their cultural endeavors, 'speak the same language.'"[204]

Personal interaction not only staked out common ground among women of different nationalities, it also inspired women to exert themselves for the cause. After spending time with her beloved Carrie Chapman Catt in the United States, Bertha Lutz promised that from the memory of those days, which she would never forget, "will come renewed enthusiasm and strength."[205] Her competitive "sister" Rosa Manus stated forthrightly that "for my love of Mrs. Catt I was inspired to give my very best."[206] In 1937 Emily Greene Balch pined for the "comfort in these anxious days" of being "among old friends, from all our countries."[207]

That personal connections and political commitment were totally intertwined is clear. In a graphic illustration, May Wright Sewall began what she called "a short private note" to her German colleague Marie Stritt and ended up blending "the discussion of public and private affairs in a curious way." But she believed that "we who work together, and who expect to work together to the end of our lives, as I suppose all of us do who believe in this International movement, will work all the better for knowing something of one another's lives and feeling mutual sympathy."[208] Only two years earlier, Sewall had apologized to Stritt for the familiarity of her address, explaining that "no other friendship equals that which is cemented by the mutual sympathy that is fostered by devotion in a common work." As a result, she concluded, "although nearly strangers we are friends."[209] Or, as Carrie Chapman Catt put it to those who gave her her birthday album, "I love you dearly because we worked together for a great Cause."[210] Marianne Hainisch, describing the 1909 ICW congress, left no doubt that the central experience was "the personal intercourse"; Helene Lange and Gertrud Baümer, in their tributes to Aberdeen in 1928, agreed that the greatest value of the ICW lay in the personal connections; a participant at a WILPF summer school rated "the personal relations" most important—and the accolades go on and on.[211]

From all sides, then, came agreement that the most significant thing about international work was the friendship or, as Egyptian feminist Saiza Nabarawi, one of the few women from beyond Europe and the United States who made it into the inner circles put it, the "sisterly comraderie."[212] Margot Badran, who knew Nabarawi in the 1960s, remembered the "special glow" that came over Nabarawi when she talked about the Alliance. The connection Egyptian leaders experienced can be read in the portraits of Carrie Chapman Catt, Rosa Manus, Germaine Malaterre-Sellier, Margery Corbett Ashby, and Marguerite de Witt Schlumberger still hanging on the walls of the Huda Sha'rawi Association library in Cairo.[213] Yet here we come full circle, back to the boundaries of an international collective identity, for the sisterly comraderie does not seem to have been reciprocal. Saiza Nabarawi merits not a mention in the paeans to family life by Catt or Manus or Corbett Ashby. But then we must remember that families exclude as well as include, that the "family circle" unites those within at the same time as it separates them from those without.

There is no question that the personal interactions of women played a crucial role in cementing their international collective identity. Women came to and stayed with the cause of internationalism because of personal connections, and they expressed their commitment by forming attachments across national borders. When Lady Aberdeen insisted, "It is in the deep meaning of these bonds, and the high purpose which unites us, that lies the secret of our strength as an organisation," she was not describing just the International Council of Women. Rather, this personalized politics characterized the international women's movement as a whole.

CONCLUSION

9

International Matters

[I]t means pouring a little drop of something into
an enormous sea the tide of which goes the other
way. But I see over and over again that people
feel encouraged that there is one body of women
who are holding up principles of right and
human law.
    (Gertrud Baer, 1938)[1]

WHAT DIFFERENCE did it all make? We have traced the development of
the International Council of Women, the International Alliance of
Women, and the Women's International League for Peace and Freedom
from their origins, and we have witnessed their interactions with the pro-
liferating transnational women's organizations in the period after the
First World War. Activity on the international stage was picking up. It
was a time when national women's movements in the Euro-American
arena—fresh from suffrage victories in some cases, frustrated by continued failure in others, and besieged by attacks on women's rights at a time
of Depression-era unemployment and the rise of fascism—slumped. At
the same time, the decline of European dominance of the world system
sparked the formation of women's movements, generally in connection
with nationalist movements of liberation, in the areas just shaking off
colonial control. Because feminist internationalists had developed an
ideology that so explicitly denied any responsibility for warmongering,
the First World War energized rather than debilitated them. The wave of
enfranchisements freed women's energies for international work and
shifted attention to goals more international than suffrage, especially
peace. And the establishment of the League of Nations, which stimulated
international organizing among a wide range of constituencies, proved
particularly enticing to women, for the doors to the diplomatic corps
within countries had traditionally slammed in their faces. Maybe, they
hoped, the League of Nations would be different.[2]

This trajectory of international activism challenges the traditional
Western-based timeline of women's movements. In the familiar scenario,
similar to that of industrialization, the United States and Britain led and
everyone else followed, some close on the heels of the leaders and others

straggling far behind. In contrast, the international women's movement evokes a more dynamic and complex vision. Understanding that national women's movements influenced each other not only directly but also through their interactions in the international arena gives us a more richly textured history of global women's movements.

We have explored the process of constructing a collective identity within the worlds of women committed to feminist internationalism. Despite the differences of character and structure and purpose and history among the three organizations, each of which extracted passionate loyalty from its members, women committed to internationalism functioned within the same universe. By the 1930s, when the coalitions brought together the broad-spectrum and cautious Council, the feminist Alliance, and the radical vanguardist Women's International League, that universe took on a structural form. Along with members of other more specialized groups, these three constituted an international women's movement. Drawing an explicit boundary that separated death-dealing men from life-giving women—as well as unintended and somewhat more permeable boundaries that favored the participation of elite, Christian, older women of European origin—women in the movement struggled over the meaning of both "feminism" and "internationalism." In that very process they affirmed their collective consciousness. Coming together at organizational headquarters, at committee meetings, and at periodic congresses or making contact through the written word, feminist internationalists pledged loyalty to leaders, made friends, and formed families across the borders of nationality. In other words, they forged an identity that cut across traditional loyalties. They did this not by submerging all differences. On the contrary, almost nothing happened without conflict. Debating everything from where they should hold conferences and what languages they should speak, to what constituted a national section and how much autonomy a section should have, to who was a feminist and what should be done about special labor legislation, internationally minded women formed a community as much through struggle as through agreement.

The increasing movement of women into the public world in industrialized societies at the turn of the century and the inclusion of members and national sections from dependent and formerly colonial countries in the 1920s and 1930s complicated the process of constructing a collective identity. Unity on the basis of political powerlessness declined after 1920 as women's fundamental difference from men came more and more into question and women's suffrage increasingly divided women into "haves" and "have-nots." Yet the international women's movement held together. Given the common assumption of women's disadvantage relative to men, gender cohesion remained firm. We can even hear the muted beginnings of the present-day call for solidarity around naming and preventing gender-specific violence against women. The bold proclamations against global violence that issued from the 1995 United Nations Fourth World Conference on Women in Beijing have roots, as we have seen, that go back to the First World War.

These new ways of viewing the history of women's movements on a global scale, however, are not the only reason why the international women's movement matters. The first, and most traditional, way of answering the question of the movement's impact looks to achievements on the stage of world politics. The second, and the one I have spent the most time exploring, considers the consequences of creating a collective identity. To conclude, I look more closely here at women's impact on public consciousness and international policy and then ponder why the construction of feminist internationalism mattered.

In the Public Eye

Were feminist internationalists voices crying in the wilderness? Although it is difficult to say for sure who was listening, scraps of evidence suggest that the international women's organizations could effectively change public consciousness. From the very founding of the ICW in 1888, British members asserted that the attention the organization attracted in Washington "would have great influence on that public opinion in England which rank & money affects."[3] When the International Council opened a Bureau of Information at the Paris Exposition of 1900, 1,500 inquirers signed the register, indicating their interest.[4] U.S. suffragist Ida Husted Harper reported in 1907 that American "magazines and newspapers are becoming more and more interested in these international meetings of women."[5]

All three organizations formed press committees or bureaus to disseminate information and turned to new technologies as they became available. Adele Schreiber called on Alliance members to harness the power of the radio in 1936, WILPF broadcast on Radio Genève as a means of "making the work of the League known in wider circles," and the ICW sponsored a series of radio talks, also on Radio Genève, in 1937.[6] The traditional print media remained crucial, however. The WILPF staff reminded the national sections that it was "extremely important to draw the attention of the masses who are the readers of the different papers of your country to the fact that there are women upholding the belief in and the work for Peace and Freedom," and insisted that press releases should be published in the political part of the paper, not on the women's page.[7]

In general, the holding of congresses seemed to rate front-page coverage in the newspapers of the host cities.[8] Not all of the publicity shed a positive light on women's activism. An American male resident of Paris complained in the New York *Herald* in 1926, just prior to the IWSA congress, that the "type of women who indulge in soap-boxing, demonstrations and parades are alien to the spirit of Paris" and regretted that "the streets, theatres, cafes and restaurants will be filled . . . with hordes of the ill-regulated and the warped."[9] On the other hand, the New York *World* reported of the same congress that "hundreds of attractive frocks showed women can work for political rights and aspire to other forms of equality with men without abandoning the feminine desire to please."[10] Perhaps as a result of this battle of images, Margery Corbett Ashby reported from Paris that "everyone in the shops restaurants & streets were aware of the Congress & interested."[11]

But whatever success congresses, newspapers, and radio programs had in spreading the word about women's international causes, such influence paled in comparison to women's direct participation in international politics through the League of Nations.

At the League of Nations

It was through the League of Nations that feminist internationalists succeeded in putting their issues on the international agenda. By exploring women's participation in the establishment of the League, organizational attitudes toward the international body, and the campaign to win women a role in League policymaking, we can see that the history of international governance would not have been the same without the participation of the transnational women's groups.

Before the formation of the League, only WILPF made serious forays into the realm of world politics. The International Woman Suffrage Alliance concentrated on winning women the vote, something that could only be secured on a nation-by-nation basis, and the ICW engaged in few concrete actions, although it did send a delegation to the Second Peace Conference at The Hague in 1907. The 1915 Congress of Women and the subsequent delegations to the warring and neutral nations represented a real departure for organized women. The resolutions passed at The Hague, including the call for a permanent international conference to settle international disputes, foreshadowed Woodrow Wilson's Fourteen Points and the proposal for the League of Nations. Wilson denied that peace activists of any stripe had influenced him, but members of WILPF plainly believed that the idea of the League of Nations had been "shaped by the women at the Hague," as Emily Greene Balch put it in 1938.[12]

Internationally minded women eagerly anticipated the silencing of the guns at the end of the great global conflagration and determined to have a hand in forging a lasting and equitable peace. But when the victorious men announced plans for the Versailles conference, women found that they had no place at the peace table. In response, the Union Française pour le Suffrage des Femmes (the French auxiliary of the International Woman Suffrage Alliance) invited delegates from other auxiliaries in the Allied countries to come to Paris in February 1919 to "bring feminist pressure," in the words of the IWSA, to bear on the men at Versailles.[13] That women from only the winning side were included caused some consternation in the IWSA, but the French suffrage group held firm in their conviction that such a gathering had to precede a more general one.[14]

The Allied suffragists decided to ask the Peace Congress to appoint a special commission of women to report on women's issues. The proposal they presented to Wilson called for international women's organizations to submit names to individual governments for inclusion on the commission. Wilson received the delegation "with the greatest sympathy" but reminded the women that only questions with "an *international* bearing" could be considered, thus ruling out suffrage.[15] He suggested that they lobby the delegates to the Peace Conference to appoint a commission to investigate the situation of women and that they themselves form a commission of women to advise and instruct "the men's commission."[16] This plan the women accepted.

The Inter-Allied Conference—what British suffragist Margery Fry called "the ladies' conference ([observing] you *can't* call them women, they are *so* well dressed!)"—went on to pass resolutions calling for equal suffrage in all countries, equal nationality and other legal rights for women, all occupations to be opened up to women, wages and salaries based on work rather than the sex of the worker, and acceptance of an equal moral standard for men and women.[17] Then the women set about lobbying the delegates to the Peace Congress. Margery Corbett Ashby, working alongside Lady Aberdeen, confided to Millicent Garrett Fawcett in March 1919 that "things are not going very well just at the moment."[18] But women did win an official hearing before the commission on the League of Nations, where, foreshadowing the later agendas of the coalitions, they called for the admission of women into all permanent bodies of the League, the granting of woman suffrage "as soon as the civilization and democratic development of each country might permit," the suppression of the traffic in women and children, and the establishment of bureaus of education and hygiene.[19] When Article 7 of the Covenant of the League of Nations proclaimed that all positions would be open to women, feminist internationalists rejoiced and rightfully claimed credit.[20] This was a victory facilitated by the connections of elite women such as Aberdeen; as political outsiders, women had to rely on personal influence over male insiders.[21]

The formation of the League of Nations, as we have seen, focused the attention of the international women's organizations on Geneva. They opened offices in the international city and formed coalitions to pursue a variety of goals. But attitudes toward the League differed from group to group. The ICW expressed the greatest enthusiasm. At the 1920 congress, the Council endorsed the principle of the League of Nations and proposed the inclusion of all self-governing states as soon as possible, but also, in accordance with its traditional concern for national autonomy, called for full consideration of "national peculiarities ... so as to prevent valuable national individuality in ethics, manners, and customs from being interfered with."[22] The ICW *Bulletin* regularly carried upbeat reports from Geneva, including praise for the entry of Germany into the League as "nothing less than a victory for civilization."[23] At the 1925 congress, Princess Gabrielle Radziwill, the League official responsible for relations with voluntary organizations, insisted that the "League needs the work of women, and we women need the League of Nations' help, because the work that we are doing can only bear fruit if it is really sanctioned by our Governments and we women must help this sanction to be given."[24] As late as 1936, in an article titled "The World Needs 'Mothering,'" an ICW member noted that they clung to the League of Nations, despite disappointments, because it represented the first milestone on the road to a system of international law.[25] Not surprisingly, League officials tended to smile upon the ICW, Radziwill describing it as "the most influential women's organization."[26]

The Alliance also evinced great enthusiasm for the work of the League of Nations at the outset, but the relationship grew more troubled, largely because of the League's dismal record on the inclusion of women. The first postwar congress proceedings reported proudly that the "Alliance has not been slow to recognise that just as hitherto its political work has had to be directed towards the education of individual national parliaments, so in future its work must also include the organising of international co-operation in order to influence the League of Nations."[27] Margery Corbett Ashby insisted in 1928 that "the organisation of the League has rendered the work of the international organisations more fruitful," and she detailed the Alliance's successes with the League in a 1940 report in *Jus Suffragii*.[28] But underneath official zeal, the leadership harbored doubts. Bertha Lutz confided to Carrie Chapman Catt that "I have no faith in any international edifice of arbitration that is built on the assumption of separate sovereign ties. The trouble with the League is not the League, it is the Nations."[29] And, true to the Alliance's central commitment to feminism, Corbett Ashby became, according to Gabrielle Radziwill, "one of the prime movers" behind the accusations that the League was not living up to the provisions of Article 7.[30]

As we have seen, skepticism about the League on almost every count thrived within the most radical of the organizations, the Women's International League. The terms of peace, which became public on the first day of WILPF's Zurich congress, prompted a vigorous denunciation by the assembly. From the beginning WILPF members divided on the question of whether or not the League as constituted could be salvaged. While one faction insisted that it represented a step toward peace, the other argued that it violated certain basic principles, especially by excluding some nations. For the critics, the League could, at best, accomplish nothing and, at worst, would simply enforce the victors' unjust peace.[31] WILPF never could resolve these differences. Jane Addams admitted that the "League is a man-made affair" but nevertheless wanted "to bring to it our woman's understanding, our warmth, our human point of view, our 'generous impulses.'"[32] Others wanted to sever all connections. According to Kathleen Courtney, the French and German members "regard the League of Nations with positive hostility and do not think that the meetings are worth attending or that it is our business to concern ourselves about them."[33] Although the French section of *Pax* carried regular reports by Emilie Gourd on League of Nations activities throughout the 1920s and 1930s, the idea that a "Commonwealth of Free Peoples" rather than the League of Nations was the only hope for the world appeared in the pages of the journal as well.[34] Conflict over WILPF's attitude toward the League erupted at the 1932 Grenoble congress, almost leading to the secession of the pro-League British section.[35]

As the League of Nations proved increasingly incapable of surmounting challenges to world peace in the troubled 1930s, discussion of alternatives took precedence within WILPF circles. Hungarian members Eugenie Miskoczy Meller and Melanie Vambery denounced the supremacy of the League's Council as "an imperialist corporation of the Great Powers" in 1933 and in 1936.[36] In calling for a true world government, Lola Maverick Lloyd of the United States proposed equal representation of "international, so-called private organisations" in the Assembly and Council of the League.[37] After the outbreak of war in Europe in 1939, WILPF declared that the League of Nations had failed because member states had not surrendered their sovereign rights.[38] So we see that internationally minded women ranged from devoted supporters to harsh critics of the League of Nations, contributing to the wider debate about the viability of the League and the possibility of alternative structures for such an international body.

At the same time, all three organizations interacted with the League of Nations in a variety of ways. In the wake of international congresses, to which the League Secretariat invariably sent representatives, officers forwarded resolutions concerning the League to the secretary-general. The three bodies as well as the coalitions sponsored luncheons, receptions, and dinners for League officials and for women delegates to the League. Lobbying took the form of both official visits and informal conversations. Until the League moved to a new building in 1937 and required passes for entry, women could buttonhole delegates in the hallways.[39]

Women from the international groups met with officers of the International Labor Organization and the League, often in joint deputations sponsored by the coalitions. In 1935 a collection of women's organizations won an hour with Eduard Benes, the new president of the Assembly, described in *Jus Suffragii* as "a good feminist." Representatives from the ICW, Alliance, WILPF, Joint Standing Committee, Liaison Committee, Consultative Committee on Nationality, and Disarmament Committee, as well as a number of other women's groups, presented Benes a wide array of positions. According to the report in *Jus Suffragii*, the women "showed the wide agreement on equality and peace, and made a moderate statement on differences in method with underlying unity in aim."[40] In contrast to such formal methods, Emily Greene Balch believed that WILPF's "best chance of putting forward our ideas is generally in conversations with one or two people, the opportunity for which arises generally suddenly and unforeseen."[41] Whatever strategy they used, internationally organized women lobbied on a variety of issues and protested when new regulations hindered their access to League delegates.[42]

What impact such visits had is hard to determine. Gertrud Baer complained about the attitude of Secretary-General Joseph Avenol, manifested during a meeting with members of the Liaison Committee: "I get completely paralyzed when men start to talk to women in that reassuring and calming way as a husband talks to his wife when she first starts to worry about his business affairs," she wrote.[43] Lady Aberdeen, not surprisingly, saw the interaction between the ICW and the League in a more positive light. She cited Secretary-General Sir Eric Drummond's praise for the ICW's "impressive record of activity" with regard to the International Labor Organization and League of Nations. And Aberdeen claimed that the ICW had earned the title of "the Mother of the League of Nations," having as early as 1888 adopted the objects, methods, and policies that the League later developed.[44] Yet a member of the British Foreign Office described the pressure from women's organizations as "embarrassing," and Radziwill's successor, Mary Craig McGeachy, noted that too often "delegates in Geneva are urged to take some action in the name of women when they have had no indication whatever that the women of their own country would be interested in such action."[45]

One way that the international organizations made a difference was to be sure that women, however few in number, had a presence at the League of Nations. Just being there mattered. Despite the official opening of all positions to women, very few governments appointed female delegates to the Assembly, and no women served on the League Council. Where women did find a place was in the League Secretariat, the civil service section, in which they held the majority of the secretarial and clerical positions.[46] The women who merited more than low-level appointments found themselves clustered in particular sections identified with "women's issues"—particularly the Fifth Committee, known as "La Commission Sentimentale," which dealt with social questions, including the traffic in women and children.[47] As the official history of WILPF put it, women's voice rose to "no more than a whisper in the assembly of nations."[48] But the connections between the international organizations and the women who did make it into the hallowed halls is notable.[49] So pervasive was the affiliation that the male colleagues of women at the League perceived them as having dual loyalties to their countries and their groups.[50]

From the time of the Inter-Allied Suffrage Conference, organized women never let up in their attempts to win women a bigger place at the League of Nations. Shortly after the formation of the League, Chrystal Macmillan devised a plan for an International Women's Office comparable to the ILO. Ultimately, however, both the international organizations and the Secretariat rejected the concept of a separate office, fearing it would undermine rather than advance Article 7.[51] All of the organizations kept vigilant on the issue of women's participation. WILPF's *News-Sheet* reminded its readers that the mere principle of inclusion was not enough, the ICW called on its member councils to urge their governments to appoint a woman delegate, and *Jus Suffragii* ridiculed the lack of women in the Secretariat.[52]

Even before the formation of the Joint Standing Committee in 1925, which, as we have seen, coordinated efforts to gain women appointments at the League, organized women worked to support specific candidates for positions. In these efforts they often worked with Dame Rachel Crowdy, chief of the Social Section from 1919 to 1930, and with Gabrielle Radziwill. In January 1925 the three major groups, along with the World Young Women's Christian Association, addressed a joint appeal to League Secretary-General Drummond urging the appointment of an additional female assessor to the Advisory Committee on Traffic in Women to help fulfill its new responsibility for the protection of children.[53] Organized women considered Avril de Saint Croix, an assessor already working on the traffic in women, one of their own. Despite public objections to the lumping together of women and children, they celebrated when Eleanor Rathbone won a place as the additional assessor.[54] The position of assessor gave women and other representatives of nongovernmental organizations the opportunity to deliver reports and address committees, even if they could not vote. When the League proposed the abolition of the system of assessors in 1936, the women's organizations and coalitions fought the move. They considered their failure to change the outcome a defeat for the participation of nongovernmental representatives.[55]

The transnational women's groups fought a number of such battles over representation, losing some and winning others. The ICW celebrated the appointment of Laura Dreyfus-Barney as a member of a special Committee of Experts to consider the education of young people about the League.[56] Rosa Manus greeted the appointment of Margery Corbett Ashby as a British delegate to the Disarmament Conference as "an immense step in advance for the women's movement."[57] And *Jus Suffragii* welcomed the appointment of Bessie Rischbieth from Australia as a substitute delegate to the Assembly in 1935.[58] At the same time, the ICW took up the cause of Florence Wilson, an American in charge of the library of the League of Nations since 1920, who was dismissed in 1927 because the United States did not belong to the League. A double standard seemed apparent because a male American colleague received reappointment at the same time. "Much patient work will still have to be done by women before the much talked of 'equal rights,' guaranteed by the Covenant of the League . . . , become a practical reality," the ICW *Bulletin* concluded.[59] Likewise WILPF lobbied to obtain an extension of Rachel Crowdy's term of service in 1929. She "is the only woman in the Secretariat occupying one of the higher positions and if her contract is not renewed there will be little encouragement for able women to enter the Secretariat where they are mostly in subordinate positions," observed Mary Sheepshanks.[60] When Princess Radziwill announced her retirement, the Liaison Committee called an emergency meeting, hoping to stave off the rumored elimination of the position and to win the appointment of a woman knowledgeable about international voluntary organizations.[61] In 1928, on the death of Mandates Section member Anna Bugge-Wicksell, the Secretariat was deluged by letters from women's organizations suggesting female replacements. Radziwill warned a male colleague that "if she is replaced by a man we shall have all the women organisations of the world on our back."[62]

In 1931 the issue of women's representation at the League won an official place on the agenda of the Assembly with what came to be known as the "Spanish Resolution," which called for greater collaboration with women's organizations in the search for peace. Ironically, given the movement's own embrace of women's difference, the resolution provoked dissatisfaction among some organized women because of its assumption of women's natural affinity for peace. Women, according to Equal Rights International member Edith Rodgers, wanted "more women in the delegations and as members of *all* the commissions," not just ones the men deemed naturally "feminine."[63] Advocates of the Equal Rights Treaty pressed for equality as a precondition for meaningful collaboration in the League. A "wave of feeling in favour of equality ... may have passed over the League," they rejoiced, pointing to "the unusual number of women delegates in the Assembly" at the time.[64] But, in fact, the conviction of Honora Enfield, head of the International Co-operative Women's Guild, turned out to be prophetic. "It is only a temporary wave and ... women are going to be caught in the backwash pretty severely," she warned.[65] Ultimately the judgment of a cartoon printed in *Jus Suffragii* in 1930 would stand. Entitled "The Assembly of the League of Nations," it portrayed an "International Chef" weighing ingredients, one side of the scale holding "Men Delegates" and the other side, far lighter, "Women Delegates." "The proportions are better this year, but there is still not enough leaven for the lump," the chef proclaims.[66]

The history of women's participation at the League of Nations, then, had its ups and downs. Although women remained seriously underrepresented and likely to be segregated in areas considered feminine, they would not have made even the limited progress they did without the agitation of the international women's organizations. Organized women's assumptions about female tendencies to pacifism, as well as the interests of the major groups in certain "women's issues," reinforced men's tendencies to consider women for only certain appointments. But at the same time the claim of speaking for a "women's bloc" amplified women's voices.[67] And in fact the League of Nations itself, on the larger world stage, took on a kind of "feminine" role, staking moral claims without any force to back them up. Perhaps the League's gendered role in world affairs helps to explain women's relatively greater participation there than in most national governments.

Setting the International Agenda

Whether from inside or outside the Palais des Nations in Geneva, feminist internationalists found that their concrete work led inexorably to the League of Nations. We look once again here at women's campaigns on behalf of peace, women's work, women's nationality, and women's rights in order to evaluate women's success in the project of policymaking. Although organized women did not directly accomplish their ambitious goals in these areas, they did manage to get their concerns on the international agenda in a way that would not have been possible without their concerted struggles.

Peace efforts in the 1930s centered on the Disarmament Conference, which began deliberations in February 1932. Four women, all members of international women's groups, sat as members. Even before the announcement of the Disarmament Conference, WILPF began a petition campaign to show support for world peace, but the global gathering provided the opportunity for a massive joint campaign—what WILPF considered "one of the most important pieces of work" it had ever undertaken.[68] In conjunction not only with other international women's organizations in the Disarmament Committee but also with labor, socialist, and religious groups, the WILPF campaign to collect signatures from around the world calling for disarmament gathered steam. In February 1932 the women's Disarmament Committee presented over seven million signatures to the Conference convened in Geneva.[69] But the women's high hopes sank as the Disarmament Conference failed to make any headway, an unsurprising development given the increasing tensions in both Europe and Asia. And in fact the British Foreign Office warned that the conference would find the women's recommendations "very tiresome."[70] Certainly the outbreak of war came as a resounding defeat, yet to focus entirely on that outcome is to overlook the widespread public support for alternatives to war, a tribute to the work of activists in the international women's movement as well as in the larger peace movement.

The far more contentious campaigns concerning women's labor legislation concentrated on the International Labor Organization, a bastion of protectionism, as well as on the League Assembly. The International Federation of Working Women planned its congresses around the International Labor Conferences of the League of Nations, and, on the other side of the question, equal rights advocates attended the ILO conferences in hopes of "get[ting] into friendly touch with as many delegates as possible."[71] When the ILO set up a Committee of Experts on Women's Work, anti–special legislation groups lobbied for representation.[72] And, as we have seen, the struggle against the Night Work for Women Convention and for the Equal Rights Treaty involved extensive lobbying at the ILO and the League. Despite the hopeless deadlock between women who favored and those who opposed special labor legislation, the fact that the conditions of women's work merited any attention on the international scene can be credited to women's activism.

The nationality issue, too, brought women to Geneva and to The Hague, site of the Codification Conference, to argue their different, if not totally contradictory, positions. Both the Alliance and the Inter-American Commission of Women sent representatives to Geneva in 1928 to urge the League to appoint women plenipotentiaries to the Hague conference. They succeeded in getting a resolution calling on governments to consider the importance of the nationality question when appointing delegates.[73] The ICW and Alliance, supported by a number of other groups, jointly called a demonstration at the Hague conference to win attention for the question of women's nationality.[74] As we have seen, the conference enshrined the principle of a woman's nationality following that of her husband, but the League did appoint the Women's Consultative Committee on Nationality. *Pax* trumpeted news of the new committee as marking "the first time in the eleven years of its existence" that the League of Nations "has voted to ask the opinion of the organized women of the world upon legislation which particularly concerns them."[75] The committee did, indeed, enjoy an unprecedented status, with the right to meet in the Secretariat and circulate its communications to the Council and Assembly of the League. That made the women's denunciations of the Hague convention all the more distasteful to League officials.[76]

Furthermore, Alice Paul's lobbying strategies in Geneva—she pretended to have the support of some countries to win over others—particularly alienated members of the League Council. According to Helen Archdale, League luminary Lord Robert Cecil "was entirely opposed to Paul . . . [and] said she was a terrible woman."[77] Despite the Inter-American Commission of Women's victory with the Equal Nationality Treaty at Montevideo in 1933, the League's support for ratification of the Hague Convention represented a great defeat for internationally organized women. Still, they managed to keep the spotlight on the nationality question and, after the Second World War, to wrest equality on the international plane.

The same divisions and defeats plagued the League-focused campaign for equal rights, but here, too, organized women made a difference. As the Depression chipped away at women's economic rights and fascism undercut their political status, the question of equality took on a new urgency. The idea of some sort of an equal rights convention originated, ironically, with international relations scholar Sir Alfred Zimmern, who told the International Federation of University Women in 1927 that it would be a long time before the League of Nations would consider such a thing.[78] In 1934 U.S. feminists working through the Inter-American Commission of Women prompted ten Latin American nations to call for a consideration of the Equal Rights Treaty at the League. Mindful of the lack of consensus among women, Gabrielle Radziwill tried to head this off by proposing instead an inquiry into the status of women. Hugh McKinnon Wood, senior member of the Legal Section of the Secretariat, opposed even this compromise, insisting that women's support for the League could not by bought by "pretending to adopt the programs they draw up for it, however impracticable." Fearing another quagmire like the Women's Consultative Committee on Nationality, he wanted to avoid anything that would give "the Alice Paul group of opinion . . . magnificent opportunities for propaganda."[79]

Despite McKinnon Wood's fears, and despite the fact that the Equal Rights Treaty got no further than its endorsement by Uruguay, Paraguay, Ecuador, and Cuba at the Pan American Conference in Montevideo, the persistence of women at the League of Nations did result in the call for a worldwide study of the status of women in 1935. International groups hustled to collect information, taking advantage of the opportunity to respond internationally to the antifeminist climate spreading across Europe.[80] The Secretariat published a fifty-page document incorporating the pleas for equality—if not for the Equal Rights Treaty—from fifteen women's organizations. In 1937, the Liaison Committee formed a "Status of Women Group" to reconsider a compromise equality convention, but the group instead lobbied the League to appoint a committee of experts to draft such a convention.[81]

As a result of such prodding, the League did call for an inquiry into women's situation, appointing a Committee of Experts on the Status of Women in 1938. Although League officials worried about how they could involve the international women's organizations without letting them run the show, the groups cooperated. Only the Women's Consultative Committee on Nationality continued, in the face of League opposition, to push for the Equal Rights and Equal Nationality Treaties.[82] The ICW, despite some skepticism, noted that four out of seven members of the Committee of Experts were women, "a fact without precedent in the records of the League."[83] Although the outbreak of war truncated the work of the committee, its existence led to the formation of the Status of Women Section of the Economic and Social Council of the United Nations. And the simple recognition that women's position was an appropriate subject for international action represented a giant leap forward from the assumption in 1919 that women's rights could be handled only on the national level.

Did the "whispers" of women make a difference? Certainly the international women's organizations, even WILPF with its serious doubts about the League of Nations, believed that their work affected what went on. With some optimism, from the Second Assembly in 1922 *Pax* reported, "It is very encouraging to find how much influence can often be exerted by just intelligently, disinterestedly and earnestly presenting the cause of justice and humanity to men who have a question in hand."[84] When Princess Radziwill asked for information about women's organizations in 1924, a WILPF staff member took heart that "the secretariat of the League of Nations is interesting itself more and more with the women's movement."[85] In the face even of the setback on nationality at the Hague Codification Conference, Maria Vérone of the ICW could greet the appointment of the Consultative Committee as "a great success" for "the feminist movement."[86] Emilie Gourd of the Alliance went even further and called the Thirteenth Assembly in 1932 "the feminist Assembly."[87] According to Louise C. A. van Eeghen, her counterpart at the ICW, "Never before has the Assembly paid so much attention to the opinion of the big international organisations."[88]

Were they accurate in their assessments? Although the international organizations did not achieve their goals of stopping war or winning women equality, however defined, there are indications that they did, indeed, exercise influence. One ironic measure can be found in the sanctions directed against the transnational groups. At the Hague Codification Conference in 1930, women from the Inter-American Commission of women found themselves barred from the Peace Palace for propagating "their ideas concerning equal rights for man and woman in nationality," spreading word in the press of supposedly confidential communications, and coming "with the hostile intention to frustrate the work of the conference."[89] Similarly, some members of the Joint Standing Committee incurred the wrath of Aristide Briand when the *Journal de Genève* printed their report of an interview with him without his authorization.[90] Had the activities of women had no impact, these violations would have had little consequence for the men of the League.

Other more positive signs of recognition can be read in the awarding of the Nobel Peace Prize to two WILPF leaders, League official Lord Robert Cecil's nomination of the Disarmament Committee for the Peace Prize, and the granting of financial support by the Nobel Committee to the Peace and Disarmament Committee.[91] In addition, League officials, as we have seen, turned to the women's organizations for information and assistance and sometimes explicitly recognized their importance. The ICW proudly reported that the president of the Eighteenth Assembly in 1937, Aga Khan, greeted deputations with congratulations for their work and indications that he had known of the organization for many years.[92] Gabrielle Radziwill and Secretary-General Sir Eric Drummond acknowledged the work women had done with the League even more explicitly. According to Radziwill, "During recent years women's organisations have contributed greatly to the forming of public opinion on international questions, and to the fostering of international understanding."[93] The secretary-general's memorandum, with a great deal more restraint, quoted a report on the Spanish Resolution by the Third Committee (which dealt with the reduction of arms) to the effect that "[i]n view of the importance of the educative and moral rôle played by women, and of their influence in the formation of public opinion, this co-operation may be of great value and produce important results."[94]

At the very least the League of Nations would not have been the same place without the insistent lobbying of organized women. They kept social and humanitarian questions on the League agenda, and though these were not considered the most pressing issues in the interwar period, they were, in fact, where the League achieved its greatest success.[95] In addition, women's agitation carried over into the formation of the League's successor, the United Nations, with lasting consequences for the international women's movement.

Toward the United Nations

The embers of women's activism, smoldering in the ashes of the League of Nations, flamed anew as the legacy of internationalism passed to the new United Nations. As we have seen, the international organizations and coalitions hoped this time to have more influence on the peacemaking process. Yet when the delegations took their seats at the founding conference, only a few included women. Bertha Lutz and Jessie Street, both Alliance members, represented Brazil and Australia, respectively. In addition, women served on the Canadian, Chinese, Dominican Republic, United States, and Uruguayan delegations.

Even before the conference, national groups began to lobby "so that when equality between races is emphasized there should also be emphasized equality between men & women."[96] Lutz and Street took up the cudgels for the inclusion of women's equality in the charter of the new organizations, but not without opposition from other women at the conference. As Lutz boasted in a letter to Catt, "Your Brazilian daughter and the Latin american women with Australia have been doing great battle to get an article into the Charter giving women representation and participation on equal terms." But to her dismay, the American woman delegate, Virginia Gildersleeve, "a very old fashioned anti-feminist," told Lutz right off that she hoped she would not be so vulgar and unladylike as to ask for anything for women in the charter. Disappointed that "the women from the countries where women have most rights are the most conservative," Lutz concluded that the "mantle is falling off the shoulder of the Anglo-Saxons and that we shall have to do the next stage of the battle for women." And, she promised, "We shall do so."[97]

Lutz found surprising not only the resistance of other women but also the opposition of the British and U.S. delegations and the support of the contingents from Russia, Ethiopia, India, Lebanon, and several Latin American countries. Making use of the intensifying rivalry between the United States and the Soviet Union, Lutz warned the American women's organizations that "[i]f we had to go home and say that only Russia had helped us we would give the message and tell the truth."[98] Of course, the intense disagreement among U.S. women over the best means of winning equality came into play. According to a World Woman's Party member in attendance at San Francisco, non-U.S. delegates blamed the division in American women's ranks for "obstruct[ing] the advancement of the status of women all over the world."[99]

In the end, the United Nations charter did include the principle of equality between women and men, to the delight of the international women's organizations. The Alliance claimed credit for the accomplishment on behalf of Lutz and Street.[100] Carrie Chapman Catt was more doubtful about who was responsible. "Now, a good many people are thinking that they started a new movement to get something of that kind into this Charter made at San Francisco," she wrote to Margery Corbett Ashby. She had met a U.S. woman who took responsibility, and naturally Lutz saw it as her victory, with the aid of Jessie Street and Isabel de Vidal of Uruguay. In any case, Catt rejoiced, believing that the San Francisco conference "pushed the women of the world a long way ahead and that was excellent."[101] Kathleen Courtney, attending as a press representative, reported to the Liaison Committee that the new Charter was in some ways better than the Covenant of the League and might even work.[102] In contrast, Lutz, despite her hard work, confided to Catt, "The real truth, and to you I can tell it, is that the United Nations have written beautifully sounding words into the Charter, or are still writing them in but have no intentions of carrying them out." Disillusioned with the structure, which she described as an oligarchy of five nations, only three of which were really great powers, she expected the conference to "peter out like the good night symphony of Haydn, where each musician gets up in turn puts out his candle and withdraws from the stage."[103]

When the question of a special women's commission arose, a long-standing debate over separating women's issues from general human rights intensified. In the flush of victory over the charter, Bertha Lutz and Jessie Street pushed for the establishment of a Commission of Women under the jurisdiction of the Social and Economic Council of the United Nations. The World Woman's Party took up the cause with gusto, sending delegates to lobby the United Nations Assembly in London in February 1946.[104] But not all organized women agreed that this was the best way to go. Dorothy Kenyon, who had served on the League of Nations committee on the status of women, reported that a batch of American women's organizations "hated to see women and women's interests segregated in a special commission."[105] The Alliance and the Liaison Committee agreed that sex discrimination should be handled by the Commission on Human Rights, not a separate Commission on the Status of Women and certainly not one consisting of only women members. Bertha Lutz regretted the Alliance's position, labeling it "too European" and not responsive to "the views and needs of women in other continents."[106] At a debate on the question, an Alliance representative called a special commission "old-fashioned" and "unnecessary."[107] On the other side, World Woman's Party members characterized the conflict as reflecting the old division between militant suffragists and their opponents. Those who objected to a women's commission, from the perspective of one World Woman's Party member, believed "that all these objects concerned with the status of women will be granted them by the men in power without any demand from women themselves."[108]

As it turned out, the Economic and Social Council set up a Sub-Commission on the Status of Women, which in May 1946 presented a report to the Commission on Human Rights stating as its goal the raising of "the status of women to equality with men in all fields of human enterprise." The World Woman's Party proclaimed it "[a] great moment in the history of the Woman Movement."[109] Taking a different view, despite a shared perspective on the desirability of identical laws for women and men, Open Door International feared that "the setting up of a sub-commission dealing with the position of women indicated an acceptance of women's rights as being something less than full human rights."[110] The raising of the subcommission to a full commission in June 1946 eliminated that objection. The international women's organizations applied for consultative status and continued to monitor UN action relevant to women. Although organized women had their doubts about their power at the United Nations—a British UN delegate described officials writing letters to their wives, reading the newspaper, and going out for coffee whenever representatives of voluntary groups stood up to speak—the formal role for nongovernmental organizations at least gave them a greater chance for a hearing than they had enjoyed in the League of Nations.[111]

Women from the great transnational organizations, then, played a critical role in winning a place for women's equal rights in the UN Charter and in fighting for the establishment of the Commission on Women. Their activism links the pre-1945 international women's movement to what might otherwise seem the "emergence" of such a movement in the 1970s. Although the UN Decade for Women conferences in Mexico City

(1975), Copenhagen (1980), and Nairobi (1985) and the UN Fourth World Conference on Women in Beijing (1995) belong to another chapter, the tale begins with the first wave of international organizing among women.[112] It is a prehistory we should not ignore.

Creating Internationalism

Even as the stories of women in the ICW, Alliance, and WILPF give the contemporary international women's movement a history, the link between past and present also returns us to the question of the consequences of creating internationalism. Certainly we can see the ways that the limits to universalism that were embedded in the functioning of the transnational women's organization shaped collective identity. Euro-American assumptions, based on a specific history of sexual differentiation in industrialized societies, underlay both the conceptualization of difference between women and men and the tradition of separatist organizing.[113] The notion of transcending nationalism assumed an independent, secure, and perhaps even powerful national existence. And the chance to partake of personal interaction depended heavily on the ability to travel, to speak and understand one of the three official languages, and to be accepted as part of the "international family."

But despite the echoes of Western domination that reverberated throughout the international women's movement, the international collective identity held the potential of wider appeal. Even though the extension of political rights to women in some parts of the world around the time of the First World War divided rather than united women, and though appeals based on women's social roles in the home struck no chords in societies where women played a central part in agriculture or trade, women's universal roles as potential mothers and the reality of worldwide violence against women might nevertheless unite them all. As we have seen, the perspectives of women from countries struggling for independence in the interwar period could shed fresh light on the meaning of internationalism. And the rituals of belonging, especially if congresses broke out of the narrow orbit of the traditional host cities (as they finally did after the Second World War), could pull in a far more varied group of women. Although universal participation without regard to economic resources was still far from a reality at Nairobi or Beijing, certainly the range of colors, nationalities, and classes of women at these two gatherings—especially at the nongovernmental meetings—would have rendered many an earlier activist—say, Lady Aberdeen—speechless.

While the bases of gender solidarity have shifted since the early twentieth century—from the unity of political powerlessness to, I would argue, a recognition of women's universal economic disadvantage and the multifaceted manifestations of violence against women—the notion of commonality across differences of class, ethnicity, religion, and other fundamental cleavages lives on.[114] Even the call for solidarity based on gender-specific violence, which seems a recent theme in the history of women's international organizing, can be traced to the pained protests of women during the First World War against the rape of women in wartime.

If we recognize that all ties among groups of people are constructed, not "natural," then we can contemplate ways that different transnational actors—organizations, institutions, and governments—can design means to facilitate the creation of a variety of international collective identities. Women within the Council, Alliance, and WILPF might not have chosen these words to describe what they did, but they recognized that they could foster internationalism through such avenues as the socialization of children and education in the history, culture, and languages of other nations. In 1919 WILPF called for the development of an international spirit through the elimination of national hatreds and rivalries from texts, the teaching of world civilization and literature, training in foreign languages and an auxiliary "world" language, education in a comparative psychology of peoples, and an exchange of students and teachers across national borders.[115] Lady Aberdeen urged the members of the ICW, as mothers and as workers, to encourage children to learn languages, to study other countries, and to refrain from using derogatory expressions about "foreigners."[116] In her New Year's message of hope in dark times, Edith Pye in 1934 asserted that it was the duty of WILPF members "to see that the children are taught rightly, that the women do not let themselves be carried away by propaganda."[117] If national hatred could be taught, feminist internationalists believed, then so could international understanding and love.

Women in the transnational organizations also worked to create internationalism through what sociologists call "prefigurative politics"—acting out the conviction that, through putting into practice desirable ways of living, a group can, in fact, help transform the old order.[118] The organizations themselves, and especially their gatherings of women from all across the globe, served as a model of what society might be. In 1922 Lady Aberdeen took the organizational relations of the International Council as a microcosm for the world. When "women of all races, creeds and classes, meet together and discuss questions which might well produce strife and dissension," their "attitude of sympathetic understanding, coupled with a sincere endeavour to realise and enter into one another's condition and circumstances," provided a glimpse of "the high road to that period of permanent peace between the nations for which we all sigh."[119] Madeleine Doty, reporting on life at the Maison in 1925, concluded, "There is no doubt about it assocation [sic] breeds tolerance."[120] Following the same line of reasoning, Gertrud Baer recommended in 1938 that workers for the cause of peace and freedom "make a practice of mixing and living for a time with people in foreign countries."[121] Sometimes women's organization members saw in the world outside their circles "here and there an attempt to live according to the principles of the New International Order," as Jane Addams described Austria's renunciation of a piece of Hungarian territory granted by the terms of the Versailles treaty, Gandhi's success in India, and the Japanese withdrawal from Shantung.[122] But certainly internationally organized women saw their own interactions as the best exemplar for the future. Had they more power, they believed, they could put into practice on a global scale what they so gloriously lived in their international circles.

Through all that participating in an international organization entailed, women in the Council, Alliance, and WILPF could, they insisted, foreshadow the kind of international understanding and cooperation they hoped would become universal. In the meantime, they could create internationalism in both mundane and lofty ways. An Australian correspondent proposed in *Pax* that when people of different nationalities married, they and their children should lose their citizenship and "enter into a superior society," called the "Terrenes," with its own laws and arrangements. Stateless persons and all who wished "to rise above nationalist prejudices" would be invited to join, under the recognition and protection of "a well-constituted League of Nations."[123] In the same vein, a proposal at the 1924 WILPF congress foresaw "the birth of an International City" where "citizens of the world," those who were internationally minded, "would be united through the convincing power of experience."[124]

But even without a society of "Terrenes" or an international city, we must recognize the earnest work of creating internationalism. Though Gertrud Baer sometimes felt "that it means pouring a little drop of something into an enormous sea," and though she knew that they did not always do "*weltbewegende Dinge* [earthshaking things]," she also insisted that "in times like ours the most important thing is to give other people the consciousness that there are at least some upright people standing for what their inarticulate wishes turn to."[125] At the Maison, at international congresses, and in the pages of *Jus Suffragii* and the *Bulletin* and *Pax*, women worked to bring a new world into being. Each small step, they believed, might make a difference.

Rethinking Identity Politics

Imagine, for a moment, a scenario in which individuals and groups across the world felt a sense of kinship, on the basis of occupation or religion or gender or politics or age or a whole host of other characteristics, with others who did not share the same nationality. The multitude of international organizations that sprang up, beginning (as with the women's groups) in the late nineteenth century but intensifying in the period between the world wars, gives witness to the myriad ways that people might feel a connection across national borders. Involvement in agriculture, common economic interests, concern with law or medicine, devotion to culture, participation in philanthropy, a career in science or education, love of sport—a vast array of commonalities served as the basis of transnational organizations. No one identity was necessarily primary; certainly none was exclusive of all others. And if the creation of such international ties has not yet shaken a world system based on national identity, that does not mean that the creation of alternative bonds is unimportant. A scientist whose worldview is more like that of a colleague halfway around the globe than a next-door neighbor's raises the same implicit challenges to national identity as the embrace of Lida Gustava Heymann and Jeanne Mélin at the 1919 Zurich congress. Yet this is an aspect of international organization that has been little attended to by existing scholarship.

The first steps in the direction of a more universal collective identity may in themselves have been insignificant, but their trailblazing role demands attention. Furthermore, the construction of internationalism within the transnational women's organizations prompts us to rethink the notion of identity politics. In line with the postmodernist and feminist recognition of multiple identities and the search for commonalities among different identity communities, we see that women's international collective identity could coexist with their identities as Germans or Egyptians, pacifists or socialists or feminists, Christians or Jews, professional women or workers.[126] If forging bonds across cultures can build on, rather than challenge, existing loyalties, the task of creating internationalism does not seem so impossible. And the model of overlapping and expansive, rather than splintering, identities suggests that the contemporary outcry against identity politics as narrow and undermining of unity and coalition needs to be rethought. An internationalist identity, however circumscribed by gender or class or politics or occupation, is not necessarily a move toward exclusion, although it can be that as well.[127] But the possibilities of multiple bonds with diverse constituencies—women, female university graduates, women professionals, male and female pacifists, Jews, socialists, advocates of women's equality—suggest that the circles of identity do not need to become smaller and smaller: they can just be drawn in myriad ways with increasing overlaps with a wider and wider range of groups.

Whether or not the multiplication of such international identities would in fact have positive consequences for the future of the world is, of course, still an open question. The history of internationalism since the late nineteenth century suggests that such redrawings of connections can be progressive or reactionary, anti-imperialist or imperialist.[128] And, as we have seen, it was not always an either/or proposition. The tensions between exclusiveness and inclusiveness, Eurocentrism and universal ideals, that simmered within the international women's organizations were, I think, characteristic of all transnational organizations.

Nevertheless, the particular construction of internationalism within transnational women's organizations did matter. Without the coalescing of discrete groups into a vibrant international women's movement, the history of intergovernmental relations at the League of Nations and United Nations would have taken a different course. Women's insistence on representation and attention to gender-specific questions did not dramatically transform those august bodies, but they did make a difference. And the dynamic and contentious process of forging bonds between women from different, even sometimes from warring, countries has consequences for both our understanding of history and our approach to contemporary identity politics. Despite its limitations, women's internationalism in the period before the Second World War points the way to one kind of global identity that we may add to the more parochial ways we view ourselves as we move into the twenty-first century.

Notes

References to congress reports appear in abbreviated form; full references appear in the bibliography under the heading "Conference Proceedings." All translations, unless otherwise indicated, are mine.

Abbreviations Used in Notes

BDIC	Bibliothèque de Documentation Internationale Contemporaine
BMD	Bibliothèque Marguerite Durand
ERI	Equal Rights International
FL	Fawcett Library
HI	Hoover Institution
HLA	Helene-Lange-Archiv
IACW	Inter-American Commission of Women
IAW	International Alliance of Women
IAssW	International Assembly of Women
IAWSEC	International Alliance of Women for Suffrage and Equal Citizenship
ICW	International Council of Women
ICW HQ	International Council of Women headquarters
ICWPP	International Committee of Women for Permanent Peace
IFBPWC	International Federation of Business and Professional Women's Clubs
IFUW	International Federation of University Women
IFWW	International Federation of Working Women
IIAV	Internationaal Informatiecentrum en Archief voor de Vrouwenbeweging
IISG	Internationaal Instituut voor Sociale Geschiedenis
ILO	International Labor Organization
I-MCPL	Indianapolis–Marion County Public Library
IWSA	International Woman Suffrage Alliance
JSC	Joint Standing Committee
LB	Landesarchiv Berlin
LBI	Leo Baeck Institute
LC	Liaison Committee
LofC	Library of Congress
NAWSA	National American Woman Suffrage Association
NCW-GB	National Council of Women of Great Britain
NCW-GB HQ	National Council of Women of Great Britain headquarters
NWP	National Woman's Party
NYPL	New York Public Library
ODI	Open Door International
PAIWC	Pan American International Women's Committee

PDC   Peace and Disarmament Committee
RUP   Rassemblement Universel pour la Paix
SCPC   Swarthmore College Peace Collection
SL   Schlesinger Library
SSC   Sophia Smith Collection
WCCN   Women's Consultative Committee on Nationality
WILPF   Women's International League for Peace and Freedom
WWP   World Woman's Party

Chapter 1

1. Smyth 1995 is writing here of Irish women.

2. On the Decade for Women, see Boulding 1977; Çagatay, Grown, and Santiago 1986; Miles 1996.

3. Hurwitz 1977.

4. Boy 1936 is an early and extremely useful study of international women's organizations; Sherrick 1982 raises provocative questions about the nature of women's international organizing; Costin 1982 and Wiltsher 1985 explore the most famous event in the history of the international women's movement. Arrington 1989, Becker 1983, and Pfeffer 1985 all focus on U.S. involvement, while Hering and Wenzel 1986 explore the participation of German women. In-house studies of the three organizations under consideration here include *Women in a Changing World* 1966 on the ICW; Whittick 1979 on the IAW; Bussey and Tims 1965 and Catherine Foster 1989 on WILPF.

5. See, for example, Luard 1966; Huntington 1973; Keohane and Nye 1973; D. Armstrong 1982; Diehl 1989; Murphy 1994; Ishay 1995; Long 1996. Recently feminist international relations theory has challenged the field of political science: see Enloe 1990; Foot 1990; Grant and Newland 1991; Peterson 1992; Sylvester 1994; Whitworth 1994. Tyrrell 1991a calls for greater attention to transnational history, including a history of organizations. Existing work on transnational organizations includes Lyons 1963; Joll 1974; van der Lindon 1987; Milner 1990; Cooper 1991; Riesenberger 1992; Strikwerda 1993; Berkowitz 1993; Herren 1993; Hoberman 1995; Hutchinson 1996.

6. Rupp 1992.

7. On this point, see Bulbeck 1988.

8. Benedict Anderson 1991 (1st ed. 1983). The literature on nationalism is, of course, extensive and has long recognized that there is no universal basis for nationalism; recent works include Isaacs 1975; J. Armstrong 1982; Gellner 1983; Chatterjee 1993 (first published 1986); Jayawardena 1986; A. Smith 1986; Greenfeld 1992; Pfaff 1993.

9. Lorde 1984, 110.

10. See Gamson 1992. On "new social movements," see Klandermans and Tarrow 1988.

11. Taylor and Whittier 1992, 105. Taylor and Whitter 1995 use the term "politicization of everyday life" to replace what is called "negotiation" in the original model. I have substituted "personalized politics" for these alternatives.

12. Minutes, Officers and Members of the ICW, London, November 14, 1944, ICW papers, NCW-GB HQ.

13. Margery Corbett Ashby to Mrs. Stansted [*sic*, for Stantial], September 23, 1954, NAWSA papers, box 2, LofC.

14. Carrie Chapman Catt to Friends of Rosa Manus, July 10, 1942, Catt papers, IIAV; Rosika Schwimmer to Carrie Chapman Catt, September 10, 1946, NAWSA papers, reel 18, LofC; "International Council of Women," November 1947, ICW papers, box 1, SSC.

15. Personal communication, Mineke Bosch, 1994.

16. See Cott 1991.

17. Rosika Schwimmer to Alice Park, January 8, 1935, Park papers, box 1, HI.

Chapter 2

1. B.P., "Farewell to Mary Dingman," November 12, 1939, Dingman papers, box 1, SL.

2. McCarthy and Zald 1977.

3. Rosa Manus to Katharine von Kardorff [German], January 15, 1930, Manus papers, IIAV; minutes, IAWSEC International Committee, Zurich, February 26, 1937, IAW papers, FL.

4. "Status of Women," *Jus Suffragii* 32, no. 6 (March 1938).

5. See Freeman 1975, 48.

6. McFadden (1988, 1990) categorizes the sources of women's early international connectedness, including such phenomena as organizations, intentional communities, the press, travel, translation, migration, and correspondence.

7. Schnetzler 1971; Evans 1977; Rasmussen 1982; Rendall 1984; Banks 1986; DuBois 1991; Bolt 1993; Holton 1994; Bonnie Anderson 1996.

8. T. Stanton 1886 reports the establishment of a permanent international committee at the 1878 conference with responsibility for advancing reforms and planning the next congress. Klejman 1989 suggests that independent congresses, especially in France, rarely transcended the national context; in general, international congresses facilitated the exchange of information but did not stimulate debate or develop plans of action. On international women's congresses, including "general women's congresses," see Wikander 1992. On the Congrès international du droit des femmes in Paris, see Klejman and Rochefort 1989.

9. Earlier, in 1868, Swiss feminist and pacifist Marie Goegg had formed the Association Internationale des Femmes, but it fell apart in 1871 in the aftermath of the repression of the Paris Commune; see Schnetzler 1971. An enduring but more focused women's organization, the World's Woman's Christian Temperance Union, technically founded in 1876, took shape in 1884; see Tyrrell 1991b.

10. 1888 ICW [NAWSA] congress report; E. C. Stanton 1886. *Women in a Changing World* 1966 is a useful in-house history of the ICW.

11. "The Birth of the I.C.W.," pamphlet, 1957, ICW papers, box 1, SSC.

12. Alice Salomon, "Character is Destiny," 61, Salomon papers, LBI.

13. Lord and Lady Aberdeen 1925, vol. 1, 295–307; Pentland 1947; Alice Salomon, "Character is Destiny," Salomon papers, LBI.

14. "Souvenir of the Pageant of Progress," ICW Congress, April 29–May 9, 1929, ICW papers, box 3, NCW-GB HQ.

15. "Presentation of an Address to the Second Peace Conference, held at The

Hague, 1907," ICW *Annual Report*, 1906–07; "To Speak and Act for 36,000,000 Women," *Christian Science Monitor*, January 13, 1925, Woman's Rights Collection, SL.

16. "Some Suggestions for the Formation of National Councils of Women," HLA, 78-315(1), LB.

17. May Wright Sewall, "Preface," ICW 1904 congress report, vol. 1. On national uses of the ICW in the United States, see Sneider 1996.

18. Minutes, Fourth and Final Business Session, ICW 1899 congress report, vol. 1, 190–91.

19. Ishbel Aberdeen and Temair, "A Christmas and New Year Message from our Hon. President," ICW *Bulletin* 15, no. 4 (December 1936).

20. Marjorie Shuler, "Women, Misunderstood, End Successful World Meeting," *Christian Science Monitor*, May 14, 1925, in Andrews papers, box 20, SL.

21. Ishbel Aberdeen and Temair, "President's Letter," ICW *Bulletin* 12, no. 2 (October 1933).

22. "Quinquennial Report," ICW 1899 congress report, vol. 1.

23. Ishbel Aberdeen, "President's Memorandum," ICW 1920 congress report, 13; L. C. A. van Eeghen, "The Mental Atmosphere at Geneva," ICW *Bulletin* 3, nos. 3–4 (November–December 1924); Alice Salomon, "Character is Destiny," 61, Salomon papers, LBI.

24. Marthe Pol Boël, "Introduction," ICW *Bulletin* 16, no. 10 (June 1938).

25. Lady Aberdeen's speech at Eighth Quinquennial in Vienna, 1930, quoted in *Women in a Changing World* 1966, 61.

26. Lady Aberdeen, "Presidential Address," ICW 1899 congress report, vol. 1, 49.

27. Teresa F. Wilson to Anna Simson, January 26, 1899, HLA, 80-319(1), LB. Simson responded testily, insisting that Germans valued accomplishment over social position; Anna Simson to Teresa Wilson [German], February 4, 1899, HLA, 83-328(5), LB.

28. May Wright Sewall to Marie Stritt, August 24, 1900, HLA, 80-309(1), LB. Apparently this plan met with the disapproval of Lady Aberdeen and the Executive Committee.

29. Secretary to Alice Thacher Post, March 19, 1925, Union Mondiale papers, SCPC.

30. Cor Ramondt-Hirschmann to Jane Addams, November 17, 1924, Addams papers, reel 16.

31. Gertrud Baer to Helen Archdale, May 18, 1933, ERI papers, box 334, FL.

32. Martina Kramers to Rosika Schwimmer [German], September 18, 1908, Schwimmer-Lloyd collection, box A-17, NYPL; Yella Hertzka to Mary Sheepshanks [German], July 12, 1930, WILPF papers, reel 2.

33. See "Report of the Meeting of the Committee of Arrangements," July 6, 1898, and "Report of Meeting" of Executive Committee, March 23, 1899, both in ICW Minute Book, ICW HQ; "Political Enfranchisement of Women,"ICW 1899 congress report, vol. 5, 115–41. On the role of Heymann and Augspurg, see May Wright Sewall to Minna Cauer, December 28, 1903, HLA, 81-323(2), LB; also Bosch 1990, 7.

34. Carrie Chapman Catt, "The History of the Origin of the IAW," Catt papers, box 7, NYPL.

35. "Constitution," IWSA 1904 and 1906 congress report. On the history of the Alliance, see Whittick 1979 and Bosch 1990.

36. In "The Council and Political Equality for Women," ICW 1904 congress report, vol. 2, Sewall attributed the Washington conference to the work of the ICW International Committee that she established. On negotiations before the Berlin congress, see Carrie Chapman Catt to May Wright Sewall, June 24, 1903, Sewall papers, I-MCPL; May Wright Sewall to Marie Stritt, December 28, 1903, January 13, 1904, and January 19, 1904, HLA, 81-323(2), LB; [Marie Stritt] to May Wright Sewall [German], February 8, 1904, HLA, 81-323(2), LB; May Wright Sewall to Marie Stritt, February 25, 1904, HLA, 81-323(4), LB.

37. May Wright Sewall to Marie Stritt, January 13, 1904, HLA, 81-323(2), LB.

38. Margery Corbett Ashby to Dr. Eder, n.d. [May 1952], draft never sent, IAW papers, FL.

39. Margery Corbett Ashby, "The History of the 'Alliance,'" *Jus Suffragii* 35, no. 1 (October–November 1940).

40. Alice Salomon, "Character is Destiny," 77, Salomon papers, LBI.

41. IWSA 1909 congress report.

42. "International Woman Suffrage Alliance," typescript, n.d., Dillon Collection, box 22, SL.

43. Carrie Chapman Catt to Aletta Jacobs, March 29, 1918, box 2; May 24, 1919, box 1, Jacobs papers, IIAV.

44. Millicent Garrett Fawcett, "The Future of the I.W.S.A.," *Jus Suffragii* 14, no. 3 (December 1919).

45. IWSA 1920 congress report, 49.

46. "Call to the 10th Congress of the IWSA," Paris, May 30–June 6, 1926, Jane Norman Smith papers, box 12, SL.

47. Chrystal Macmillan, "The Future of the IWSA," *Jus Suffragii* 14, no. 5 (February 1920).

48. Annie Furuhjelm to Aletta Jacobs, February 12, 1920, Jacobs papers, box 1, IIAV.

49. Helen Douglas Irvine to Editor, December 12, 1927, *Jus Suffragii* 22, no. 4 (January 1928).

50. C. Nina Boyle to Editor, December 15, 1927, *Jus Suffragii* 22, no. 4 (January 1928).

51. Marie Stritt to Mrs. Bompas, February 13, 1928, *Jus Suffragii* 22, no. 6 (March 1928). For other responses, see nos. 7–9.

52. C. Nina Boyle to Editor, March 15, 1928, *Jus Suffragii* 22, no. 7 (April 1928).

53. Margery Corbett Ashby to Josephine Schain, March 3, 1937, Schain papers, box 4, SSC.

54. Carrie Chapman Catt to Aletta Jacobs, March 3, 1918, postscript to March 1 letter, Jacobs papers, box 2, IIAV.

55. Carrie Chapman Catt to Margery Ashby, January 31, 1933, NAWSA papers, reel 11, LofC.

56. Ishbel Aberdeen and Temair to Presidents [German], October 16, 1931, HLA, 85-334(1), LB; "Postponement of the Athens Congress," *Jus Suffragii* 26, no. 2 (November 1931).

57. Carrie Chapman Catt to Rosa Manus, May 25, 1932, Catt papers, reel 4, LofC; Rosa Manus to Carrie Chapman Catt, October 5, 1932, Catt papers, reel 4, LofC.

58. Margery I. Corbett Ashby, "Courage and Vision," *Jus Suffragii* 27, no. 4 (January 1933).

59. Minutes, IAW board meeting, Brussels, April 3–5, 1939, IAW papers, FL; see also minutes, IAW board meeting, Paris, December 6–9, 1938, IAW papers, FL.

60. The first two phrases are from Lily van der Schalk-Schuster to Helen Archdale, July 21, 1930, ERI papers, box 331, FL; the third is from Doris Stevens's deposition, August 23, 1933, Stevens papers, carton 9, SL.

61. See, for example, Aletta Jacobs to Rosika Schwimmer [German], n.d. [postmarked November 1905], Schwimmer-Lloyd collection, box A-8, NYPL.

62. ICW 1920 congress report, 201.

63. Carrie Chapman Catt to Jane Addams, August 18, 1922, Addams papers, reel 14.

64. Mrs. Ogilvie Gordon, "The International Woman Suffrage Alliance Congress at Rome," ICW *Bulletin* 1, no. 11 (May 1923); "President's Report" and "Interim Report for business period between May 1922 and July 1923," ICW Executive Minute Book, ICW HQ; "Resolutions Adopted at the Rome Congress," *Jus Suffragii* 17, no. 9 (July 1923); Margery Corbett Ashby to Anna Lord Strauss, n.d. [ca. 1962], Corbett Ashby papers, box 483, FL; Margery Corbett Ashby interview, conducted by Brian Harrison, November 23, 1976, cassette #8, FL.

65. Margery Ashby to Carrie Chapman Catt, December 31, 1925, NAWSA papers, reel 11, LofC.

66. On the Hague congress and WILPF, see Bussey and Tims 1965; Costin 1982; Catherine Foster 1989; Vellacott 1987; Wiltsher 1985.

67. Ishbel Aberdeen to Gertrud Bäumer [German], April 1915, HLA, 84-330(8), LB.

68. Anna Backer, "Annual Report of the Corresponding Secretary," ICW *Annual Report*, 1920–22.

69. "President's Report," ICW 1920 congress report, 76.

70. "'Jus Suffragii' and the Crisis," *Jus Suffragii* 9, no. 1 (October 1, 1914); Aletta Jacobs to Rosika Schwimmer, October 18, 1914, and Anita Dobelli Zampetti to Schwimmer, October 19, 1914, Schwimmer-Lloyd collection, box A-46, NYPL; Jessie Innes to Aletta Jacobs, May 5, 1915, Jacobs papers, box 1, IIAV.

71. Carrie Chapman Catt to Millicent Garrett Fawcett, Adela Stanton Coit, and Chrystal Macmillan, September 24, 1914, NAWSA papers, box 11, LofC.

72. Aletta Jacobs to Miss Macmillan, Miss Sheepshanks, Rosika, and other suffrage friends, August 16, 1914, Schwimmer-Lloyd collection, box A-40, NYPL; also printed in *Jus Suffragii* 8, no. 13 (September 1, 1914).

73. Aletta Jacobs to Rosika Schwimmer, December 29, 1914, Schwimmer-Lloyd collection, box A-52, NYPL.

74. Carrie Chapman Catt to Aletta Jacobs, December 15, 1914, Jacobs collection, box 2, IIAV.

75. Anna Howard Shaw to Aletta Jacobs, January 4, 1915, Jacobs papers, box 2, IIAV.

76. Carrie Chapman Catt to Aletta Jacobs, November 13, 1914, Jacobs papers, box 2, IIAV; on the role of Heymann and Augspurg, see Gerhard 1990, 310.

77. Anita Augspurg to Rosika Schwimmer [German], February 23, 1915, Schwimmer-Lloyd collection, box A-54, NYPL.

78. "Call to the Women of all Nations," [February 1915], Schwimmer-Lloyd papers, box A-53, NYPL; 1915 Congress of Women [WILPF] report.

79. Anita Augspurg to Rosika Schwimmer [German], February 23, 1915, Schwimmer-Lloyd collection, box A-54, NYPL.

80. "Some Letters from Those Not Adhering to the Congress," 1915 Congress of Women [WILPF] report, 306–10; *Mitteilungen des Deutschen Frauenstimmrechtsbundes* 2, no. 3–4 (March–April 1915); C. L. Brunschwicg to [Rosika Schwimmer] [French], March 28, [1915], Schwimmer-Lloyd collection, box A-57, NYPL. On the German context, see Hering 1990.

81. Annie Furuhjelm to Aletta Jacobs, April 14, 1915, Schwimmer-Lloyd collection, box A-57, NYPL.

82. "Preamble and Resolutions Adopted," 1915 Congress of Women [WILPF] report, 35–41.

83. *Monthly News-Sheet No. 4*, October 1, 1915; "Propositions de la Section Française C.I.F.P.P.," November 7, 1915, WILPF papers, reel 9; Aletta Jacobs to Jane Addams, December 4, 1915, Addams papers, reel 9; Chrystal Macmillan to Jane Addams, January 14, 1916, Addams papers, reel 9; Emily Hobhouse to [Aletta Jacobs], Easter Day, 1916, Jacobs papers, box 2, IIAV.

84. On Schwimmer, see Rauther 1984 and Wenger 1990. Conflicting interpretations are offered by Wynner 1974 and Wiltsher 1985, who both lionize Schwimmer (Wynner served for many years as Schwimmer's secretary and is the literary executor of her estate), and by Kraft 1978, who sees Schwimmer as far more the villain of the story.

85. Rosika Schwimmer to Annie Furuhjelm, September 27, 1914, Schwimmer-Lloyd collection, box A-45, NYPL; Rosika Schwimmer to Mrs. John Jay White, February 16, 1915, Schwimmer-Lloyd collection, box A-54, NYPL.

86. Rosika Schwimmer to Lola Lloyd, August 20, 1915, Schwimmer-Lloyd collection, box A-61, NYPL.

87. See, for example, Rosika Schwimmer to Lola Lloyd, September 14, 1915, Schwimmer-Lloyd collection, box O-106, NYPL; telegram from Rosika Schwimmer to Jane Addams, January 26, 1916, Addams papers, reel 9; Carrie Chapman Catt to Rosika Schwimmer, January 6, 1926, Catt papers, reel 6, LofC; Aletta Jacobs to Lucy Anthony, July 21, 1928, Jacobs papers, IIAV; Rosa Manus to Carrie Chapman Catt, December 7, 1937, Catt papers, reel 4, LofC. On this conflict, see Bosch 1990, 295–96.

88. Draft of telegram from Rosika Schwimmer to Aletta Jacobs, November 23 or 24, 1914, Schwimmer-Lloyd collection, box A-64, NYPL; Aletta Jacobs to Jane Addams, December 4, 1915, Addams papers, reel 9; Chrystal Macmillan to Jane Addams, December 17, 1915, WILPF papers, reel 35.

89. Chrystal Macmillan to Jane Addams, December 17, 1915, WILPF papers, reel 35; Thora Daugaard to Rosika Schwimmer, December 30, 1915, Schwimmer-Lloyd collection, box A-69, NYPL; Chrystal Macmillan to Jane Addams, January 14, 1916, Addams papers, reel 9.

90. Rosika Schwimmer to Lola Lloyd, January 26, 1916, Schwimmer-Lloyd collection, box A-72, NYPL; Chrystal Macmillan to Rosika Schwimmer, January 15, 1916, Schwimmer-Lloyd collection, box A-71, NYPL; Aletta Jacobs, Chrystal Macmillan, Rosa Manus to Jane Addams, January 22, 1916, and Rosika Schwimmer to Jane Addams, January 26, 1916, Addams papers, reel 9; Jane Addams to Rosika Schwimmer, February 18, 1916, Schwimmer-Lloyd collection, box A-76, NYPL.

91. See Vellacott 1993b, which contrasts the Paris and Zurich conferences, pointing out that most of the women who went to Paris had opposed the convening of the Hague Congress in 1915.

92. Aletta Jacobs and Rosa Manus to Members of International Committee of Women for Permanent Peace, June 5, 1919, Fannie Fern Andrews papers, box 30, SL.

93. On Balch, see Randall 1964 and Alonso 1995.

94. Lida Gustava Heymann to Jane Addams [German], September 16, 1919, Addams papers, reel 12.

95. Aletta Jacobs to Emily Greene Balch, June 22, 1919, WILPF papers, reel 36.

96. "How Many Members Has the W.I.L.?" Pax 1, no. 6 (April 1926); reported also in Bussey and Tims 1965, 77. This is an estimate based on reports from some of the national sections, ranging from a high of 10,000 for Denmark to a low of 30 for Belgium, plus a guess for other sections.

97. News-Sheet 1 (May 26, 1919), WILPF papers, reel 18; "Circular Letter to Executive Committee," April 30, 1920, WILPF papers, reel 9.

98. "Questionnaire," n.d. [1928], WILPF papers, reel 2; minutes, WILFP VIth International Congress, Prague, [1929], WILPF papers, reel 19.

99. Minutes, WILPF International Executive Committee, Geneva, September 4–8, 1931, WILPF papers, reel 10.

100. Kathleen Courtney to Jane Addams, November 20, 1924, Addams papers, reel 16; M.T. [Myrrha Tunas], "National Sections: 1924," WILPF papers, reel 2.

101. Anita Augspurg, Lida Gustava Heymann, Magda Hoppstock, Auguste Kirchhoff, Frida Perlen to Andrée Jouve, February 28, 1925, Addams papers, reel 17.

102. "President's Report," ICW, "Combined Third and Fourth Annual Report of the Seventh Quinquennial Period," 1922–24, ICW papers, ICW HQ.

103. Bertha Lutz to Carrie Chapman Catt, May 14, 1936, NAWSA papers, reel 12, LofC.

104. Partial copy of resolutions, WILPF papers, reel 19; Emily Greene Balch to Jane Addams, September 30, [1919], Addams papers, reel 12.

105. Minutes, International Women's Congress, Zurich [German], May 12–17, 1919, WILPF papers, reel 17.

106. Emily Greene Balch to Jane Addams, November 7, 1922, Addams papers, reel 15.

107. Vida Goldstein to Emily Greene Balch, December 18, 1919, WILPF papers, reel 36.

108. M[ary] Sheepshanks to Members of Executive, January 16, 1929, Jane

Addams papers, reel 20; Mary Sheepshanks to Jane Addams, April 23, 1929, Addams papers, reel 20.

109. Edith Pye to Camille Drevet, June 27, 1932, and Camille Drevet to Executive Committee members [French], June 29, 1932, WILPF papers, reel 10.

110. Jane Addams to Kathleen Courtney, August 15, 1932, and Jane Addams to Edith Pye, August 17, 1932, Courtney papers, box 454, FL. On Addams and Kollontai, see R[aissa] Lomonossoff to Jane Addams, November 30, 1923; Jane Addams to [Raissa] Lomonossoff, January 9, 1924; and R[aissa] Lomonossoff to Jane Addams, February 15, 1924: all in Addams papers, reel 16.

111. Minutes, WILPF International Executive Committee, September 29, [1933], WILPF papers, reel 10.

112. E. Horscroft to International Executive Committee, January 27, 1933, WILPF papers, reel 10.

113. Minutes, WILPF 8th International Congress, Zurich, September 3–8, 1934, WILPF papers, reel 20; "French and German Section. Proposals for Revision of Constitution as a whole," [1934], Palthe-Broese van Groenau papers, IIAV.

114. Camille Drevet, "Geneva Letter," *Pax* 7, no. 10 (October 1932).

115. *Charts Representing the Soviet Organisations Working for Revolution in All Countries*, October 1928, WILPF papers, reel 9.

116. Report, "Conference tenue au Bureau de M. Aubert," December 3, 1928, WILPF papers, reel 2; Clara Ragaz to Mary Sheepshanks and Gabrielle Duchêne, December 10, 1928, WILPF papers, reel 9; partial letter to M. J. Le Fort [French], December 12 1928, WILPF papers, reel 2; Albert Picot to Madame [French], January 2, 1929, WILPF papers, reel 10; Emily Greene Balch to Jane Addams, May 18, 1932, and June 19, 1932, Addams papers, reel 23.

117. Albert Picot to Mesdames [French], March 25, 1929, WILPF papers, reel 10; Madeleine Z. Doty, "The Attack on the W.I.L.," *Pax* 4, no. 4 (February 1929).

118. Pauline Chaponnière-Chaix's remarks are reported in M. Sheepshanks to Lida Gustava Heymann and Gabrielle Duchêne, February 14, 1929, Dossiers Duchêne, F Rés. 207, BDIC; minutes, WILPF meeting at City Hotel, Zurich, February 25, 1929, WILPF papers, reel 10.

119. Clara Ragaz to Cor Ramondt and Gertrud Baer [German], October 17, 1936, WILPF papers, reel 3; minutes, WILPF International Executive Committee, Geneva, September 4–8, 1931, WILPF papers, reel 10; M. Aubert to Mme. Hilja Rupinen [French], January 13, 1933, WILPF papers, reel 2; minutes, WILPF International Executive Committee, Sept. 26, [1933], WILPF papers, reel 10; "The W.I.L. Falsely Charged with Communist Activity," *Pax* 8, no. 10 (December 1933); Clara Ragaz to Lotti Birch [German], June 24, 1936, WILPF papers, reel 3.

120. Kathleen Courtney to Jane Addams, June 22, 1932, Addams papers, reel 23; on the struggle with Swiss authorities, see [Edith Pye] to Mr. Henderson, June 16, 1933, WILPF papers, reel 2; Camille Drevet to Jane Addams, June 23, 1933, Addams papers, reel 24; Gabrielle Duchêne to [Gertrud Baer] [German], June 24, 1933, Dossiers Duchêne, F Rés. 351, BDIC; Gertrud Baer and Edith Pye to Friends, July 1, 1933, Addams papers, reel 24; Camille Drevet, "Secrétariat,

Rapport C. Drevet, May 1932–May 1934," WILPF papers, reel 21. Drevet left WILPF in 1936–37 and devoted her considerable energies to the Ligue internationale des combattants de la paix; see Drefus 1986.

121. Letter of the Chairmen to the Sections, draft, n.d. [September 1933], WILPF papers, reel 10.

122. Draft, Gertrud Baer to Frau Karavelova and Frau Kerteva [German], n.d. [February 1937], WILPF papers, reel 3.

123. See, for example, Käte Marcus, "Campaign against Hitler Party," *Jus Suffragii* 25, no. 6 (March 1931); Camille Drevet to Friends, March 6, 1933, WILPF papers, reel 10; Carrie Chapman Catt to Rosa Manus, April 7, 1933, Catt papers, reel 4, LofC.

124. Ishbel Aberdeen to Agnes von Zahn-Harnack [German], May 12, 1933 and June 2, 1933, HLA, 85-334(2), LB; minutes, ICW Executive Committee, Stockholm, June 30, 1933, and minutes, ICW Board of Officers, Paris, May 13, 1936, ICW Minute Book, ICW HQ.

125. Dorothee von Velsen to Katherine Bompas, June 7, 1933, Catt papers, reel 4, LC; D.v.V., *Jus Suffragii* 28, no. 2 (November 1933).

126. On Heymann and Augspurg, see Heymann 1972.

127. Lola Hanauskova to Gertrud Baer [German], August 24, 1933, WILPF papers, reel 2; [Yella Hertzka and Olga Misar?] to Emily Greene Balch [German], May 1934, WILPF papers, reel 21; Clara Ragaz to Lotti Birch [German], November 6, 1936, WILPF papers, reel 3.

128. Draft of letter from Gertrud Baer to Frau Karavelova and Frau Kerteva [German], n.d. [February 1937], WILPF papers, reel 3; Gertrud Baer to Cor Ramondt and Clara Ragaz [German], February 22, 1937, WILPF papers, reel 3.

129. On different kinds of organizations and various schemes of classification, see C. Miller 1992 and Boy 1936.

130. See C. Miller 1992 and Skjelsbaek 1971.

131. Alice Salomon, "Character is Destiny," 35, Salomon papers, LBI; Ottilie Baader to Sehr geehrte Frau [German], January 16, 1904, HLA, 81-323(2), LB.

132. "Erste Internationale Konferenz sozialistischer Frauen," August 17, 1907, Second International papers, no. 486, IISG. On the Socialist Women's International, see Evans 1977 and DuBois 1991.

133. Martina Kramers to May Wright Sewall, September 16, 1901, Sewall papers, I-MCPL.

134. Martina Kramers to Carrie Chapman Catt, June 2, 1913, Schwimmer-Lloyd collection, box A-33, NYPL. On Kramers's relationship with her lover, Bobbie, and the consequences within the Alliance, see Bosch 1990.

135. Martina Kramers to Rosika Schwimmer, August 31, 1911, Schwimmer-Lloyd collection, box A-26, NYPL.

136. Martina Kramers to Rosika Schwimmer, August 31, 1911, Schwimmer-Lloyd collection, box A-26, NYPL; Anna Lindemann to Rosika Schwimmer, January 27, 1913, Schwimmer-Lloyd collection, box A-32, NYPL.

137. See the greetings, read in German by Hélène Ankersmit of the Dutch Union of Socialist Women's Clubs, in "Report of Business Session," 1915 Congress of Women [WILPF] report, 118–19.

138. "Manifesto Issued by the International Conference of Anti-War Socialists, at Zimmerwald, September 1915," appendix, *News-Sheet* 5 (November 1, 1915).

139. Minutes, WILPF Executive Committee, May 1919, WILPF papers, reel 9.

140. Cor Ramondt-Hirschmann to Vice Presidents, July 20, 1934, WILPF papers, reel 20.

141. Gabrielle Duchêne, "Rapport," RUP papers, no. 69, IISG.

142. Emily Greene Balch, "pour le groupe des déléguées pacifistes," [1934], WILPF papers, reel 20.

143. "Report of Hon. International Secretary" [Balch], Appendix A. [1934], WILPF papers, reel 21.

144. See Hermon 1993.

145. "Some Highlights of 1935," PDC papers, SCPC; minutes, Liaison Committee, May 15, 1936, LC papers, no. 2, IISG.

146. "Appel aux Femmes," [1936], and "Ce que les Femmes Peuvent Faire," [1936], xeroxes from Duchêne papers, in RUP papers, no. 24, IISG.

147. Section Féminine (Margery Corbett Ashby, Germaine Malaterre-Sellier, Mary Dingman, Gabrielle Duchêne, Clara Ragaz) to Mme. La Présidents, n.d. [1936], xerox from Duchêne papers, in RUP papers, no. 24, IISG; Clara Ragaz to Chairmen [German], July 7, 1936, WILPF papers, reel 3; G. Duchêne, "Rassemblement Universel pour la Paix," and minutes, Section Féminine du R.U.P. [French], July 22, 1936, xeroxes from Duchêne papers, in RUP papers, no. 24, IISG.

148. Mary Dingman to Dame Adelaide Livingstone, July 27, 1936, ICW papers, box 3, LofC.

149. Rosa Manus to Mary Dingman, July 28, 1936, ICW papers, box 4, LofC.

150. Helen Archdale to Flora Drummond, July 8, 1931, ERI papers, box 331, FL; "An International Feminist Centre in Geneva," *Jus Suffragii* 27, nos. 11–12 (August–September 1933); Mary Dingman to Laura Dreyfus-Barney, February 25, 1936, ICW papers, box 4, LofC.

151. Elizabeth Abbott to Emily Greene Balch, October 13, 1919, WILPF papers, reel 35; Jane Addams to Emily Greene Balch, [ca. November 24, 1920], Addams papers, reel 13; IWSA 1923 congress report, 49; Emilie Gourd, "Resume of Report of the Chairman of the Co-operation Sub-Committee," IAWSEC, 1935, Josephine Schain papers, box 8, SSC.

152. Emily Greene Balch to Jane Addams, January 8, 1921, Addams papers, reel 13.

153. Marchioness of Aberdeen and Temair, "International Council of Women," *Jus Suffragii* 16, no. 9 (June 1922).

154. The ICW, Alliance, WILPF, and World Young Women's Christian Association sent delegates. Minutes, JSC, July 7, 1925, LC papers, no. 1, IISG.

155. Minutes, JSC, March 18, 1927, LC papers, no. 1, IISG.

156. Minutes, JSC, April 27, 1926; March 18, 1927; May 9, 1927; and June 4, 1927: LC papers, no. 1, IISG.

157. Minutes, Emergency Meeting of JSC, November 29, 1927; minutes, Special Urgency Meeting, JSC, December 16, 1927; and "Report of the Joint Standing Committee," n.d. [1927?]: LC papers, no. 1, IISG. See C. Miller 1991.

158. Minutes, JSC, February 7, 1928, LC papers, no. 1, IISG.

159. "Copy of report to be presented by Miss Zimmern to the Liaison Committee of WIO on March 17, 1931," and Margery Corbett Ashby to International Organisations, April 14, 1931, both in ICW papers, box 12, NCW-GB; Lily van der Schalk to Helen Archdale, April 11, 1931, ERI papers, box 331, FL.

160. Alice Paul to Anna Godyevatz, January 7, 1932; Katherine Bompas to Alice Paul, December 23, 1931; Marta Vergara to Alice Paul [French], January 2, 1932; Hélène Granitsch to Alice Paul [French], January 13, 1932; and Louise van Eeghen to Alice Paul, January 13, 1932: all in Jane Norman Smith papers, box 12, SL. On Alice Paul in the U.S. movement, see Lunardini 1986; Cott 1987; Rupp and Taylor 1987. Becker 1981 includes a chapter on the Woman's Party in the international arena.

161. In fact, the Liaison Committee and the Joint Standing Committee merged in 1936, taking on the name of the former. See "Communique on the Amalgamation of the Joint Standing and Liaison Committees of Women's International Organisations," n.d. [1936?], Balch papers, reel 10.

162. Minutes, Temporary LC, November 4, 1930; [Katherine Bompas] to Kathleen Courtney, November 28, 1930; minutes, Temporary LC, December 2, 1930; and Lady Aberdeen to Katherine Bompas, December 15, 1930: all in LC papers, no. 1, IISG.

163. Lady Aberdeen to May Ogilvie Gordon, April 28, 1932, ICW papers, box 12, NCW-GB HQ.

164. M.M. Ogilvie Gordon to Lady Aberdeen, February 5, 1932, March 8, 1932, and June 10, 1932, ICW papers, box 12, NCW-GB HQ; "Memorandum on the Function and Organisation of the LC of WIO," n.d. [1932], and minutes, LC, June 9, 1932, both in LC papers, no. 1, IISG; minutes, LC, September 12, 1934, and May 15, 1936, LC papers, no. 2, IISG.

165. CRH [Cor Ramondt-Hirschmann] to Jane Addams, October 8, 1931, WILPF papers, reel 20.

166. Mary Dingman to May Ogilvie Gordon, January 14, 1932, ICW papers, box 4, LofC; minutes, LC, January 26, 1932, LC papers, no. 1, IISG.

167. Minutes, PDC, September 14, 1935, PDC papers, SCPC.

168. Gertrud Baer to Clara Ragaz and K. E. Innes, May 25, 1938, WILPF papers, reel 3.

169. Minutes, PDC, September 5, 1932 [sic, for 1931], January 21, 1932, and Rosa Manus, "Letter to Member Organisations re petitions," November 25, 1931, both in PDC papers, SCPC; "Official Record of the Declarations and Petitions presented by the Disarmament Committee . . . ," [1932], Kathleen Courtney papers, box 454, FL.

170. Mary Dingman to Absent Colleagues, October 1, 1932, ICW papers, box 4, LofC; minutes, PDC, June 21, 1932, and September 22, 1932, ICW papers, box 2, LofC.

171. Kathleen Courtney et al. to Laura Dreyfus-Barney, June 17, 1935, ICW

papers, box 3, LofC; minutes, PDC, September 14, 1935, PDC papers, SCPC; "Women for World Peace," ICW *Bulletin* 14, no. 3 (November 1935).

172. PDC papers, SCPC.

173. "Plan for Bringing Economic Forces into Co-operation with the Women's Peace Movement," [1935]; "The Peace-Roll of Industry," [1937], PDC papers, SCPC.

174. Clara Ragaz to K. E. Innes and Gertrud Baer [German], May 22, 1938, WILPF papers, reel 3.

175. Margery Corbett Ashby to Carrie Chapman Catt, July 25, 1923, NAWSA papers, reel 10, SL; Carrie Chapman Catt to Maud N. Parker, May 21, 1945, Catt papers, box 2, NYPL.

176. Martina [Kramers] to Rosika Schwimmer, September 10, 1917, Schwimmer-Lloyd collection, box A-92, NYPL.

177. C. Ramondt-Hirschmann to Friends, November 6, 1935, WILPF papers, reel 2.

178. Rosa Manus to Carrie Chapman Catt, June 8, 1939; and Carrie Chapman Catt to Rosa Manus, March 9, 1939; both in Catt papers, reel 4, LofC; Bertha Lutz to Carrie Chapman Catt, January 14, 1939, NAWSA papers, reel 12, LofC.

179. Emily Greene Balch to Jane Addams, September 30, 1919, WILPF papers, reel 35.

180. P. Chaponnière-Chaix to Emily Greene Balch, June 28, 1921, WILPF papers, reel 18.

181. Renée Girod to Alice Paul, March 24, 1939, WWP papers, reel 173.

182. Clara Ragaz to K. E. Innes and Gertrud Baer [German], January 8, 1939, WILPF papers, reel 4.

183. Cor Ramondt-Hirschmann to Jane Addams, May 22, 1930, Addams papers, reel 21.

184. Margery Corbett Ashby interview, conducted by Brian Harrison, September 21, 1976, cassette #6, FL.

185. Emily Greene Balch to Mrs. Villard, April 1, 1920, Jane Addams papers, reel 13.

186. Doris Stevens to Helen Archdale, July 14, 1934, Stevens papers, carton 4, SL.

187. Alice Paul to Lola Maverick Lloyd, October 6, 1939, WWP papers, reel 173.

188. Marthe Boël, "To the Members of the I.C.W. Executive Committee," ICW *Bulletin* 18, no. 1 (October 1939).

189. Marthe Boël to Friends and Presidents of National Councils, May 10, 1940, ICW papers, box 10, NCW-GB HQ; minutes, ICW Office [French], February 7, 1940, ICW papers, box 3, NCW-GB HQ.

190. Renée Girod, "Dear Readers and Friends of the I.C.W.," ICW *Bulletin* 21, no. 1 (September 1942); Dorothy M. Arnold to Kathleen Courtney, November 8, 1940, Courtney papers, box 456, FL.

191. Marthe Boël to Members of Executive Committee, December 12, 1945, ICW papers, box 10, NCW-GB HQ.

192. M. I. Corbett Ashby, "War," *Jus Suffragii* 34, no. 1 (October 1939).

193. Margery Corbett Ashby to Carrie Chapman Catt, June 6, 1940; Katherine Bompas to Carrie Chapman Catt, July 11, 1940; and Carrie Chapman Catt to Margery Corbett Ashby and Katherine Bompas, June 30, 1943: all in Catt papers, box 3, NYPL; IAW 1946 congress report, 42–48.

194. Margery Corbett Ashby to Members of the Board and Presidents of Auxiliaries, October 15, 1940, Catt papers, box 3, NYPL.

195. Carrie Chapman Catt to Katherine Bompas, February 25, 1942; Katherine Bompas to Carrie Chapman Catt, November 4, 1942; and Carrie Chapman Catt to Margery Corbett Ashby and International Board, April 9, 1945: all in NAWSA papers, reel 11, LofC; Lena Madesin Phillips to Renée Girod, January 19, 1943, Phillips papers, carton 5, SL.

196. On Plamínková and Manus, see Bosch 1990.

197. Minutes, IAWSEC International Executive Committee, Geneva, October 1945, Corbett Ashby papers, box 483, FL; minutes, IAWSEC Board Meeting, London, March 4–7, 1946, IAW papers, FL; IAW 1946 congress report.

198. Minutes, WILPF International Executive Committee, March 24, [1934], WILPF papers, reel 10; minutes, WILPF International Emergency Executive Committee Meeting, Paris, April 22–26, 1939, WILPF papers, reel 33.

199. Minutes, WILPF International Executive Committee, Geneva, April 11–14, 1933, WILPF papers, reel 10. Rosika Schwimmer worked to help get affidavits to allow European suffragists and pacifists to enter the United States before the war, and the International Federation of Business and Professional Women and the World Woman's Party also worked along these lines.

200. Emily Greene Balch to International Executive Meeting, November 21, 1939, WILPF papers, reel 4.

201. Cor Ramondt-Hirschmann to Friends, September 8, 1939, WILPF papers, reel 4; Gertrud Baer, "A Christmas Letter to International Members and Sections," November 25, 1940, WILPF papers, reel 11.

202. E Gd. [Emilie Gourd], "Lettre de Genève," *Jus Suffragii* 34, no. 2 (November 1939).

203. Carrie Chapman Catt to Rosika Schwimmer, October 15, 1946, Catt papers, reel 6, LofC.

204. "Plan for an International Assembly of Women," IAssW papers, SL. That the concern was to keep out women who belonged to the Communist Party was clearly stated in minutes, 6th meeting of Steering Committee, March 27, 1946, IAssW papers, SL.

205. Margery Corbett Ashby to Brian Ashby, October 13, 1946, October 16, 1946, Corbett Ashby papers, box 477, FL.

206. Rosika Schwimmer to Carrie Chapman Catt, October 22, 1946, November 4, 1946, NAWSA papers, reel 18, LofC.

207. Minutes, IAWSEC International Committee, Geneva, October 1945, IAW papers, FL.

208. Katherine Bompas to Carrie Chapman Catt, November 8, 1945, Catt papers, box 3, NYPL. Catt's complaint is in Carrie Chapman Catt to Rosika Schwimmer, October 15, 1946, Catt papers, reel 6, LofC.

209. M. Corbett Ashby, "International Congress of Women, Paris 1945," *Jus Suffragii* 40, no. 4 (January 1946).

210. "Memorandum on Closer Cooperation Between International Council of Women & International Alliance of women," n.d., IAW papers, FL; see also Bussey and Tims 1965.

211. See, for example, Jayawardena 1986; Basu and Ray 1990; Hahner 1990; Johnson-Odim 1991; Stoner 1991; Badran 1995.

212. The term "neo-Europes" comes from Crosby 1987.

Chapter 3

1. Statement by Mary Dingman, *Our Common Cause* 1933.

2. "The Constitution and Standing Orders of the ICW," ICW papers, box 1, SSC.

3. [Martina Kramers], "Announcements," *Jus Suffragii* 5, no. 6 (February 15, 1911); Emily Hobhouse, "Foreword," 1915 Congress of Women [WILPF] report, ix.

4. Matilda Gage to My dear Son, March 27, 1888, Gage papers, box 2, SL.

5. Aberdeen 1909, x.

6. Rosa Aberson to Madeleine Z. Doty [French], May 31, 1926, WILPF papers, reel 19.

7. Carrie Chapman Catt to Margery Corbett Ashby, December 19, 1925, NAWSA papers, reel 10, LofC; Bertha Lutz to Carrie Chapman Catt, May 6, 1936, NAWSA papers, reel 12, LofC.

8. Minutes, WILPF International Congress, Grenoble, May 15–19, 1932, WILPF papers, reel 20.

9. Minutes, WILPF 8th International Congress, Zurich, September 3–8, 1934, WILPF papers, reel 20.

10. Mme. Avril de Sainte-Croix to Madame la Présidente [French], November 8, 1905, Dossier Avril de Sainte-Croix, BMD.

11. Catherine Marshall to Gabrielle Duchêne, January 28, [1926], Dossiers Duchêne, F Rés. 206, BDIC.

12. Margery Corbett Ashby interview, conducted by Brian Harrison, September 21, 1976, cassette #4, FL.

13. Cor Ramondt-Hirschmann to Jane Addams, June 15, 1924, Addams papers, reel 16.

14. Emily Greene Balch to Elisabeth Waern-Bugge, December 12, 1934, WILPF papers, reel 2.

15. "Treasurer's Report" and "Minutes of Council Meeting," ICW 1899 congress report, vol. 1, 91, 162–64; Lady Aberdeen to Presidents of National Councils of Women, August 1897, ICW papers, box 3, NCW-GB HQ.

16. "The Meeting of the I.C.W. Executive Committee in Paris," [June 15–18, 1906], ICW *Annual Report*, 1905–06; "Report of the Executive Committee," July 5, 1898, ICW Executive Minute Book, ICW HQ.

17. "Resolutions Passed at the Quinquennial Meeting of the ICW," September 8–18, ICW *Annual Report*, 1920–22.

18. Minutes, WILPF Chairmen's Meeting at Zurich, March 24, 1936, reel 33, WILPF papers; Mabel L. Sippy to Rosika Schwimmer, March 14, 1915, box A-55, Schwimmer-Lloyd collection, NYPL.

19. Lida Gustava Heymann to Vilma Glücklich [German], June 4, 1925, reel 2, WILPF papers.

20. Clara Guthrie d'Arcis, "Treasurer's Report," PDC, n.d., Corbett Ashby papers, box 484, FL.

21. See, for example, Rosika Schwimmer to Lola Lloyd, August 4, 1915, Schwimmer-Lloyd collection, box A-60, NYPL; Rosika Schwimmer to Mien Palthe, December 3, 1917, Schwimmer-Lloyd collection, box A-95, NYPL.

22. Rosa Manus to Josephine Schain, January 2, 1935, Schain papers, box 6, SSC.

23. "Announcements," *Jus Suffragii* 7, no. 5 (January 15, 1913).

24. By considering the obstacles to the participation of Jewish and Muslim women under the rubric "religion," I do not mean to downplay either the impact of racial anti-Semitism on Jewish women under fascism or the orientalism that pervaded the dealings of Euro-American women with Muslim women. Yet I am reluctant to use the terms "race" or "ethnicity" in this context, especially since religion and ethnicity often constituted distinct and significant identities among internationally organized women (e.g., in the case of Christian Arabs or Tunisian Jews). Although women of other religious traditions belonged to the international women's organizations, the sources are silent about their experiences.

25. May Wright Sewall to Marie Stritt, April 15, 1900, HLA, 83-329(1), LB.

26. May Wright Sewall to Marie Stritt, March 19, 1904, HLA, 83-329(5), LB.

27. Stenographic report of 2nd Congress, October 24, 1921, IFWW papers, folder 6, SL; Ishbel Aberdeen and Temair, "A New Year's Message from the I.C.W. President," ICW *Bulletin* 3, nos. 5–6 (January–February 1925).

28. On the "Catechism," see Maria M. Gordon to Marie Stritt, September 29, 1905, and [Marie Stritt] to Maria Gordon [German], October 5, 1905, HLA, 83-329(7), LB.

29. *Pax* 1, no. 3 (January 1926); Ishbel Aberdeen and Temair, "President's Letter," ICW *Bulletin* 10, no. 4 (December 1931).

30. "Toronto Arrangements for the Quinquennial Meetings of the ICW and for the Congress Connected Therewith," ICW 1909 congress report, vol. 1.

31. Minutes, ICW Executive Committee, London, July 8–9, 1897, ICW Executive Minute Book, ICW HQ; Anna Simson to May Wright Sewall [German], May 19, 1898, HLA, 83-328(4), LB; "Report of the Executive Committee," July 5, 1898, ICW Executive Minute Book, ICW HQ; May Wright Sewall, "Memorandum Sent to Presidents of National Councils of Women," August 22, 1898, ICW HQ; "Report of Meeting," ICW Executive Committee, London, March 23, 1899, ICW HQ; minutes, ICW Executive Committee, July 8, 1899, ICW HQ.

32. See Jacobs 1996 on Aletta Jacobs's Jewish identity. On anti-Semitism in the Alliance, see Bosch 1990, 219–24. For an analysis of how anti-Semitism functioned in the U.S. women's movement, see Lerner 1986.

33. Martina Kramers to Rosika Schwimmer [German], August 31, 1907, Schwimmer-Lloyd collection, box A-13, NYPL.

34. Emily Greene Balch to Jane Addams, January 8, 1921, Addams papers, reel 13; Emily Greene Balch to Gabrielle Duchêne [French], September 2, 1920, Dossiers Duchêne, F Rés. 296, BDIC.

35. Alice Salomon, "Character is Destiny," 192–93, Salomon papers, LBI.

36. Mia Boissevain, typescript tribute to Rosa Manus, Manus papers, IIAV.

37. Emily Greene Balch to Jane Addams, n.d. [October 1930], Addams papers, reel 21. On Baer, see Pinkus 1978.

38. Edith Pye to Camille Drevet, July 13, 1933, WILPF papers, reel 2. This is the only reference to this incident I have found.

39. Margery Corbett Ashby to Josephine Schain, March 3, 1937, and Dorothy Heneker to Josephine Schain, March 27, 1937, Schain papers, box 4, SSC; Rosa Manus to Carrie Chapman Catt, April 1, 1937, Catt papers, reel 4, LofC.

40. Alice Salomon, "Character is Destiny," 303, Salomon papers, LBI.

41. Carrie Chapman Catt to Rosa Manus, May 29, 1939, Catt papers, reel 4, LofC.

42. Mia Boissevanin, typescript tribute to Rosa Manus, n.d., Manus papers, IIAV; discussion of concentration camps in Mary Dingman to Family and Friends, November 4, 1939, Dingman papers, box 1, SL; Dorothy M. Arnold to Kathleen Courtney, November 8, 1940, Courtney papers, box 456, FL; Rosika Schwimmer to Alice Park, March 30, 1944, Park papers, box 1, HI.

43. On Sha'rawi, known in Alliance records as "Hoda Charoui," see Shaarawi 1987 and Badran 1995.

44. The classic text on orientalism is Said 1978.

45. Carrie Chapman Catt, "The Holy Land" [part 2], *Jus Suffragii* 6, no. 6 (February 15, 1912).

46. Rosa Welt Straus and V. M. Neufam to Carrie Chapman Catt, April 26, 1920, *Jus Suffragii* 14, no. 9 (July 1920).

47. "A Glimpse of Egypt and a Journey through Palestine," *Jus Suffragii* 15, no. 9 (June 1921).

48. See Lucy Mair, "The Conflict in Palestine," *Jus Suffragii* 24, no. 5 (February 1930).

49. Elisabeth Waern-Bugge, "Report on Palestine," [April 1931], WILPF papers, reel 10; Emily Greene Balch to Jane Addams, [January-February 1931], Addams papers, reel 22; Elisabeth Waern-Bugge, "Rapprochment in Palestine," *Pax* 6, no. 3 (February 1931).

50. M. Corbett Ashby to Josephine Schain, February 5, 1935, Schain papers, box 4, SSC; G. Mallaterre-Sellier and C. Bakker van Bosse, "Rapport de notre voyage en Proche-Orient," 1935, Schain papers, box 4, SSC; M. I. Corbett Ashby, "An International Pilgramage," *Jus Suffragii* 29, no. 6 (March 1935).

51. Minutes, WILPF Executive Committee, September 12, 1922, WILPF papers, reel 9; minutes, Liaison Committee, January 13, 1942, LC papers, no. 3, IISG.

52. Margery Corbett Ashby to Carrie Chapman Catt, June 9, 1926, NAWSA papers, reel 11, LofC.

53. Minutes, Disarmament Committee, October 31, 1933, ICW papers, box 2, LofC; "Palestine," *Jus Suffragii* 33, no. 2 (November 1938).

54. Minutes [French], IAWSEC Executive Committee, Copenhagen, July 5, 1939, IAW papers, FL.

55. Rosa Manus to Carrie Chapman Catt, July 31, 1939, Catt papers, reel 4, LofC; on this incident, see Bosch 1990, 221–22, 251; Whittick 1979, 144. Margot Badran has emphasized that anti-Zionism did not translate into anti-Semitism for Sha'rawi and that Saiza Nabarawi always fondly recalled Rosa Manus, whose portrait still hung in the Huda Sha'rawi Association library in Cairo after the 1967 war. Personal communication, December 29, 1995.

56. Alice Salomon, "Character is Destiny," 43, Salomon papers, LBI.

57. "Abridged Minutes of the Meetings of the IWSA, August 1906," IWSA 1904 and 1906 congress report.

58. Margery Corbett Ashby to Mother, n.d., and Margery Corbett Ashby to Father, May 15, 1923, Corbett Ashby papers, box 477, FL.

59. Aletta Jacobs to Rosika Schwimmer [German], January 1, 1906, Schwimmer-Lloyd collection, box A-8, NYPL. On generational issues in the Alliance, see Bosch 1990, 179–83.

60. See, for example, Carrie Chapman Catt to Rosika Schwimmer, March 30, 1906, Schwimmer-Lloyd collection, box A-9, NYPL; Marie Stritt to Rosika Schwimmer [German], November 6, 1911, Schwimmer-Lloyd collection, box A-27, NYPL; Anna Howard Shaw to Aletta Jacobs, March 23, 1909, Jacobs papers, IIAV; Aletta Jacobs to Carrie Chapman Catt, May 28, 1929, Catt papers, reel 4, LofC.

61. Carrie Chapman Catt to Rosa Manus, September 18, 1931, Catt papers, reel 4, LofC.

62. Madeleine Doty to Jane Addams, January 6, 1926, Addams papers, reel 17.

63. Shoshana Zelmans, "An Appeal of a Young Leader," Jus Suffragii 31, no. 1 (October 1936).

64. Anna Howard Shaw to Aletta Jacobs, April 1, 1910, Jacobs papers, IIAV.

65. Carrie Chapman Catt to Aletta Jacobs, May 24, 1919, Jacobs papers, IIAV.

66. Andrée Jouve, "The Summer-School at Podebrady," WILPF Bulletin, July and October 1923.

67. Julie Bernocco Fava-Paravis [French], in Aberdeen 1909, 44–48.

68. Germaine Malaterre-Sellier to Margery Corbett Ashby [French], October 19, 1938, Corbett Ashby papers, box 483, FL.

69. On Sha'rawi's giving, see interview with Margery Corbett Ashby, conducted by Brian Harrison, November 23, 1976, cassette #8, Corbett Ashby papers, FL.

70. "Digest of the Executive Committee Meeting," Geneva, September 9–13, 1927, WILPF papers, reel 9; Cor Ramondt-Hirschmann to Executive Committee [French], August 1930, WILPF papers, reel 10.

71. Frances M. Sterling to Carrie Chapman Catt, October 1, 1928, NAWSA papers, reel 11, LofC.

72. "Editorial Notes," Jus Suffragii 7, no. 10 (July 15, 1913).

73. Katherine Karaveloff quoted in [Mary Sheepshanks] to Executive Member, November 5, 1927, WILPF papers, reel 2.

74. [Ishbel Aberdeen], "President's Memorandum," 1914, ICW papers, box 1, SSC; I.A.&T. [Ishbel Aberdeen and Temair], "President's Notes," ICW *Bulletin*, 6, no. 10 (June 1928).

75. Alice Masaryk, quoted in Emily Greene Balch to Jane Addams, April 12, 1921, Addams papers, reel 13; minutes, [WILPF] Third International Congress of Women, Vienna, July 10–16, 1921, WILPF papers, reel 18.

76. May Wright Sewall, "Introduction to volume I," ICW 1904 congress report, vol. 1; minutes, June 12, 1913, IWSA 1913 congress report, 57–58.

77. Martina Kramers to Rosika Schwimmer [German], May 31, 1907, Schwimmer-Lloyd collection, box A-12, NYPL.

78. Minutes, ICW Executive Committee, Copenhagen, May 27, 1924, ICW HQ; ICW, *President's Memorandum*, 1929, 7; "Eighth Quinquennial Meeting of the International Council of Women," ICW *Bulletin* 8, no. 10 (June 1930).

79. Amanda Labarca Hubertson to Mrs. Glen Levin Swiggett, English translation, April 9, 1918, PAIWC papers, box 1, LofC.

80. [Ishbel Aberdeen], "President's Memorandum," 1914, ICW papers, box 1, SSC; "Report of Business Sessions," 1915 Congress of Women [WILPF] report, 74.

81. "Business Session of the ICW," June 22, 1909, ICW 1909 congress report, vol. 1.

82. Benedict Anderson 1991 and Hollinger 1993 both make the point that Esperanto is an international language only in a limited sense.

83. "The Paper," *Jus Suffragii* 27, no. 1 (October 1932).

84. Chiyin Chen to Anne Zueblin [German], May 14, 1932, WILPF papers, reel 20.

85. Anne Furuhjelm to Aletta Jacobs, February 12, 1920, Jacobs papers, IIAV.

86. Alice Salomon, "Character is Destiny," 106–7, Salomon papers, LBI; Marie Popelin, "Impressions et Souvenirs du Canada," in Aberdeen 1909, 76–81; ICW, "Combined Third and Fourth Annual Report of the Seventh Quinquennial Period," 1922–24, ICW HQ; minutes, ICW Executive Committee, Copenhagen, May 24, [1924], ICW HQ.

87. Annie Furuhjelm to Aletta Jacobs, February 12, 1920, Jacobs papers, IIAV; minutes, WILPF International Executive Committee, Geneva, September 10–14, 1936, and Basle, January 5–9, 1938, WILPF papers, reel 11; Gertrud Baer to Lola Hanouskova [German], February 8, 1937, WILPF papers, reel 21.

88. Marguerite Gobat to Gabrielle Duchêne [French], March 7, 1927, Dossiers Duchêne, F Rés. 206, BDIC.

89. Gertrud Baer, "A Christmas Letter to International Members and Sections," November 25, 1940, WILPF papers, reel 11.

90. "Business Session of the ICW," June 22, 1909, ICW 1909 congress report, vol. 1.

91. Terrell 1968, 204, 331–32. Terrell, who had studied in Europe, created a sensation at the 1904 ICW meeting in Berlin when she responded to complaints about delegates speaking in English during long, hot night meetings by translating and delivering her own speech in German.

92. Mary Church Terrell to Jane Addams, March 18, 1921; Jane Addams to Mary Church Terrell, March 29, 1921; Emily Greene Balch to [Mary White]

Ovington, March 16, 1921: all in Addams papers, reel 13; Emily Greene Balch to President of Permanent Advisory Commission for Military, Naval, and Air Questions, League of Nations, December 14, 1920, WILPF papers, reel 1; Terrell 1968, 360–67. See the discussion in Alonso 1993, 102; Carrie Foster 1995, 159–60. In response to such critiques, the League's position shifted to a protest against the injustice of conscripting "native troops" for use as cannon fodder.

93. See Neverdon-Morton 1989, 198.

94. Quoted in "200 Negro Singers Refuse to Appear at Music Festival," *Washington Post*, May 6, 1925; see also "Social Upsets Stir Women's Council," *New York Times*, May 7, 1925: both in Andrews papers, box 20, SL.

95. Minutes, VIth International Congress, Prague, [1929], WILPF papers, reel 19; Mabelle Byrd, speech at 1929 congress, August 26, 1929, WILPF papers, reel 19. The International Council of Women of the Darker Races, established by U.S. members of the National Association of Colored Women, remained largely American in membership, although its conventions in the 1920s attracted delegates from Africa, the Caribbean, and the Pacific region. See Barnett 1978; Neverdon-Morton 1989, 198–201.

96. Zonana 1993 coined the term "feminist Orientalism," with reference to Said 1978. Melman 1992 and Lewis 1996 extended Said's analysis by considering women's contributions to the construction of a complex and multivocal orientalist vision. Zonana focuses on feminist orientalism as one strand in this discourse. Other scholars use the term "imperial feminism" to describe the centrality of dominant assumptions about colonized and dependent countries to the Western feminist project. See Amos and Pramar 1984; Mohanty 1984; Tyrrell 1991b; Burton 1991, 1994, 1995; Ramusack 1990; Donaldson 1992; Sinha 1994; Badran 1995; Weber 1996. I use "feminist orientalism" here to refer not just to attitudes toward "Eastern" women but to all women outside the Euro-American arena.

97. In the terms of Immanuel Wallerstein's world system, the core is the dominant region of the world system, the semiperipheries the intermediate zones, and the peripheries the economically and/or politically subordinated regions. See Wallerstein 1974.

98. Countess van Heerdt-Quarles to Carrie Chapman Catt, *Jus Suffragii* 15, no. 4 (January 1921); "Rhodesia," *Jus Suffragii* 20, no. 4 (January 1926); cartoon no. 15, *Jus Suffragii* 25, no. 9 (June 1931).

99. Minutes, Liaison Committee, July 25, 1939, LC papers, no. 2, IISG; "Congo," *Jus Suffragii* 18, no. 11 (August 1924); Nour Hamada, "The Oriental Women's Congress in Damascus," *Jus Suffragii* 24, no. 12 (September 1930); Deutsch 1929; Carrie Chapman Catt to Lady Aberdeen, June 27, 1927, NAWSA papers, reel 12, LofC.

100. Deutsch 1929, 18. On the Catt-Jacobs world tour, see Bosch 1990, 95–98.

101. "Editorial Notes," *Jus Suffragii* 7, no. 10 (July 15, 1913).

102. Carrie Chapman Catt, "Burmah," *Jus Suffragii* 6, no. 10 (June 15, 1912); 6, no. 11 (July 15, 1912). Catt noted the economic and political rights of women in Sumatra and Java as well, a phenomenon that she attributed to the vestiges of an older matriarchal society.

103. Carrie Chapman Catt, "Java," *Jus Suffragii* 7, no. 1 (September 15, 1912).

104. "Women of the Gold Coast," *Jus Suffragii* 18, no. 6 (March 1924); "The Turkish Woman of To-Day," *Jus Suffragii* 20, no. 4 (January 1926); E. S. Stevens, "The Woman Movement in Iraq," *Jus Suffragii* 24, no. 2 (November 1929); Kodsieh Ashraf, "Some Glimpses of the Past History and Present Progress of the Woman's Movement in Persia," ICW *Bulletin* 9, no. 5 (January 1931); "Position of Women of Native Races," *Jus Suffragii* 29, no. 10 (July 1935); Eleanor Hawarden, "The Status of Women in Africa," *Jus Suffragii* 30, no. 4 (January 1936).

105. Grace Johnson, notes on WILPF conference, May 1924, Woman's Rights Collection, box 25, SL.

106. See, for example, Carrie Chapman Catt, "India" [part 2], *Jus Suffragii* 6, no. 11 (July 15, 1912); "India," *Jus Suffragii* 19, no. 6 (March 1925). I am grateful to Anene Ejikeme, who first noted the use of the term "truly international" for a later period in Ejikeme 1992.

107. "Editorial Notes," *Jus Suffragii* 7, no. 10 (July 15, 1913); "A Message to Chinese Women," *Pax* 2, no. 6 (April 1927), and "The Honolulu Congress," *Pax* 3, no. 5 (April 1928); "The Alliance Board," *Jus Suffragii* 27, no. 8 (May 1933); Lotti Birch to Congress Committee [German], April 28, 1937, WILPF papers, reel 21.

108. "Proposed Amendments to the Constitution," *Jus Suffragii* 7, no. 7 (March 15, 1913); "Editorial Notes," *Jus Suffragii* 7, no. 10 (July 15, 1913).

109. Minutes, WILPF Executive Committee, Vienna, July 4–9, 1921, WILPF papers, reel 9; M.T. [Myrrha Tunas], "National Sections: 1924," WILPF papers, reel 2.

110. ICW, *President's Memorandum*, 1930, 11; "List of Resolutions Passed by the Council Meeting," ICW, *President's Memorandum*, 1938, 85.

111. Sophie Sanford, "Mrs. Sanford's Visit to India and Japan," ICW *Annual Report*, 1907–08.

112. Carrie Chapman Catt, untitled MS, 1913, Catt papers, box 7, NYPL.

113. Katherine Bompas to Louisa Fast, November 6, 1934, and Margery Corbett Ashby to Louisa Fast, November 6, 1934, IAW papers, box 1, SSC.

114. Carrie Chapman Catt to Margery Ashby, February 7, 1925, NAWSA papers, reel 10, LofC.

115. Gabrielle Duchêne to Madeleine Doty [French], November 10, 1925, WILPF papers, reel 2; "International Summer School of the W.I.L. for 1927," *Pax* 2, no. 4 (February 1927); Madeleine Rolland, "Report of the Colonial Commission," draft, [1932], WILPF papers, reel 20; minutes, WILPF International Executive Committee, Grenoble, May 20–22, 1932, WILPF papers, reel 10; minutes, IXth World Congress, Luhacovice, July 27–31, 1937, WILPF papers, reel 21.

116. On Haiti, see Bussey and Tims 1965, 58–59.

117. Hilda Clark to Jane Addams, December 13, 1924; Jane Addams to Vilma Glücklich, December 31, 1924; Vilma Glücklich to Jane Addams, December 19, 1924, and January 19, 1925: all in Addams papers, reel 16.

118. Minutes, WILPF International Executive Committee, Geneva, April 25, [1930], WILPF papers, reel 10.

119. On India, see Mathrani 1996.

120. Taraknath Das to Jane Addams, April 12, 1921, Addams papers, reel 13.

121. Agnes Smedley for the Secretary, Pandurgang Khanko, Indian News Service and Information Bureau, to Emily Greene Balch, April 28, 1921, WILPF papers, reel 1.

122. "Report of Secretary-Treasurer," May 1920–July 1921, WILPF papers, reel 9; Lotti Birch, "Report on Activities at Geneva Headquarters since September 1936," WILPF papers, reel 21.

123. Margaret Cousins to Alice Paul, March 17, 1942, WWP papers, reel 174. On Cousins, see Ramusack 1990; Burton 1991; Candy 1991; Jayawardena 1995.

124. [Mary Sheepshanks] to Caris E. Mills, March 12, 1929, WILPF papers, reel 19.

125. "Survey of the Activities, 1915–1937," typescript, n.d., WILPF papers, reel 11; "Tunis Branch," *Pax* 5, no. 7 (May 1930); Camille Drevet, "The Women of Tunis," *Pax* 6, no. 7 (June 1931); minutes, WILPF International Congress, Grenoble, May 15–19, 1932, WILPF papers, reel 20.

126. Alice Kandaleft, "The World as It Is and as It Could Be—Continued," *Our Common Cause* 1933, 148–54, 161, 168–69.

127. Shareefeh Hamid Ali, "East and West in Co-operation," 1935, IAW papers, box 1, SSC.

128. Minutes, WILPF IXth World Congress, Luhacovice, July 27–31, 1937, WILPF papers, reel 21.

Chapter 4

1. Julie Siegfried to Lady Aberdeen [French], August 9, 1914, ICW papers, box 10, NCW-GB HQ.

2. Netherlands Women's League for International Disarmament to American Sisters, April 24, 1899, Sewall papers, I-MCPL.

3. Martina Kramers to Mesdames et chères Collègues [French], January 9, 1917, Schwimmer-Lloyd collection, box A-84, NYPL.

4. The problematic nature of the concept of "international sisterhood" is lucidly discussed in Sherrick 1982; Bosch 1990, 21–23; Tyrrell 1991b.

5. Louise C. A. van Eeghen, "Highlights in the History of the I.C.W.," June 11, 1954, and "The Birth of the I.C.W.," 1957, both in ICW papers, box 1, SSC.

6. Netherlands Women's League for International Disarmament to American Sisters, April 24, 1899; Anna Philosophoff to May Wright Sewall, May 27, 1899; and Cora di Brazza to May Wright Sewall, September 17, 1900: all in Sewall papers, I-MCPL; Teresa Wilson, "Quinquennial Report," ICW 1899 congress report, vol. 1, 90; Lady Aberdeen to Marie Stritt [German], June 2, 1905, HLA, 83-329(7), LB; [Marie Stritt] to P. Chaponnière-Chaix [German], October 6, 1905, HLA, 83-329(7), LB; "First Public Meeting of the Third Quinquennial," June 8, 1904, ICW 1904 congress report, vol. 2; Carrie Chapman Catt to Clara

Schlingheyde, February 10, 1911, Catt papers, reel 4, LofC; Rosika Schwimmer, *Jus Suffragii* 7, no. 7 (March 15, 1913).

7. Matsuyo Takizawa to Jane Addams, July 6, 1921, Addams papers, reel 13; Miss T. G. Ho, speech at 1929 congress, August 26, 1929, WILPF papers, reel 19; PDC, "Communiqué No. 204" [French], February 1938, WILPF papers, reel 11.

8. "Message of the WILPF to the Women of Japan," n.d. [1924], WILPF papers, reel 2; [Camille Drevet] to [Agnes] von Zahn-Harnack [French], September 23, 1931, WILPF papers, reel 2; Rosa Manus and C. Ramondt-Hirschmann, "To the Women of China," November 1932, WILPF papers, reel 10; minutes, WILPF International Executive Committee, Geneva, September 10–14, 1936, WILPF papers, reel 11.

9. There is an enormous scholarship on the history of "difference" versus "sameness" assumptions and arguments in women's organizing. See, for example, Schott 1985a; Cott 1987, 1989; Offen 1988; J. Scott 1988; Black 1989; C. Miller 1992; Alonso 1993.

10. Minutes, WILPF International Congress, September 3–8, 1934, WILPF papers, reel 20; speech of Lida Gustava Heymann, WILPF Zurich Congress, [1919], WILPF papers, reel 17.

11. Minutes, WILPF 8th International Congress, Zurich, September 3–8, 1934, WILPF papers, reel 20.

12. "Glad Tidings for Pacifists," *Pax* 1, no. 9 (August 1926).

13. Mary Sheepshanks, "Peace," *Jus Suffragii* 13, no. 3 (December 1918).

14. Huda Sha'rawi, "L'Orient et l'Occident en coopération," *La République*, April 20, 1935, Corbett Ashby papers, box 484, FL.

15. "Man Made Wars," *Pax* 6, no. 6 (May 1931).

16. Paula Pogány to Mary Sheepshanks, February 8, 1915, Schwimmer-Lloyd collection, box A-54, NYPL.

17. Anna Howard Shaw to Aletta Jacobs, August 22, 1915, and April 18, 1916, Jacobs papers, IIAV.

18. Carrie Chapman Catt to Margery Corbett Ashby and Katherine Bompas, June 16, 1942, Catt papers, box 3, NYPL.

19. Rosika Schwimmer to Isabella Ford, January 30, 1915, Schwimmer-Lloyd collection, box A-53, NYPL.

20. Minutes, WILPF International Executive Committee, Bruges, April 6–10, 1937, WILPF papers, reel 11; Gertrud Baer, "To Women in Ecuador and Peru," July 31, 1941, WILPF papers, reel 11.

21. Rosa Manus to Josephine Schain, April 19, 1932, Schain papers, box 6, SSC.

22. See Koven and Michel 1990; Weiner et al. 1993.

23. "A Call to the Congress," *Jus Suffragii* 20, no. 4 (March 1926).

24. Milena Rudnycka, "The National Question and Its Peaceful Solution," draft text, August 26, 1929, WILPF papers, reel 19.

25. "Die Waffen nieder! Aufruf an alle Frauen der ganzen Erde," [n.d.], WILPF papers, reel 9.

26. ICW 1899 congress report, vol. 1, 78.

27. Jane Addams, "Address to the Pan-Pacific Women's Conference," *Pax* 3, no. 11 (October 1928).

28. "To Women of Palestine Who Love Peace," September 1920, WILPF papers, reel 1.

29. Text of telegram in Marthe Boël, "To the Members of the I.C.W. Executive Committee," ICW *Bulletin* 18, no. 1 (Octoer 1939).

30. Minutes, WILPF Fourth Biennial Congress, May 1–8, 1924, WILPF papers, reel 18.

31. Marie Hoheisel, "The World Needs 'Mothering,'" ICW *Bulletin* 14, no. 6 (February 1936).

32. Rosika Schwimmer, "War and Women," n.d. [1914], Schwimmer-Lloyd collection, box A-48, NYPL.

33. Quotations from Emily Hobhouse, "To Women throughout Europe," Schwimmer-Lloyd collection, box A-51, NYPL; Milena Rudnycka, "The National Question and Its Peaceful Solution," August 26, 1929, WILPF papers, reel 19; Ishbel Aberdeen and Temair, "A New Year's Message from the I.C.W. President," January 1925, ICW *Bulletin* 3, nos. 5–6 (January–February 1925; "International Manifesto of Women," *Jus Suffragii* 8, no. 13 (September 1, 1914); Skandinavische Vorbereitungskom. to "Werte Frau," n.d. [August 1917], Schwimmer-Lloyd collection, box A-91, NYPL; minutes, Internationaler Frauenkongress, May 12–17, 1919, WILPF papers, reel 17; Aletta Jacobs to Rosika Schwimmer, August 18, 1914, Schwimmer-Lloyd collection, box A-41, NYPL; Gertrude G. Bussey and Marie Lous-Mohr to Secretary-General of the United Nations, September 9, 1946, reel 4, WILPF papers.

34. Emily Balch to Elisabeth Waern-Bugge, December 12, [1934], WILPF papers, reel 2.

35. Mrs. F. W. Pethick-Lawrence to Rosika Schwimmer, August 25, 1914, Schwimmer-Lloyd collection, box A-39, NYPL.

36. Winifred Harper Cooley, "The Internationalism of the International," *Jus Suffragii* 7, no. 10 (July 15, 1913).

37. "Memorandum of the Meeting of the Executive and Standing Committees," May 20–27, 1913, ICW *Annual Report*, 1912–13; "Resolutions Adopted at the Quinquennial Council Meeting of the ICW," 1914, ICW papers, box 1, SSC.

38. Rosika Schwimmer, "The Women of the World Demand Peace, n.d. [September 1914], Schwimmer-Lloyd collection, box A-42, NYPL; "The Atrocities of War," September 1914, Catt papers, box 3, NYPL.

39. "An International Conference of Women," [1915], WILPF papers, reel 16.

40. "Women in Earnest, Says Jane Addams," *New York Times*, April 29, 1915.

41. Mary Sheepshanks to Rosika Schwimmer, December 15, 1914, Schwimmer-Lloyd collection, box A-50, NYPL.

42. "The Atrocities of War," *Jus Suffragii* 9, no. 1 (October 1, 1914); Rosika Schwimmer to Florence Holbrook, January 26, 1915, Schwimmer-Lloyd collection, box A-53, NYPL; Emily J. Robinson to Emily Balch, December 14, 1920, WILPF papers, reel 54; "La Liberation des femmes et enfants non-musulmans en Turquie," n.d., WILPF papers, reel 54; Muriel Lester to Clara Ragaz, April 1, 1938, WILPF papers, reel 3.

43. "The Atrocities of War," *Jus Suffragii* 9, no. 11 (October 1, 1914).

44. "The Presidential Addresses Delivered by the Countess of Aberdeen During the Visit of the I.C.W. Executive Committee to Paris," June 1906, ICW HQ.

45. Annie Furuhjelm, "Our Alliance," *Jus Suffragii* 8, no. 9 (May 1, 1914).

46. NAWSA [ICW] 1888 congress report, 33.

47. Carrie Chapman Catt to Editor, *Sun* (New York), January 11, 1913, Catt papers, box 1, NYPL; Carrie Chapman Catt, "Congress Announcements," *Jus Suffragii* 7, no. 6 (February 15, 1913).

48. Carrie Chapman Catt, "President's Address," IWSA 1913 congress report, 87–98.

49. Mary Sheepshanks, "Is Internationalism Dead?" *Jus Suffragii* 10, no. 9 (June 1, 1916).

50. Siao-Mei Djang to M[ary] Sheepshanks, July 30, 1929, WILPF papers, reel 19.

51. Carrie Chapman Catt to Aletta Jacobs, December 21, 1915, Jacobs papers, IIAV.

52. Mary Sheepshanks, "Peace," *Jus Suffragii* 13, no. 3 (December 1918).

53. International Executive Committee, "Statement on Fascism," April 11–15, 1933, WILFP papers, reel 10.

54. "The Third Public Meeting of the Quinquennial," June 10, 1904, ICW 1904 congress report, vol. 2.

55. "Report of Business Sessions," 1915 Congress of Women [WILPF] report, 128–29.

56. M. Slieve McGowan, "Women and Politics," *Jus Suffragii* 17, no. 5 (February 1923); "To What Extent Does a Differentiated Sex Psychology Exist?" *Jus Suffragii* 19, no. 8 (May 1925).

57. Bertha Lutz to Carrie Chapman Catt, August 25, 1933, NAWSA papers, reel 12, LofC.

58. Rosika Schwimmer to Gabrielle Duchêne, n.d. [1934], WILPF papers, reel 20.

59. "Report of the Meeting of the Committee of Arrangements," July 6, 1898, ICW Executive Minute Book, ICW HQ.

60. Teresa Wilson to Anna Simson, n.d. [1899], HLA, 83-328(6), LB.

61. Lady Aberdeen, "Presidential Address," ICW 1899 congress report, vol. 1, 49.

62. "Official Announcements," *Jus Suffragii* 5, no. 10 (July 15, 1911); W. A. E. Mansfeldt, "Men's International Alliance for Women Suffrage," *Jus Suffragii* 7, no. 2 (October 15, 1912); "Men's International Alliance for Woman Suffrage," *Jus Suffragii* 7, no. 3 (November 15, 1912).

63. Margery Corbett Ashby interview, September 21, 1976, conducted by Brian Harrison, Corbett Ashby papers, cassette #6, FL.

64. "Report of Business Sessions," April 29, May 1, [1915], 1915 Congress of Women [WILPF] report, 111–17, 162–63.

65. Emily Greene Balch to Aletta Jacobs, November 15, 1916, Jacobs papers, IIAV.

66. Circular Letter to Executive Committee, April 30, 1920, WILPF papers, reel 9.

67. "What Is This League?" [1920–21], WILPF papers, reel 9.

68. "[Excerpt] from letter from Eleanor M. Moore, June 12, 1920," WILPF papers, reel 1.

69. Minutes, Liaison Committee, September 12, 1938, LC papers, no. 2, IISG.

70. Minutes, Disarmament Committee, January 15, 1932, ICW papers, box 2, LofC.

71. May Wright Sewall to Marie Stritt, March 19, 1904, and Marie Stritt to May Wright Sewall [German], April 20, 1904, both in HLA, 83-329(5), LB.

72. "Women Arraign 'Jungle' Morality," *Evening Star* (Washington), May 12, 1925, clipping in Andrews papers, box 20, SL; "List of Resolutions Passed at the 7th Quinquennial Council Meeting," ICW 1925 congress report.

73. Minutes, June 17, 1911, IWSA 1911 congress report, 42–43; articles in *Jus Suffragii* 7, no. 1 (September 15, 1912); 7, no. 2 (October 15, 1912); 7, no. 3 (November 15, 1912); 7, no. 4 (December 15, 1912); minutes, June 21, 1913, IWSA 1913 congress report, 60–61.

74. Foreword, IWSA 1923 congress report, 26.

75. Isabella Grassi to Madame, July 21, 1919, WILPF papers, reel 36; M[ary] Sheepshanks to Gabrielle Duchêne [French], January 16, 1929, Dossiers Duchêne, F Rés. 296, BDIC; "Non-Party Character of the W.I.L.P.F.," *Pax* 10, no. 2 (March–April 1935).

76. Eva Fichet to Emily Balch [French], August 19, 1934, WILPF papers, reel 20.

77. Catherine E. Marshall to Vilma Glücklich, May 14, [1923], Addams papers, reel 15. On Marshall, see Vellacott 1993a.

78. May Ogilvie Gordon to [Emma Ender?] [German], December 1, 1926, HLA, 84-331(6), LB; Ishbel Aberdeen and Temair, "A Message from the President," ICW *Bulletin* 5, no. 10 (June 1927). On the Aberdeens' relationship, see Lord and Lady Aberdeen 1925.

79. Alice Salomon, "To Lord and Lady Aberdeen on the Occasion of Their GOLDEN WEDDING, November 7th, 1927," ICW *Bulletin* 6, no. 3 (November 1927).

80. Lady Aberdeen to Emma Ender [German], January 31, 1928, HLA, 78-315(1), LB.

81. Emma Ender to Lady Aberdeen [German], February 13, 1928, HLA, 85-333(2), LB.

82. "Lady Aberdeen's Response to Toast Proposed by Baroness Boël," July 13, 1938, ICW, *President's Memorandum*, 1938, 15–17. On Aberdeen see also Pentland 1952.

83. Aletta Jacobs to Rosika Schwimmer [German], November 18, 1903, Schwimmer-Lloyd collection, box A-4, NYPL; see Bosch 1990, 9–12, 53–55; Jacobs 1996.

84. Anna Howard Shaw to Aletta Jacobs, February 24, 1905, Jacobs papers, IIAV.

85. Aletta Jacobs to Rosika Schwimmer [German], [July 1905], Schwimmer-Lloyd collection, box A-7, NYPL; see Bosch 1990, 62.

86. Lydia Kingsmill Commander to Aletta Jacobs, June 24, 1907, Jacobs

papers, IIAV; Carrie Chapman Catt to Aletta Jacobs, December 1905, Jacobs papers, IIAV.

87. Madeleine Doty to Gabrielle Duchêne, July 27, 1925, Dossiers Duchêne, F Rés. 207, BDIC.

88. Madeleine Doty to Jane Addams, March 26, 1927, Addams papers, reel 18.

89. Madeleine Doty to Mary Sheepshanks, February 8, 1927, Addams papers, reel 18.

90. Madeleine Doty to Jane Addams, February 10, 1927, Addams papers, reel 18.

91. Carrie Chapman Catt to Martina Kramers, May 21, 1913, Schwimmer-Lloyd collection, box A-32, NYPL [reprinted in Bosch 1990, 126–27].

92. Martina Kramers to Rosika Schwimmer [German], May 27, 1913, and June 2, 1913, Schwimmer-Lloyd collection, boxes A-32 and A-33, NYPL; Martina Kramers to Carrie Chapman Catt, June 2, 1913, Schwimmer-Lloyd collection, box A-33, NYPL [reprinted in Bosch 1990, 127–29].

93. Martina Kramers to Rosika Schwimmer [German], May 27, 1913, box A-32, NYPL.

94. Martina Kramers to Rosika Schwimmer [German], November 30, 1908, Schwimmer-Lloyd collection, box A-18, NYPL.

95. Adele Schreiber-Krieger to Rosika Schwimmer [German], March 28, 1910, and June 15, 1910, Schwimmer-Lloyd collection, boxes A-22 and A-23, NYPL. See Evans 1976, 115–39; Hackett 1984; Wickert 1991; Grossmann 1995.

96. Aletta Jacobs to Rosika Schwimmer [German/English], August 5, 1910, Schwimmer-Lloyd collection, box A-23, NYPL.

97. Bertha Lutz to Carrie Chapman Catt, February 12, 1934; July 7, 1936; and July 15, 1936: NAWSA papers, reel 12, LofC. On Stevens, see Rupp 1989.

98. Bertha Lutz to Carrie Chapman Catt, February 12, 1934; December 1, 1934; and July 15, 1936: NAWSA papers, reel 12, LofC.

99. Bosch 1990 focuses on women's relationships within the International Woman Suffrage Alliance; Tyrrell 1991b, 116–20, discusses couples within the World Woman's Christian Temperance Union; Alberti 1989 describes women's love for other women within the British women's movement; Gerhard, Klausmann, and Wischermann 1993 analyze women's ties within the German women's movement; Rupp and Taylor 1987 emphasize the centrality of coupled women in the U.S. women's rights movement in the 1950s; Taylor and Rupp 1993 discuss women's relationships within the contemporary U.S. women's movement.

100. On the emergence of the category and identity "lesbian" at the turn of the century, see Chauncey 1982–83 and Duggan 1993. On romantic friendship, see Faderman 1981 and Lützen 1990.

101. Anna Rühling, "Welches Interesse hat die Frauenbewegung an der Lösung des homosexuellen Problems?"; translated as Anna Rueling, "What Interest Does the Women's Movement Have in the Homosexual Question?" in Faderman and Eriksson 1980, 81–91. See Pieper 1984.

102. Kokula 1981, 31, cites Hackett 1976 on the reference to Schleker and Schirmacher. See also Bosch 1990, 85, 287. For Kramers's comment, see Martina

Kramers to Carrie Chapman Catt, June 2, 1913, Schwimmer-Lloyd collection, box A-33, NYPL.

103. Aletta Jacobs to Rosika Schwimmer [German], February 16, 1905, Schwimmer-Lloyd collection, box A-6, NYPL; Aletta Jacobs to Rosika Schwimmer [German], April 20, 1905, Schwimmer-Lloyd collection, box A-7, NYPL. Jacobs, whose German was not perfect, used the male form of "friend" with the feminine endings on the article and adjective. Since Dutch is similar to German in having different endings on the words for male and female friends, I assume she meant a male friend.

104. [Rosika Schwimmer] to Wilhelmina [van Wulfften Palthe], July 29, 1917, Schwimmer-Lloyd collection, box A-90, NYPL, for "fairies" and "queer"; MG [Marguerite Gobat] to Vilma Glücklich [French], October 27, 1924, WILPF papers, reel 1, for "perverse au point de vue sexuel"; Aletta Jacobs to Rosika Schwimmer, May 3, 1909, Schwimmer-Lloyd collection, box A-20, NYPL, for "MANLY-LOOKING"; Helen Archdale to Anna Nilsson, May 17, 1933, ERI papers, box 331, FL, for cropped hair and mannish dress; Mia Boissevain, tribute to Rosa Manus, n.d., Rosa Manus papers, IIAV.

105. Heymann 1972, 76. See also Braker 1995.

106. Lida Gustava Heymann to Rosika Schwimmer [German], October 3, 1919, Schwimmer-Lloyd collection, box A-119, NYPL; [no signature] to Lida Gustava Heymann, July 29, 1921, WILPF papers, reel 1.

107. Lida Gustava Heymann to Jane Addams, November 4, 1924, Addams papers, reel 16.

108. Emily Greene Balch to Aletta Jacobs, November 15, 1916, Jacobs papers, IIAV; Emily Hobhouse to Aletta Jacobs, April 24, 1920, Jacobs papers, IIAV; "List of individuals expected in Innsbruck" [German], n.d. [1925], WILPF papers, reel 2; Lida Gustava Heymann to Gabrielle Duchêne, February 17, 1926, Dossiers Duchêne, F Rés. 206, BDIC.

109. Anne Zueblin to Jane Addams, January 17, 1930, Addams papers, reel 21.

110. Clara Ragaz to K. E. Innes and Gertrud Baer, April 18, 1940, WILPF papers, reel 4.

111. Emily Greene Balch to Alice Paul, September 17, 1943, WWP papers, reel 174.

112. Rosika Schwimmer to Alice Park, January 7, 1944 [?], Park papers, box 1, HI.

113. Lida Gustava Heymann to Mary Rozet Smith [German/English], June 5, 1924, Addams papers, reel 16; Lida Gustava Heymann to Jane Addams [German], n.d. [ca. March 15, 1929], Addams papers, reel 20. On the relationship of Addams and Smith, see Cook 1977.

114. Anne Zueblin to M. Illova, June 10, 1929, WILPF papers, reel 19; [Mary Sheepshanks] to Mary Rozet Smith, July 5, 1929, Addams papers, reel 20.

115. [Jane Addams] to Lida Gustava Heymann, February 23, 1924, Addams pappers, reel 16.

116. Aletta Jacobs to Jane Addams, December 23, 1915, Addams papers, reel 9; Aletta Jacobs to Jane Addams and Alice Hamilton, Sept. 26, 1919, Addams papers, reel 12; Aletta Jacobs to Jane Addams, June 12, 1923, Addams papers, reel 15.

117. See Fowler 1986. Fowler finds Catt's heterosexual credentials so impressive that he barely entertains the idea that Catt may have loved women. See Bosch 1990, 291, for criticism of Fowler. Catt also carried on a romantic relationship with Peck, who herself lived with another woman. Catt wrote to Peck's partner, "Miss Peck and I are making love to one another but with you to watch her and Miss Hay to keep her eye on me, I expect it will be some time before an elopement can be successfully planned!" (Catt to Frances Squire Potter, n.d., quoted in Bosch 1990, 38).

118. Martina Kramers to Rosika Schwimmer [German], September 24, 1906, Schwimmer-Lloyd collection, box A-10, NYPL.

119. Rachel Foster Avery to Aletta Jacobs, July 14, 1910, and Anna Howard Shaw to Aletta Jacobs, February 8, 1909, both in Jacobs papers, IIAV.

120. Anna Howard Shaw to Aletta Jacobs, April 7, 1911, Jacobs papers, IIAV.

121. Martina Kramers to Rosika Schwimmer [German], September 24, 1906, Schwimmer-Lloyd collection, box A-10, NYPL; Anna Howard Shaw to Aletta Jacobs, December 14, 1908, Jacobs papers, IIAV.

122. Rachel Foster Avery to Aletta Jacobs, July 14, 1910, Jacobs papers, IIAV.

123. Anna Manus-Jacobi, tribute to Carrie Chapman Catt [German], March 11, 1947, Manus papers, IIAV.

124. Emily Greene Balch quoted in Randall 1964, 299.

125. Lida Gustava Heymann to Jane Addams [German], September 16, 1919, Addams papers, reel 12.

126. Helen Cheever to Jane Addams, September 13, 1922, Addams papers, reel 15.

127. Emily Greene Balch quoted in Randall 1964, 397.

128. Emily Greene Balch quoted in Randall 1964, 399.

129. Elisabeth Busse quoted in Pieper 1984, 120–21. The German reads "sie leben frauenbündlerisch." I am grateful to Helen Fehervary for suggesting this wording.

130. Alice Salomon, "Character is Destiny," 218, 39–42, Salomon papers, LBI. On Salomon, see Kaplan 1991, 214–17.

131. Alice Salomon, "The Unmarried Woman of Yesterday and To-day," ICW *Bulletin* 11, no. 2 (October 1932).

132. Lena Madesin Phillips to Carrie Probst, May 28, 1935, Phillips papers, carton 4, SL. On Phillips's relationship with Marjory Lacy-Baker, see Rupp and Taylor 1987, 121–24.

133. Helen Archdale to Doris Stevens, February 14, 1936, Stevens papers, carton 4, SL.

134. On Lady Rhondda's relationships with women, see Eoff 1991, 107–16.

135. Alice Salomon, "Character is Destiny," 218, Salomon papers, LBI.

136. Rosa Manus to Clara Hyde, April 28, 1923, Catt papers, reel 4, LofC.

137. Emily Greene Balch to Jane Addams, [1928?], Addams papers, reel 19.

138. Martina Kramers to Carrie Chapman Catt, June 2, 1913, Schwimmer-Lloyd collection, box A-33, NYPL. Bosch 1990 makes this point about different attitudes toward sexuality on the two sides of the Atlantic.

139. "What Is This League?" [1920–21], WILPF papers, reel 9.

140. Elizabeth Baelde, "Impressions of the Visit of the I.C.W. to Canada," in Aberdeen 1909, 31–34.

141. Eline Hansen to Rosika Schwimmer, March 12, 1915, Schwimmer-Lloyd collection, box A-55, NYPL; Edna Münch to Rosika Schwimmer, March 18, 1915, Schwimmer-Lloyd collection, box A-57, NYPL.

142. "Stenographic Report of 2nd Congress," October 17, 1921, IFWW papers, SL.

143. Lena Madesin Phillips, "Unfinished History of the International Federation of Business and Professional Women," Phillips papers, carton 9, SL.

144. Katherine Bompas to Carrie Chapman Catt, November 29, 1945, Catt papers, box 3, NYPL.

145. Margery Corbett Ashby to Josephine Schain, February 5, 1935, Schain papers, box 4, SSC.

146. [Mrs. Bader Dimeschquie], "Delegates and Friends," 1935, IAW papers, box 1, SSC.

147. [Mary Sheepshanks] to Yella Hertzka, July 16, 1930, WILPF papers, reel 2.

148. Idola Saint-Jean to Helen Archdale, September 15, 1931, ERI papers, box 334, FL; minutes, meeting of the IAWSEC board, Paris, December 6–9, 1938, IAW papers, FL.

Chapter 5

1. Lida Gustava Heymann to Vilma Glücklich [German], August 12, 1925, WILPF papers, reel 2.

2. "The International Character of the Y.W.C.A.," in "News of the YWCA throughout the World," supplement to *Jus Suffragii* 27, no. 9 (June 1933).

3. Teresa Wilson to Anna Simson, December 1, 1898, HLA, 83-328(1), LB.

4. Emily Greene Balch to Jane Addams, February 16, 1921, Addams papers, reel 13; [Anna Wössner] to Emily Greene Balch [German], May 5, 1922, WILPF papers, reel 1.

5. Helene Granitsch to Helen Archdale [German], June 18, 1931, ERI papers, box 334, FL.

6. Rosa Manus to Clara Hyde, October 8, 1923, Catt papers, reel 4, LofC.

7. Pentland 1947.

8. Carrie Chapman Catt, "Address," IWSA 1909 congress report, 63; Marianne Beth, "The Woman Movement in Europe," in *Our Common Cause* 1933, 96–101.

9. Carrie Chapman Catt, "Address," IWSA 1909 congress report, 63.

10. Annie Furuhjelm, "Our Alliance," *Jus Suffragii* 8, no. 9 (May 1, 1914).

11. Annie Furuhjelm, "Our Alliance," *Jus Suffragii* 8, no. 9 (May 1, 1914).

12. "Compte rendu de la conference internationale des femmes à Zurich," [1919], WILPF papers, reel 17.

13. G. Duchêne [French], "Messages of Europe, Christmas 1924," WILPF papers, reel 18.

14. Bosch 1990, 18–19, describes the IWSA congresses as "cultural manifestations of the political ideal of international sisterhood," emphasizing that the

romanticization of difference supported the idea of an essential unity and equality of women. Tyrrell 1991b, 49–50, also emphasizes the use of hymns, emblems, slogan, badges, flags, and banners to strengthen the notion of women united in temperance work around the globe.

15. The Committee on Peace and Arbitration of the ICW in 1904 recommended the adoption of a peace flag; see "The International Committee," ICW *Annual Report*, 1905–06. All three of the organizations considered the adoption of an international song, and the ICW accepted one in 1913; see Eva Upmark, "Miscellaneous," ICW *Bulletin* 1, no. 11 (May 1923).

16. Alice Salomon, "Character is Destiny," 129–30, Salomon papers, LBI.

17. Carrie Chapman Catt to Friends of Rosa Manus, July 10, 1942, Catt papers, IIAV.

18. *Jus Suffragii* 5, no. 8 (April 15, 1911); [Madeleine Doty] to Delegates to Congress, June 10, 1926, reel 19, WILPF papers.

19. Minutes, JSC, September 7, 1928, LC papers, IISG.

20. Madeleine Doty, "Story of the Congress," *Pax* 1, no. 9 (August 1926).

21. "The Berlin Congress," Congress Supplement to *Jus Suffragii* 23, no. 9 (July 1929).

22. Carrie Chapman Catt to Rosika Schwimmer, March 4, 1905, Schwimmer-Lloyd collection, box A-6, NYPL. See Powell 1996.

23. Margery Corbett Ashby interview, conducted by Brian Harrison, September 21, 1976, cassette #4, Corbett Ashby papers, FL.

24. Minutes, May 1, 1909, IWSA 1909 congress report.

25. Minutes, June 21, 1913, IWSA 1913 congress report; Foreword, IWSA 1923 congress report; Foreword, IAWSEC 1926 congress report.

26. 1888 constitution, printed in Sewall 1914; "The International Council of Women, 1888–1924," typescript, ICW papers, box 11, NCW-GB.

27. Minutes, May 1, 1909, IWSA 1909 congress report.

28. "Memorandum of the Meeting of General Officers," July 26–27, 1905, ICW *Annual Report*, 1904–05; "The Meeting of the I.C.W. Executive Committee in Paris," [June 15–18, 1906], ICW *Annual Report*, 1905–06.

29. *Jus Suffragii* 9, no. 2 (November 1, 1914); minutes of ICW Board of Officers, Brussels, March 28, 1939, ICW papers, box 3, NCW-GB.

30. "Denmark and Norway," *Jus Suffragii* 34, no. 8 (May 1940).

31. "Constitution and Standing Orders of the ICW," drawn up at Washington, 1888. Revised at Dubrovnik, 1936, and at Helsinki, 1954, ICW papers, box 1, SSC.

32. "Copy of Extracts from a Letter to Lady Aberdeen Commenting on Memorandum of the Hague Conference," [1901], HLA, 80-319(1), LB; minutes, ICW Executive Committee, Dresden, August 18, 1903, HLA, 80-319(2), LB.

33. "The International Committees," ICW *Annual Report*, 1905–06; Camille Vidart, "Rapport de la sous-Commission pour les Races et Nationalités," ICW *Annual Report*, 1907–08.

34. Carrie Chapman Catt, "President's Address," IWSA 1913 congress report; "Abridged Minutes of the Meetings of the IWSA, August 1906," IWSA 1904 and 1906 congress report.

35. Annie Furuhjelm, "Our Alliance," *Jus Suffragii* 8, no. 9 (May 1, 1914);

Martina Kramers to Officers of the IWS Alliance and Presidents of its Auxiliaries, February 17, 1910, Schwimmer-Lloyd collection, box A-22, NYPL; Van Voris 1987, 62–63.

36. "Proceedings of the Quinquennial Meeting," May 4, 1925, ICW HQ. See Bohachevsky-Chomiak 1988, 262–80.

37. "Eighth Quinquennial Meeting of the ICW," ICW *Bulletin* 8, no. 10 (June 1930).

38. "First Meeting of Council Workers under Mrs. Sewall's Administration," July 6, 1899, ICW 1899 congress report, vol. 1.

39. "Resolutions of the Zurich Congress, 1919," WILPF papers, reel 17; Louie Bennett to [Chrystal] Macmillan, January 5, 1916, WILPF papers, reel 9; Olga Misar, "Nationaler Frauen Ausschuss für dauernden Frieden in Oesterreich gibt folgende Punkte für die Agenda," January 14, 1916, WILPF papers, reel 9.

40. Minutes, WILPF Executive Committee, June 1920, WILPF papers, reel 9.

41. "Constitution, By-Laws and Rules of Order," [1929], WILPF papers, reel 19; minutes, extraordinary meeting of the [WILPF] Executive Committee, London, February 4–5, 1924, WILPF papers, reel 9.

42. Minutes, WILPF 8th International Congress, Zurich, September 3–8, 1934, WILPF papers, reel 20.

43. Summary of minutes of the [WILPF] Executive Committee meeting, Freiburg, September 6–12, 1922, WILPF papers, reel 9. On the history of Czech nationalism, see David 1991.

44. Lida Gustava Heymann to Vilma Glücklich [German], February 14, 1925, WILPF papers, reel 2.

45. Mary Sheepshanks to Executive Committee members, June 19, 1928, Addams papers, reel 20.

46. M. Sheepshanks to Gabrielle Duchêne [French], January 16, 1929, Dossiers Duchêne, F Rés. 296, BDIC; [Mary Sheepshanks] to Lida Gustava Heymann and Gabrielle Duchêne, February 5, 1929, WILPF papers, reel 19.

47. M. Sheepshanks to Lida Gustava Heymann and Gabrielle Duchêne, February 14, 1929, Dossiers Duchêne, F Rés. 207, BDIC; minutes, WILPF International Executive Committee, Geneva, April 16–19, 1929, WILPF papers, reel 10.

48. Minutes, International Executive Committee, Geneva, April 16–19, 1929, WILPF papers, reel 10.

49. Lida Gustava Heymann to Jane Addams, November 1, 1929, Addams papers, reel 20.

50. Minutes, WILPF International Executive Committee, Lille, April 8–13, 1931, WILPF papers, reel 10; notes from Executive Committee meeting in Lille [German], April 1931, WILPF papers, reel 10; minutes, WILPF International Executive Committee, Grenoble, May 20–22, 1932, WILPF papers, reel 10.

51. Clara Ragaz to Kathleen Innes and Gertrud Baer, October 29, 1937, WILPF papers, reel 3.

52. Milena Illová to Mary Sheepshanks, February 11, 1929, WILPF papers, reel 19.

53. "French Suffragists and the War," letter from de Witt Schlumberger to Sisters of the Union, *Jus Suffragii* 8, no. 13 (September 1, 1914). At the same time, Schlumberger objected to the portrayal of French women as opposed to interna-

tional collaboration; see copy of extract from "La Revue," September 15, 1915 [French], Dossier de Witt Schlumberger, BMD.

54. Le Bureau du Comité Central, l'Union Française pour le Suffrage des Femmes to Carrie Chapman Catt [French], December 23, 1914, reel 20, NAWSA papers, LofC.

55. "Report of Business Sessions" [French], April 30, 1915, 1915 Congress of Women [WILPF] report.

56. Gertrud Baümer, April 4, 1915, "Some Letters from Those Not Adhering to the Congress" [German], 1915 Congress of Women [WILPF] report, 306–10.

57. "Memorial Presented by the Polish Delegation at the Women's International Peace Congress," April 28, 1915, Schwimmer-Lloyd collection, box A-57, NYPL.

58. "President's Memorandum," ICW 1920 congress report.

59. Carrie Chapman Catt to Aletta Jacobs, December 21, 1915, Jacobs papers, box 2, IIAV.

60. Margery Corbett Ashby to Mother, February 14, 1921, Corbett Ashby papers, box 477, FL; Marguerite de Witt Schlumberger to Carrie Chapman Catt [French], March 14, 1921, St. Joan's International Alliance papers, box 506, FL.

61. Carrie Chapman Catt, diary, October–November 1922, Catt papers, reel 2, LofC.

62. Anna Garlin Spencer to Jane Addams, May 2, 1920, Addams papers, reel 13.

63. Henri de La Fontaine to Emily Greene Balch [French/English], February 27, 1920, WILPF papers, reel 36; [Marguerite Gobat] to Mlle. La Fontaine [French], November 10, 1919, WILPF papers, reel 36.

64. Jane Addams, "President's Address," Fourth International Congress, May 1–7, 1924, WILPF papers, reel 18.

65. M.S. [Mary Sheepshanks], "The Women's International League Congress," *Jus Suffragii* 20, no. 10 (August–September 1926).

66. Mosa Anderson, "Bulgarian Problems and the Bulgarian Section of the W.I.L.," [1928], WILPF papers, reel 9.

67. Emily Balch to Mme. Dobredieva [French], September 13, 1919, WILPF papers, reel 1; telegram from Halina Sujkowska, Dr. Budzinska Tylicka, Sophie Prauss to Jane Addams, [August 9, 1920], Addams papers, reel 13.

68. Emily Greene Balch to Mme. Dr. Budzinska-Tylicka [French], March 1, 1922, WILPF papers, reel 1. See Bohachevsky-Chomiak 1988, 262–80.

69. Clara Ragaz to Cor Ramondt-Hirschmann [German], July 12, 1937, WILPF papers, reel 3.

70. [K. D. Courtney], notes, October 21, 1923, WILPF papers, reel 1.

71. Lida Gustava Heymann to Clara Ragaz, Emily Greene Balch, and Gertrud Baer [German], July 6, 1931, WILPF papers, reel 10.

72. "Report of Emily G. Balch on her journey in Eastern Europe," 1925, WILPF papers, reel 9.

73. Mosa Anderson, "Report of Visit to Yugo-Slavia and Bulgaria," December 16, 1927–February 6, 1928, and "Prospects for the Women's International League in Yugo-Slavia," [1928], WILPF papers, reel 9.

74. Miléva Petrovitch to [Mary Sheepshanks] [French], July 19, 1929, WILPF

papers, reel 19; minutes, WILPF International Executive Committee, Geneva, April 25, [1930], WILPF papers, reel 10; Mme. Topalourts to Executive Committee [French], October 14, 1930, WILPF papers, reel 10.

75. Camille Drevet, "Notes pour l'Exécutif," [1929], WILPF papers, reel 10.

76. "Camille Drevet's Tour," *Pax* 4, no. 6 (May 1929); "Rapport de C. Drevet sur le voyage en Bulgarie, Roumanie, Hongrie et Autriche," May 13–June 19, [1927], WILPF papers, reel 9.

77. Bohachevsky-Chomiak 1988, 262, makes this point.

78. Milena Rudnycka, "The National Question and Its Peaceful Solution," draft text of speech to 1929 congress, August 26, 1929, WILPF papers, reel 19.

79. Madeleine Z. Doty, "The Sixth International Congress of the W.I.L.," *Pax* 4, no. 5 (April 1929).

80. Alice Salomon, "Character is Destiny," 4, Salomon papers, LBI.

81. "Verbatim Report of Mass Meeting Held in The Round Room, Mansion House, Dublin," July 12, 1926, WILPF papers, reel 19.

82. "Rosika Schwimmer's Case," *Pax* 4, no. 8 (July 1929).

83. Heymann 1972, 292. See also L.G.H., "International Community—World Citizenship," *Pax* 14, no. 2 (February 1939); Lotti Birch to Clara Ragaz and Gertrud Baer [German], March 6, 1940, WILPF papers, reel 4.

84. "To the International Woman Suffrage Alliance," *Jus Suffragii* 9, no. 3 (December 1, 1914).

85. "Extract from the Forthcoming Report of the International Congress of Women" [French], May 12–17, 1919, WILPF papers, reel 17; "Zum Internationalen Frauenkongress," [1919], WILPF papers, reel 17.

86. "Sechster Verhandlungstag," [1919], WILPF papers, reel 17; "Compte rendu de la conference internationale des femmes à Zurich," [1919], WILPF papers, reel 17.

87. Van Voris 1987.

88. Alice Park, diary entry, June 3, 1926, Park papers, box 25, HI; extract from letter of Editha Philps to Rosika Schwimmer, June 7, 1926, Palthe-Broese van Groenau papers, IIAV.

89. Drefus 1986.

90. "Communiqué," Section française de la Ligue internationale des Femmes pour la Paix et la Liberté," n.d. [1931], F Rés. 296, Dossiers Duchêne, BDIC.

91. [Mary Sheepshanks] to Marie Ursule Ferrari [French], August 13, 1930, WILPF papers, reel 21.

92. "Towards Peace and Freedom," August 1919, WILPF papers, reel 17; "Women and War in the Far East," *Pax* 7, no. 6 (May 1932); see Iinuma 1996.

93. "A New Peace: Report of the International Conference of Women at The Hague, 7 to 9 December, 1922," WILPF papers, reel 9.

94. Sophie Sturge to Aletta Jacobs, November 8 [1915], WILPF papers, reel 9.

95. Anna M. Graves to Emily Greene Balch, [August 31, 1923], Addams papers, reel 15; Emily Greene Balch to Jane Addams, September [1923], Addams papers, reel 15.

96. Minutes, WILPF Executive Committee Meeting, Swarthmore, April 25–29, 1924, and Washington, May 8, 1924, WILPF papers, reel 9; Vilma

Glücklich to Jane Addams, October 8, 1924, Addams papers, reel 16; MT [Myrrha Tunas], "National Sections: 1924," WILPF papers, reel 2; "The World Section," *Pax* 2, no. 1 (November 1926); Vilma Glücklich to Gabrielle Duchêne [French], November 26, 1924, Dossiers Duchêne, F Rés. 207, BDIC.

97. Madeleine Z. Doty, "The W.I.L. World Section," *Pax* 5, no. 3 (January 1930).

98. The author may have been Anna Graves. "Suprainternational Republic," n.d., Balch papers, reel 8.

99. Minutes, 8th International Congress, Zurich, September 3–8, 1934, WILPF papers, reel 20; minutes, International Executive Committee, London, March 25–30, 1935, WILPF papers, reel 11.

100. WILPF *Bulletin*, December 1, 1920.

101. Cor Ramondt-Hirschmann to Jane Addams, November 17, 1924, Addams papers, reel 16.

102. E.GD [Emilie Gourd], "La 'Saison de Geneve,'" *Jus Suffragii* 23, no. 1 (October 1928).

103. Mary Dingman used the term "International Colony"; Mary Dingman to Family and Friends, April 5, 1937, Dingman papers, box 1, SL.

104. Lady Aberdeen, quoted by Marthe Boël, "President's Opening Address," ICW, *President's Memorandum*, 1938, 8.

105. Emily Greene Balch, "Our Call," WILPF *Bulletin*, February 1922.

106. Jane Addams, "President's Address," Fourth International Congress, May 1–7, 1924, WILPF papers, reel 18.

107. Minna Cauer, "Treue," *Zeitschrift für Frauenstimmrecht*, January 1, 1915.

108. Anita Augspurg, Lida Gustava Heymann, Frida Perlen, and Elise von Schlumberger, "Internationaler Frauenkongress 1915," [1915], WILPF papers, reel 1.

109. Emily Greene Balch to Mme. Dr. Budzinska-Tylicka [French], March 1, 1922, WILPF papers, reel 1.

110. "Memorandum zu unterbreiten der Executive der IFFF," 1937, Palthe-Broese van Groenau papers, IIAV; "Memorandum über die Zusammenarbeit unter Nachbar-Staaten," *Pax* 12, no. 6 (July 1937).

111. Minutes, WILPF VIth International Congress, Prague, [1929], WILPF papers, reel 19.

112. Minutes, Disarmament Committee, February 23, 1932, ICW papers, box 2, LofC.

113. I am indebted to Mala Mathrani for first bringing to my attention the tendency in colonized countries to view nationalism and internationalism as complementary. See Mathrani forthcoming.

114. Margery Corbett Ashby to Josephine Schain, February 5, 1935, Schain papers, box 4, SSC; Corbett Ashby also described Huda Sha'rawi as "terrifically nationalist"; Margery Corbett Ashby to Carrie Chapman Catt, June 9, 1926, NAWSA papers, reel 11, LofC.

115. Sofia R. de Veyra to Emily Greene Balch, June 3, 1920, WILPF papers, reel 1.

116. Edith M. Pye, "A Visit to Canton," *Pax* 3, no. 6 (May 1928).

117. L. Muthulakshmi Reddi to Helen Archdale, March 1, 1934, ERI papers, box 333, FL.

118. "L'Orient et l'Occident en coopération," *La République*, April 20, 1935, Corbett Ashby papers, box 484, FL.

119. Minutes, WILPF IXth World Congress, Luhacovice, July 27–31, 1937, WILPF papers, reel 21.

120. Egyptian section, "Propositions pour le Congres de Luhacovice," [April 1937], WILPF papers, reel 2; A. Jacot to Madame [French], April 15, 1937, WILPF papers, reel 3.

121. Lotti Birch to Clara Ragaz and Cor Ramondt-Hirschmann [German], May 1, 1937, WILPF papers, reel 3; Cor Ramondt-Hirschmann to Lotti Birth [German], May 7, 1937, WILPF papers, reel 3; Clara Ragaz to Alice Jacot [French], May 12, 1937, WILPF papers, reel 3; Lotti Birch to Congress Committee [German], May 12, 1937, WILPF papers, reel 21; Cor Ramondt-Hirschmann to Clara Ragaz [German], May 20, 1937, WILPF papers, reel 3.

122. Alice Jacot to Clara Ragaz [French], May 22, 1937, WILPF papers, reel 3.

123. Clara Ragaz to Cor Ramondt-Hirschmann [German], June 24, 1937, WILPF papers, reel 3; minutes, WILPF Executive Committee meeting, Luhacovice, July 26–August 3, 1937, WILPF papers, reel 21.

124. Hanna Bieber-Bohm to Members of the BdF [German], December 13, 1898, HLA, 83-328(3), LB.

125. Anna Simson to Teresa Wilson [German], November 14, 1898, HLA 83-328(3), LB.

126. Alexandra Gripenberg to Marie Stritt, May 17, 1904, HLA, 81-323(4), LB.

127. "Third Business Session," July 4, 1899, ICW 1899 congress report, vol. 1, 168–69.

128. May Wright Sewall to Auguste Schmidt, July 21, 1899, HLA, 83–329(1), LB.

129. H. M. Swanwick to Jane Addams, July 26, 1916, Addams papers, reel 9; Frances M. Sterling to Katharina von Kardorff, March 7, 1930, Manus papers, IIAV; minutes, IAWSEC Board, Brussels, September 9–10, 1936, IAW papers, FL.

130. Minutes, June 29, 1899, ICW 1899 congress report, vol. 1, 154–61.

131. Auguste Schmidt and Marie Stritt to ICW [German], June 8, 1899, HLA, 83–329(1), LB.

132. "Gleanings from the Council Meetings," ICW *Bulletin* 3, nos. 9–10 (June–July 1925).

133. "Circular Letter to [WILPF] Executive Committee," April 30, 1920, WILPF papers, reel 9.

134. Untitled typescript, [1929], WILPF papers, reel 19.

135. M. de Saint-Prise to Madame [French], June 28, 1921, WILPF papers, reel 18.

136. Madeleine Doty to Jane Addams, December 31, 1926, Addams papers, reel 18.

137. Minutes, WILPF 5th Biennial Congress, Dublin, July 9–15, 1926,

WILPF papers, reel 19; "Digest of the Executive Committee Meeting," Geneva, September 9–13, 1927, WILPF papers, reel 9.

138. British Section to National Sections, January 25, 1928, WILPF papers, reel 2.

139. [Gabrielle Duchêne], "Raisons pour lesquelles nous restons fermement attachées à la constitution actuelle," [1927], Dossiers Duchêne, F Rés. 206, BDIC.

140. Minutes, WILPF International Executive Committee, Geneva, March 22, 1928, WILPF papers, reel 9; "Questionnaire," [1928], WILPF papers, reel 2.

141. Emily Greene Balch to Jane Addams, September 28, 1920, Addams papers, reel 13.

142. "Object of the WILPF," [1924], WILPF papers, reel 19; Eleanor M. Moore, "The Two Wings of the Peace Movement," *Pax* 1, no. 1 (February 1920); minutes, WILPF Executive Committee, Paris, February 6–10, 1926, WILPF papers, reel 9; Catherine Marshall to Jane Addams, February 17, 1926, Addams papers, reel 17; Minutes, WILPF Executive Committee, Dublin, July 6, 1926, WILPF papers, reel 9.

143. Madeleine Doty to Jane Addams and Emily Balch, September 16, 1927, Addams papers, reel 19.

144. Minutes, WILPF International Executive Committee, September 26, [1933], WILPF papers, reel 10; minutes, WILPF International Executive Committee, March 27, [1934], WILPF papers, reel 10; minutes, WILPF International Executive committee, Zurich, August–September 1934, WILPF papers, reel 10.

145. [Gabrielle Duchêne], "Raisons pour lesquelles nous restons fermement attachées à la constitution actuelle," [1927], Dossiers Duchêne, F Rés. 206, BDIC.

146. Emily Greene Balch to Gertrud Baer, September 4, 1933, WILPF papers, reel 2.

147. Clara Ragaz to members of Executive Committee and consultative members [German], [end of 1937], WILPF papers, reel 3; minutes, WILPF International Executive Committee, Bruges, April 6–10, 1937, WILPF papers, reel 11; minutes, WILPF IXth World Congress, Luhacovice, July 27–31, 1937, WILPF papers, reel 21.

148. Vilma Glücklich to Jane Addams, December 12, 1924, Addams papers, reel 16.

149. [Gabrielle Duchêne] to Kathleen Courtney [French], May 25, 1927, Addams papers, reel 18. On the China incident, see Madeleine Doty to Jane Addams, May 19, 1927, Addams papers, reel 18; Minutes, WILPF Officers' Meeting, Geneva, May 24–26, [1927], Addams papers, reel 19.

150. Madeleine Z. Doty, "The Sixth International Congress of the W.I.L.," *Pax* 4, no. 5 (April 1929).

151. Madeleine Doty to Jane Addams, January 6, 1926, Addams papers, reel 17.

152. Minutes, WILPF International Congress, Grenoble, May 15–19, 1932, WILPF papers, reel 20.

153. Catherine Marshall to Gabrielle Duchêne, January 29, 1926, Dossiers Duchêne, F Rés. 206, BDIC.

154. [Madeleine Doty] to Edith Pye, July 19, 1930, Balch papers, reel 8.

155. Lillian Wald to Jane Addams, October 5, 1927, Addams papers, reel 19; Emily Greene Balch to Jane Addams, October 14, [1927], Addams papers, reel 19.

156. Gerhard 1994 raises this issue in considering the German women's movement before 1933.

Chapter 6

1. "Women Voters," *Jus Suffragii* 17, no. 10 (August 1923). The title of this chapter is adapted from Hollinger 1993.

2. Boy 1936 classified one subset of international women's groups as "feminist," including in this category the ICW and Alliance. (WILPF earned the designation "pacifist organization.") She did note that "almost all of the organizations are more or less 'feminist' in the large sense in which we have defined the word" (50).

Cott 1989 distinguishes "feminist," "female," and "communal" consciousness. Other scholars have also approached the problem of definition by establishing different categories of feminism, such as "individual" and "relational" (Offen 1988) or "equity" and "social" (Black 1989). C. Miller 1992 emphasizes the conflict between "equal rights" and "social" feminists in the international women's organizations, arguing that it destroyed the unity of the 1920s by the next decade and undermined women's relationships with the League of Nations. In contrast, I see the disagreement among women as part of the process of constructing an internationalist and feminist consciousness.

3. This is the argument made, persuasively, by Wikander 1992.

4. C. L. Brunschwicg to Maria Rutgers-Hoitsema [French], June 19, 1912, Rutgers-Hoitsema papers, IIAV.

5. "Report of the Liaison Committee," [1932], ERI papers, box 330, FL.

6. "Report of the Delegates to the Liaison Committee of Women's International Organisations from the ERI," [1934], ERI papers, box 330, FL.

7. Untitled notes, in folder marked "Pamphlet 1932–1933," ERI papers, box 332, FL.

8. "Report of Operations at Geneva in September 1929 for Filing at Headquarters," [1929], ERI papers, box 330; Doris Stevens to Margareta Robles de Mendoza, June 28, 1930, Stevens papers, carton 10, SL; Florence Barry to Helen Archdale, March 14, 1934, ERI papers, box 333, FL; Margery Corbett Ashby interview, conducted by Brian Harrison, September 21, 1976, cassette #6, Corbett Ashby papers, FL; Ruth Van der Litt to Mabel Vernon, April 28, 1930, Smith papers, box 3, SL.

9. "Resolutions Adopted," IWSA 1920 congress report, 49–50.

10. Chrystal Macmillan, "The Future of the IWSA," *Jus Suffragii* 14, no. 5 (February 1920).

11. Chrystal Macmillan to Editor, *Jus Suffragii*, March 1, 1916, copy in Schwimmer-Lloyd collection, box A-75, NYPL; "The Mandate from Geneva," *Jus Suffragii* 14, no. 10 (August 1920).

12. Margery I. Corbett Ashby, "Courage and Vision," *Jus Suffragii* 27, no. 4 (January 1933).

13. Rosika Schwimmer to Gertrud Woker [German], August 25, 1915, Schwimmer-Lloyd collection, box A-61, NYPL.

14. "Towards Peace and Freedom," August 1919, congress pamphlet, WILPF papers, reel 17.

15. Avril de Sainte-Croix, "Rapport du Comité contre la traite des blanches et pour l'unité de la morale," ICW *Annual Report*, 1907–08.

16. ICW *Bulletin* 18, no. 8 (May 1939).

17. Minutes, JSC, July 7, 1925, LC papers, IISG; "When the Assembly of the League of Nations Meets," ICW *Bulletin* 16, no. 1 (July 1937).

18. Rosika Schwimmer to Fraülein T. Eschholz [German], July 20, 1912, Schwimmer-Lloyd collection, box A-29, NYPL.

19. Helen Archdale to Alice Paul, April 1, 1931, ERI papers, box 331, FL.

20. Helen Archdale to Doris Stevens, August 11, 1929, Stevens papers, carton 4, SL.

21. C. Miller 1992, 200–201.

22. Carrie Chapman Catt, "What Is the Alliance?" *Jus Suffragii* 22, no. 8 (May 1928).

23. M. I. Corbett Ashby, "The Woman Pilgrim's Progress," *Jus Suffragii* 33, no. 9 (June 1939).

24. Margery I. Corbett Ashby, "What Is the Alliance?" *Jus Suffragii* 22, no. 5 (February 1928).

25. Marie Stritt to Mrs. Bompas, February 13, 1928, printed in *Jus Suffragii* 22, no. 6 (March 1928).

26. Helen A. Archdale to Editor, *Jus Suffragii* 22, no. 9 (June 1928); see also [Helen Archdale] to Ada Sacchi Simonetta [French], February 24, 1934, ERI papers, box 334, FL.

27. E. Gd. [Emilie Gourd], "Lettre de Geneve," *Jus Suffragii* 26, no. 3 (December 1931); Germaine Malaterre Sellier, "Vers l'Avenir," *Jus Suffragii* 33, no. 9 (June 1939).

28. M. I. Corbett Ashby, "Message from the President and Board," *Jus Suffragii* 31, no. 1 (October 1936).

29. "The Month's Miscellany," *Jus Suffragii* 19, no. 5 (February 1925).

30. Quoted in C. Miller 1992, 161 [French].

31. Katherine Bompas, "The Rise and Fall of the Women's Movement," *Jus Suffragii* 35, no. 9 (July 1941).

32. Mathrani 1995.

33. Emily Newell Blair, "Have Women Contributed to the Crisis?" *Our Common Cause* 1933, 71–80.

34. "Status of Women at Geneva. Meeting of the Committee of Experts," [1938], LC papers, IISG.

35. Margaret Hickey, "The Individual Responsibility of Women in Meeting the Critical Issues of Today," *International Women's Conference* 1950, 8–9.

36. "Memorandum of the Meeting of the Executive and Standing Committees," The Hague, May 20–27, 1913, ICW *Annual Report*, 1912–13.

37. May Wright Sewall to Minna Cauer, December 28, 1903, HLA, 81-323(2), LB.

38. Anna Howard Shaw to Aletta Jacobs, February 24, 1905, Jacobs papers, IIAV.

39. Annie Furuhjelm, "Our Alliance," *Jus Suffragii* 8, no. 9 (May 1, 1914).

40. Anna Howard Shaw to Aletta Jacobs, January 28, 1908, Jacobs papers, IIAV.

41. Anna Howard Shaw to Millicent Farrett Fawcett, March 25, 1909, Fawcett papers, box 89, FL.

42. Anna Howard Shaw, "Report on Rome ICW Meeting," 1914, Dillon collection, box 23, SL.

43. Anna Howard Shaw, "Women Suffrage Triumphant in the Eternal City," speech, 1914, Dillon collection, box 23, SL; Anna Howard Shaw, "Report on Rome ICW Meeting," 1914, Dillon collection, box 23, SL.

44. Martina G. Kramers, "Announcements," *Jus Suffragii* 5, no. 4 (December 15, 1910).

45. Carrie Chapman Catt to Presidents, May 4, 1911, Schwimmer-Lloyd collection, box A-26, NYPL.

46. Minutes, June 17, 1911, IWSA 1911 congress report.

47. Lucy Anthony to Aletta Jacobs, April 27, 1908, Jacobs papers, IIAV; Aletta Jacobs to Rosika Schwimmer, May 13, 1908, Schwimmer-Lloyd collection, box A-16, NYPL.

48. Carrie Chapman Catt to Rosika Schwimmer, May 22, 1908, Schwimmer-Lloyd collection, box A-16.

49. Rosa Manus to Catharine McCulloch, June 2, 1909, Dillon collection, box 18, SL.

50. Minna Cauer to Rosika Schwimmer [German], November 6, 1909, Schwimmer-Lloyd collection, box A-21, NYPL.

51. "The Meeting of the International Board of Officers," *Jus Suffragii* 8, no. 12 (August 1, 1914).

52. Carrie Chapman Catt to Aletta Jacobs, July 16, 1910, Jacobs papers, IIAV; Anna Howard Shaw to Aletta Jacobs, August 5, 1910, Jacobs papers, IIAV.

53. Carrie Chapman Catt to Editor of the *Sun* (New York), January 11, 1913, Catt collection, box 1, NYPL.

54. Minutes, April 30, 1909, IWSA 1909 congress report, 47–48.

55. Minutes, June 16, 1913, IWSA 1913 congress report, 31–32.

56. K.B., "Obituary: Emmeline Pankhurst," *Jus Suffragii* 22, no. 10 (July 1928).

57. Doris Stevens, "Memo to FM, Rambouillet and the Sorbonne," April 29, 1958, Stevens papers, carton 10, SL; "Notes on the Personnel of the Committee," [1928], Stevens papers, carton 10, SL.

58. "Protest by Mme. Maria Verone [*sic*] after the Arrest at Rambouillet," August 20, 1928, Stevens papers, carton 10, SL.

59. Doris Stevens to Alice Paul, September 1, 1928, Stevens papers (83-M106), carton 2, SL.

60. Alva Belmont to Alice Paul, August 29, 1928, Stevens papers, carton 9, SL; Elizabeth Rogers to Alice Paul, September 30, 1928, Stevens papers (83-M106), carton 2, SL.

61. "Equal Rights and the Peace Pact," *Jus Suffragii* 23, no. 1 (October 1928).

62. Margery Corbett Ashby interview, conducted by Brian Harrison, November 23, 1976, cassette #7, Corbett Ashby papers, FL.

63. Wikander 1992, 1995, 1996.

64. See Lubin and Winslow 1990; Wikander, Kessler-Harris, and Lewis 1995.

65. Maria Rutgers-Hoitsema to Chère Madame [French], March 9, 1911, Rutgers-Hoitsema papers, IIAV.

66. See J. Scott 1988.

67. "Stenographic report of 1st conference," November 5, 1919, IFWW papers, SL.

68. Louise C. A. van Eeghen to Miss Mayo, April 22, 1931, ERI papers, box 334, FL.

69. Katherine Bompas to Anna Lord Strauss, September 4, 1947, LWV papers, box 744, Lof C.

70. Helen A. Archdale to Editor, October 30, 1928, *Jus Suffragii* 23, no. 3 (December 1928).

71. "The Open Door Versus Protection," *Jus Suffragii* 4, no. 9 (August 1929).

72. A.M.R., "Legislation for Women in Industry: 'Protective' or 'Restrictive?'" *Jus Suffragii* 24, no. 9 (June 1930).

73. Margery Corbett Ashby diary entry, May 8, 1925, Corbett Ashby papers, box 484, FL; Carrie Chapman Catt to Margery Ashby, September 17, 1925, NAWSA papers, reel 10, LofC; Carrie Chapman Catt to Margery Ashby, March 19, 1926, NAWSA papers, reel 11, LofC. On this struggle, see Becker 1981, 161–95.

74. Carrie Chapman Catt to Margery Ashby, November 21, 1925, NAWSA papers, reel 10, LofC.

75. Margery Ashby to Alice Paul, December 15, 1925, NAWSA papers, reel 11, LofC; Alice Paul to Margery Ashby, February 1, 1926, NAWSA papers, reel 11, LofC; "Report of the Committee on Admissions," IAWSEC 1926 congress report, 58–60.

76. "Rival Suffragists Take Row to Paris," *World* (New York), May 26, 1926, Smith papers, box 12, SL.

77. "Report on Morning Session of 10th Congress of IWSA," May 31, 1926, Smith papers, box 12, SL.

78. "British Leader Hits Woman's Party Ban," *New York Post*, June 3, 1926, Smith papers, box 12, SL.

79. "World Suffragists Bar American Group; British Party Quits," *New York Times*, June 1, 1926, and "Mrs. Belmont Holds Mrs. Catt Is the Foe," *New York Times*, June 2, 1926, both in Smith papers, box 12, SL, raise the possibility, which the Woman's Party denied, that a rival organization might emerge. "Suffrage Congress Stirs French Women," *New York Times*, June 8, 1926, and Jane Norman Smith, "Report on 10th Congress of IWSA," 1926, in Smith papers, box 1, SL, report the formation of the Open Door Committee in the last days of the Congress. The Open Door Council, organized in Britain, called the meeting that founded ODI in Berlin; see Crystal Macmillan to Jane Norman Smith, Feb-

ruary 19, 1929, Smith papers, box 3, SL. On the ODI, see Constitution, ODI, June 15, 1929, ODI papers, box 461, FL.

80. ODI, "Report of the Third Conference," Prague, July 24–28, 1933, ODI papers, box 460, FL.

81. Winifred Le Sueur to Madam, October 31, 1929, Jane Norman Smith papers, box 3, SL; Anna Kelton Wiley to Alva Belmont, December 19, 1929, Doris Stevens papers, carton 9, SL.

82. "Address Made by Mrs. Jane Norman Smith in Behalf of Equal Rights Treaty before Unofficial Plenary Session of 6th Pan American Conference, Havana," February 7, 1928, Smith papers, box 1, SL; "Draft Letter to Women Abroad about Equal Rights Treaty," [1929], ERI papers, box 331, FL; Helen Archdale to Doris Stevens, June 10, 1929, Stevens papers, carton 4, SL; "Constitution of Equal Rights International," November 17, 1930, Stevens papers, carton 4, SL; ERI, "Secretary's Report," [1931], ERI papers, box 330, FL. See C. Miller 1994.

83. Doris Stevens, "Notes on 1927," Stevens papers, carton 9, SL.

84. Helen Archdale to Alice Paul, April 1, 1931, ERI papers, box 331, FL, used the term "we left wing feminists." On vanguardism, see Helen Archdale to Mrs. Reddi, July 24, 1933, ERI papers, box 333, FL.

85. Flora Drummond to Helen Archdale, June 13, 1932, ERI papers, box 331, FL; Helen Archdale to Jessie Street, n.d., ERI papers, box 334, FL.

86. The ERI papers are full of indications of conflict with the Woman's Party and, particularly, with Alice Paul, who resigned in 1932. See C. Miller 1994.

87. Helen Archdale to Jessie Street, n.d., ERI papers, box 334, FL.

88. Untitled document, [September 1940], WWP papers, reel 173.

89. Untitled document, [September 1940], WWP papers, reel 173.

90. Doris Stevens to Madeleine Doty, July 6, 1926, WILPF papers, reel 18; minutes, 5th [WILPF] Biennial Congress, Dublin, July 9–15, 1926, WILPF papers, reel 19; Alice Park, diary entry, July 15, 1926, Park papers, box 25, HI.

91. "Two Meetings at the Maison Internationale," Pax 5, no. 3 (January 1930).

92. Minutes, IXth World Congress, Luhacovice, July 27–31, 1937, WILPF papers, reel 21. On different national positions, see the excellent essays in Wikander, Kessler-Harris, and Lewis 1995.

93. Gerturd Baer to Dorothy Evans, April 4, 1938, WILPF papers, reel 110. At the 1937 congress, Gabrielle Duchêne stated that she opposed special legislation except for the protection of maternity, and Thora Daugaard reponded that in Denmark that was considered protection of the child, not the woman. See minutes, IXth World Congress, Luhacovice, July 27–31, 1937, WILPF papers, reel 21.

94. Ingeborg Walin to Presidents of Auxiliaries and members of Committee on Like Conditions of Work for Men and Women, December 5, 1929, Nationaal Bureau voor Vrouwenarbeid papers, no. 881, IIAV.

95. "Industrial Legislation for Women," Jus Suffragii 28, no. 1 (October 1933).

96. Josephine Schain to Ruth Woodsmall, March 23, 1935, Woodsmall papers, box 37, SSC.

97. Minutes, IAWSEC board meeting, Amsterdam, May 9–11, 1936, IAW papers, FL; minutes, IAWSEC board meeting, Brussels, September 9–10, 1936, IAW papers, FL; minutes, IAWSEC board Meeting, Zurich, February 25 and March 1–2, 1937, IAW papers, FL; "Like Conditions of Work for Men and Women," *Jus Suffragii* 31, no. 7 (April 1937).

98. "The Eighth Congress of the I.W.S.A.," IWSA 1920 congress report, 39; Foreword, IWSA 1923 report, 26; *Women in a Changing World* 1966, 58–59.

99. Resolutions, Open Door International 2nd conference, Stockholm, August 1931, ODI papers, box 460, FL.

100. "The Industrial Woman and Protective Legislation," *Jus Suffragii* 15, no. 8 (May 1921), reply to "Some Notes on Equal Pay and the Position of Women in Industry," 15, no. 6 (March 1921).

101. Mary Sheepshanks to Lida Gustava Heymann, August 5, 1929, WILPF papers, reel 19.

102. "Debate on Protective Legislation," December 11, 1929, WILPF papers, reel 10.

103. International Federation of Working Women, "Report Presented by the Secretariat at the Biennial Congress," Vienna, August 14–18, 1923, Anderson papers, box 4, SL.

104. *Women in a Changing World* 1966, 58–59.

105. K. Popprová to Helen Archdale, November 3, 1933, ERI papers, box 331, FL.

106. May Ogilvie Gordon, "The Washington Night Work Convention," ICW *Bulletin* 12, no. 5 (January 1934).

107. Helen Archdale to May Oung, July 5, 1933, ERI papers, box 334, FL.

108. "Report of the Delegates to the Liaison Committee of Women's International Organisations from the ERI," [1934], ERI papers, box 330, FL; "The Council Sessions of the International Council of Women in Paris, July 2nd to 12th, 1934," ICW *Bulletin* 13, no. 1 (July 1934); Lubin and Winslow 1990, 43–44.

109. See F. Miller 1990.

110. Minutes, WILPF International Executive Committee, Geneva, September 4–8, 1931, WILPF papers, reel 10.

111. Summary of Congress Proceedings, IAWSEC 1935 congress report, 14–15.

112. See C. Miller 1994.

113. Chrystal Macmillan, "The Nationality of Married Women," *Jus Suffragii* 11, no. 10 (July 1, 1917); *Jus Suffragii* 12, no. 9 (June 1, 1918). See Page 1984.

114. See C. Miller 1992, 201–14.

115. "Minutes of Round Table Discussion called together on invitation of the Chairman of the IACW," April 16, 1929, Stevens papers, carton 10, SL; Doris Stevens to Helen Archdale, August 29, 1929, carton 4, Stevens papers, SL.

116. "Rough Draft for Programme," Joint Demonstration of the Nationality of Married Women, March 14, 1930, Palthe-Broese van Groenau papers, IIAV; Margery I. Corbett Ashby, "The Board Meets in Holland," *Jus Suffragii* 24, no. 7 (April 1930); Page 1984.

117. May Ogilvie Gordon to Lady Aberdeen, December 6, 1930; minutes, International Committee for Action on the Nationality of Married Women, Geneva, January 25, 1931: both in ICW papers, box 12, NCW-GB.

118. M. M. Ogilvie Gordon to Lady Aberdeen, January 28, 1931, ICW papers, box 12, NCW-GB. "Feminists before the League of Nations," *Pax* 6, no. 2 (December 1930), and Lily van der Schalk, "The Nationality Campaign," *Jus Suffragii* 25, no. 6 (March 1931), gave credit for persuading the League of Nations to take up the issue to the Nationality Committee of the Inter-American Commission of Women. That League representatives from Guatemala, Venezuela, and Peru introduced and supported the resolution would support this claim.

119. [Lady Aberdeen] to Katherine Bompas, February 3, 1931, and Chrystal Macmillan and Lily v. d. Schalk Schuster to [Lady Aberdeen], February 12, 1931, both in ICW papers, box 12, NCW-GB.

120. "Women's Consultative Committee on Nationality," *Pax* 6, no. 8 (August 1931); Margery I. Corbett Ashby, "Nationality at Geneva," *Jus Suffragii* 25, no. 11 (August 1931); E.Gd. [Emilie Gourd], "Les Activities féministes à Geneve," *Jus Suffragii* 25, no. 13, no. 1 (October 1931).

121. Margery I. Corbett Ashby, "Nationality at Geneva," *Jus Suffragii* 25, no. 11 (August 1931).

122. Alice Livermore to Helen Archdale, February 27, 1934, ERI papers, box 333, FL.

123. Lady Aberdeen to [May Ogilvie] Gordon, March 15, 1932, ICW papers, box 12, NCW-GB; A.Z.F[orsythe], "Nationality of Married Women," *Pax* 8, no. 1 (December 1932).

124. Gabrielle Radziwill, quoted in C. Miller 1992, 205.

125. C. Miller 1992, 205–9.

126. Page 1984.

127. Lily van der Schalk-Schuster to Helen Archdale, October 26, 1930, May 4, 1931, ERI papers, box 331, FL. There is extensive documentation of this conflict in the ERI papers.

128. Helen Archdale to Anna Nilsson, May 31, 1933, ERI papers, box 331, FL.

129. Helen Archdale to Doris Stevens, May 22, 1932, Stevens papers, carton 4, SL.

130. Quoted in C. Miller 1994, 235.

131. Eugenie Miskoczy Meller to Executive Committee of WILPF, May 28, 1933, WILPF papers, reel 2.

132. Chrystal McMillan [*sic*] to Jane Norman Smith, copy, February 10, 1934, Smith papers, box 4, SL.

133. Jane Norman Smith to Chrystal Macmillan, March 7, 1934, Smith papers, box 4, SL.

134. Minutes, Liaison Committee, September 14, 1934, LC papers, no. 2, IISG; minutes, WILPF International Executive committee, London, March 25–30, 1935, WILPF papers, reel 11; May Ogilvie Gordon, "The Congress of the International Alliance for Women Suffrage at Istanbul," ICW *Bulletin* 13, no. 8

(April 1935); "List of Resolutions Passed by the Council Meeting," Dubrovnik, September 28–October 9, 1936, ICW, *President's Memorandum*, 1926, 14.

135. Draft speech of Chrystal Macmillan, Joint Demonstration on the Nationality of Married Women, March 14, 1930, Palthe-Broese van Groenau papers, IIAV.

136. On the World WCTU, see Tyrrell 1991b; on imperialism and prostitution, see Burton 1994; on the traffic in women, see C. Miller 1992.

137. Cartoon no. 12, *Jus Suffragii* 25, no. 6 (March 1931).

138. Avril de Sainte-Croix, "Committee on 'White Slave Traffic' and Equal Moral Standard," ICW *Annual Report*, 1906–07.

139. "Editorial Notes," *Jus Suffragii* 7, no. 10 (July 15, 1913).

140. A. Maud Royden, "Solidarity," *Jus Suffragii* 7, no. 10 (July 15, 1913).

141. "Replies from the National Councils to the First Draft of the Preliminary Agenda," [1909], HLA, 80-319(3), LB; "Resolutions Adopted at the Quinquenniel Council Meeting of the ICW," ICW 1909 congress report, vol. 1; Carrie Chapman Catt to Aletta Jacobs, December 7, 1912, Jacobs papers, IIAV; A. Maud Royden, "Solidarity," *Jus Suffragii* 7, no. 10 (July 15, 1913).

142. M. I. Corbett-Ashby [*sic*], "League of Nations," *Jus Suffragii* 15, no. 6 (March 1921); Emily Greene Balch to the President of the Assembly of the League of Nations, December 9, 1920, WILPF papers, reel 1; [Emily Greene Balch?] to Gabrielle Duchêne [French/English], [1920], WILPF papers, reel 1.

143. Quoted in C. Miller 1992, 155.

144. Aletta Jacobs to Rosika Schwimmer [German], September 10, 1906, Schwimmer-Lloyd collection, box A-10, NYPL.

145. Aletta H. Jacobs, "Resolution on the White Slave Traffic," August 22, 1913, *Jus Suffragii* 8, no. 1 (September 1, 1913).

146. Nina Boyle to Editor, *Jus Suffragii* 16, no. 9 (June 1922).

147. C. Nina Boyle to Editor, *Jus Suffragii* 22, no. 7 (April 1928).

148. C. Miller 1992, 165.

149. Alison Neilans to Margery Corbett Ashby, February 22, 1937, Appendix D to minutes, IAWSEC board, Zurich, February 25 and March 1–2, 1937, IAW papers, FL.

150. "Resolutions Passed at the Quinquennial Meeting of the ICW Held in Cristiana September 8th–18th, 1920," ICW *Annual Report*, 1920–22; "Resolutions Regarding Questions of Morality and the Equal Moral Standard," ICW 1920 congress report, 38–39.

151. P. Chaponnière-Chaix, "The International Council of Women at The Hague, May 14–22, 1922," ICW *Bulletin* 1, no. 6 (August 1922).

152. "Meetings of the Board and Presidents' Council," *Jus Suffragii* 18, no. 9 (June 1924).

153. L. de Alberti, "The Paris Congress," *Jus Suffragii* 20, no. 9 (July 1926).

154. Editor, "The Month's Miscellany," *Jus Suffragii* 19, no. 5 (February 1925).

155. Aletta Jacobs to Rosika Schwimmer [German], September 10, 1906, Schwimmer-Lloyd collection, box A-10, NYPL.

156. de Witt Schlumberger to Editor, *Jus Suffragii* 11, no. 8 (May 1, 1917);

see also, in addition to articles cited below, de Witt Schlumberger, "Neo-Malthusianism Criticised," *Jus Suffragii* 11, no. 12 (September 1, 1917); and letters in *Jus Suffragii* 12, no. 1 (October 1, 1917).

157. Edith How Martyn to Editor, May 1917, *Jus Suffragii* 11, no. 9 (June 1, 1917).

158. M. W. W. Rutgers-Hoitsema to Editor, October 2, 1917, *Jus Suffragii* 12, no. 2 (November 1, 1917).

159. Edith How Martyn to Editor, *Jus Suffragii* 30, no. 2 (November 1935).

160. Vera Laughton Mathews to Editor, *Jus Suffragii* 30, no. 3 (December 1935). See also Isabel Donzé to Editor, same issue.

161. K.B., "A Controversial Question," *Jus Suffragii* 32, no. 1 (October 1937).

162. Leonora de Alberti to Jeanne Eder-Schwyzer, August 29, 1921, June 28, 1923, and August 18, 1923; Florence Barry to Jeanne Eder-Schwyzer, September 15, 1921; and [Jeanne Eder-Schwyzer], "Die Internationale Liga der katholischen Frauenbünde und der Pariser Kongress": all in Eder-Schwyzer papers, IIAV; A. L. P. Dorman, "Suffrage and the International Catholic Women's Leagues," *Jus Suffragii* 16, no. 11 (August 1922); "The I.W.S.A. and the Catholic Women's League," *Jus Suffragii* 18, no. 3 (December 1923); minutes, Liaison Committee, December 4, 1928, and February 5, 1929, LC papers, no. 1, IISG.

163. Minutes, ICW Executive Committee [German], May 10–13, 1932, Geneva, HLA, 85-336(1), LB; Lady Aberdeen to Presidents [German], June 27, 1932, HLA, 85-334(1), LB.

164. Printed resolutions and proposals, [1929?], WILPF papers, reel 19.

Chapter 7

1. Marie Stritt to Lady Aberdeen [German], December 3, 1927, HLA, 78-315(1), LB.

2. Ishbel Aberdeen, "President's Report," ICW *Annual Report*, 1905–06; "The Delegates at Hotel Wittsburg," [informal Executive Committee meeting, June 1907], ICW *Annual Report*, 1906–07; May Wright Sewall to Marie Stritt, August 14, 1908, HLA, 84-330(2), LB; "Business Transacted at the Special Session of the ICW," September 1–5, 1908, ICW *Annual Report*, 1907–08; ICW *Annual Report*, 1913–14, 152.

3. May Wright Sewall, "The Report on Council Insignia," [August 17–19, 1903], in ICW 1909 congress report, vol. 1.

4. May Wright Sewall to Co-Workers, December 31, 1903, HLA, 83-329(5), LB.

5. Minutes, first business meeting of the Quinquennial Council, May 6, 1925, "Report on the Quinquennial Meeting," edited by the Marchioness of Aberdeen and Temair, ICW HQ.

6. IWSA 1904 and 1906 congress report.

7. Carrie Chapman Catt, "Announcements," *Jus Suffragii* 5, no. 9 (May 15, 1911).

8. "Competition for a New Alliance Emblem," *Jus Suffragii* 22, no. 9 (June 1928).

9. Minutes, IAWSEC International Committee, July 8-9, 1938, IAW papers, FL.

10. Minutes, Third International WILPF Congress, July 10-16, 1921, WILPF papers, reel 18.

11. [Emily Greene Balch] to Lucy Biddle Lewis, June 10, 1919, WILPF papers, reel 36.

12. Minutes, ICW Executive Committee, July 5, 1898, ICW Executive Minute Book, ICW HQ; minutes, Fourth and Final Business Session, ICW 1899 congress report, vol. 1, 178-79.

13. [Elsie Zimmern], ICW, "Biennial Report," 1925-27, ICW papers, box 1, SSC.

14. *Women in a Changing World* 1966, 100.

15. K.B. [Katherine Bompas], "International Communications," *Jus Suffragii* 30, no. 2 (November 1935).

16. [Emily Greene Balch], "Report of the Secretary-Treasurer of the W.I.L.P.F. to June 1920," WILPF papers, reel 1.

17. Emily Greene Balch to Jane Addams, December 4, 1919, Addams papers, reel 12.

18. Vilma Glücklich, "Report of Vilma Glücklich on the work done by the Geneva office between . . . May, 1924, and . . . July, 1925," WILPF papers, reel 2.

19. WILPF, "What Is This League?" [1920-21], WILPF papers, reel 9.

20. "La Maison Internationale," WILPF *Bulletin*, June and August 1922.

21. "Geneva Headquarters," *Pax* 1, no. 11 (October 1926); Madeleine Doty, "International Headquarters," *Pax* 1, no. 1 (November 1925).

22. Madeleine Doty to Jane Addams, November 2, 1925, Addams papers, reel 17.

23. Mary Sheepshanks quoted in Alberti 1989, 201.

24. Lida Heymann and Anita Augspurg, "Maison Internationale," *Pax* 1, no. 2 (December 1925).

25. Madeleine Doty to Jane Addams, April 16, 1928, Addams papers, reel 19.

26. "Report of the Officer's Meeting," Zurich, October 4-5, 1932, WILPF papers, reel 10; E. G. Balch, "London, March 25-30," *Pax* 10, no. 2 (March-April 1935); minutes, WILPF International Executive Committee, September 24, [1933], WILPF papers, reel 10; minutes, International Executive Committee, Geneva, September 7-11, 1938, WILPF papers, reel 11; Lotti Birch to Chairmen [German], March 31, 1939, WILPF papers, reel 4.

27. Minutes, Executive Committee, Geneva, September 12-16, 1935, WILPF papers, reel 11.

28. Lotti Birch to Clara Ragaz [German], July 22, 1938, WILPF papers, reel 3.

29. "Das internationale Heim 'Maison Internationale' in Genf," *Die Frau*, October 1920.

30. Minutes, WILPF Executive Committee, July 4-9, 1921, WILPF papers, reel 9.

31. Minutes, WILPF International Executive Committee, Geneva, September 10-14, 1936, WILPF papers, reel 11.

32. "Preliminary Report of Discussions and Decisions of Informal Executive Meeeting," London, February 4–5, 1924, WILPF papers, reel 1; Vilma Glücklich to Jane Addams, June 26, 1924, Addams papers, reel 16.

33. Sophie H. R. [Hattinga-Raven] to Vilma Glücklich [German], January 23, 1925, WILPF papers, reel 9; Cor Ramondt-Hirschmann to Vilma Glücklich, February 4, 1925, WILPF papers, reel 9.

34. Minutes, WILPF International Executive Committee, March 27, [1934], WILPF papers, reel 10.

35. Minutes, WILPF International Executive Committee, Dresden, September 1–5, 1923, WILPF papers, reel 9; "Proposals of C. Drevet," [1931], WILPF papers, reel 10; minutes, WILPF International Executive Committee, March 27, [1934], WILPF papers, reel 10.

36. Mary Sheepshanks to Alice Hamilton, December 12, 1928, Addams papers, reel 20; Emily Greene Balch to Anna Wössner, September 21, 1921, WILPF papers, reel 1.

37. [Mary Sheepshanks] to Executive Member, December 29, 1927, WILPF papers, reel 2.

38. [Emily Balch?] to [no addressee], July 7, 1922, WILPF papers, reel 1.

39. Marie Stritt to May Wright Sewall [German], August 7, 1903, HLA, 80-319(2), LB.

40. [Margery Corbett Ashby], "Relationship of International Alliance and the International Council," [March 1953], IAW papers, FL.

41. "Practical Suggestions for International Executive Meetings," [1930?], WILPF papers, reel 10; [Edith Pye] to Camille Drevet, February 17, 1933, WILPF papers, reel 2; minutes, WILPF International Executive committee, Geneva, April 11–14, 1933, WILPF papers, reel 10; Edith Pye to Gertrud Baer, August 14, 1933, WILPF papers, reel 2.

42. Christine Touaillon to International Executive Committee, February 2, 1928, WILPF papers, reel 2.

43. Gabrielle Duchêne to National Sections [French], February 1928, WILPF papers, reel 2; "Section Française aux Sections Nationales," February 1928, WILPF papers, reel 2.

44. [Mary Sheepshanks] to Yella Hertzka [German], February 18, 1930, WILPF papers, reel 2; Yella Hertzka to Mary Sheepshanks [German], March 3, 1930, WILPF papers, reel 2; [Mary Sheepshanks] to Yella Hertzka, March 24, 1930, WILPF papers, reel 2.

45. Edith Pye to Gertrud Baer, July 11, 1933, WILPF papers, reel 2; [Edith Pye] to Lida Gustava Heymann, July 12, 1933, WILPF papers, reel 2.

46. Emily Balch to Fellow Members of the International Executive committee, [March 4, 1934], WILPF papers, reel 2.

47. Minutes, WILPF International Executive, Prague, August 30, 1929, WILPF papers, reel 10; E. Eaton, "A Newcomer's Impression of the International Executive Committee," *Pax* 11, no. 6 (November 1936).

48. May Wright Sewall to Carrie Chapman Catt, June 4, 1904, NAWSA papers, reel 18, LofC.

49. Lady Aberdeen to Marie Stritt, July 6, 1905, HLA, 83-329(7), LB.

50. "Board Meeting," *Jus Suffragii* 18, no. 11 (August 1924).

51. "Alliance Board Meeting in Brussels," *Jus Suffragii* 31, no. 1 (October 1936).

52. Vilma Glücklich to Friends, August 16, 1923, WILPF papers, reel 1; "W.I.L. International Executive Committee," *Pax* 6, no. 1 (November 1930).

53. Minutes, WILPF International Executive Committee, Prague, April 29–May 4, 1936.

54. Madeleine Doty to Mme. Beskow, February 24, 1926, WILPF papers, reel 2.

55. Mary Sheepshanks to Jane Addams, March 28, 1928, Addams papers, reel 19.

56. See WILPF *Bulletin*, December 1, 1920.

57. Notes on Executive Committee meeting, [Innsbruck, July 10–15, 1925], WILPF papers, reel 2.

58. I.A.&T. [Ishbel Aberdeen and Temair], "President's Notes," ICW *Bulletin* 6, no. 10 (June 1928).

59. "Headquarters Notes," ICW *Bulletin* 15, nos. 5–6 (January–February 1937).

60. Minutes, Disarmament Committee, May 7, 1934, ICW papers, box 2, LofC.

61. May Wright Sewall to Marie Stritt, March 28, 1903, HLA, 83-329(3), LB; "President's Memorandum," [August 19, 1903], ICW 1909 congress report, vol. 1.

62. "The Meeting of the International Board of Officers," *Jus Suffragii* 8, no. 12 (August 1, 1914).

63. Emily Balch to Helena Swanwick, March 31, 1920, Addams papers, reel 12.

64. Vilma Glücklich to Executive Members, National Sections and Referents of Special Committees, July 20, 1923, WILPF papers, reel 1.

65. "Report of Meeting," ICW Executive Committee, London, March 23, 1899, ICW Executive Minute Book, ICW HQ; minutes, Fourth and Final Business Session, ICW 1899 congress report, vol. 1, 188–90.

66. Minutes, WILPF Congress Committee, Brussels, January 30, 1937, WILPF papers, reel 21.

67. Alice Salomon, "Character is Destiny," 133–34, Salomon papers, LBI.

68. Sewall 1894, 65–67.

69. Minutes, WILPF Prague Congress Committee, January 7, [1929], WILPF papers, reel 19; minutes, IAWSEC board, Paris, December 6–9, 1938, IAW papers, FL.

70. Rosika Schwimmer to Fräulein Müller [German], March 15, 1912, Schwimmer-Lloyd collection, box A-28, NYPL.

71. *Jus Suffragii* 7, no. 10 (July 15, 1913).

72. "Editoral Notes," *Jus Suffragii* 7, no. 10 (July 15, 1913); Carrie Chapman Catt, "Fraternal Delegates," *Jus Suffragii* 7, no. 10 (July 15, 1913).

73. Margery Corbett Ashby to Carrie Chapman Catt, June 30, 1929, NAWSA papers, reel 11, LofC.

74. Minutes, IXth WILPF World Congress, Luhacovice, July 27–31, 1937, WILPF papers, reel 21.

75. Cor Ramondt-Hirschmann to Gertrud Baer [German], February 18, 1937, WILPF papers, reel 3.

76. [Emily Balch], untitled typescript, [1926], WILPF papers, reel 19.

77. L. de Alberti, "How Rome Welcomed the Congress," *Jus Suffragii* 17, no. 9 (July 1923).

78. Ishbel Aberdeen and Temair, "Foreword," ICW *Bulletin* 13, no. 1 (July 1934).

79. Jane Addams to Edith Pye, August 17, 1932, Addams papers, reel 24.

80. Ishbel Aberdeen, "President's Report," ICW *Annual Report*, 1907-08.

81. May Wright Sewall, "Introduction to volume I," ICW 1904 congress report, vol. 1.

82. Ishbel Aberdeen and Temair, "President's Letter," ICW *Bulletin* 11, no. 2 (October 1932).

83. Hon. International Secretary to Mrs. W. F. Osborne, April 27, 1934, WILPF papers, reel 20; Greta Engkvist to Vice Presidents, July 12, 1934, WILPF papers, reel 20.

84. Anna Howard Shaw to Aletta Jacobs, July 11, 1913, Jacobs papers, IIAV.

85. "Quinquennial Tours," brochure, 1930, HLA, 84-332(4), LB; CRH [Cor Ramondt-Hirschmann] to Gabrielle Duchêne [French], October 5, 1931, WILPF papers, reel 20.

86. Carrie Chapman Catt, "Announcements," *Jus Suffragii* 5, no. 9 (May 15, 1911).

87. Mrs. Ogilvie Gordon, "Impressions of the Quinqennial Meeting in Kristiana by Some of the Delegates," ICW 1920 congress report, 231.

88. "The Tenth Congress of the Alliance, Paris, 1926," *Jus Suffragii* 19, no. 9 (June 1925).

89. Minutes, WILPF VIth International Congress, Prague, [1929], WILPF papers, reel 19.

90. Quoted in Gerhard 1990, 211.

91. Crystal Eastman Benedict, "A Comment," *Jus Suffragii* 7, no. 10 (July 15, 1913).

92. Margery Corbett Ashby, diary entry, May 9, 1925, Corbett Ashby papers, box 484, FL.

93. Minutes, WILPF International Executive Committee, September 26–29, 1928, WILPF papers, reel 9; [Mary Sheepshanks] to Milena Illova, May 9, 1929, WILPF papers, reel 19.

94. Marie Stritt to Lady Aberdeen, December 3, 1927, HLA, 78-315(1), LB.

95. Julie Siegfried to Lady Aberdeen [French], August 9, 1914, ICW papers, box 10, NCW-GB.

96. Louie Bennett to Gertrud [Baer], May 8, 1934, WILPF papers, reel 20.

97. May Wright Sewall to Anna Simson, August 13, 1899, HLA, 83-329(1), LB.

98. Carrie Chapman Catt to Rosa Manus, July 19, 1929, Catt papers, reel 4, LofC.

99. Minutes, IAWSEC International Committee, Zurich, February 26, 1937, IAW papers, FL.

100. Lady Aberdeen to Fannie Fern Andrews, August 10, 1920, Andrews

papers, box 119, SL; Rosa Manus to Carrie Chapman Catt, November 12, 1939, Catt papers, IIAV.

101. Ishbel Aberdeen and Temair, "President's Memorandum," ICW *Bulletin* 3, nos. 9–10 (June–July 1925).

102. Aino Kallas quoted in "Gleanings from the Council Meetings," ICW *Bulletin* 3, nos. 9–10 (June–July 1925).

103. "Meeting of the Board of Officers of the Alliance," *Jus Suffragii* 19, no. 11–12 (August–September 1925); Madeleine Doty, "Story of the Congress," *Pax* 1, no. 9 (August 1926).

104. Anna Howard Shaw to Aletta Jacobs, December 11, 1909, Jacobs papers, IIAV.

105. Elizabeth Abbott to Emily Greene Balch, October 8, 1920, and November 2, 1920, WILPF papers, reel 35; "Brief von Frl. Heymann," December 4, 1920, WILPF papers, reel 36; letter to members of the Executive Committee and Consultative Members, January 12, 1921, WILPF papers, reel 18; "News of the Young Women's Christian Association throughout the World," supplement to *Jus Suffragii* 15, no. 4 (January 1921).

106. Minutes, Fourth and Final Business Session, ICW 1899 congress report, vol. 1, 191–92; "The International Committees," ICW *Annual Report*, 1904–05; Emily Cummings, "The 'Press Committee,'" ICW *Annual Report*, 1906–07; "President's Memorandum," ICW 1920 congress report, 13–17; "President's Report," ICW *Annual Report*, 1920–22.

107. "12. Sendschreiben, An die Mitglieder des Internationalen Frauenausschusses für dauernden Frieden," February 5, 1916, Schwimmer-Lloyd collection, box A-73, NYPL.

108. Emily Greene Balch to Signora Grassi, July 31, 1919, WILPF papers, reel 36; Emily Greene Balch to Jane Addams, October 11, 1919, Addams papers, reel 12.

109. Madeleine Z. Doty, "Pax International to Continue," *Pax* 3, no. 5 (April 1928); minutes, WILPF International Executive committee, September 24, [1933], WILPF papers, reel 10.

110. [Gertrud Baer] to Klara [sic] Ragaz [German], January 23, 1936, WILPF papers, reel 2.

111. [Emily Greene Balch], "Report of the Secretary-Treasurer of the W.I.L.P.F. to June 1920," WILPF papers, reel 1.

112. Minutes, IAWSEC Board meeting, Amsterdam, May 9–11, 1936, IAW papers, FL.

113. Minutes, WILPF 5th Biennial Congress, Dublin, July 9–15, 1926, WILPF papers, reel 19.

114. Helen Wilson, "The Prevention of Venereal Disease," *Jus Suffragii* 11, no. 1 (October 1, 1916); "Simplification de la Toilette Feminine," *Jus Suffragii* 19, no. 7 (April 1925) and no. 8 (May 1925); "Editorial Notes," ICW *Bulletin* 6, no. 3 (November 1927).

115. Martina G. Kramers, "Dear Correspondents and Readers," *Jus Suffragii* 4, no. 5 (January 15, 1910); "Meetings of the I.W.S.A. Board of Officers," *Jus Suffragii* 15, no. 11 (August 1921).

116. Editor, "The Month's Miscellany," *Jus Suffragii* 19, no. 5 (February 1925).

117. "Miscelleanous [*sic*], ICW *Bulletin* 1, no. 8 (December 1922).

118. Anna Backer, "Report for the Quinquennial Period," 1925, ICW Executive Minute Book, ICW HQ.

119. ICW *Bulletin* 6, no. 1 (September 1927).

120. G. M. Günther, "Editor's Report," ICW, *President's Memorandum*, 1938, 51–55.

121. Bussey and Timms 1965, 53; M. Z. Doty, "Report on Pax," [1931], WILPF papers, reel 10; Lotti Birch, "Report on Activities at Geneva Headquarters from May 1st, 1936–July 15th, 1937," WILPF papers, reel 21.

122. "The Paper," *Jus Suffragii* 27, no. 1 (October 1932).

123. "The Paper," *Jus Suffragii* 24, no. 5 (February 1930).

124. Marthe Boël, "Report on the Activities of the ICW since the Last Council Meeting," ICW, *President's Memorandum*, 1938.

125. *Internationaal* 3, no. 4 (October–November–December 1918); Harriet C. Newcomb to Editor, November 11, 1918, *Jus Suffragii* 13, no. 3 (December 1918).

126. Lena Madesin Phillips to Renée Girod, May 7, 1941, Phillips papers, carton 5, SL; Marthe Boël, "President's Open Letter," ICW *Bulletin* 18, no. 5 (February 1940).

127. "*Jus* Report," IWSA 1923 congress report, 50.

128. "Pax International," *Pax* 6, no. 4 (March 1931).

129. "Interim Report of Corresponding Secretary," ICW *Annual Report*, 1905–06.

130. Annie B. Sterritt, "Unmet Friends," *Pax* 3, no. 2 (December 1927).

131. Mary Sheepshanks to Rosika Schwimmer, December 15, 1914, Schwimmer-Lloyd collection, box A-50, NYPL.

Chapter 8

1. Ishbel Aberdeen and Temair, "A Christmas and New Year Message from Our Hon. President," ICW *Bulletin* 15, no. 4 (December 1936).

2. Madeleine Z. Doty to International Member, [December 1927], WILPF papers, reel 9.

3. Lola Hanouskova to Gertrud Baer [German], January 18, 1937, WILPF papers, reel 21.

4. Sewall 1894.

5. Rosika Schwimmer to Aletta Jacobs [German], August 5, 1908, and Rosika Schwimmer to Helene Lazarovich [German], August 7, 1908, both in Schwimmer-Lloyd collection, box A-15, NYPL.

6. [Mary Sheepshanks] to Executive Member, November 24, 1927, WILPF papers, reel 2; Naima Sahlbom to Gabrielle Duchêne, March 11, 1921, Dossiers Duchêne, F Rés. 296, BDIC.

7. Anita Augspurg to Rosika Schwimmer [German], May 14, 1904, Schwimmer-Lloyd collection, box A-5, NYPL; Whittick 1979, 34.

8. Margery Corbett Ashby, "1920: Geneva," n.d., Corbett Ashby papers, box 483, FL.

9. Clara Ragaz to Lotti Birch [German], May 16, 1937, WILPF papers, reel 3; Clara Ragaz to K. E. Innes and Gertrud Baer [German], February 21, 1938, WILPF papers, reel 3.

10. Carrie Chapman Catt to Aletta Jacobs, November 19, 1907; March 1, 1909; September 27, 1909; and July 16, 1910: all in Jacobs papers, IIAV.

11. Carrie Catt to Aletta Jacobs, December 15, 1908; January 27, 1909; and July 16, 1910: all in Jacobs papers, IIAV.

12. [Madeleine Doty] to Louie Bennett, June 23, 1926, WILPF papers, reel 18.

13. Vilma Glücklich to Gabrielle Duchêne [French], November 26, 1924, Dossiers Duchêne, F Rés. 207, BDIC.

14. Quoted in Pentland 1947.

15. ICW 1899 congress report, vol. 1, 56.

16. Carrie Catt to Rosa Manus, February 17, 1933, Catt papers, reel 4, LofC; Ishbel Aberdeen, ICW *President's Memorandum*, 1930; Rosa Manus to Katharine von Kardorff [German], [November 19, 1931], Manus papers, IIAV; Rosa Manus to Josephine Schain, April 19, 1932, Schain papers, box 6, SSC.

17. Aletta Jacobs to Rosika Schwimmer [German], February 10, 1904, Schwimmer-Lloyd collection, box A-5, NYPL.

18. Carrie Catt to Rosika Schwimmer, June 24, 1913, Schwimmer-Lloyd collection, box A-7, NYPL.

19. "Report of the Board of the Alliance," IAWSEC 1926 congress report, 52.

20. Josephine Schain to Rosa Manus, November 30, 1934, September 14, 1939, Schain papers, box 5, SSC.

21. M. I. Corbett Ashby, "The President's New Year Message," *Jus Suffragii* 32, no. 4 (January 1938).

22. Anna Howard Shaw to Aletta Jacobs, November 15, 1905, Jacobs papers, IIAV.

23. Anna Howard Shaw to Mien van Wulfften Palthe-Broese van Groenau, Saturday 1913, Palthe-Broese van Groenau papers, IIAV; Anna Howard Shaw to Aletta Jacobs, [October 4, 1915], Jacobs papers, IIAV.

24. Countess van Heerdt-Quarles to Carrie Chapman Catt, Christmas 1920, *Jus Suffragii* 15, no. 4 (January 1921).

25. Margery Corbett Ashby, notes on "Berlin Congress, 1904," n.d., Corbett Ashby papers, box 483, FL.

26. Marianne Hainisch to Aletta Jacobs [German], October 26, 1906, Jacobs papers, IIAV.

27. "The Impressions of the Swedish Delegation Concerning the Meeting of the I.C.W. in Canada," in Aberdeen 1909, 15–18.

28. Rosa Manus to Clara Hyde, December 18, 1923, Catt papers, reel 4, LofC.

29. Emily Hobhouse to Jane Addams, November 4, 1915, Jacobs papers, IIAV.

30. Rosika Schwimmer to Emily Balch, January 26, 1916, Schwimmer-Lloyd collection, box A-72, NYPL.

31. Camille Drevet to Jane Addams, February 6, 1928, Addams papers, reel 19.

32. Bertha Lutz to Carrie Chapman Catt, January 14, 1939, NAWSA papers, reel 12, LofC.

33. Cor Ramondt-Hirschmann to Lotti Birch, June 30, 1937, and Gertrud Baer to Cor Ramondt-Hirschmann [German], July 4, 1937, both in WILPF papers, reel 3.

34. P. Chapponniére-Chaix to Lady Aberdeen, November 8, 1911, ICW papers, box 10, NCW-GB.

35. Marie Stritt to Rosika Schwimmer [German], November 6, 1911, Schwimmer-Lloyd collection, box A-27, NYPL; Marie Stritt, "What We Owe to the Alliance," *Jus Suffragii* 8, no. 9 (May 1, 1914).

36. "Sechster Verhandlungstag," 1919, WILPF papers, reel 17.

37. Rosa Manus to Laura Dreyfus-Barney, April 22, 1932, ICW papers, box 3, LofC.

38. Minutes, WILPF Executive Committee, Paris, February 6–10, 1926, WILPF papers, reel 9.

39. C. Ramondt-Hirschmann to Executive Committee members and national sections [French], August 1930, WILPF papers, reel 10.

40. Winifred Giles to Emily Greene Balch, February 28, 1920, WILPF papers, reel 1; Dorothy Evans to Jane Addams, March 2, 1925, Addams papers, reel 17.

41. Adele Schreiber to Rosika Schwimmer [German], Schwimmer-Lloyd collection, box A-6, NYPL; Rosika Schwimmer to Frau Eschholz [German], January 2, 1912, Schwimmer-Lloyd collection, box A-28, NYPL.

42. Alice Salomon to Jane Addams, January 7, 1919 [*sic*, for 1920], Addams papers, reel 12; Josephine Erkeus to Margery Ashby [German], November 22, 1933, Corbett Ashby papers, box 483, FL.

43. Carrie Catt to Rosika Schwimmer, June 24, 1913, Schwimmer-Lloyd collection, box A-33, NYPL; Aletta Jacobs to Rosika Schwimmer [German], June 23, 1906, Schwimmer-Lloyd collection, box A-9, NYPL.

44. Rosika Schwimmer to Carrie Catt, September 10, 1946, NAWSA papers, reel 18, LofC.

45. Rosa Manus to Clara Hyde, March 20, 1924, Catt papers, reel 4, LofC; Rosa Manus to Carrie Catt, January 24, 1932, Catt papers, reel 4, LofC.

46. Aletta Jacobs to Rosika Schwimmer [German], December 28, 1904, Schwimmer-Lloyd collection, box A-6, NYPL.

47. Kate Waller Barrett, "Impressions of Canada Received during the Quinquennial Meeting of the ICW at Toronto," in Aberdeen 1909, 1–5.

48. Anna Lindemann to Rosika Schwimmer [German], August 19, 1911, Schwimmer-Lloyd collection, box A-26, NYPL.

49. Dorothy North to Jane Addams, June 5, 1920, Addams papers, reel 13.

50. Lida Gustava Heymann to Jane Addams [German], January 6, 1927, Addams papers, reel 18.

51. Katharine von Kardorff to Rosa Manus [German], February 27, 1935, Manus papers, IIAV.

52. Anna Howard Shaw to Aletta Jacobs, May 22, 1908, Jacobs papers, IIAV.

53. Carrie Catt to Frances and Pan, October 15, 1910, Catt papers, reel 5, LofC.

54. Fowler 1986, 27.

55. Rachel Foster Avery to Aletta Jacobs, July 17, 1906, Jacobs papers, IIAV.

56. Margery Corbett to Emilia Coops-Broese van Groenau, November 3, 1909, Coops-Broese van Groenau papers, IIAV.

57. Fannie Fern Andrews, diary of European trip of 1915, Andrews papers, SL; Alice Park, diary entry, June 3, 1926, Park papers, box 25, HI.

58. Lida Gustava Heymann to Gabrielle Duchêne, February 14, 1926, Dossiers Duchêne, F Rés. 206, BDIC.

59. Carrie Catt to Aletta Jacobs, September 7, 1905, and December 1905, both in Jacobs papers, IIAV.

60. Charlotte Perkins Gilman to Aletta Jacobs, November 22, 1905, Jacobs papers, IIAV.

61. Carrie Chapman Catt to Vilma Glücklich, December 5, 1905, Schwimmer-Lloyd collection, box A-8, NYPL.

62. Emily Balch to Jane Addams, December 1, 1932, Addams papers, reel 24; Vilma Glücklich to Jane Addams, September 17, 1924, Addams papers, reel 16.

63. Rosa Manus to Katharine von Kardorff [German], February 4, 1930, Manus papers, IIAV; Rosika Schwimmer to Carrie Catt, February 9, 1939, NAWSA papers, reel 18, LofC.

64. Pentland 1947.

65. Alice Salomon, "Character is Destiny," 67, Salomon papers, LBI.

66. Anna Howard Shaw to Aletta Jacobs, September 6, 1909, Jacobs papers, IIAV.

67. Notes from Martha Connole's diary, 1938, Phillips papers, carton 5, SL.

68. Elisabeth Zellweger, "What She Was to Us," ICW *Bulletin* 17, no. 8 (May 1939).

69. Alice Salomon, "Character is Destiny," 67, Salomon papers, LBI.

70 Hertha Sprung to Emma Ender [German], December 28, 1929, HLA, 85-333(9), LB.

71. Rosa Manus to Carrie Chapman Catt, June 22, 1926, Catt papers, reel 4, LofC. For Alice Salomon's comment, see "Character is Destiny," 83, Salomon papers, LBI.

72. Rose Scott to Lady Aberdeen, January 16, 1911, ICW papers, box 10, NCW-GB.

73. Eva Upmark to Lady Aberdeen, October 2, 1911, ICW papers, box 10, NCW-GB.

74. Countess Albert Apponyi to Lady Aberdeen, December 22, 1911, ICW papers, box 10, NCW-GB.

75. Marie Michelet, "The Farewell Banquet," ICW 1920 congress report, 220–22.

76. "The Council Sessions of the ICW at Dubrovnik," ICW *Bulletin* 15, no. 3 (November 1936).

77. Marthe Boël, "To Lady Aberdeen, on Her 80th Birthday," ICW *Bulletin* 15, no. 7 (March 1937); Marthe Boël, "A Message of Goodbye," ICW *Bulletin* 17, no. 8 (May 1939).

78. Clara Mende, "A Visit to Mrs. Chapman Catt," *Jus Suffragii* 20, no. 4 (January 1926), reprinted from the ICW *Bulletin*.

79. Swiss page [German], Birthday Memorial Book, 1929, Catt papers, IIAV;

M.A.D. [Mary A. Dingman] to Rosa Manus, December 6, 1940, Manus papers, IIAV.

80. Carrie Chapman Catt to Rosika Schwimmer, August 4, 1908, Schwimmer-Lloyd collection, box A-15, NYPL.

81. Carrie Chapman Catt to Rosika Schwimmer, [June 1913], Schwimmer-Lloyd collection, box A-33, NYPL.

82. Annie Furuhjelm, "Our Alliance," *Jus Suffragii* 8, no. 9 (May 1, 1914).

83. Martina Kramers to Rosika Schwimmer, March 20, 1913, Schwimmer-Lloyd collection, box A-32, NYPL.

84. Anna Lindemann to Rosika Schwimmer [German], March 29, 1913, Schwimmer-Lloyd collection, box A-32, NYPL.

85. Chrystal Macmillan to Dear ———, December 12, 1914, Schwimmer-Lloyd collection, box A-50, NYPL.

86. Martina Kramers to Rosika Schwimmer [German], November 5, 1907, Schwimmer-Lloyd collection, box A-14, NYPL.

87. Anna Howard Shaw to Aletta Jacobs, July 11, 1913, Jacobs papers, IIAV. On the relationship between Catt and Shaw, see Bosch 1990.

88. [no signature] to Miss Leckie, August 18, 1917, Schwimmer-Lloyd collection, box A-91, NYPL.

89. Carrie Chapman Catt to Aletta Jacobs, December 21, 1921, Jacobs papers, IIAV; Carrie Catt, diary of tour of Europe, October–November 1922, Catt papers, reel 2, LofC.

90. Dutchie [Rosa Manus] to Clara Hyde, December 2, 1922, Catt papers, reel 4, LofC.

91. Rosa Manus to Catharine McCulloch, June 2, 1909, Dillon collection, SL.

92. [Clara Hyde] to Rosa Manus, September 13, 1922, Catt papers, reel 4, LofC.

93. Rosa Manus to Dear Colleagues and Friends, [1928], Manus papers, IIAV; E[milie] Gourd to [Rosa Manus] [French], September 25, 1928, Manus papers, IIAV.

94. "Extract from greetings presented by Maud Wood Park," [1929], Manus papers, IIAV; Dutch pages, birthday memorial book, 1929, Catt papers, IIAV.

95. Rosa Manus to Friends of the Alliance, *Jus Suffragii* 28, no. 2 (November 1933); *Jus Suffragii* 33, no. 2 (November 1938).

96. Annie Furuhjelm to Carrie Chapman Catt, December 17, 1930, Catt papers, reel 3, LofC.

97. Bertha Lutz to Carrie Chapman Catt, July 26, 1945, NAWSA papers, reel 12, LofC.

98. Else Lüders to Carrie Chapman Catt, May 10, 1947, Catt papers, IIAV.

99. Rosika Schwimmer to Carrie Chapman Catt, December 16, 1914, Schwimmer-Lloyd collection, box A-50, NYPL. On Addams's reception in Japan, see Sugimori 1996.

100. Hermine C. Schützinger to Jane Addams [German], April 15, 1916, Addams papers, reel 9; Zedenka Smrekar to Jane Addams [German], August 7, 1921, Addams papers, reel 14; Alice Salomon to Jane Addams, april 12, 1922, Addams papers, reel 14.

101. Chrystal Macmillan to Jane Addams, January 14, 1916, Addams papers, reel 9.

102. Aletta Jacobs to Jane Addams, October 26, 1922, Addams papers, reel 15.

103. Lida Gustava Heymann to Jane Addams, December 10, 1928, Addams papers, reel 20.

104. Lida Gustava Heymann to Jane Addams, March 1, 1929, Addams papers, reel 20.

105. Minutes, WILPF VIth International Congress, Prague, [1929], WILPF papers, reel 19.

106. Aletta Jacobs and Rosa Manus to Jane Addams, March 24, 1919, WILPF papers, reel 1.

107. Aletta Jacobs to Carrie Catt, May 14, 1924, Catt papers, box 1, NYPL; "Messages of Europe, Christmas 1924," pamphlet, WILPF papers, reel 18.

108. Madeleine Doty, "Story of the Congress," *Pax* 1, no. 9 (August 1926).

109. Andrée Jouve, "Impressions of the Grenoble Congress," *Pax* 7, no. 7 (June 1932).

110. Chrystal Macmillan to Rosa Manus, March 21, 1915, WILPF papers, reel 25; "Central Bureau Notes," *Internationaal* 3, no. 2 (April–May–June 1918); *Internationaal* 3, no. 4 (October–November–December 1918).

111. Anna Howard Shaw to Aletta Jacobs, April 18, 1916, Jacobs papers, IIAV.

112. Rosika Schwimmer to Alice Park, June 4, 1926, Park papers, box 1, HI.

113. Jane Addams to Emily Balch, April 30, 1920, Addams papers, reel 12.

114. Clara Ragaz, "Jane Addams Nobel Prize Winner," *Pax* 7, no. 3 (January 1932).

115. *Pax* 7, no. 3 (January 1932); Addams papers, reel 22. On the Nobel Prize, and the relationship between Addams and Balch, see Alonso 1995, 1996; Deegan 1996.

116. Olga Misar to Jane Addams, August 19, 1921, Addams papers, reel 14.

117. Genevieve F. Tapping to Jane Addams, April 8, 1922, WILPF papers, reel 1.

118. Minutes, WILPF Executive Committee, Paris, February 6–10, 1926, WILPF papers, reel 9; Madeleine Doty to Jane Addams, [ca. September 10, 1926], Addams papers, reel 18.

119. Irma Tischer to Jane Addams, June 11, 1927, Addams papers, reel 19; Andrée Jouve to Jane Addams, January 6, 1928, Addams papers, reel 19.

120. Eleanor M. Moore to Jane Addams, October 4, 1928, Addams papers, reel 20.

121. Emily Greene Balch to Jane Addams, September 4, 1930, Addams papers, reel 21.

122. Minutes, WILPF Executive Committee, Geneva, September 12–16, 1935, WILPF papers, reel 11; *Pax* 10, nos. 3–4 (May–June 1935).

123. Clara Ragaz, "Opening Address," IXth World Congress of the WILPF, July 25–31, 1937, Palthe-Broese van Groenau papers, IIAV.

124. Rosa Manus to Clara Hyde, April 28, 1923, Catt papers, reel 4, LofC.

125. Cor Ramondt-Hirschmann to Jane Addams, November 25, 1924,

Addams papers, reel 16; Jane Addams to Emily Balch, February 14, 1922, Addams papers, reel 14.

126. Vilma Glücklich to Executive Committee, February 27, 1925, Addams papers, reel 17; V. Glücklich to Jane Addams, February 16, 1925, Addams papers, reel 17.

127. Vilma Glücklich to Jane Addams, October 30, 1925, Addams papers, reel 17.

128. [Gabrielle Duchêne] to Madeleine Doty [French], August 29, 1925, Dossiers Duchêne, F Rés. 207, BDIC.

129. Madeleine Doty to Jane Addams, October 28, 1925, Addams papers, reel 17.

130. Cor Ramondt-Hirschmann to Jane Addams, May 4, 1926, Addams papers, reel 18.

131. Extract from Marguerite Gobat's letter to Rosika Schwimmer, June 21, 1926, Palthe-Broese van Groenau papers, IIAV.

132. Alice Salomon, "Character is Destiny," 61, Salomon papers, LBI.

133. Cora di Brazza to May Wright Sewall, September 17, 1900, Sewall papers, I-MCPL.

134. Hanna K. Korany to May Wright Sewall, [1893], Sewall papers, I-MCPL.

135. Cath. van Rennes to Anna Howard Shaw, February 23, 1913, Dillon collection, box 20, SL.

136. Estelle Davis Williams to Rosika Schwimmer, March 22, 1915, Schwimmer-Lloyd collection, box A-56, NYPL.

137. Minna Cauer, "An meine Freunde!" November 1920, Jacobs papers, IIAV.

138. Bosch 1990 elaborates these friendships.

139. Anna Howard Shaw to Aletta Jacobs, July 17, 1906, Jacobs papers, IIAV.

140. Anna Howard Shaw to Aletta Jacobs, September 23, 1908, Jacobs papers, IIAV.

141. Anna Howard Shaw to Aletta Jacobs, December 14, 1908, Jacobs papers, IIAV.

142. Anna Howard Shaw to Aletta Jacobs, February 8, 1909, and January 4, 1915, both in Jacobs papers, IIAV.

143. Anna Howard Shaw to Aletta Jacobs, January 16, 1917, and Thanksgiving Day 1918, both in Jacobs papers, IIAV.

144. Aletta Jacobs to Lucy Anthony, July 5, 1919, Dillon collection, box 18, SL.

145. Aletta Jacobs to Lucy Anthony, September 26, 1919, Dillon collection, box 18, SL.

146. Aletta Jacobs to Lucy Anthony, February 21, 1920, Dillon collection, box 18, SL.

147. Carrie Chapman Catt to Aletta Jacobs, November 15, 1906, Jacobs papers, IIAV; Carrie Chapman Catt to Millicent Garrett Fawcett, [1909], Fawcett papers, box 89, FL.

148. Carrie Chapman Catt, "To Aletta," July 18, 1912, Jacobs papers, IIAV.

149. Carrie Chapman Catt to Aletta Jacobs, December 21, 1921, Jacobs papers, IIAV.

150. Rosa Manus to Clara Hyde, November 24, 1922, Catt papers, reel 4, LofC.

151. Rosa Manus to Clara Hyde, April 28, 1923; Rosa Manus to Carrie Chapman Catt, August 6, 1926; and Rosa Manus to Carrie Chapman Catt, May 14, 1927: all in Catt papers, reel 4, LofC.

152. Rosa Manus to Selma Lagerlöf [German], October 4, 1928, Manus papers, IIAV.

153. Laura Dreyfus-Barney to Rosa Manus [French], July 6, 1933, ICW papers, box 3, LofC.

154. Carrie Chapman Catt to Rosa Manus, July 19, 1929, and Rosa Manus to Carrie Chapman Catt, January 9, 1932, both in Catt papers, reel 4, LofC.

155. Rosa Manus to Carrie Chapman Catt, June 20, 1938, Catt papers, reel 4, LofC.

156. Dutchie [Rosa Manus] to Clara Hyde, December 21, 1922, Catt papers, reel 4, LofC.

157. Bertha Lutz to Carrie Chapman Catt, July 7, 1922, Catt papers, reel 4, LofC.

158. Bertha Lutz to Carrie Chapman Catt, July 29, 1931, NAWSA papers, reel 12, LofC.

159. Carrie Chapman Catt to Bertha Lutz, September 8, 1938, NAWSA papers, reel 12, LofC.

160. Carrie Chapman Catt to Rosika Schwimmer, September 7, 1905, Catt papers, reel 6, LofC.

161. Martina Kramers to Rosika Schwimmer [German], March 15, [1907], Schwimmer-Lloyd collection, box A-11, NYPL.

162. Lola Lloyd to Rosika Schwimmer, November 24, 1915, Schwimmer-Lloyd collection, box A-65, NYPL.

163. Lola Lloyd to Rosika Schwimmer, June 2, [1915], Schwimmer-Lloyd collection, box A-59, NYPL.

164. Lola Lloyd to Rosika Schwimmer, June 2, [1915], Schwimmer-Lloyd collection, box A-59, NYPL; Rose Morgan French to Rosika Schwimmer, March 21, 1915, Schwimmer-Lloyd collection, box A-56, NYPL; RMF [Rose Morgan French] to Rosika Schwimmer, June 10, 1915, Schwimmer-Lloyd collection, box A-59, NYPL.

165. Anna Wicksell to Rosika Schwimmer, February 24, 1916, Schwimmer-Lloyd collection, box A-74, NYPL.

166. Rosika Schwimmer to Naima Sahlbom [German], Schwimmer-Lloyd collection, box A-96, NYPL.

167. Rosika Schwimmer to Mien Palthe, August 17, 1918, Schwimmer-Lloyd collection, box A-99, NYPL; Mien Palthe to Rosika Schwimmer, November 15, 1917, Schwimmer-Lloyd collection, box A-94, NYPL.

168. Aletta Jacobs to Rosika Schwimmer [German], November 18, 1903, Schwimmer-Lloyd collection, box A-4, NYPL; Aletta Jacobs to Rosika Schwimmer, January 4, 1912, Schwimmer-Lloyd collection, box A-28, NYPL; Aletta Jacobs to Rosika Schwimmer, November 13, 1912, Schwimmer-Lloyd collection,

box A-31, NYPL; Martina Kramers to Rosika Schwimmer, October 17, 1911, Schwimmer-Lloyd collection, box A-27, NYPL.

169. Lola Lloyd to Rosika Schwimmer, [May 1915], Schwimmer-Lloyd collection, box A-58, NYPL; Lola Lloyd to Rosika Schwimmer, [June 7, 1915], Schwimmer-Lloyd collection, box A-59, NYPL.

170. Emily Greene Balch to Jane Addams, June 9, 1919, Addams papers, reel 12; Aletta Jacobs to Jane Addams, December 12, 1927, Jacobs papers, IIAV.

171. Rosa Manus to Katharine von Kardorff [German], February 4, 1930; Katharine von Kardorff to Rosa Manus [German], March 1, 1930; Katharine von Kardorff to Rosa Manus [German], February 7, 1930; all in Manus papers, IIAV.

172. Carrie Chapman Catt to Aletta Jacobs, April 20, 1914, and July 16, 1910, Jacobs papers, IIAV.

173. Emily Hobhouse to Jane Addams, November 4, 1915, Jacobs papers, IIAV.

174. Mia Boissevain, tribute to Rosa Manus, Manus papers, IIAV.

175. Aletta Jacobs to Emily Balch, August 10, 1919, WILPF papers, reel 36.

176. Alice Salomon, "To Lord and Lady Aberdeen," ICW *Bulletin* 6, no. 3 (November 1927).

177. Marthe Boël, "President's Message," ICW *Bulletin* 15, no. 3 (November 1936).

178. Ishbel Aberdeen and Temair, "A Christmas and New Year Message from Our Hon. President," ICW *Bulletin* 15, no. 4 (December 1936).

179. Marthe Boël, "A Message of Goodbye"; F. F. Plaminkova, "Now that Death has closed her eyes"; and Karen M. Glaesel, "Our Grannie": all in ICW *Bulletin* 17, no. 8 (May 1939).

180. "Carrie Chapman Catt," *Jus Suffragii* 23, no. 4 (January 1929).

181. Rosika Schwimmer to Carrie Chapman Catt, May 18, 1912, Schwimmer-Lloyd collection, box A-29, NYPL.

182. Rosa Manus to Catharine McCulloch, June 2, 1909, Dillon collection, box 18, SL.

183. Rosa Manus to Carrie Chapman Catt, February 21, 1939, Catt papers, reel 4, LofC.

184. Bertha Lutz to Carrie Chapman Catt, August 25, 1933; February 12, 1934; July 26, 1945; and July 29, 1931: all in NAWSA papers, reel 12, LofC.

185. Bertha Lutz to Rosa Manus, November 20, 1928, Manus papers, IIAV.

186. Marguerite Gobat to Jane Addams, October 3, 1929, Addams papers, reel 20; "Messages of Europe, Christmas 1924," WILPF paper, reel 18.

187. Jane Addams to Emily Greene Balch, March 20, [1920], Addams papers, reel 12.

188. Vilma Glücklich to Jane Addams, December 12, 1924, Addams papers, reel 16.

189. Rosika Schwimmer to Mrs. Illingworth, August 18, 1914, Schwimmer-Lloyd collection, box A-41, NYPL; Stella Davis Williams to Rosika Schwimmer, [received December 18, 1914], Schwimmer papers, box 1, HI; Stella Williams to Rosika Schwimmer, [February 12, 1915], Schwimmer-Lloyd collection, box A-54, NYPL; Stella Williams to [Rosika Schwimmer], [November 1915], Schwimmer-Lloyd collection, box A-63, NYPL.

190. Ishbel Aberdeen, "Dear Bulletin," ICW *Bulletin* 1, no. 7 (October 1922); [Madeleine Doty], partial statement on *Pax*, n.d., Dossiers Duchêne, F Rés. 206, BDIC; Margery Ashby to Carrie Catt, January 30, 1931, NAWSA papers, reel 11, LofC; Edith Pye to Jane Addams, May 24, 1932, Addams papers, reel 23.

191. Marchioness of Aberdeen and Temair, "International Council of Women," *Jus Suffragii* 16, no. 9 (June 1922); Mrs. Philip North Moore, "Ceremonial Meeting of Welcome," May 4, 1925, ICW Executive Minute Book, ICW HQ.

192. "Notes," ICW *Bulletin* 2, nos. 4–5 (December–January 1923–24); Ishbel Aberdeen and Temair, "President's Message," ICW *Bulletin* 8, no. 9 (May 1930).

193. Marthe Boël, "President's Opening Address," ICW, *President's Memorandum*, 1938, 8.

194. [Marguerite Gobat] to Emily Greene Balch [French], April 17, [1921], WILPF papers, reel 1.

195. Anna Wössner to Marguerite Gobat [German], April 26, 1921, WILPF papers, reel 1.

196. Vilma Glücklich to Myrrha Tunas [German], July 10, 1925, WILPF papers, reel 2.

197. Emily Greene Balch to Jane Addams, December 18, 1919, Addams papers, reel 12; Marguerite Gobat to Emily Greene Balch [French], June 17, 1921, WILPF papers, reel 1; Anna Wössner to Marguerite Gobat [German], July 25, 1921, WILPF papers, reel 1; Emily Greene Balch to "Famille Internationale," September 28, [1921], WILPF papers, reel 1.

198. Jane Addams to Kathleen Courtney, August 15, 1932, Addams papers, reel 24; Gertrud Baer, "A Christmas Letter to International Members and Sections," November 25, 1940, WILPF papers, reel 11.

199. [Emily Greene Balch] to Jessie Hughan, December 11, 1919, WILPF papers, reel 36.

200. K. D. Courtney to Madeleine Doty, October 30, [1925?], WILPF papers, reel 2.

201. Rosika Schwimmer to Miel Coops [German], May 27, 1930, Coops-Broese van Groenau papers, IIAV.

202. May Wright Sewall, "Preface to Chapter IV," ICW 1909 congress report, vol. 2.

203. Mrs. Mitsu Fujisawa, "My Impressions in Lugano," WILPF *Bulletin*, October and December 1922.

204. Emma Ender to Lady Aberdeen [German], December 1927, HLA, 78-315(1), LB.

205. Bertha Lutz to Carrie Chapman Catt, July 7, 1922, Catt papers, reel 4, LofC.

206. Rosa Manus to Lucy Anthony, November 15, 1926, Anna Manus Jacobi papers, IIAV.

207. Emily Greene Balch to Friends, July 1, 1937, WILPF papers, reel 3.

208. May Wright Sewall to Marie Stritt, October 16, 1903, HLA, 80-319(2), LB.

209. May Wright Sewall to Marie Stritt, January 22, 1901, HLA, 83-329(3), LB.

210. Carrie Chapman Catt to Friends, May 1, 1929, Catt papers, IIAV.

211. Marianne Hainisch, "Erinnerungen an die Gereralversammlung des I.C.W. in Toronto," in Aberdeen 1909, 53–58; Helene Lange to Lady Aberdeen [German] and Gertrud Baümer to Lady Aberdeen, January 7, 1928, HLA, 78-315(1); Berta Kamm, "The W.I.L. Summer School in England," *Pax* 3, no. 10 (September 1928).

212. Quoted in Badran 1995, 109.

213. Margot Badran, personal communication, December 29, 1995.

Chapter 9

1. Gertrud Baer to Kathleen Innes and Clara Ragaz, May 18, 1938, WILPF papers, reel 3.

2. See C. Miller 1991, 1992.

3. Matilda Gage to My dear Children, April 8, 1888, Gage papers, box 2, SL.

4. "Review of Work at Paris Headquarters and Conferences," ICW 1904 congress report, vol. 1.

5. Ida Husted Harper to Aletta Jacobs, October 5, 1907, Jacobs papers, IIAV.

6. Adele Schreiber, "Feminists and the Radio," *Jus Suffragii* 30, no. 9 (June 1936); Lotti Birch to Chairmen [German], November 13, 1936, WILPF papers, reel 3; "When the Assembly of the League of Nations Meets," ICW *Bulletin* 16, no. 1 (July 1937).

7. Lotti Birch and Gertrud Baer, Circular-Letter no. 3 on Congress, February 23, 1937, WILPF papers, reel 21; minutes, WILPF Executive Committee, Basle, January 5–9, 1938, WILPF papers, reel 11.

8. Collections of organizational and individual papers contain numerous clippings on the congresses.

9. Clipping in Alice Park diary, March 8, 1926, Park papers, box 25, HI.

10. "Suffragists Meet in Paris Congress," *World* (New York), May 31, 1926, clipping in Smith papers, box 12, SL.

11. Margery Corbett Ashby to Carrie Chapman Catt, June 9, 1926, NAWSA papers, reel 11, LofC.

12. [Incomplete minutes, WILPF International Executive committee,] September 9, [1938], WILPF papers, reel 11. I am grateful to Carl Strikwerda for stimulating me to think about women's impact on Wilson and to Ayfer Stump for researching the question. See Wiltsher 1985; MacFarland 1990; Knock 1992. MacFarland (164) cites the work of an anonymous Swarthmore College student in the 1950s who argued the similarities between the Hague Congress proposals, the Fourteen Points, and the Covenant of the League of Nations; although MacFarland believes that organized women did have impact on U.S. foreign policy, she is not convinced of WILPF's impact on Wilson or the Versailles treaty. Wiltsher (192) suggests, without providing evidence, that the women pacifists did influence Wilson. Knock argues that the progressive internationalists sometimes shaped, sometimes reinforced, and sometimes confirmed Wilson's ideas about peace.

13. "Report of Headquarters Committee," IWSA 1920 congress report, 34.

14. Marguerite de Witt Schlumberger to Madam, January 10, 1919; Marguerite de Witt Schlumberger to Millicent Garrett Fawcett [French], January 11, 1919; and Mary Sheepshanks to Marguerte de Witt Schlumberger, January 23, 1919: all in Fawcett papers, box 90, FL.

15. Mrs. Oliver Strachey, "The Inter Allied Conference," n.d., and Millicent Garrett Fawcett, diary entry, February 7–15, 1919, both in Fawcett papers, box 90, FL.

16. Millicent Garrett Fawcett to Carrie Chapman Catt, February 19, 1919, Fawcett papers, box 90, FL; Suzanne Grinberg, "Women at the Peace Congress," *Jus Suffragii* 13, no. 6 (March 1919).

17. Margery Fry to Mrs. Hubback, March 29, 1919, Fawcett papers, box 90, FL.

18. Margery Corbett Ashby to Millicent Garrett Fawcett, March 24, 1919, Fawcett papers, box 90, FL.

19. "Women's Deputation Heard," *Evening Post* (New York), April 11, 1919; "Women's Petitions to League Framers," *New York Times*, April 13, 1919.

20. Mary Sheepshanks, "Features of the Month," *Jus Suffragii* 13, no. 7 (April 1919), and 18, no. 8 (May 1919).

21. C. Miller 1992, 20–24. Miller's dissertation, on the work of international women's organizations at the League of Nations, is based heavily on documents from the League of Nations archives and thus proved a valuable resource for this section.

22. "Resolutions Regarding the League of Nations," ICW 1920 congress report, 33–34.

23. Laura Dreyfus Barney, "The Seventh Assembly of the League of Nations," ICW *Bulletin* 5, no. 2 (October 1926).

24. Gabrielle Radziwill, quoted in *Women in a Changing World* 1966, 54.

25. Marie Hoheisel, "The World Needs 'Mothering,'" ICW *Bulletin* 14, no. 6 (February 1936).

26. Gabrielle Radziwill quoted in C. Miller 1992, 46.

27. "Introduction," IWSA 1920 congress report, 22.

28. Margery Corbett Ashby to Carrie Chapman Catt, October 28, 1928, NAWSA papers, reel 11, LofC; Margery Corbett Ashby, "The History of the 'Alliance,'" *Jus Suffragii* 35, no. 1 (October–November 1940).

29. Bertha Lutz to Carrie Catt, April 29, 1936, NAWSA papers, reel 12, LofC.

30. Gabrielle Radziwill quoted in C. Miller 1992, 47–48.

31. Minutes, ICWPP, Zurich, May 6, 1919, WILPF papers, reel 9; Wiltsher 1985, 201–2.

32. Jane Addams quoted in Madeleine Doty, "New Year Resolutions," *Pax* 2, no. 2 (December 1926).

33. K. D. Courtney to Emily Balch, January 2, 1928, Balch papers, reel 8.

34. "World Events," *Pax* 6, no. 9 (September 1931).

35. Minutes, WILPF International Executive Committee, Grenoble, May 20–22, 1932, WILPF papers, reel 10.

36. Eugenie Miskoczy Meller and Melanie Vambery to Camille Drevet, March 20, 1933, WILPF papers, reel 10.

37. Minutes, WILPF International Executive Committee, Prague, April 29–May 4, 1936, WILPF papers, reel 11; minutes, WILPF IXth World Congress, Luhacovice, July 27–31, 1937, WILPF papers, reel 21.

38. Minutes, WILPF International Executive Committee, Geneva, December 5–9, 1939, WILPF papers, reel 33; "Sovereign Rights," WILPF *News Letter* 15, no. 1 (January 1940).

39. C. Miller 1992, 72–75.

40. "Events in Geneva," *Jus Suffragii* 30, no. 1 (October 1935).

41. Emily Greene Balch to Gabrielle Duchêne, December 3, 1920, Dossiers Duchêne, F Rés 296, BDIC.

42. Minutes, Liaison Committee, September 19, [1936], LC papers, IISG; Joint Chairmen to J. Avenol, January 15, 1938, WILPF papers, reel 3.

43. Gertrud Baer to Kathleen Innes and Clara Ragaz, January 7, 1939, WILPF papers, reel 4.

44. Ishbel Aberdeen and Temair, "President's Letter," ICW *Bulletin* 11, no. 1 (September 1932); "President's Memorandum Regarding the Business Transacted by the I.C.W. Executive Held at Geneva," June 7–17, 1927, ICW papers, box 1, SSC.

45. Member of British Foreign Office and Mary Craig McGeachy, both quoted in C. Miller 1992, 121, 74.

46. C. Miller 1992, 77–100; C. Miller 1991, 65–66.

47. C. Miller 1992, 153; see Alberti 1989, on Helena Swanwick's appointment in 1924.

48. Bussey and Tims 1965, 73.

49. C. Miller 1992, 109. Bussey and Tims 1965, 73, make the same point. By 1929, fifteen women attended the Tenth Assembly as delegates and technical advisors, and seven of these belonged to WILPF.

50. C. Miller 1992, 113.

51. C. Miller 1992, 30–34.

52. Constance Drexel, "Representation of Women in the League," *News-Sheet* 5 (November 17, 1919); "President's Memorandum," ICW 1920 congress report, 13–17; E.A., "Women in the League of Nations Secretariat," *Jus Suffragii* 16, no. 5 (February 1922).

53. [Margery Corbett Ashby] to Sir Eric Drummond, January 12, 1925, Addams papers, reel 16.

54. Margery Corbett Ashby to Vilma Glücklich, February 13, 1925, WILPF papers, reel 2; "Protection of Children," *Jus Suffragii* 19, no. 6 (March 1925); "The League of Nations," *Jus Suffragii* 19, no. 7 (April 1925).

55. Minutes, Liaison Committee Emergency Meeting, May 6, 1936, LC papers, IISG; minutes, IAWSEC board, Brussels, September 9–10, 1936, IAW papers, FL; minutes, Liaison Committee, September 21, 1936, LC papers, IISG; "The League of Nations," *Jus Suffragii* 31, no. 9 (June 1937). See C. Miller 1992, 119.

56. "Editorial Notes," ICW *Bulletin* 5, no. 1 (September 1926).

57. Rosa Manus to Margery Corbett Ashby, December 15, 1931, Corbett Ashby papers, box 483, FL.

58. "Assembly of the League of Nations," *Jus Suffragii* 29, no. 10 (July 1935).

59. "Editorial Notes, ICW *Bulletin* 5, no. 5 (January 1927).

60. [Mary Sheepshanks], "Report of Headquarters for the Last Six Months," April 1929, WILPF papers, reel 10.

61. Minutes, Liaison Committee Emergency Meeting, December 6, 1938, LC papers, IISG.

62. Gabrielle Radziwill quoted in C. Miller 1992, 159–61.

63. Edith Rodgers to Helen Archdale, October 7, 1931, ERI papers, box 333, FL.

64. A. Honora Enfield to Helen Archdale, October 21, 1932, ERI papers, box 333, FL; Helen Archdale to Doris Stevens, May 30, 1932, Stevens papers, carton 4, SL; [Helen Archdale] to Honora Endfield, October 15, 1932, ERI papers, box 333, FL.

65. A. Honora Enfield to Helen Archdale, October 21, 1932, ERI papers, box 333, FL.

66. Cartoon no. 7, "The Assembly of the League of Nations: 1930," *Jus Suffragii* 24, no. 12 (September 1930).

67. C. Miller 1992 makes this point.

68. "News of the W.I.L. Disarmament Campaign," *Pax* 6, no. 5 (April 1931).

69. "Official Record of the Declarations and Petitions Presented by the Disarmament Committee of the Women's International Organisations to the Disarmament Conference, Geneva, February 6th, 1932," Courtney papers, box 454, FL.

70. Member of British Foreign Office quoted in C. Miller 1992, 243.

71. Elizabeth Abbott to Jane Norman Smith, May 21, 1928, Smith papers, box 12, SL; "Call to the 2nd Meeting of the ICWW," 1921, IFWW papers, SL.

72. Alice Paul to Jane Norman Smith, April 8, 1932, Smith papers, box 11, SL; Chrystal Macmillan to Jane Norman Smith, February 10, 1934, Smith papers, box 4, SL.

73. Doris Stevens to Alva Belmont, September 13, 1928; "Feminist Victory.....Women Plenipotentiaries to the Hague Codification Conference," press release, September 14, 1928: both in Stevens papers, 76–246, carton 9, SL.

74. "Rough draft for Programme, Joint Demonstration on the Nationality of Married Women," and "Notice, Invitation and Appeal," printed circular, March 14, 1930, Palthe-Broese van Groenau papers, IIAV.

75. "League of Nations Ask Women's Aid," *Pax* 6, no. 4 (March 1931).

76. C. Miller 1992, 194–99.

77. Helen Archdale quoted in C. Miller 1992, 200.

78. C. Miller 1992, 184–85.

79. Both quotations from Hugh McKinnon Wood in C. Miller 1992, 214. See also C. Miller 1994.

80. Minutes, Liaison Committee, October 28, 1935, LC papers, IISG; "Status of Women," ICW *Bulletin* 14, no. 3 (November 1935); Mrs. Spiller, "Rough Notes on the Status of Women Campaign," n.d. [1935], WILPF papers, reel 2; minutes, IAWSEC Board, Zurich, February 25–March 1-2, 1937, IAW papers, FL.

81. C. Miller 1992, 223–24.

82. C. Miller 1992, 226.

83. Renée Girod, "The Status of Women," ICW *Bulletin*, 16, no. 9 (May 1938); "Once Again: The Status of Women," ICW *Bulletin* 16, no. 5 (January 1938).

84. "News from Headquarters," WILPF *Bulletin* February 1922.

85. Irma M. Tunas Tischer to Jane Addams, May 9, 1924, Addams papers, reel 16.

86. Maria Vérone, "The Nationality of Married Women," ICW *Bulletin* 9, no. 8 (April 1931).

87. E.GD. [Emilie Gourd], "La 'Saison feministe de Geneve," *Jus Suffragii* 27, no. 2 (November 1932).

88. L. C. A. van Eeghen, "Women's Activities at Geneva during the Sessions of the League of Nations Assembly," ICW *Bulletin* 11, no. 3 (November 1932).

89. [Excerpt from letter from Mr. Heemskerk]; Doris Stevens to Mr. Heemskerk, April 8, 1930; Stevens papers, 76-246, carton 10, SL

90. K. D. Courtney, "Joint Standing Committee," n.d., WILPF papers, reel 10.

91. "Women for World Peace," ICW *Bulletin* 14, no. 6 (February 1936); on Addams and Balch as winners of the Nobel Peace Prize, see Alonso 1995.

92. "I.C.W. Deputation to the President of the 18th Assembly of the League of Nations," ICW *Bulletin* 16, no. 2 (October 1937).

93. Gabrielle Radziwill to Lady Aberdeen, November 20, 1931, HLA, 85-334(1), LB.

94. Memorandum by the Secretary-General, "Collaboration of Women in the Organisations of Peace," November 22, 1931, HLA, 85-334(1), LB.

95. C. Miller 1992, 134.

96. Margery Corbett Ashby to Carrie Chapman Catt, March 10, 1945, Catt collection, box 3, NYPL; Jessie Street to Margery Corbett Ashby, April 11, 1945, Corbett Ashby papers, box 483, FL.

97. Bertha Lutz to Carrie Chapman Catt, May 21, 1945, NAWSA papers, reel 12. See also Bertha Lutz, "Reminiscences of the San Francisco conference that founded the United Nations," n.d., Corbett Ashby papers, box 483, FL.

98. Bertha Lutz to Carrie Chapman Catt, May 21, 1945, NAWSA papers, reel 12, LofC.

99. Edith Goode to Laura E. W. Kendall, May 23, 1945, WWP papers, reel 174.

100. [Margery Corbett Ashby], "Relationship of International Alliance and the International Council," [March 1953], IAW papers, FL.

101. Carrie Chapman Catt to Margery Corbett Ashby, July 6, 1945, NAWSA papers, reel 11, LofC.

102. Minutes, Liaison Committee, July 11, 1945, LC papers, IISG.

103. Bertha Lutz to Carrie Chapman Catt, June 3, 1945, NAWSA papers, reel 12, LofC.

104. Emmeline Pethick-Lawrence to Alice Paul, February 5, 1946, WWP papers, reel 175; Betty Gram Swing to Alice Paul, [February 1946], WWP papers, reel 175.

105. Dorothy Kenyon to Margery Ashby, October 1, 1945, NAWSA papers, reel 11, LofC.

106. Minutes, IAW Board, London, March 4–7, 1946, IAW papers, FL.

107. Amelia Himes Walker, "Mission to the First Assembly," [February 1946], WWP papers, reel 175.

108. Amelia Himes Walker, "Mission to the First Assembly," [February 1946], WWP papers, reel 175.

109. WWP, "United Nations Sub-Commission On Status of Women Reports," [1946], Smith papers, box 12, SL.

110. ODI, "Report of the Board and President's Meeting and Summerschool," Arnakhus, Hellebaek, Denmark, June 12–16, 1946, ODI papers, box 460, FL.

111. *International Women's Conference* 1950, 95–96.

112. On these developments, see Stephenson 1982; Tinker and Jaquette 1987; Pietilä and Vickers 1990; Stienstra 1994; Peters and Wolper 1995; Winslow 1995.

113. My thinking on these issues has been much influenced by the scholarship of U.S. women of color who have critiqued the Eurocentric bias of these aspects of feminist thought and practice. See, for some of the classic statements, B. Smith 1979 and the essays in Moraga and Anzaldúa 1981. See also Bulbeck 1988.

114. See Peters and Wolper 1995.

115. "Towards Peace and Freedom," August 1919, WILPF papers, reel 17.

116. Ishbel Aberdeen and Temair, "President's Letter to the Members of the I.C.W.," ICW *Bulletin* 1, no. 6 (August 1922).

117. [Edith Pye] to Friends, January 1934, WILPF papers, reel 2.

118. See Breines 1982; Epstein 1991; Weigand 1995; Whittier 1995.

119. Ishbel Aberdeen and Temair, "President's Letter to the Members of the I.C.W.," ICW *Bulletin* 1, no. 6 (August 1922).

120. Madeleine Doty to Jane Addams, November 17, [1925], Addams papers, reel 17.

121. Gertrud Baer, "The WILPF Executive Meeting, Basle, 1938," *Pax* 13, no. 1 (February 1938).

122. Jane Addams, "President's Address," May 1–7, 1924, WILPF papers, reel 18.

123. *Pax et Libertas* 1, no. 1 (February 1920).

124. "For a New International Order, A 'Cahier of Peace' Presented to the Washington Congress," 1924, WILPF papers, reel 18.

125. Gertrud Baer to Kathleen Innes and Clara Ragaz, May 18, 1938, WILPF papers, reel 3; Gertrud Baer to Kathleen Innes, June 11, 1938, WILPF papers, reel 3.

126. For theoretical perspectives on these issues, see Hollinger 1993; Seidman 1993; Nagel 1994; J. Smith 1994; Gamson 1995.

127. On this point, see Hoberman 1995, 1996.

128. On the reactionary and imperialist aspects of internationalism, see Tyrrell 1991b; Burton 1994; Badran 1995; Hoberman 1995. All of these scholars have also influenced my thinking on this point through further conversation and correspondence.

Bibliography

Manuscript Collections

Bibliothèque de Documentation Internationale Contemporaine, Universités de Paris, Nanterre
    Dossiers Gabrielle Duchêne
Bibliothèque Marguerite Durand, Paris
    Dossier Isabelle Bogelot
    Dossier Camille Drevet
    Dossier Avril de Sainte-Croix
    Dossier Marguèrite de Witt Schlumberger
Fawcett Library, London Guildhall University, London
    Margery Corbett Ashby Papers
    Kathleen Courtney Papers
    Equal Rights International Papers
    Millicent Garrett Fawcett Papers
    International Alliance of Women Papers
    Open Door International Papers
    St. Joan's International Alliance Papers
Hoover Institution, Stanford University, Stanford, California
    Alice Park Papers
    Rosika Schwimmer Papers
    Clara Zetkin Papers
Indianapolis–Marion County Public Library, Indianapolis, Indiana
    May Wright Sewall Papers
Internationaal Informatiecentrum en Archief voor de Vrouwenbeweging, Amsterdam
    Carrie Chapman Catt Papers
    Emilia Coops-Broese van Groenau Papers
    Jeanne Eder-Schwyzer Papers
    E. Welmoet Wijnaendts Francken-Dyserinck Papers
    Aletta Jacobs Papers
    Rosa Manus Papers
    Nationaal Bureau voor Vrouwenarbeid Papers
    Mien van Wulfften Palthe-Broese van Groenau Papers
    Maria W. H. Rutgers-Hoitsema Papers
Internationaal Instituut voor Sociale Geschiedenis, Amsterdam
    Liaison Committee of the Women's International Organisations Papers
    E. Sylvia Pankhurst Papers
    Rassemblement Universel pour la Paix Papers
    Second International Papers
International Council of Women Headquarters, Paris
    International Council of Women Papers

Landesarchiv Berlin, Berlin
  Helene-Lange-Archiv
Leo Baeck Institute, New York
  Marie Munk Papers
  Alice Salomon Papers
Library of Congress, Washington, D.C.
  Carrie Chapman Catt Papers
  International Council of Women Papers
  National American Woman Suffrage Association Papers
  Pan American International Women's Committee Papers
Microfilmed Collections
  Jane Addams Papers, microfilmed and distributed by University Microfilms
    International
  Emily Greene Balch Papers, microfilmed and distributed by Scholarly
    Resources
  Women's International League for Peace and Freedom Papers, microfilmed
    and distributed by the Microfilming Corporation of America
  World Woman's Party Papers, series VII, National Woman's Party Papers,
    microfilmed and distributed by the Microfilming Corporation of America
National Council of Women of Great Britain Headquarters, London
  International Council of Women Papers
New York Public Library, Rare Books and Manuscripts Division, Astor, Lenox
  and Tilden Foundations, New York
  Carrie Chapman Catt Collection
  Schwimmer-Lloyd Collection
Schlesinger Library, Radcliffe College, Cambridge, Massachusetts
  Corinne Marie Allen Papers
  Mary Anderson Papers, series III
  Fannie Fern Andrews Papers
  Theodora Bosanquet Papers
  Dillon Collection, series XI
  Mary Agnes Dingman Papers
  Matilda Joslyn Gage Papers
  International Assembly of Women Papers
  International Federation of Working Women Papers
  Lena Madesin Phillips Papers
  Jane Norman Smith Papers
  Somerville-Howorth Papers
  Doris Stevens Papers
  Mary Winslow Papers
  Mary Winsor Papers
  Woman's Rights Collection
Sophia Smith Collection, Smith College, Northampton, Massachusetts
  Carrie Chapman Catt Papers
  International Alliance of Women Papers
  International Congress of Working Women Papers
  International Council of Women Papers

Josephine Schain Papers
Ruth Woodsmall Papers
Swarthmore College Peace Collection, Swarthmore College, Swarthmore, Pennsylvania
Peace and Disarmament Committee of the Women's International Organisations Papers
Union Mondiale de la Femme pour la concorde Internationale Papers

Conference Proceedings, by Year

International Council of Women

National Woman Suffrage Association. *Report of the International Council of Women, 1888*. Washington: Rufus H. Darby, 1888.

ICW. *Report of Transactions of Second Quinquennial Meeting Held in London July 1899*, edited by the Countess of Aberdeen. 7 vols. London: T. Fisher Unwin, 1900.

ICW. *Report of Transactions During the Third Quinquennial Term Terminating with the Third Quinquennial Meeting Held in Berlin, June, 1904*, edited by May Wright Sewall. 2 vols. Boston: n.p., 1909.

ICW. *Report of Transactions of the Fourth Quinquennial Meeting Held at Toronto, Canada, June, 1909*, edited by the Countess of Aberdeen. London: Constable, 1910.

ICW. *Report on the Quinquennial Meetings, Rome 1914*, edited by the Countess of Aberdeen. Karlsruhe: G. Braunsche Hofbuchdruckerei und Verlag, n.d.

Aberdeen, Ishbel. *President's Memorandum Regarding the Quinquennial Meeting of the ICW at Rome*. [no publication information].

ICW. *Quinquennial Report of the Corresponding Secretary Presented at the Quinquennial Sessions, 1914*. [no publication information].

ICW. *Resolutions Adopted at the Quinquennial Council Meeting of the ICW, 1914*. [no publication information].

ICW. *Report on the Quinquennial Meeting, Kristiania 1920*, edited by the Marchioness of Aberdeen and Temair. Aberdeen, Scotland: Rosemount, 1921.

ICW. *Report on the Quinquennial Meeting. Washington, 1925*, edited by the Marchioness of Aberdeen and Temair. [no publication information].

ICW. *President's Memorandum Regarding the business transacted by the I.C.W. Executive Held in London, April 29th–May 9th, 1929*. [no publication information].

ICW. *President's Memorandum Regarding the 8th Quinquennial Meeting of the ICW Held at Vienna, May 26th to June 7th, 1930*. [no publication information].

ICW. *President's Memorandum Regarding the Meeting of the Executive and Standing Committees of the ICW at Stockholm, June 26–July 6, 1933*. [no publication information].

ICW. *President's Memorandum Regarding the Council Meeting of the ICW Held at Dubrovnik, September 28th to October 9th, 1936*. [no publication information].

ICW. *President's Memorandum Regarding the Council Meeting of the ICW Held at Edinburgh (Scotland), July 11th to 21st, 1938.* [no publication information].

ICW. *Report of First Post-War Council Meeting, Philadelphia, 1947.* [no publication information].

International Alliance of Women

IWSA. *Report, First International Woman Suffrage Conference, February 12–18, 1902.* [no publication information].

IWSA. *Report of Second and Third Conferences, Berlin, Germany, June 3, 4, 1904, Copenhagen, Denmark, August 7, 8, 9, 10, 11, 1906.* Copenhagen: Bianco Luno, 1906.

IWSA. *Report of the Fourth Conference of the International Woman Suffrage Alliance, Amsterdam, Holland, 1908.* Amsterdam: F. Van Rossen, 1908.

IWSA. *Report of Fifth Conference and First Quinquennial, London, England, 1909.* London: Samuel Sidders, 1909.

IWSA. *Report of Sixth Congress, Stockholm, Sweden, 1911.* London: Women's Printing Society, 1911.

IWSA. *Report of Seventh Congress, Budapest, 1913.* Manchester: Percy Brothers, 1913.

IWSA. *Report of Eighth Congress, Geneva, Switzerland, 1920.* Manchester: Percy Brothers, 1920.

IWSA. *Report of Ninth Congress, Rome, Italy, 1923.* Dresden: B. G. Teubner, 1923.

IAWSEC. *Report of Tenth Congress, Paris, France, 1926.* London: London Caledonian, 1926.

IAWSEC. *Report of the Eleventh Congress, Berlin, 1929.* [no publication information].

IAWSEC. *Report of the Twelfth Congress, Istanbul, 1935.* [no publication information].

IAWSEC. *Report of the Thirteenth Congress, Copenhagen, 1939.* [no publication information].

IAW. *Report of the Fourteenth Congress, Interlaken, 1946.* [no publication information].

Women's International League for Peace and Freedom

International Committee of Women for Permanent Peace. *International Congress of Women, The Hague—April 28th to May 1st 1915: Report.*

Other conference proceedings can be found in the WILPF papers; see microfilmed collections, above.

Organizational Periodicals

ICW *Annual Report*
ICW *Bulletin*
Jus Suffragii
Pax

Other Published Primary Sources

Aberdeen and Temair, Ishbel Maria Gordon. 1960. *Canadian Journal of Lady Aberdeen, 1893–1898*, edited by John T. Saywell. Toronto: Champlain Society.

————, ed. 1909. *Our Lady of the Sunshine and Her International Visitors*. London: Constable.

Aberdeen, Lord and Lady. 1925. *"We Twa": Reminiscences of Lord and Lady Aberdeen*. 2 vols. London: W. Collins and Sons.

Adams, Mildred, ed. 1946. *"The World We Live In—The World We Want": The Record of the International Assembly of Women Held at South Kortright, N.Y., USA, October 1946*. [privately published].

Addams, Jane, Emily G. Balch, and Alice Hamilton, eds. 1972. *Women at The Hague: The International Congress of Women and Its Results*. 1915. Reprint, New York: Garland.

Annuaire des organisations internationales/Yearbook of International Organizations. 1949. Geneva: Éditions de l'Annuaire des Organisations Internationales.

Anthony, Susan B., and Ida Husted Harper, eds. 1902. *History of Woman Suffrage*. Vol. 4. Indianapolis: Hollenbeck.

Deutsch, Regine. 1929. *The International Woman Suffrage Alliance: Its History from 1904–1929*. N.p.: London.

Harper, Ida Husted, ed. 1922. *History of Woman Suffrage*. Vol. 6. New York: J. J. Little and Ives.

Heymann, Lida Gustava, with Anita Augspurg. 1972. *Erlebtes-Erschautes: Deutsche Frauen kämpfen für Freiheit, Recht und Frieden, 1850–1940*, edited by Margrit Twellman. Meisenheim am Glan: Anton Hain.

International Women's Conference. 1950. Bad Reichenhall, Germany, September 25–30. [no publication information].

Jacobs, Aletta. 1996. *Memories: My Life as an International Leader in Health, Suffrage, and Peace*, edited by Harriet Feinberg, translated by Annie Wright. New York: Feminist Press.

Kohut, Rebekah. 1925. *My Portion (An Autobiography)*. New York: Thomas Seltzer.

League of Nations. 1929. *Handbook of International Organisations*. Geneva: League of Nations.

Our Common Cause—Civilization: Report of the International Congress of Women Including the Series of Round Tables, July 16–22, 1933, Chicago, Illinois. 1933. New York: National Council of Women of the United States.

Report to the President on the Results of the San Francisco Conference by the Chairman of the United States Delegation, the Secretary of State. 1945. Department of State, Publication 2349, Conference Series 71. Washington, D.C.: U.S. Government Printing Office.

Schreiber, Adele, and Margaret Mathieson. 1955. *Journey towards Freedom. Written for the Golden Jubilee of the International Alliance of Women*. Copenhagen: I.A.W.

Sewall, May Wright, ed. 1894. *The World's Congress of Representative Women*. Chicago: Rand, McNally.

Sewall, May Wright. 1914. *Genesis of the ICW and the Story of Its Growth, 1888–1893*. N.p.: Indianapolis.

Shaarawi, Huda. 1987. *Harem Years: The Memoirs of an Egyptian Feminist*, edited by Margot Badran. New York: Feminist Press.

Shaw, Anna Howard. 1915. *Story of a Pioneer*. New York: Harper.

Stanton, Elizabeth Cady. 1886. "Reminiscences." In *History of Woman Suffrage*, edited by Elizabeth Cady Stanton et al., vol. 3, 922–53. Rochester, N.Y.: Charles Mann.

Stanton, Theodore. 1886. "Continental Europe." In *History of Woman Suffrage*, edited by Elizabeth Cady Stanton et al., vol. 3, 896–99. Rochester, N.Y.: Charles Mann.

Swanwick, Helena Maria. 1935. *I Have Been Young*. London: Gollancz.

Swiggett, Mrs. Glen Levin, ed. 1916. *Report on the Women's Auxiliary Conference held in the City of Washington, U.S.A., in Connection with the Second Pan American Scientific Congress, December 28, 1915–January 7, 1916*. Washington: Government Printing Office.

Terrell, Mary Church. 1968. *A Colored Woman in a White World*. Washington: National Association of Colored Women's Clubs.

Secondary Sources

Alberti, Johanna. 1989. *Beyond Suffrage: Feminists in War and Peace, 1914–28*. London: Macmillan.

Alonso, Harriet Hyman. 1989. *The Women's Peace Union and the Outlawry of War, 1921–1942*. Knoxville: University of Tennessee Press.

———. 1993. *Peace as a Women's Issue: A History of the U.S. Movement for World Peace and Women's Rights*. Syracuse: Syracuse University Press.

———. 1995. "Nobel Peace Laureates, Jane Addams and Emily Greene Balch: Two Women of the WILPF." *Journal of Women's History* 7, no. 2: 6–26.

———. 1996. "A Response from Harriet Hyman Alonso" [to Deegan 1996]. *Journal of Women's History* 8, no. 2: 126–29.

Amos, Valerie, and Pratibha Pramar. 1984. "Challenging Imperial Feminism." *Feminist Review* 17 (July): 3–19.

Anderson, Benedict. 1991. *Imagined Communities: Reflections on the Origin and Spread of Nationalism*. Rev. ed. London: Verso.

Anderson, Bonnie S. 1996. "Joyous Greetings to Distant Lands: Creating an International Women's Movement, 1840–1860." Paper presented at the annual meeting of the American Historical Association, Atlanta, January.

Armstrong, David. 1982. *The Rise of the International Organisation: A Short History*. London: Macmillan.

Armstrong, John A. 1982. *Nations before Nationalism*. Chapel Hill: University of North Carolina Press.

Aronson, Emary C. 1991. "Fabian Socialism and the International Sisterhood." Paper presented at the annual meeting of the American Historical Association, Chicago, December.

Arrington, Leonard J. 1989. "Modern Lysistratas: Mormon Women in the International Peace Movement, 1899–1939." *Journal of Mormon History* 15: 89–104.

Badran, Margot. 1995. *Feminists, Islam, and Nation: Gender and the Making of Modern Egypt*. Princeton: Princeton University.

Banks, Olive. 1986. *Faces of Feminism: A Study of Feminism as a Social Movement*. New York: Basil Blackwell.

———. 1987. *Becoming a Feminist: The Social Origins of "First Wave" Feminism*. Athens: University of Georgia Press.

Bard, Christine. 1995. *Les filles de Marianne: Histoire des féminismes 1914–1940*. Paris: Fayard.

Barnett, Evelyn Brooks. 1978. "Nannie Burroughs and the Education of Black Women." In *The Afro-American Woman*, edited by Sharon Harley and Rosalyn Terborg-Penn, 97–108. Port Washington, N.Y.: National University Publications.

Barry, Kathleen. 1981. "International Feminism: Sexual Politics and the World Conference of Women in Copenhagen." *Feminist Issues* 1: 37–50.

Basu, Aparna, and Bharati Ray. 1990. *Women's Struggle: A History of the All-India Women's Conference, 1927–1990*. New Delhi: Manohar.

Batho, Edith C. 1968. *A Lamp of Friendship: A Short History of the International Federation of University Women, 1918–1968*. N.p.: IFUW.

Becker, Susan. 1981. *The Origins of the Equal Rights Amendment: American Feminism Between the Wars*. Westport, Conn.: Greenwood.

———. 1983. "International Feminism between the Wars: The NWP versus the LWV." In *Decades of Discontent: The Women's Movement 1920–1940*, edited by Lois Scharf and Joan M. Jensen, 225–42. Westport, Conn.: Greenwood.

Berkowitz, Michael. 1993. *Zionist Culture and Western European Jewry before the First World War*. New York: Cambridge University Press.

Black, Naomi. 1989. *Social Feminism*. Ithaca: Cornell University Press.

Bohachevsky-Chomiak, Martha. 1988. *Feminists Despite Themselves: Women in Ukrainian Community Life, 1884–1939*. Edmonton: Canadian Institute of Ukrainian Studies, University of Alberta.

Bolt, Christine. 1993. *Women's Movements in the United States and Britain from the 1790s to the 1920s*. Amherst: University of Massachusetts Press.

Bosch, Mineke. 1989. "Gossipy Letters in the Context of International Feminism." In *Current Issues in Women's History*, edited by Arina Angerman, Geerte Binnema, Annemieke Keunen, Vefie Poels, and Jacqueline Zirkzee, 131–52. London: Croom Helm.

Bosch, Mineke, and Annemarie Kloosterman. 1985. *Lieve Dr. Jacobs: Brieven uit de Wereldbond voor Vrouwenkiesrecht, 1902–1942*. Amsterdam: Feministische Uitgeverij Sara.

———. 1990. *Politics and Friendship: Letters from the International Woman Suffrage Alliance, 1902–1942*. Columbus: Ohio State University Press.

Boulding, Elise. 1977. *Women in the 20th Century World*. New York: Halsted.

Boy, Magdeleine. 1936. *Les associations internationales féminines*. Thesis, Faculty of Law, University of Lyon. Lyon: Paquet.

Boyd, Nancy. 1986. *Emissaries: The Overseas Work of the American WYCA, 1895–1970*. New York: Woman's Press.

Braker, Regina. 1995. "Bertha von Suttner's Spiritual Daughters: The Feminist Pacifism of Anita Augspurg, Lida Gustava Heymann, and Helene Stöcker at the International Congress of Women at the Hague, 1915." *Women's Studies International Forum* 18, no. 2: 103–12.

Breines, Wini. 1982. *Community and Organization in the New Left, 1962–68.* New York: Praeger.

Bulbeck, Chilla. 1988. *One World Women's Movement.* London: Pluto.

Burton, Antoinette. 1991. "The Feminist Quest for Identity: British Imperial Suffragism and 'Global Sisterhood,' 1900–1915." *Journal of Women's History* 3, no. 2: 46–81.

———. 1992. "The White Woman's Burden: British Feminists and 'The Indian Woman,' 1865–1915." In *Western Women and Imperialism: Complicity and Resistance,* edited by Nupur Chaudhuri and Margaret Strobel, 137–57. Bloomington: Indiana University Press.

———. 1994. *Burdens of History: British Feminists, Indian Women, and Imperial Culture.* Chapel Hill: University of North Carolina Press.

———. 1995. "Colonial Encounters in Late-Victorian England: Pandita Ramabai at Cheltenham and Wantage 1883–6." *Feminist Review* 49 (Spring): 29–49.

Bussey, Gertrude, and Margaret Tims. 1965. *Women's International League for Peace and Freedom, 1915–1965.* London: George Allen and Unwin.

Çagatay, Nilüfer, Caren Grown, and Aida Santiago. 1986. "The Nairobi Women's Conference: Toward a Global Feminism?" *Feminist Studies* 12: 401–12.

Candy, Catherine. 1991. "Margaret Cousins, 'Mother India,' and the Ideal 'Femaculine': An Irish Orientalist Feminist in India." Paper presented at the annual meeting of the American Historical Association, Chicago, December.

Chafetz, Janet Saltzman, and Anthony Gary Dworkin. 1986. *Female Revolt: Women's Movements in World and Historical Perspective.* Totowa, N.J.: Rowman and Allanheld.

Chatterjee, Partha. 1993. *Nationalist Thought and the Colonial World: A Derivative Discourse.* 1986. Reprint, Minneapolis: University of Minnesota Press.

Chaudhuri, Nupur, and Margaret Strobel, eds. 1992. *Western Women and Imperialism: Complicity and Resistance.* Bloomington: Indiana University Press.

Chauncey, George, Jr. 1982–83. "From Inversion to Homosexuality: Medicine and the Changing Conceptualization of Female Deviance." *Salmagundi,* nos. 58–59: 114–46.

Combahee River Collective. 1982. "A Black Feminist Statement." In *All the Women Are White, All the Blacks Are Men, But Some of Us Are Brave,* edited by Gloria T. Hull, Patricia Bell Scott, and Barbara Smith, 13–22. Old Westbury, N.Y.: Feminist Press.

Cook, Blanche W. 1977. "Female Support Networks and Political Activism: Lillian Wald, Crystal Eastman, and Emma Goldman." *Chrysalis* 3 (Autumn): 43–61.

Cooper, Sandi E. 1984. "The Work of Women in 19th-Century Continental European Peace Movements." *Peace and Change* 9: 11–28.

———. 1991. *Patriotic Pacifism: Waging War on War in Europe, 1815–1914.* New York: Oxford University Press.

Costin, Lela B. 1982. "Feminism, Pacifism, Internationalism, and the 1915 International Congress of Women." *Women's Studies International Forum* 5: 301–15.

Cott, Nancy F. 1987. *The Grounding of Modern Feminism*. New Haven: Yale University Press.

———. 1989. "'What's in a Name?' The Limits of 'Social Feminism'; or, Expanding the Vocabulary of Women's History." *Journal of American History* 76: 809–29.

———. 1991. *A Woman Making History: Mary Ritter Beard through Her Letters*. New Haven: Yale University Press.

Crosby, Alfred. 1987. *Ecological Imperialism*. New York: Cambridge University Press.

Daley, Caroline, and Melanie Nolan, eds. 1994. *Suffrage and Beyond: International Feminist Perspectives*. New York: New York University Press.

David, Katherine. 1991. "Czech Feminists and Nationalism in the Late Habsburg Monarchy: 'The First in Austria.'" *Journal of Women's History* 3, no. 2: 26–45.

Deegan, Mary Jo. 1996. "A Very Different Vision of Jane Addams and Emily Greene Balch" [comment on Alonso 1995]. *Journal of Women's History* 8, no. 2: 121–25.

Diehl, Paul F. 1989. *The Politics of International Organizations: Patterns and Insights*. Chicago: Dorsey.

Donaldson, Laura E. 1992. *Decolonizing Feminisms: Race, Gender, and Empire Building*. Chapel Hill: University of North Carolina Press.

Drefus, M. 1986. "Camille Drevet." In *Dictionnaire biographique du mouvement ouvrier français*, vol. 26, 14–16. Paris: les éditions ouvrières.

DuBois, Ellen Carol. 1991. "Woman Suffrage and the Left: An International Socialist-Feminist Perspective." *New Left Review*, no. 186 (March–April): 20–44.

———. 1994. "Woman Suffrage around the World: Three Phases of Suffragist Internationalism." In *Suffrage and Beyond: International Feminist Perspectives*, edited by Caroline Daley and Melanie Nolan, 252–74. New York: New York University Press.

Duggan, Lisa. 1993. "The Trials of Alice Mitchell: Sensationalism, Sexology, and the Lesbian Subject in Turn-of-the-Century America." *Signs: Journal of Women in Culture and Society* 18: 791–814.

Ejikeme, Anene. 1992. "'One Big Family': Nigerian Women and WILPF, 1950–70." M.A. thesis, Ohio State University.

Eldorado: Homosexuelle Frauen und Männer in Berlin, 1850–1950. 1984. Berlin: Frölich und Kaufmann.

Enloe, Cynthia. 1990. *Bananas, Beaches, and Bases: Making Feminist Sense of International Politics*. Berkeley: University of California Press.

Eoff, Shirley M. 1991. *Viscountess Rhondda: Equalitarian Feminist*. Columbus: Ohio State University Press.

Epstein, Barbara. 1991. *Political Protest and Cultural Revolution: Nonviolent Direct Action in the 1970s and 1980s*. Berkeley: University of California Press.

Evans, Richard J. 1976. *The Feminist Movement in Germany, 1894–1933*. London: Sage.

———. 1977. *The Feminists: Women's Emancipation Movements in Europe, America and Australasia 1840–1920*. London: Croom Helm.

Evans, Richard J. 1987. *Comrades and Sisters: Feminism, Socialism and Pacifism in Europe, 1870–1945.* New York: St. Martin's.

Faderman, Lillian. 1981. *Surpassing the Love of Men: Romantic Friendship and Love between Women from the Renaissance to the Present.* New York: William Morrow.

Faderman, Lillian, and Brigitte Eriksson, eds. 1980. *Lesbian-Feminism in Turn-of-the-Century Germany.* [Weatherby Lake, Mo.]: Naiad.

Foot, Rosemary. 1990. "Where Are the Women? The Gender Dimension in the Study of International Relations." *Diplomatic History* 14: 615–22.

Forcey, Linda Rennie. 1991. "Women as Peacemakers: Contested Terrain for Feminist Peace Studies." *Peace and Change* 16: 331–54.

Foster, Carrie A. 1995. *The Women and the Warriors: The U.S. Section of the Women's International League for Peace and Freedom, 1915–1946.* Syracuse: Syracuse University Press.

Foster, Catherine. 1989. *Women for All Seasons: The Story of the Women's International League for Peace and Freedom.* Athens: University of Georgia Press.

Fowler, Robert Booth. 1986. *Carrie Catt: Feminist Politician.* Boston: Northeastern University Press.

Freeman, Jo. 1975. *The Politics of Women's Liberation.* New York: Longman.

Gamson, William A. 1992. "The Social Psychology of Collective Action." In *Frontiers in Social Movement Theory*, edited by Aldon Morris and Carol McClurg Mueller, 53–76. New Haven: Yale University Press.

———. 1995. "Hiroshima, the Holocaust, and the Politics of Exclusion." *American Sociological Review* 60 (February): 1–20.

Gellner, Ernest. 1983. *Nations and Nationalism.* Oxford: Blackwell.

Gerhard, Ute. 1990. *Unerhört: Die Geschichte der deutschen Frauenbewegung.* Reinbek bei Hamburg: Rowohlt.

———. 1994. "National oder International. Die internationalen Beziehungen der deutschen bürgerlichen Frauenbewegung." *Feministische Studien* 12, no. 2: 34–52.

Gerhard, Ute, Christina Klausmann, and Ulla Wischermann. 1993. "Frauenfreundschaften—ihre Bedeutung für Politik und Kultur der alten Frauenbewegung." *Feministische Studien* 11, no. 1: 21–37.

Grant, Rebecca, and Kathleen Newland, eds. 1991. *Gender and International Relations.* Buckingham: Open University Press.

Greenfeld, Liah. 1992. *Nationalism: Five Roads to Modernity.* Cambridge, Mass.: Harvard University Press.

Grossmann, Atina. 1995. *Reforming Sex: The German Movement for Birth Control and Abortion Reform, 1920–1950.* New York: Oxford University Press.

Hackett, Amy. 1976. "The Politics of Feminism in Wilhelmine Germany, 1890–1918." Ph.D. diss., Columbia University.

———. 1984. "Helene Stöcker: Left-Wing Intellectual and Sex Reformer." In *When Biology Became Destiny*, edited by Renate Bridenthal, Atina Grossmann, and Marion Kaplan, 109–30. New York: Monthly Review.

Hahner, June E. 1990. *Emancipating the Female Sex: The Struggle for Women's Rights in Brazil, 1850–1940.* Durham: Duke University Press.

Hamann, Brigitte. 1986. *Bertha von Suttner: Ein Leben für den Frieden*. Munich: R. Piper.

Harrison, Brian. 1987. *Prudent Revolutionaries: Portraits of British Feminists between the Wars*. Oxford: Clarendon.

Hering, Sabine. 1990. *Die Kriegsgewinnlerinnen*. Pfaffenweiler: Centaurus-Verlagsgesellschaft.

Hering, Sabine, and Cornelia Wenzel. 1986. *Frauen Riefen, aber Man Hörte sie Nicht: Die Rolle der Deutschen Frauen in der Internationalen Frauenfriedensbewegung zwischen 1892 und 1933*. 2 vols. Kassell: Archiv der deutschen Frauenbewegung.

Herman, Sondra R. 1993. "From International Feminism to Feminist Internationalism: The Emergence of Alva Myrdal, 1936–1955." *Peace and Change* 18: 325–46.

Hermann, Ursula. 1985. "Sozialdemokratische Frauen in Deutschland im Kampf um den Frieden vor und während des Ersten Weltkrieges." *Zeitschrift für Geschichtswissenschaft* 33: 213–30.

Hermon, Elly. 1993. "Une ultime tentative de sauvetage de la Société des Nations: La campagne du Rassemblement Universel pour la Paix." In *Le Pacifisme en Europe des années 1920 aux années 1950*, edited by Maurice Vaïsse, 193–221. Brussels: Bruylant.

Herren, Madeleine. 1993. *Internationale Sozialpolitik vor dem Ersten Weltkrieg: Die Anfänge europäischer Kooperation aus der Sicht Frankreichs*. Berlin: Duncker und Humblot.

Hoberman, John. 1995. "Toward a Theory of Olympic Internationalism." *Journal of Sport History* 22: 1–37.

———. 1996. "The International Olympic Committee as a Supranational Elite." Paper presented at the annual meeting of the American Historical Association conference, Atlanta, January.

Hollinger, David A. 1993. "How Wide the Cirle of the 'We'? American Intellectuals and the Problem of the Ethnos since World War II." *American Historical Review* 98: 317–37.

Holton, Sandra Stanley. 1994. "'To Educate Women into Rebellion': Elizabeth Cady Stanton and the Creation of a Transatlantic Network of Radical Suffragists." *American Historical Review* 99: 1112–36.

hooks, bell. 1984. *Feminist Theory: From Margin to Center*. Boston: South End.

Huntington, Samuel P. 1973. "Transnational Organizations in World Politics." *World Politics* 25: 333–68.

Hurwitz, Edith F. 1977. "The International Sisterhood." In *Becoming Visible: Women in European History*, edited by Renate Bridenthal and Claudia Koonz, 325–45. Boston: Houghton Mifflin.

Hutchinson, John F. 1996. *Champions of Charity: War and the Rise of the Red Cross*. Boulder, Colo.: Westview.

Iinuma, Takeko. 1996. "Women Organize for Peace in the Face of Fascism: The Women's Peace Association of Japan." Paper presented at the annual meeting of the American Historical Asociation, Atlanta, January.

Isaacs, Harold R. 1975. *Idols of the Tribe: Group Identity and Political Change*. Cambridge, Mass.: Harvard University Press.

Ishay, Micheline R. 1995. *Internationalism and Its Betrayal*. Contradictions of Modernity, edited by Craig Calhoun, vol. 2. Minneapolis: University of Minnesota Press.

Jayawardena, Kumari. 1986. *Feminism and Nationalism in the Third World*. London: Zed.

———. 1995. *The White Woman's Other Burden: Western Women and South Asia During British Rule*. New York: Routledge.

Johnson-Odim, Cheryl. 1991. "Common Themes, Different Contexts: Third World Women and Feminism." In *Third World Women and the Politics of Feminism*, edited by Chandra Talpade Mohanty, Ann Russo, and Lourdes Torres, 314–27. Bloomington: Indiana University Press.

Joll, James. 1974. *The Second International, 1889–1914*. Rev. ed. London: Routledge and Kegan Paul.

Kaplan, Marion A. 1979. *The Jewish Feminist Movement in Germany*. Westport, Conn.: Greenwood.

———. 1991. *The Making of the Jewish Middle Class: Women, Family, and Identity in Imperial Germany*. New York: Oxford Univesity Press.

Kennedy, Kathleen. 1995. "Declaring War on War: Gender and the American Socialist Attack on Militarism, 1914–1918." *Journal of Women's History* 7, no. 2: 27–51.

Keohane, Robert O., and Joseph S. Nye, Jr., eds. 1973. *Transnational Relations and World Politics*. Cambridge, Mass.: Harvard University Press.

Klandermans, Bert, and Sidney Tarrow. 1988. "Mobilization into Social Movements: Synthesizing European and American Approaches." In *From Structure to Action: Comparing Movement Participation across Cultures*, edited by Bert Klandermans, Hanspeter Kriesi, and Sidney Tarrow, 1–38. Greenwich, Conn.: JAI.

Klausmann, Christina, Reinhild Schäfer, Elke Schüller, and Ulla Wischermann. 1994. "International Kongresses der alten und neuen Frauenbewegung." *Feministische Studien* 12, no. 2: 100–36.

Klejman, Laurence. 1989. "Les Congrès féministes internationaux." *Mil neuf cent: Cahiers Georges Sorel: Revue d'histoire intellectuelle* 7: 71–86.

Klejman, Laurence, and Florence Rochefort. 1989. *L'égalité en marche: Le féminisme sous la Troisième République*. Paris: Presses de la Foundation nationale des sciences politique.

Knock, Thomas J. 1992. *To End All Wars: Woodrow Wilson and the Quest for a New World Order*. New York: Oxford University Press.

Kokula, Ilse. 1981. *Weibliche Homosexualität um 1900 in zeitgenössischen Dokumenten*. Munich: Verlag Frauenoffensive.

Koven, Seth, and Sonya Michel. 1990. "Womanly Duties: Maternalist Politics and the Origins of the Welfare States in France, Germany, Great Britain, and the U.S., 1880–1920." *American Historical Review* 95: 1076–108.

Kraft, Barbara S. 1978. *The Peace Ship*. New York: Macmillan.

Kuzmack, Linda Gordon. 1990. *Woman's Cause: The Jewish Woman's Movement in England and the U.S., 1881–1933*. Columbus: Ohio State University Press.

Lerner, Elinor. 1986. "American Feminism and the Jewish Question, 1890–

1940." *Anti-Semitism in American History*, edited by David A. Gerber, 305–28. Urbana: University of Illinois Press.

Lewis, Reina. 1996. *Gendering Orientalism: Race, Femininity, and Representation*. New York: Routledge.

Long, David. *Towards a New Liberal Internationalism: The International Theory of J. A. Hobson*. New York: Cambridge University Press.

Lorde, Audre. 1984. *Sister/Outsider*. Trumansburg, N.Y.: Crossing.

Luard, Evan, ed. 1966. *The Evolution of International Organizations*. New York: Frederick A. Praeger.

Lubin, Carol Riegelman, and Anne Winslow. 1990. *Social Justice for Women: The International Labor Organization and Women*. Durham: Duke University Press.

Lunardini, Christine A. 1986. *From Equal Suffrage to Equal Rights*. New York: New York University Press.

Lützen, Karin. 1990. *Was das Herz begehrt: Liebe und Freundschaft zwischen Frauen*, translated from Danish by Gabriele Haefs. Hamburg: Ernst Kabel Verlag.

Lyons, F. S. L. 1963. *Internationalism in Europe, 1815–1914*. Leyden: A. W. Sythoff.

MacFarland, Susan May. 1990. "Anti-War Women: The Role of the Feminist-Pacifist-Internationalist Movement in American Foreign Policy and International Relations, 1898–1930." Ph.D. diss., University of Oklahoma.

Mathrani, Mala. 1995. "Constructing an Asian Identity: Organized Indian Women and the Search for an 'Asian' Sisterhood, 1930–1947." Paper presented at the annual meeting of MAR/Association of Asian Studies conference, Towson, Maryland.

———. 1996. "Nationalism or Internationalism? All-India Women's Conference, 1927–1947." Paper presented at the annual meeting of the American Historical Association, Atlanta, January.

———. Forthcoming. "Nationalism or Internationalism? Indian Women and Their International Connections, 1880s–1947." Ph.D. diss., Ohio State University.

McCarthy, John D., and Mayer N. Zald. 1977. "Resource Mobilization and Social Movements: A Partial Theory." *American Journal of Sociology* 82: 1212–41.

McFadden, Maggie. 1988. "Weaving the Cloth of International Sisterhood." Paper presented at the annual meeting of the National Women's Studies Association, Minneapolis, June.

———. 1990. "Weaving the Delicate Web: The Origins of Women's International Networks, 1820–1880." Paper presented at the Berkshire Conference on the History of Women, New Brunswick, N.J., June.

Melman, Billie. 1992. *Women's Orients: English Women and the Middle East, 1718–1918*. Ann Arbor: University of Michigan Press.

Miles, Angela. 1996. *Integrative Feminisms: Building Global Visions, 1960s-1990s*. New York: Routledge.

Miller, Carol. 1991. "Women in International Relations? The Debate in Interwar Britain." In *Gender and International Relations*, edited by Rebecca Grant and Kathleen Newland, 64–82. Buckingham: Open University Press.

Miller, Carol. 1991. 1992. "Lobbying the League: Women's International Organisations and the League of Nations." D.Phil. diss., Oxford University.
——. 1994. "'Geneva—the Key to Equality': Inter-war Feminists and the
League of Nations." *Women's History Review* 3: 219–45.
Miller, Francesca. 1986. "The International Relations of Women of the Americas, 1890–1928." *Americas* 43 (October): 171–82.
——. 1990. "Latin American Feminism and the Transnational Arena." In
Women, Culture, and Politics in Latin America, edited by Emilie Bergmann et
al., 10–26. Berkeley: University of California Press.
Milner, Susan. 1990. *The Dilemmas of Internationalism: French Syndicalism and
the International Labour Movement, 1900–1914.* New York: Berg.
Mohanty, Chandra Talpade. 1984. "Under Western Eyes: Feminist Scholarship
and Colonial Discourses." *Boundary 2* 12, no. 4–13, no. 1: 333–58.
Moraga, Cherríe, and Gloria Anzaldúa, eds. 1981. *This Bridge Called My Back:
Writings by Radical Women of Color.* Watertown, Mass.: Persephone.
Morgan, Robin, ed. 1984. *Sisterhood Is Global: The International Women's
Movement.* Garden City, N.Y.: Anchor.
Murphy, Craig N. 1994. *International Organization and Industrial Change:
Global Governance since 1850.* New York: Oxford University Press.
Nagel, Joane. 1994. "Constructing Ethnicity: Creating and Recreating Ethnic
Identity and Culture." *Social Problems* 41 (February): 152–76.
Neverdon-Morton, Cynthia. 1989. *Afro-American Women of the South and the
Advancement of the Race, 1895–1925.* Knoxville: University of Tennessee
Press.
Offen, Karen. 1988. "Defining Feminism: A Comparative Historical Approach."
Signs: Journal of Women in Culture and Society 14: 119–57.
——. 1995. "Reflections on National Specificities in Continental European
Feminism." *U.C.G. Women's Studies Centre Review* 3: 53–61.
Oldfield, Sybil. 1984. *Spinsters of This Parish: The Life and Times of F. M.
Mayor and Mary Sheepshanks.* London: Virago.
Page, Dorothy P. 1984. "'A Married Woman, or a Minor, Lunatic or Idiot': The
Struggle of British Women against Disability in Nationality, 1914–1933."
Ph.D. diss., University of Otago, Dunedin, New Zealand.
Pedersen, Susan. 1991. "National Bodies, Unspeakable Acts: The Sexual Politics
of Colonial Policy-making." *Journal of Modern History* 63: 647–80.
Pentland, Marjorie. 1947. *In the Nineties: Ishbel Aberdeen and the I.C.W..* Lon-
don: Caxton.
——. 1952. *A Bonnie Fechter: Life of Ishbel Marjoribanks, Marchioness of
Aberdeen.* London: Batsford.
Peters, Julie, and Andrea Wolper, eds. 1995. *Women's Rights, Human Rights:
International Feminist Perspectives.* New York: Routledge.
Peterson, V. Spike. 1992. *Gendered States: Feminist (Re)Visions of International
Relations Theory.* Boulder, Colo.: Lynne Rienner.
Pfaff, William. 1993. *The Wrath of Nations: Civilization and the Furies of
Nationalism.* New York: Simon and Schuster.
Pfeffer, Paula F. 1985. "'A whisper in the assembly of nations'—United States'
Participation in the International Movement for Women's Rights from the

League of Nations to the United Nations." *Women's Studies International Forum* 8: 459–72.

Pieper, Mecki. 1984. "Die Frauenbewegung und ihre Bedeutung für lesbische Frauen (1850–1920)." In *Eldorado: Homosexuelle Frauen und Männer in Berlin, 1850–1950*, 116–24. Berlin: Frölich und Kaufmann.

Pietilä, Hilkka, and Jeanne Vickers. 1990. *Making Women Matter: The Role of the United Nations*. London: Zed.

Pinkus, Gertrud. 1978. "Gertrud Baer: Fauenbewegung bis 1920." *Frauenoffensive* 10: 30–46.

Pois, Anne Marie. 1988. "The Politics and Process of Organizing for Peace: The U.S. Section of the Women's International League for Peace and Freedom, 1919–1939." Ph.D. diss., University of Colorado.

Powell, Cynthia. 1996. "The Persistence of the Nation in International Woman Suffrage: Carrie Chapman Catt and the International Woman Suffrage Alliance." Paper presented at the annual meeting of the Organization of American Historians, Chicago, March.

Pugh, Martin. 1992. *Women and the Women's Movement in Britain, 1914–1959*. New York: Paragon House.

"Die Radikalen in der alten Frauenbewegung." 1984. Special issue of *Feministische Studien* 3, no. 1.

Ramusack, Barbara. 1990. "Cultural Missionaries, Maternal Imperialists, Feminist Allies: British Women Activists in India, 1865–1945." *Women's Studies International Forum* 13: 309–21.

Randall, Mercedes M. 1964. *Improper Bostonian: Emily Greene Balch*. New York: Twayne.

Rasmussen, Janet E. 1982. "Sisters across the Sea: Early Norwegian Feminists and Their American Connections." *Women's Studies International Forum* 5: 647–54.

Rauther, Rosa. 1984. "Rosika Schwimmer. Stationen auf dem Lebensweg einer Pazifistin." *Feministische Studien* 3, no. 1: 63–76.

Reinalda, Bob, and Natascha Verhaaren. 1989. *Vrouwenbeweging en Internationale Organisaties, 1868–1986*. Nijmegen: Ariadne.

Rendall, Jane. 1984. *The Origins of Modern Feminism: Women in Britain, France, and the United States, 1780–1860*. New York: Schocken.

Rice, Anna V. 1947. *A History of the World's Young Women's Christian Association*. New York: Woman's Press.

Riesenberger, Dieter. 1992. *Für Humanität in Krieg und Frieden: Das Internationale Rote Kreuz, 1863–1977*. Göttingen: Vandenhoeck und Reprecht.

Rubinstein, David. 1991. *A Different World for Women: The Life of Millicent Garrett Fawcett*. Columbus: Ohio State University Press.

Ruddick, Sara. 1989. *Maternal Thinking: Toward a Politics of Peace*. New York: Ballantine.

Rupp, Leila J. 1989. "Feminism and the Sexual Revolution in the Early Twentieth Century: The Case of Doris Stevens." *Feminist Studies* 15: 289–309.

———. 1992. "Eleanor Flexner's *Century of Struggle*: Women's History and the Women's Movement." *NWSA Journal* 4: 157–69.

———. 1994a. "Constructing Internationalism: The Case of Transnational

Women's Organizations, 1888–1945." *American Historical Review* 99: 1571–600.

Rupp, Leila J. 1994b. "Zur Organisationsgeschichte der internationalen Frauen-bewegung vor dem Zweiten Weltkrieg," translated by Beate L. Menzel. *Femi-nistische Studien* 12, no. 2: 53–65.

———. 1996. "Challenging Imperialism in International Women's Organiza-tions." *NWSA Journal* 8: 8–27.

———. Forthcoming. "Sexuality and Politics in the Early Twentieth Century: The Case of the International Women's Movement." *Feminist Studies*.

Rupp, Leila J., and Verta Taylor. 1987. *Survival in the Doldrums: The American Women's Rights Movement, 1945 to the 1960s*. New York: Oxford University Press.

Said, Edward W. 1978. *Orientalism*. London: Routledge and Kegan Paul.

Scarborough, Neve. 1953. *History of the Associated Country Women of the World*. London: ACWW.

Schnetzler, Barbara. 1971. *Die frühe amerikanische Frauenbewegung und ihre Kontakte mit Europa (1936–1869)*. Bern: Herbert Lang.

Schott, Linda. 1985a. "Women against War: Pacifism, Feminism, and Social Jus-tice in the U.S." Ph.D. diss., Stanford University.

———. 1985b. "The Women's Peace Party and the Moral Basis of Women's Pacifism." *Frontiers* 8: 18–24.

Scott, George. 1973. *The Rise and Fall of the League of Nations*. New York: Macmillan.

Scott, Joan W. 1988. "Deconstructing Equality-Versus-Difference: or, The Uses of Poststructuralist Theory for Feminism." *Feminist Studies* 14: 33–50.

Seidman, Steven. 1993. "Identity and Politics in a 'Postmodern' Gay Culture: Some Historical and Conceptual Notes." In *Fear of a Queer Planet: Queer Politics and Social Theory*, edited by Michael Warner, 105–42. Minneapolis: University of Minnesota Press.

Sherrick, Rebecca L. 1982. "Toward Universal Sisterhood." *Women's Studies International Forum* 5: 655–61.

Sinha, Mrinalini. 1994. "Reading Mother India: Empire, Nation, and the Female Voice." *Journal of Women's History* 6, no. 2: 6–44.

Skjelsbaek, Kjell. 1971. "The Growth of International Nongovernmental Orga-nization in the 20th Century." *International Organization* 25: 420–42.

Smith, Anthony D. 1986. *The Ethnic Origins of Nations*. New York: Basil Black-well.

Smith, Barbara. 1979. "Notes for Yet Another Paper on Black Feminism, or Will the Real Enemy Please Stand Up?" *Conditions: five*: 123–27.

Smith, Joan. 1994. "The Creation of the World We Know: The World-Economy and the Re-Creation of Gendered identities." In *Identity Politics and Women: Cultural Reassertions and Feminism in International Perspective*, edited by Valentine M. Moghadam, 27–41. Boulder, Colo.: Westview.

Smyth, Ailbhe. 1995. "Paying Our Disrespects to the Bloody States We're In: Women, Violence, Culture, and the State." *Journal of Women's History* 6, no. 4–7, no. 1: 190–215.

Sneider, Allison. 1996. "Constructing National Citizenship in International Arenas: U.S. Women's Suffrage and the International Council of Women, 1876–1904." Paper presented at the annual meeting of the Organization of American Historians, Chicago, March.

Steinson, Barbara J. 1982. *American Women's Activism in World War I.* New York: Garland.

Stephenson, Carolyn J. 1982. "Feminism, Pacifism, Nationalism, and the United Nations Decade for Women." *Women's Studies International Forum* 5: 287–300.

Stevenson, Janet. 1980. "Lola Maverick Lloyd: 'I must do something for peace!'" *Chicago History* 9: 47–57.

Stienstra, Deborah. 1994. *Women's Movements and International Organizations.* New York: St. Martin's.

Stocks, M. D. 1949. *Eleanor Rathbone: A Biography.* London: Victor Gollancz.

Stoner, K. Lynn. 1991. *From the House to the Streets: The Cuban Woman's Movement for Legal Reform, 1898–1940.* Durham: Duke University Press.

Strikwerda, Carl. 1993. "The Troubled Origins of European Economic Integration: International Iron and Steel and Labor Migration in the Era of World War I." *American Historical Review* 98: 1106–29.

Sugimori, Nagako. 1996. "Jane Addams in Japan: Jane Addams and the Development of Feminist-Pacifism in Japan." Paper presented at the annual meeting of the Organization of American Historians, Chicago, March.

Sylvester, Christine. 1994. *Feminist Theory and International Relations in a Postmodern Era.* New York: Cambridge University Press.

Taylor, Verta, and Leila J. Rupp. 1993. "Women's Culture and Lesbian Feminist Activism: A Reconsideration of Cultural Feminism." *Signs: Journal of Women in Culture and Society* 19: 32–61.

Taylor, Verta, and Nancy Whittier. 1992. "Collective Identity in Social Movement Communities: Lesbian Feminist Mobilization." In *Frontiers of Social Movement Theory,* edited by Aldon D. Morris and Carol McClurg Mueller, 104–29. New Haven: Yale University Press.

———. 1995. "Analytical Approaches to Social Movement Culture: The Culture of the Women's Movement." In *Social Movements and Culture,* edited by Hank Johnston and Bert Klandermans, 163–87. Minneapolis: University of Minnesota Press.

Tinker, Irene, and Jane Jaquette. 1987. "UN Decade for Women: Its Impact and Legacy." *World Development* 15: 419–27.

Tyrrell, Ian. 1991a. "American Exceptionalism in an Age of International History." *American Historical Review* 96: 1031–55.

———. 1991b. *Woman's World, Woman's Empire: The Woman's Christian Temperance Union in International Perspective, 1880–1930.* Chapel Hill: University of North Carolina Press.

van der Lindon, W. H. 1987. *The International Peace Movement, 1815–1874.* Amsterdam: Tilleul.

Van Voris, Jacqueline. 1987. *Carrie Chapman Catt: A Public Life.* New York: Feminist Press.

Vellacott, Jo. 1987. "Feminist Consciousness and the First World War." *History Workshop: A Journal of Socialist and Feminist Historians* 23: 81–101.

Vellacott, Jo. 1993a. *From Liberal to Labour with Women's Suffrage: The Story of Catherine Marshall.* Buffalo, N.Y.: McGill-Queen's University Press.

————. 1993b. "A Place for Pacifism and Transnationalism in Feminist Theory." *Women's History Review* 2: 23–56.

A Venture in Faith: A History of St. Joan's Social and Political Alliance, Formerly the Catholic Women's Suffrage Society, 1911–1961. [no publication information].

Wallerstein, Immanuel. 1974. *The Modern World-System.* Vol. 1. New York: Academic Press.

Walters, F. P. 1952. *A History of the League of Nations.* London: Oxford University Press.

Ware, Vron. 1992. *Beyond the Pale: White Women, Racism, and History.* London: Verso.

Weber, Charlotte. 1996. "Unveiling Scheherazade: The Intersection between Feminism and Orientalism within the International Women's Movement, 1911–1950." M.A. thesis, Ohio State University.

Weigand, Kate. 1995. "Vanguards of Women's Liberation: The Old Left and the Continuity of the Women's Movement in the U.S., 1945–1970s." Ph.D. diss., Ohio State University.

Weiner, Lynn Y., Ann Taylor Allen, Eileen Boris, Molly Ladd-Taylor, Adele Lindenmeyer, and Kathleen Uno. 1993. "Maternalism as a Paradigm." *Journal of Women's History* 5, no. 2: 95–131.

Wenger, Beth S. 1990. "Radical Politics in a Reactionary Age: The Unmaking of Rosika Schwimmer, 1914–1930." *Journal of Women's History* 2, no. 2: 66–99.

White, L. 1951. *Non-governmental Organizations: Their Purposes, Methods, and Accomplishments.* New Brunswick, N.J.: Rutgers University Press.

Whitelaw, Lis. 1990. *The Life and Rebellious Times of Cicely Hamilton: Actress, Playwright, Suffragette.* Columbus: Ohio State University Press.

Whittick, Arnold. 1979. *Woman into Citizen.* London: Atheneum with Frederick Mueller.

Whittier, Nancy. 1995. *Feminist Generations: The Persistence of the Radical Women's Movement.* Philadelphia: Temple University Press.

Whitworth, Sandra. 1994. *Feminism and International Relations: Towards a Political Economy of Gender in Interstate and Non-Governmental Institutions.* New York: St. Martin's.

Wickert, Christl. 1991. *Helene Stöcker, 1869–1943: Frauenrechtlerin, Sexualreformerin, Pazifistin: eine Biographie.* Bonn: Verlag J. H. W. Dietz.

Wikander, Ulla. 1992. "International Women's Congresses, 1878–1914: The Controversy over Equality and Special Labour Legislation." In *Rethinking Change: Current Swedish Feminist Research*, edited by Maud L. Eduards et al., 11–26. Uppsala: Humanistisk-samhällsvetenskapliga forskningsradet.

————. 1995. "Some 'Kept the Flag of Feminist Demands Waving': Debates at International Congresses on Protecting Women Workers." In *Protecting Women: Labor Legislation in Europe, the United States, and Australia, 1880–1920*, edited by Ulla Wikander, Alice Kessler-Harris, and Jane Lewis, 29–62. Urbana: University of Illinois Press.

——. 1996. "A Free and Equal Labour Market for Women? European Women at Congresses in London and Berlin, 1899 and 1904." Paper presented at the European Social Science History Conference, Noordwijkerhout, the Netherlands, May.

Wikander, Ulla, Alice Kessler-Harris, and Jane Lewis, eds. 1995. *Protecting Women: Labor Legislation in Europe, the United States, and Australia, 1880–1920.* Urbana: University of Illinois Press.

Wilkins, Wyona H. 1975. "The Paris International Feminist Congress of 1896 and Its French Antecedents." *North Dakota Quarterly* 43 (Autumn): 5–28.

Wiltsher, Anne Wiltsher. 1985. *Most Dangerous Women: Feminist Peace Campaigners of the Great War.* London: Routledge and Kegan Paul.

Winslow, Anne. 1995. *Women, Politics, and the United Nations.* Westport, Conn.: Greenwood.

Women in a Changing World: The Dynamic Story of the International Council of Women since 1888. 1966. London: Routledge and Kegan Paul.

Wynner, Edith. 1974. "Schwimmer, Rosika." In *Dictionary of American Biography*, edited by John A. Garraty and Edward T. James, suppl. 4, 724–28. New York: Charles Scribner's Sons.

Zonana, Joyce. 1993. "The Sultan and the Slave: Feminist Orientalism and the Structure of *Jane Eyre.*" *Signs: Journal of Women in Culture and Society* 18: 592–617.

Index

About the Author

Leila Rupp is Professor of History at Ohio State University. She is the author of *Mobilizing Women for War: German and American Propaganda, 1939–1945* (Princeton) and coauthor, with Verta Taylor, of *Survival in the Doldrums: The American Women's Rights Movement.*